The Formative Assessment Handbook

The Formative Assessment Handbook

Resources to Improve Learning Outcomes for All Students

Marine Freibrun, MEd and
Sandra Brunet, MEd

JOSSEY-BASS™
A Wiley Brand

Published by John Wiley & Sons, Inc., Hoboken, New Jersey.
Published simultaneously in Canada.

For general information on our other products and services or for technical support, please contact our Customer Care Department within the United States at (800) 762-2974, outside the United States at (317) 572-3993 or fax (317) 572-4002.

Wiley also publishes its books in a variety of electronic formats. Some content that appears in print may not be available in electronic formats. For more information about Wiley products, visit our web site at www.wiley.com.

Library of Congress Control Number is Available:

ISBN 9781394170739 (Paperback)
ISBN 9781394170746 (ePDF)
ISBN 9781394170753 (ePub)

Cover Design: Wiley
Cover Image: © Shutterstock
Author Photo: Courtesy of the Author

Contents

Introduction: The *Why* for Our Book   vii

Acknowledgments   xiii

About the Authors   xv

List of Resources in the Book   xvii

PART I   **Before Instruction: Setting Up Your Classroom for Success**   **1**

CHAPTER 1   Formative Assessment Overview: What the Research Says   3

CHAPTER 2   Setting Up the Classroom for Successful Implementation   17

CHAPTER 3   Selecting Learning Targets and Developing Success Criteria   29

CHAPTER 4   Utilizing Pre-Assessments   57

PART II   During Instruction: Effective "In-the-Moment" Formative Assessment Instructional Practices and Resources   **89**

CHAPTER 5   Effective Formative Assessment Instructional Practices and Resources   91

CHAPTER 6   In-the-Moment Formative Instruction: Collaborative Routines   161

CHAPTER 7   Dialogic Teaching and Dialectic Synergy   189

CHAPTER 8   Common Formative Assessments and Your PLC   207

PART III   **Formative Assessment After Instruction**   **231**

CHAPTER 9   Formative Assessment Resources in Practice: Student Self-Assessment   233

CHAPTER 10   Formative Assessment After Instruction   255

CHAPTER 11   Concluding Thoughts   269

References   271

Bibliography   273

Index   275

Introduction:
The *Why* for Our Book

If you are reading this book and you have worked in education for some time now, you know that education in our country sometimes can feel a little bipolar. As educators and teachers in the classroom, we constantly feel like shifts are happening, new training is taking place, and those once coveted "best practices" are being replaced by newer and better practices. It is no wonder teachers in America are suffering from initiative fatigue; they are feeling worn out, and they are completely overwhelmed by the expectations being placed on them every day in classrooms across this country. Once we add to that plate, the global pandemic of 2020 and the challenges across America's classroom as we begin to recover and rebuild, it is no wonder teachers are tired.

The role of the teacher has grown exponentially in the last 25 years, and those of us who started in education many years ago barely recognize the profession as the one we entered as bright-eyed youths.

When many current veteran teachers began in the profession, teaching still had a myriad of elements of its traditional roots. At its inception, the education system was designed to churn out excellent factory workers who could sit still for hours and respond to bells for the breaks during their nine-hour shifts.

Teachers who taught the youngsters of the nineteenth and twentieth centuries were often told what to teach and how to teach. There was also an expectation that the most remarkable success could be garnered when every student was taught similarly. Those nineteenth- and twentieth-century teachers also did not face criticism or sanctions if and when their students failed to achieve academic success. Concepts of creative instruction and innovation were discouraged, and the sage on the stage was born in education circles across this country.

Moreover, we would like to *assume* that because we now know better, we do better, yet the remnants of this era still permeate more classes across our nation than we may like to admit. The challenge therein lies in the changing need of our student populations. We no longer train our youth to work in factories and respond to bells.

In addition, as the face of our nation and our classrooms become increasingly pluralistic, it is incumbent upon our teachers to understand, recognize, and honor the backgrounds of each individual in the classroom. While education could once be described as a one-size-fits-all model, current classrooms require teachers to know and understand the unique learning styles of various students. Teachers must adjust their instruction, often mid-lesson, to meet their student populations' ever-changing and ever-growing needs.

This is not the only way that the face of education has changed. Teachers in classrooms across America are now expected to counsel students on social, emotional, and intellectual growth and to seek, understand, and utilize students' unique backgrounds to meet their learning needs more effectively.

Today's teachers must understand and recognize when learning is not happening and be able and ready to intervene immediately and differentiate their instruction. While we still expect teachers to have mastery of their content, we have added much to the ever-growing workload of the teacher. The sage on the stage can no longer meet the needs of our current educational landscape.

In addition to the shifts already shared, current classroom teachers face the following additional challenges:

- An increased system of school-wide accountability for teachers and students based on performance metrics.
- An expectation of higher levels of knowledge for classroom teachers of the content they teach, as well as of pedagogy, including knowledge of deeper learning, project-based learning, and the ability to help students develop the ability to apply content to novel problems.
- Understanding of the adoption of and shifts in national and state standards.
- Added inclusion movements promoting that general education teachers have a more significant role in educating students from neurodiverse backgrounds.
- Increased use of performance-based evaluation systems.
- The expectation that teachers serve as a bridge between the school and families and communities, with the expectation of frequent and immediate communication with parents.
- Increased responsibility for ensuring student safety in the classrooms.

Teaching was once viewed as a profession where the job ended at 3:00 p.m., and the job promised our teachers the ultimate work-life balance.

More often than not these days, our teachers can be found at school late into the evenings and often on their weekends. Most teachers spend a large part of their summers working alongside their grade level or department teams, attending professional development on the new book adoption, or training on the amendments or additions to current standards.

Gone are the days of the 7:30 a.m. to 2:30 p.m. educator. The teacher role in 2023 and beyond is complex, multifaceted, and dynamic.

With that in mind, the *why* behind *The Formative Assessment Handbook: Resources to Improve Learning Outcomes for All Students* is to offer teachers an easy-to-implement, practical, data-driven, and research-based handbook that will *not* be "one more thing."

Our goal is to provide educators across America with easy-to-implement, formative assessments that they can select from, matching their current instructional standards and goals.

We believe teachers who use (with fidelity) these pre-made tools alongside the data and strategies shared in this book can significantly impact student achievement. It is our goal and sincere hope that this book can take one burden off the shoulders of the twenty-first-century educator while simultaneously honoring the teaching professional in best serving the needs of their learners.

As educators, we believe teachers are the lifeblood of education and they have a direct hand in the future of our nation. We hope this handbook provides value to those entering the profession and those who have positively impacted the lives of children for many years.

How to Use This Book

We know all of the work that is on a teacher's plate in the current education landscape, so our goal with this book is that it serves as both a guide and a resource. While you can read it cover to cover to get all the details of implementing formative assessment, you can also dog-ear, highlight, tab, and mark up the pages and resources within the book that serve a specific practical function for you in your classroom. Our goal is to create a resource that, in the end, will serve to save the classroom teacher from expending undo time, energy, and resources on unnecessary elements of the role. We want this book to be something a teacher can open up, determine a specific need or want, and flip to the section most closely correlated to addressing that need. We have kept things simple for this book by focusing on three main areas of formative assessment, outlined by the parts within this book.

Part I: Before Instruction: Setting Up Your Classroom for Success

In Part I, we dive into a general overview of all of the things that you need to know, do, and prepare *before* you begin your instruction to create the ideal environment to implement the formative assessment. We begin in Chapter 1 by giving an overview of the research behind formative assessment to develop a compelling reason why formative assessment is an essential component of high-quality academic instructional delivery. In Chapter 2, we present information and tips on setting up systems for the successful implementation of formative assessment. Finally, Chapters 3 and 4 provide teachers with support in selecting learning targets and developing success criteria as well as utilizing pre-assessments.

We hope that the combination of this background information serves to provide a solid basis of knowledge of all of the practices that will make your classroom successful as you begin to implement formative assessments.

Part II: During Instruction: Effective "In-the-Moment" Formative Assessment Instructional Practices and Resources

In Part II, we focus on "in-the-moment" formative assessment. This means the formative assessment you complete as a teacher in real-time while instruction is happening. In this section, you will find specific and actionable plans for implementing formative assessment and grab-and-go resources to utilize formative assessment across various content areas effectively. Chapter 5 introduces graphic organizers, picture notes, think-pair-share, Jigsaws, doodle it, and running records. Chapter 6 dives into collaborative routines. Chapter 7 explores the concepts of Dialogic Teaching and Dialectic Synergy as a way to enhance formative assessment. Finally, in Chapter 8 we explore the role of CFA's and your PLC.

Part III: Formative Assessment After Instruction

In Part III, we focus on what formative assessment looks like after instruction. Chapter 9 provides formative assessments such as exit tickets, muddiest points, and summaries you can utilize after you have completed instruction and need to check for understanding and/or re-teaching prior to a summative assessment or moving on to the next unit. In Chapter 10 we share what formative assessments can look like after instruction. It is our sincere hope that these resources and chapters assist you in meeting your classroom and yearlong goals and are able to provide you with the insight needed to successfully create many opportunities to engage your students in their learning, develop meaningful connections, determine the levels of student learning throughout your instructional sequence, and better assist you in creating opportunities to re-teach to mastery.

Acknowledgments

The writing of this book was an amalgamation of inspiration from the many amazing teachers who have allowed us to serve as their leader and mentor. To the teachers of Bridgeport Elementary School, North Park Elementary School, Hawaii Technology Academy, and Switzerland Point Middle School, you all are truly what is great about education. Your continued dedication to serving children and your love and passion for meeting student needs are the hallmark of our amazing profession. To every teacher out there, working daily far beyond your contract hours, your hard work does not go unnoticed. Thank you for giving all you have and all you are for the kids! There is no greater profession!

About the Authors

Sandra Brunet is a seasoned school administrator and Executive Coach with over 15 years' of experience leading schools in California, Hawaii, and Florida. She has distinguished herself by following her passion for putting students first and has been recognized for her efforts to transform school culture by building positive relationships and increasing school achievement. Most recently, Sandy has moved into an executive coaching role where she works and coaches principals and superintendents across the United States on data-driven instruction, improving instructional outcomes, meeting the needs of multilingual learners, and best practices in diversity, equity, and inclusion (DEI).

Sandra holds a Master's in Educational Administration and a Bachelor's in Communication Studies from UCLA. She is also the co-author of *Leading with Administrator Clarity*. Sandy currently calls the Gulf Coast of Florida home, and if you can't find her at home, she is surely out at a beach or riding her paddleboard in the nearby Gulf of Mexico.

Marine Freibrun, MEd, began her career as an elementary school teacher in Southern California, teaching grades 2, 3, and 5.

Throughout her career, she also had the opportunity to support and serve teachers as an instructional coach, English Language Development (ELD) coach, and Positive Behavior Interventions and Supports (PBIS) coach.

Marine also served as the English Language Arts and Literacy Assessment Coordinator for the Idaho State Department of Education. As the assessment coordinator, she supported teachers and district leaders in the implementation of the Idaho Literacy Achievement and Accountability Act, legislation designed to establish an extended-time literacy intervention program to support students' literacy achievement. In doing so, Marine worked with teachers and district leadership to evaluate assessment data from the state's literacy assessment and define the next steps for effective instructional practices.

Most recently, Marine is a Manager of Educational Partnerships for the Center for the Collaborative Classroom and supports schools in Idaho, Utah, and Wyoming with curriculum implementations.

Marine is also the author of *Getting Started with Teacher Clarity* and co-author of *Leading with Administrator Clarity*. Marine received her Bachelor's in Elementary Education from the University of California, Irvine, and her Master's in Educational Leadership and Policy Studies from California State University, Northridge.

She lives in the Boise area with her husband and two sons.

List of Resources
in the Book

Number	Title
Resource 3.1	SAMPLE Deconstructing the Standards: Teacher Template
Resource 3.2	BLANK Deconstructing the Standards: Teacher Template
Resource 3.3	Steps to Co-Creating Success Criteria
Resource 4.1	How to Create a Pre-Assessment in Google Forms
Resource 4.2	4 Corners
Resource 4.3	Chat Log Sample Card Secondary
Resource 4.4	Chat Log Sample Card Primary
Resource 4.5	Show What You Know—Gallery Walk
Resource 4.6	Show What You Know—ABC Brainstorm
Resource 4.7	Show What You Know—ABC Brainstorm (Sample Completed)
Resource 4.8	Sample Entrance Ticket
Resource 4.9	Blank, Editable Sample Entrance Tickets
Resource 4.10	Animal Adaptations Anticipation Guide
Resource 4.11	Blank, Editable Anticipation Guide
Resource 5.1	KWL Chart

(Continued)

Resource 5.2   One-Minute Essay

Resource 5.3   Light Bulb Moments

Resource 5.4   Formative Classroom Mastery Deck Cards

Resource 5.5   Student Mastery Tracker

Resource 5.6   Clarify This!

Resource 5.7   Think-Pair-Share

Resource 5.8   Questions for My Teacher

Resource 5.9   Learning Logs

Resource 5.10   Anonymous No

Resource 5.11   Sheet Protector Boards

Resource 5.12   What Are Your Wonderings?

Resource 5.13   Learning Target Tickets

Resource 5.14   Quick Writes

Resource 5.15   Doodle It!

Resource 5.16   Red, Yellow, Green

Resource 5.17   Parking Lot

Resource 5.18   Levels of Questioning

Resource 5.19   Anchor Charts

Resource 5.20   Fist to Five

Resource 5.21   3-2-1

Resource 5.22   Visual Maps

Resource 5.23   Picture Notes

Resource 5.24   Error Analysis

Resource 5.25a   2-Column Charts

Resource 5.25b   3-Column Charts

Resource 6.1   Jigsaw

Resource 6.2   Inside/Outside Circle

Resource 6.3   Structured Language Talk

Resource 6.4   Pass It On!

Resource 6.5   Think-Aloud

Resource 6.6   Collaboration Board

Resource 6.7   Goals and Steps

Resource 6.8   One-Minute Shares

Resource 6.9   Lingering Questions

Resource 6.10   Give One, Get One

Resource 7.1   Developing Conversation Ground Rules

Resource 7.2   Classroom Stems Poster

Resource 7.3   Dialogic Classroom Stems Bookmarks (Grades 3–10)

Resource 7.4   Analysis of Classroom Rules for Discussion

Resource 7.5   Peer Thinking Analysis/Observational Tool

Resource 8.1   Developing Team Commitments

Resource 8.2   Team Norm Development Activity

Resource 8.3   Formative Assessment in the PLC

Resource 8.4   PLC Common Formative Protocol, Shortened Protocol

Resource 8.5   PLC Common Formative Protocol, Detailed Protocol

Resource 9.1a   Student Self-Assessment Checklist (Primary)

Resource 9.1b   Student Self-Assessment Checklist (Upper Elementary)

Resource 10.1   Formative Post-Instruction, Basic Exit Tickets 3-2-1

Resource 10.2   Formative Post-Instruction, Procedural Exit Tickets, Strategy

Resource 10.3   Formative Post-Instruction, Declarative Exit Ticket, Message in a Bottle

Resource 10.4   Formative Post-Instruction, Metacognitive Exit Ticket, Thinking Head

Resource 10.5   Formative Post-Instruction, Reflection

Resource 10.6   Formative Post-Instruction—3 Times Summary

Before Instruction: Setting Up Your Classroom for Success

CHAPTER 1

Formative Assessment Overview: What the Research Says

If you have been in education for any period of time, you may have noticed the buzz around formative assessment getting louder with each passing school year. There are many reasons why formative assessment is considered critical in student learning and practical instruction. This chapter will spend some time diving into the research behind formative assessment to lay the groundwork for the rest of this book.

Like all good practitioners, we believe that the more time we spend on high-yield, research-based strategies, the better off our students will be as a result of our efforts. We spent a great deal of time reviewing the large body of research on the most effective educational practices and firmly believe that spending time and energy on formative assessment and feedback is time well spent.

Creating a Common Language

Before diving into all the types and forms of formative assessment, we must develop a shared understanding of what formative assessment is and a common language around this critical educational practice. Once we have completed that, we will dive into what the research tells us about why formative assessment matters.

This handbook defines formative assessment as

> Any assessment task designed to promote students' learning.
> The purpose of these tasks is to provide feedback for teachers
> and students so that in-the-moment adjustments can be made
> to teaching and learning opportunities to more effectively enable
> students to reach proficiency.

It is important to note that for this conversation, there are two critical components of formative feedback:

- Formative feedback is an in-the-moment assessment that can provide immediate information to students and educators about the learning taking place in the classroom.

- This information must be used to make adjustments to and drive future instruction within the school.

If either of these elements is missing, an authentic formative assessment has yet to occur.

While we imagine the vast majority of readers have a highly developed understanding of assessment, it is crucial to take a moment and make sure we are all speaking the same language when we talk about assessment.

- Summative assessment—or *assessment of learning*—is exactly as it sounds. When teachers provide an assessment to the students at the end of a defined learning cycle, after which the material has been taught, re-taught, and mastery is expected, they engage in summative assessment. Common summative assessment examples include end-of-course exams, district benchmark testing, standard end-of-unit tests, and end-of-the-school-year statewide exams, which help create school grades and ratings.

- Formative assessment—or *assessment for learning*—is focused on identifying students' needs *and* responding to those learning needs. Formative assessment requires teachers to make frequent, interactive, and feedback-driven assessments to better adjust their instruction to help *all* students reach high standards. The most effective formative assessments work to involve the students in the process actively and to take ownership of their learning.

One main reason that formative assessment has become an education "go-to" is that it can produce more significant results than many other current strategies. It is often more time and cost-effective than many other options to boost student achievement. Suppose a school leader on a tight budget has the option to reduce class size or provide solid professional development (PD) on formative assessment and work toward fidelity of implementation. In that case, I can tell you which one their budget would probably dictate needs to be selected.

A Brief Overview of the Research Supporting Formative Assessment

While the purpose of this book is not to complete an exhaustive research review, we feel that any time teaching methods are discussed, that conversation should be squarely framed around what the research tells us is best for student learning and performance. To that end, we will dive into a brief but essential overview of the research behind the formative assessment.

One of the main reasons that education has felt, at times, like a pendulum, shifting from one new idea to initiative to the next, is because the most recent "new idea" was just that—one person's idea of what would work best with kids.

If John Hattie taught us anything in his work on effect sizes, it is that, by and large, what we are doing in education works. Over 95% of the 256 influences related to student achievement that he analyzed in his meta-analysis had a positive impact on student achievement, and those that did not were pretty obvious. No one is surprised by the idea that bullying or moving harms student learning (Hattie, 2015). So *if* it can be said that, by and large, most of what we are doing in education works, it is incumbent upon us, the practitioners, to utilize data to determine what works *best*.

In his review of meta-analyses on classroom feedback, Hattie (2015) found that formative feedback can significantly contribute to students' achievements, averaging an effect size of .73 (or nearly two years' growth in one year). As a classroom teacher, you know that you cannot focus your time everywhere, so it makes sense to look at those strategies that have the most significant overall impact on student achievement. Formative assessment and feedback are two areas where student growth exceeds the expected annual growth of "one year's growth in one year" and instead falls into "the zone of desired effects," where influences significantly exceed anticipated annual growth expectations.

In addition to Hattie's work, many other researchers, educational organizations, and institutions have studied the impact of formative assessment on student learning outcomes. There is also a large body of past and present research that has served to remind all educators that education is both an art and a science.

According to a policy brief from the OECD Observer and the Centre for Educational Research and Innovation (CERI), *achievement gains* associated with formative assessment have been described as "among the largest ever reported for educational interventions" (OECD, 2005).

Furthermore, the study concluded that using formative assessments positively impacts equity. According to CERI, "formative assessment also improves equity of student outcomes. Schools that use formative assessment show not only general gains in academic achievement but also exceptionally high gains for previously underachieving students. Attendance and retention of learning are also improved, as well as the quality of students' work" (OECD, 2005).

In their article "Inside the Black Box: Raising Standards Through Classroom Assessment," Black and Wiliam conducted a thorough research review. They determined that practical formative assessment includes teachers adjusting theory teaching in response to student learning and students receiving feedback with specific information about how they can improve their academic outcomes, including the integration of self-assessment. Their research review concluded that formative assessment can account for the largest ever reported gains as an educational intervention for lower-achieving students (Black and Wiliam, 1998).

Goertz, Olah, and Riggan, in their 2009 policy brief titled "Can Interim Assessments be Used for Instructional Change?" dove into a study of 45 elementary school teachers across nine schools and two districts. Their goal was to determine how well formalized formative assessments (specifically, interim assessments in math) impacted teachers' use of data in a cycle of instructional improvement. The goal was to determine how teachers gathered or accessed evidence about student learning; next, how they analyzed and interpreted that evidence, and how they used evidence to plan instruction and carry out improved instruction. While they found interim assessments to be effective in guiding instruction, their main conclusion was that interim assessments designed for instructional purposes are helpful but insufficient to inform instructional change. Essentially, those quarterly assessments are not happening often enough, and the data is not utilized widely enough to guide classroom practices. This truly speaks to the need for real-time, moment formative assessment as the most effective way to meet the needs of all students and impact instructional practice.

Grant Wiggins and Jay McTighe (2005) reflect heavily on the importance of "beginning with the end in mind" and the critical role of both backward planning and authentic, timely, and specific feedback as key components of meaningful learning. In *Understanding by Design*, Wiggins and McTighe argue that backward design is focused primarily on student learning and understanding. When teachers are designing lessons, units, or courses, they often focus on the activities and instruction rather than the outputs of the instruction. They suggest instead that beginning with the *know* and *show* output from the instruction allows for teachers to develop formative assessment, which helps build the level of student understanding and assists teachers in developing appropriate formative assessments throughout the learning sequence.

Renowned education researcher Robert Marzano dives deep into citing the significant impact that instructional feedback has on formative and summative assessment scores. Throughout this book, we will be referring to their work, as appropriate, to point out the places that it ties into the instructional practices that we present. In his 2010 work *Formative Assessment & Standards-Based Grading,* Marzano details specific benefits of formative assessment. He dives into the true importance of formative assessment as it relates to student performance, growth, and grading. He spends a large amount of time reminding his readers that formative scores are not an accurate way to determine student grades. Specifically, he shares that when a teacher tracks a student's formative scores for one unit, the student's scores will generally show a progression of learning and therefore a student's scores likely will be lower at the beginning of a unit than at the end. If a teacher averages a student's formative scores to calculate a summative score, the resulting summative score would be lower than the student's actual current level of skill, as it would give early scores the same weight as later scores. Marzano suggests instead that teachers should give more weight to scores at the end of the unit, which generally best reflect students' level of mastery. He also puts a lot of emphasis on the importance of oral responses and teachers' discussions as a form of formative assessment, a concept we dive into in our chapter on dialogic teaching and dialectic synergy.

While most of our educational research review was focused on the United States, it is essential to note that formative assessment is widely embraced nationally. While formative assessment has become so commonplace that it is used at schools in 25 U.S. states as an official policy (Altman et al., 2010), it is not simply a U.S. education phenomenon. Nations across the globe, including Scotland, England,

New Zealand, Canada, Finland, Germany, Singapore, Sweden, and Spain, have all encouraged teachers to use formative assessment in the teaching and learning process.

The Benefits of Formative Assessment in the Classroom and Across the District

We would not have written this book had we not seen the substantial benefits of formative assessment firsthand. We believe, and the research supports, that utilizing formative assessment can increase student learning and teachers' feelings of efficacy. We have seen firsthand how formative assessment has increased student outcomes, increased student engagement, and improved teachers' instructional practices in the following areas:

- **Response to Intervention (RTI) and Multi-Tiered Systems of Support (MTSS)**. Teachers can gauge student learning continually, create intervention groups, differentiate instruction, re-teach as needed, and scaffold learning by utilizing daily, weekly, monthly, and quarterly formative assessment practices.

- **Small group rotations for individualized instruction**. Research supports using small groups to tailor learning based on student needs.

- **Student agency**. When formative assessment is coupled with frequent and authentic feedback, students are more engaged in their learning and feel a true sense of ownership.

While most districts are talking about formative assessment, and many districts claim to utilize formative assessment, a deep dive into classrooms across America would tell a different story. *By and large, formative assessment has* not *been adopted to the level it needs to be to impact student outcomes*. It seems formative assessment is sprinkled into the curriculum and across classrooms, but teachers still feel the pressure for grades in the grade book and are moving on to "cover" their material.

Table 1.1 might help give insight into what a "typical" classroom looks like now and what it *could* look like if the formative assessment truly were embraced across the nation.

Table 1.1   Average classroom with and without formative assessment.

Topic	Current "average" classroom	Potential "average classroom" if formative feedback were embraced widely
Tests	While students may engage in some pre-assessment reviews and games/activities, students are given formal summative assessments, roughly once per week to once per unit, in all content areas.	Formal summative assessments would be given on an as-needed basis and may occur for different groups at different times. Teachers could focus on instruction to mastery *even if* it meant fewer assignments were graded. By and large, daily in-the-moment formatives would guide instruction and provide informal data for re-teaching.
Grades	The frequent assessments help teachers to have plenty of grades to put in the grade book to provide precise feedback to parents on student progress.	Grade books would have far fewer grades, but the hope is that students would have a higher degree of mastery overall.
Engagement	Students have varying levels of engagement, from the authentically engaged to the ritual compliance and rebellion. Typically, these levels of engagement closely mirror academic performance.	All students have increased levels of engagement as they can begin to see how they can be successful in their learning and have a hand in their success.
Feedback	Feedback is provided regularly on assessments, although the frequency varies by teacher. Typically, when students receive feedback, it is on a summative assignment and a grade has been entered.	Feedback is provided regularly on low-stake activities. Students are pushed to learn and change, provided success criteria, and given a clear indication of what is needed to succeed when a grade is assigned.

Topic	Current "average" classroom	Potential "average classroom" if formative feedback were embraced widely
Instruction	Teachers begin each school year with a pacing guide and a set of lessons they intend to teach. As the year goes on, they make minor adjustments based on changes to the school calendar, but by and large, they closely align with the pacing guide.	While teachers begin each school year with a pacing guide and a set of lessons they intend to teach, they administer pre-assessments and formative assessments as the year progresses. They can adjust the pacing of their instruction based on student and classroom needs. Some content can be skipped over, while other content is given additional time so students reach mastery.
Differentiation	At the beginning of the school year, the teacher reviews testing data and creates groups based on a student's overall academic profile. When and if students are provided small group instruction, they attend with a homogeneous group of students.	Rather than rely on the beginning-of-the-year assessments or previous test scores, teachers use in-the-moment formative data to create small intervention and enrichment groups based on student understanding of the specific content. These groups can change within each unit and vary from standard to standard.

The following are some key benefits of integrating formative assessment (with fidelity) into your everyday practice!

- **Clear expectations for student performance.** By implementing formative assessment regularly in your classroom, students have clear objectives, and teachers can intervene "at the moment" to clear up confusion and redirect student learning.

- **Frequent opportunities for feedback.** After setting clear expectations, the formative assessment process allows teachers to provide students with frequent, specific, and targeted feedback.

- **Improved student performance.** With clear expectations and the ability to receive regular, specific, and targeted feedback, this feedback via formative assessment helps students narrow the divide between what they can do and the lesson expectations. By teaching students how to self-monitor (a key component of formative assessment), they can become self-regulated, independent, and autonomous in reviewing and correcting their work.

- **Increases in student engagement and agency.** Throughout the formative assessment process, students are called on to set their own learning goals and measure their progress; this directly impacts levels of student motivation and increases their agency in their learning.

- **More effective differentiation and scaffolding.** The formative assessment practice helps teachers better understand student needs. With this understanding, they can increase rigor and differentiate up or determine gaps and scaffold accordingly, which leads to more personalized learning opportunities.

- **Data-based instruction.** With formative assessment and multiple data points, teachers can better incorporate data in their decisions on how to re-teach, skip, and adjust their instruction.

Formative Assessment and Feedback

In his journal article "Formative Assessment and the Design of Instructional Systems," D. Royce Sadler discussed the critical role of feedback in formative assessment. Sadler (1989) defined the formative assessment system as containing a feedback loop to minimize the gap between a learner's current knowledge and the desired learning outcomes. He also clarified that information becomes valid only when a learner actively uses new information (feedback) to close any preexisting gaps (p. 121).

Sadler's model works as described in Figure 1.1.

Figure 1.1
Critical role of feedback in formative assessment.

Teacher receives information from formative assessment

Teacher modifies instruction based on information

Teacher provides feedback to students about how they can improve their learning.

Formative Assessment and the Ongoing Feedback Loop

The ongoing feedback loop and formative assessment are closely related, as they both focus on providing regular, ongoing feedback to students to help them improve their learning and progress. While formative assessment is a type of assessment that is designed to provide feedback to students and teachers throughout the learning process, to help students improve their learning and progress, the ongoing feedback loop is a key component of the formative assessment process. It involves regularly providing students with feedback on their learning and using that feedback to help them improve. This can take many forms, including teacher feedback on student work, peer feedback, and self-assessment. By providing regular feedback to students, teachers can help them understand what they are doing well and where they need to improve.

One of the key benefits of the ongoing feedback loop is that it allows students to receive regular feedback on their learning, which can help them stay on track and make progress. When students receive regular feedback, they are more likely to be engaged and motivated in their learning, and they are more likely to be successful. This is because regular feedback helps students to understand what they are doing well and where they need to focus their efforts to improve.

The ongoing feedback loop also helps teachers to understand their students' learning needs. By providing regular feedback to students, teachers can identify areas where students are struggling and provide targeted support and intervention. This can help to ensure that students receive the support they need to succeed and can help to prevent learning gaps from developing.

Overall, the ongoing feedback loop and formative assessment are closely related, and they both play an important role in helping students to learn and progress. By providing regular, ongoing feedback to students, teachers can help them to understand their learning needs, and provide the support they need to succeed. This, in turn, can help to improve student achievement and ensure that students are well prepared for the challenges of the future.

Summary

In this chapter, we began by creating a common language around formative assessment. We determined, for this book, formative assessment was any assessment task designed to promote students' learning. The purpose of these tasks is to provide feedback for both the teachers and the students so that "in-the-moment" adjustments can be made to teaching and learning opportunities to more effectively enable students to reach proficiency.

Next, we spent some time differentiating between summative assessment (assessment of learning) and formative assessment (assessment for learning). Finally, we did a shallow dive into some of the research supporting formative assessment, including work from John Hattie, The Centre for Educational Research and Innovation (CERI), Black and Wiliam, and Goertz, Olah, and Riggan (CERI, n.d.). Finally, we reviewed what a classroom looks like with and without authentically embedded formative assessment and reviewed the overall benefits of a classroom that strategically embeds formative assessment throughout the learning sequence.

Key Takeaways

- I can define formative assessment.
- I can recognize the difference between formative and summative assessments.
- I understand some of the research supporting formative assessment and how utilizing formative assessment in my classroom can benefit my students in a variety of ways.
- I understand some of the research supporting formative assessment and how utilizing formative assessment in my classroom can benefit me as a teacher and my ability to gauge student progress.

Setting Up the Classroom for Successful Implementation

To effectively administer and use formative assessment in your classroom, it is important that you set the stage for a successful rollout. In this chapter, we will dive into how you can organize your classroom and students to have the maximum opportunity for success.

Nancy Frey says, "When learning is organized and intentional, and when the learner knows what he or she is learning, great things can happen" (Fisher et al., 2018). This is what we want our classroom organization and management to embody.

In this chapter, we will focus on "clarity of organization." These are the lesson tasks, assignments, and activities that link the learning goals and student outcomes.

Where to Begin—Start Small!   When you start thinking about all that goes into organizing your classroom for formative assessment (planning, explicit instruction, success criteria, target responses, etc.), it may feel a little overwhelming. Starting with something manageable can help lessen the stress and help you integrate teacher clarity more seamlessly into your daily teaching routine.

Where to Begin—Create Goals!   Think about where you want to be in two to three months. Do you want to have a solid plan for formative assessments? Do you want to have your learning intentions and success criteria planned out for a math unit? Do you want to create target responses for a writing standard in your grade level?

When you think about where you want to be in a short period, you can start backward, planning your path.

Where to Begin—Do the Work Collaboratively!   Great things happen for your students when you work with your grade-level team. Through collaboration and the common goal of creating teacher clarity comes collective teacher efficacy, the belief of teachers in their ability to positively affect student outcomes.

When it comes to formative assessment and measuring student success, we need to look at where students are in the learning process.

Organizing Your Classroom

Classroom organization and management are essential to incorporate formative assessment into your daily classroom routine intentionally. We will address some helpful hacks that will support your quest to incorporate additional formative assessment into your classroom.

Setting up routines in your classroom is essential for students to know what to expect every day. This lowers anxiety and gives students predictable routines while also helping them succeed. Routines are also essential to ensuring your formative assessment practices are intentional and run smoothly.

The following are some examples of routines you can set up in your classroom.

Turn-In Bins

Turn-in bins can be used for more than just turning in work. Change your turn-in bins into Self-Assessment Turn-in Bins. This will encourage your students to choose their Level of Understanding when completing their work.

Get your students to turn in their work and acknowledge their Level of Understanding. This also will help get you into the routine of using turn-in bins as a formative assessment.

Whether it is an independent practice page or a quick assessment, students can turn in their work according to their level of understanding. This supports you as the classroom teacher in ensuring that you understand your students' feelings about an assignment (Freibrun, 2021).

It is effortless to set up in your classroom.

Use four different bins and label them with each Level of Understanding. Here's an example of how you can label your bins (see Figure 2.1):

- 4 – I understand and can teach my peers.

- 3 – I almost have it, but I may need a little more practice.

Figure 2.1 Turn-in bins.

- 2 – I am a little confused and need some clarification.
- 1 – I am lost. Please re-teach me.

Set them up so they are visible to students and easily accessible as they turn in their work.

Students will know where their work goes, and you will know how students are doing and how *they think* they are doing.

Classroom Library

Use your classroom library. A well-stocked classroom library can be a valuable resource for formative assessment. You can use books to assess students' reading levels, interests, and comprehension skills, and you can use them as a starting point for discussions, writing assignments, and other formative assessment activities.

Physical Space

Use the physical space in your classroom wisely. Consider how you can arrange the furniture and other physical elements in your classroom to support formative assessment. For example, you might set up small group workstations, create a quiet reading area, or designate a space for student presentations.

Small Group Rotations

Setting up small group rotations in your classroom can be an effective way to provide personalized instruction and support to students. It allows you to differentiate instruction and meet the individual needs of each student in a more focused and efficient way.

To set up small group rotations, start by dividing your students into small groups based on their ability levels or other factors, such as their learning styles or interests. You can use a variety of methods to group your students, including pre-assessment, ongoing formative assessment, or other techniques.

Once your students are grouped, you can plan out the rotations for each group. This might involve setting up different stations or activities for each group or assigning each group a specific task or project to work on.

When planning your rotations, it's important to consider the amount of time you have available and the goals you want to achieve. For example, you might want to spend more time with struggling students or focus on a specific skill or concept.

To embed formative assessment in the teacher-led rotation, you can use a variety of strategies. One effective approach is to incorporate formative assessment tasks into the activities and tasks that students are working on during the rotation.

For example, you might ask students to complete a quiz or quizlet on a specific topic or have them work on a project that involves applying the skills and knowledge they have learned. You can then use the results of these formative assessments to adjust your instruction and provide additional support to students as needed.

Another strategy is to incorporate formative assessment into the feedback you provide to students during the rotation. For example, you might provide students with regular feedback on their progress and offer suggestions for improvement based on their performance.

Instructional rotations are typically when we meet with small groups of students while the rest of our class works on something independently. Our time with small groups is vital because we are re-teaching or extending concepts for specific students.

Formative assessment helps us determine which groups of students we meet with and what skills students work on independently. It is also a critical time for students to work independently because they should be doing more than just "busy work." It should be purposeful.

Picture this:

You have just taught a whole group lesson on identifying a character's traits. You have taken your small group back to support them in understanding this new learning goal. The other students are sitting at their desks working on independent work. This is their opportunity to practice the same skill and not just complete busy work that is not aligned with the learning goal.

So, how can we make that work in our classrooms?

Here are some ideas for ensuring we are intentional with our time and students work on purposeful skills while in instructional rotations.

It is important to use differentiated lessons during small group rotation. Differentiated instruction is a teaching approach that focuses on meeting the individual needs of each student in the classroom. This approach recognizes that every student learns at their own pace and has unique learning styles and abilities. As a result, it is important for teachers to provide a range of options for students to choose from during independent work time, to accommodate their diverse needs and interests.

One way to create differentiated work for students during independent work time is to offer a variety of activities for them to choose from. These activities should be designed to meet the needs of students with different learning styles, abilities, and interests. For example, some students may prefer hands-on activities, while others may prefer to read or write. Some students may work on reinforcing basic skills, while others may work on more advanced concepts.

To create these activities, teachers can use a variety of resources, including books, websites, and games. They can also incorporate technology, such as computers and tablets, to provide interactive and engaging options for students. In addition, teachers can use graphic organizers, such as Venn diagrams and concept maps, to help students organize their thoughts and ideas.

When creating the activities, it is important for teachers to provide clear instructions and examples for students to follow. This will help students understand what is expected of them and how to complete the activity successfully. Teachers also can provide support and guidance as needed, to help students who may be struggling or need additional assistance.

Another way to create differentiated work for students during independent work time is to offer a range of options for students to choose from. This can include activities that are designed for different ability levels, as well as activities that focus on different content areas, such as math, science, or social studies. Teachers also can provide options that allow students to work independently, in pairs, or in small groups. This will give students the opportunity to choose the type of activity that best meets their needs and interests.

In addition to providing a range of options, teachers also can provide support and accommodations for students who may need extra help. This can include providing additional resources or materials, offering one-on-one support, or providing modifications to the activity. For example, a student who is working on a math activity may need extra support with the concepts, so the teacher could provide additional examples or explanations to help the student understand.

Overall, creating differentiated work for students during independent work time requires a thoughtful and intentional approach. By offering a range of activities and options, providing clear instructions and support, and providing accommodations as needed, teachers can create an environment that is conducive to learning for all students.

Overall, incorporating formative assessment into small group rotations can help you better understand each student's needs and adjust your instruction accordingly, providing a more effective and personalized learning experience for all of your students.

Setting Behavior Expectations

Part of classroom routines is setting behavior expectations. Students should know what you expect throughout the school day. Once you have explicitly taught your students what you expect, your classroom instruction should go off without a hitch. Table 2.1 gives you some tips to set expectations.

Table 2.1 Tips on setting behavior expectations.

Tip	Explanation	Example
Make them activity-specific	Think about your instructional day and your daily schedule. Break up those activities/daily lessons into sections.	Think about the expectations you have for each of these activities in your classroom and list them under each activity. Some of the same expectations might fall under multiple activities, which is okay! Independent Work Whole Group Lessons Small Group/Partner Work Entering/Exiting Morning Meeting
Phrase them positively	Write the behavior expectations in a positive way. Stay away from saying "don't" or "no" and phrase them in a way that tells students what to do instead of what not to do.	Instead of "Don't talk while others are talking," say, "Use a voice level 0 while others are talking." Instead of "No shouting out," say, "Use our classroom sign language to share an idea with our class."

Call out the action with specificity	We often see classroom rules listed as subjective phrases like:
	    Have fun.
	    Listen while others talk.
	    Raise your hand to share.
	They do not give students a specific instance to understand how to behave or know what is expected.
	To help your students be successful, it is essential to be specific about what action or expectation you want to see.
		Here are four specific, concise, and positively written expectations that are easy for students to follow for independent work:
		    Use a voice level of 0 while working.
		    Use our classroom sign language while raising your hand to ask a question.
		    Write your level of understanding of your independent work.
		    Choose an early finisher to complete if you finish your work early.

While you must spend time carefully creating behavioral expectations, it is equally important that you are strategic in implementing these expectations.

- **Post them in a visible location.** It is essential to have these expectations posted in a visible location for students to see at all times and for you to refer to throughout the day.

- **Explicitly teach the expectations and review them daily/weekly.** You should use the first few weeks of school to teach behavior expectations, but it does not stop there. Review expectations before whole group lessons, prior to students working independently, while entering and exiting the classroom, and especially when you return from breaks.

- **Teach and review expectations.** We cannot assume our students remember or understand what behavior should look like during certain situations, so take the time to remind them what you expect. They will more than likely live up to that expectation.

Instructional Planning

Routines aren't just for students. As teachers, we also should plan for the day, week, month, and school year with intention. Get into the routine of planning out times for formative assessment throughout your instructional day.

Self-Assessment

Here are some things to consider as you plan your lessons.

Self-Assessment Tickets

Are you incorporating self-assessment tickets? We will dive more deeply into this strategy in a later chapter, but for now, consider knowing how many lessons you will be using for self-assessment. Make copies of those tickets to have them ready before each lesson. If you are doing something digitally, use our digital form in your lesson to give students a chance to self-assess before you teach and after the lesson is done.

Assess with Intention

What is the purpose of your assessments for the week or the unit you are planning? When you are planning out your assessments, be sure to use backward planning strategies to ensure you are planning and assessing with intention. In backward planning, teachers work to be intentional in not only knowing the curriculum standards, but also in creating formative and summative assessments to meet student needs and abilities, and finally in designing lessons that integrate these standards and assessments.

Learning Goals

Outline the learning goals for your small group rotations, also known as learning objectives. These should be visible to your students, so they know their learning goals in their small groups. This is also important for your formative assessment of student learning so you can tailor the next lesson's goals to fit all your students' needs. These same learning goals should be used for students working independently. The work they complete should be aligned with a learning goal that has been communicated.

Summary

We began the chapter with a quote by Nancy Fray: "When learning is organized and intentional, and when the learner knows what he or she is learning, great things can happen." It is our belief that by organizing your classroom with turn-in bins, developing a classroom library, paying careful attention to physical space, creating a plan for small group rotations, and establishing solid behavioral expectations, you will spend time to save time. All of this will assist you in creating an environment where academic success and success with formative assessment can thrive.

Key Takeaways

- I have created turn-in bins or an effective system of collecting work.
- I have developed and refined clear behavior expectations for students.
- I outline learning goals for in-class rotations.
- I have differentiated independent work for students to complete during small group rotations.

Selecting Learning Targets and Developing Success Criteria

Many teachers believe that formative assessment begins when they administer an assessment to their students and utilize the data from those assessments to create intervention and enrichment-based instructional groups. In reality, formative assessment is an ongoing process that begins before a teacher ever begins a lesson. Authentic formative assessment is a process that begins the moment a teacher begins to think about their upcoming lesson. The lesson design phase, which they engage in, will include two critical elements of formative assessment: selecting the learning targets and developing the success criteria.

Very few current practitioners, including us, had the benefit, when we were in elementary school, of teachers who were provided with the most current research on best practices and utilized learning targets and success criteria to guide their learning. The introduction to a new lesson may have looked something like the scenario below for us.

> "Today, we are beginning our new class book, *Charlotte's Web*. We will start by reading the first three chapters. I think all of you boys and girls will enjoy this book. It takes place on a farm, and the main characters are a pig and his best friend, a spider, Charlotte. They develop a magical friendship. I think this book will be a fun read for us all. At the end of the book, we will do some fun projects and create some dioramas and journals about our reading!

While our teachers may have done a great job of getting us interested in what we were going to read and selecting reading that would be engaging for us, they did not always know to clearly articulate *what* we were doing, *why* we were doing it, and *how* we would have our outcomes measured once we completed these tasks. Compare the lesson intro above to the one provided below:

"Today, we are beginning our new class book, *Charlotte's Web*. To begin, we will read the first three chapters of the novel. We will be paying particular attention to standard 3.3 as we read (**RL.3.3** — Describe characters in a story [e.g., their traits, motivations, or feelings] and explain how their actions contribute to the sequence of events). More specifically, we will do the following in each chapter:

Chapter 1—Defend our opinion about whether or not all the family members have the same perspective as Wilbur.

Chapter 2—Complete an analysis of the author's use of details to help us understand how each family member views Wilbur.

Chapter 3—Describe Wilbur's interaction with the goose and explain how this interaction helps us better understand Wilbur.

Once we finish these three chapters, you will complete a writing task focused on how character traits contribute to the events in a story based on these three chapters. At that time, you will be provided with a specific rubric to self-assess your writing along with specific language standards, which you will be asked to integrate into your writing, Li3.1h and Li3.1i (using coordinating conjunctions and producing a simple compound and complex sentences). I am excited to dive into this new book with you, so let us start.

It is obvious to recognize the differences between the introduction of this novel and these two third-grade classrooms. While both teachers take the time to give the students a little peek into what is to come, they do it dramatically differently. To be entirely successful at formative assessment, it is essential to understand why the second introduction is far more effective in setting the stage for learning for the students.

Two key components are missing from the first example and present in the second example: *learning targets* and *success criteria*. This chapter will provide a working definition and common language around these two concepts. Next, we will dive deeper into why these matter based on the research. Then, we will provide pointers on easy ways to create these and implement them within your classroom. Finally, we will share resources and images to refer to when beginning the implementation process.

Creating a Common Language Around Learning Targets and Success Criteria

First, we must develop a common language about what we mean when we use these two terms. For this book, when we use the term *learning targets*, we are directly addressing the targets teachers use to determine what they will teach the students *and* what the students will learn as a result of their instruction. Teachers use these learning targets to decide what successful mastery of knowledge and skills looks like. When we discuss the concept of "success criteria," we refer to the specific guidance and feedback provided directly to the student. This feedback is provided so that they may know what success looks like for them and be more actively engaged in their learning. Success criteria allow students to measure their progress and assess their learning.

Learning Intentions: A Deeper Dive

In this section, we will dive deeper into learning targets, why they matter (what the research says about them), and provide specific steps for beginning implementation.

Learning targets, also referred to as learning intentions, are what we expect a student should be able to know, do, or understand after our lesson or group of lessons. Typically, as a teacher, it helps to focus on what we want students to learn and not what we want them to be able to produce (success criteria). As teachers, we spend time thinking about how the students learn the material we are teaching. Typically, this is done most effectively by linking these to standards or disaggregated portions of the most prominent standards. They are often provided to students in the first person and in student-friendly language. Providing learning intentions to students at the onset of a lesson encourages students to begin being metacognitive.

The Benefits of Learning Intentions

There are many benefits of explicit learning intentions for teachers and students. First and foremost, John Hattie's visible learning research has found that the effect size of having clear learning intentions versus not having them is an effect size of .68 (Hattie, 2012). This preliminary step in the formative assessment process can impact overall learning and achievement significantly, in addition to the research-based benefits of creating clear learning intentions.

Clarity for the Teacher

By creating clear learning intentions, a teacher knows what to teach, what to assess, what instructional activities to plan, how to interpret and use data and assessment results, how to monitor and report progress, and to work in PLC with other teachers with common learning intentions.

Clarity for the Student

By providing students with clear learning intentions, you give them a road map of where you are going. All too often, in education, we as teachers hold the map, but we do not allow students to have an idea of our direction and how all of their learning ties together. Creating learning intentions assists students in knowing the direction of their learning. As a result of knowing the direction of their learning (via learning intentions), there is also a significant increase in student autonomy. They can become more actively engaged in assessing their learning because they know what they are responsible for learning and how to react to feedback. Essentially, their autonomy is increased because they can self-assess, reflect on, and track their progress.

Clarity of the Content

Teaching can be overwhelming. A tremendous amount of content *and* new pacing plans and accountability measures have made teaching feel like a very high pressure profession. We never seem to have the time to "cover" all that we are asked to cover during a school year. The successful use of learning targets can help a teacher truly drill down on the "what" and the "how" of the expected learning and free teachers to systematically abandon superfluous content that does not directly relate to the learning intention.

Expert Advice

Writing the learning intention on the board does not magically make students process it. You, as the teacher, need to review, refer to it, and revisit it.

Types of Learning Intentions

Some of you may be reviewing this section and thinking, "This is all fine and good, but there is more than one type of learning that takes place in my classroom," and this is true. To be most effective at creating learning intentions, it is essential to understand the different types of learning intentions and the best way to examine and assess each learning intention.

In their 2012 book *Classroom Assessment for Learning*, authors Stiggins, Arter, Chappuis, and Chappuis assert that learning targets can fall into one of four categories: knowledge, reasoning, skill, and product (Stiggins et al., 2012, pp. 44–58).

Table 3.1 outlines these four types of learning intentions.

Table 3.1   Types of learning intentions and effective ways to assess them.

Type of learning intention	Purpose	Example	Multiple choice	Written response	Performance task
Knowledge	Simple and basic conceptual understanding or procedural knowledge.	Identify factors that determine the reliability of internet sources.	Y	Y	N
Reasoning	Focused on thinking and reasoning. The thought process students learn can apply to various content areas.	I can use data points from a random sample to draw inferences about voting patterns in a particular geographic region.	Y	Y	Y
Skill and product targets	Real-time demonstration of the creation of a product is the focus of the learning intention.	I can draft a friendly letter. I can dribble the soccer ball 50 yards.	N	N	Y

Type of learning intention	Purpose	Example	Multiple choice	Written response	Performance task
Disposition	The type of attitude one could or should have toward particular learning.	"Math Mindset"	N	Y	N

Source: Adapted from *Student-Involved Assessment for Learning* (4th Edition) by R.J. Stiggins. Upper Saddle River, NJ: Merrill Prentice Hall. Copyright 2005 Pearson Education Inc.

Sample Learning Intentions in the same content area—Content Area: Fine Arts

- *Knowledge*—I can identify how artists use wavy lines to create the illusion of movement in their artwork.

- *Reasoning*—I can evaluate the quality of my drawings by utilizing this technique to refine them.

- *Skill or Product*—I can use my brush to make wavy lines and create the illusion of movement in my artwork.

- *Disposition*—I place great value on the contributions art makes to our larger world.

Creating Learning Intentions: A Step-by-Step Guide

While creating a learning intention is not hard at all, it can feel daunting for a teacher new to employing this strategy. In this section, we will provide a two-step guide on how to create effective learning intentions for your students.

Step 1: Deconstruct the Standard into Teachable Chunks (Learning Targets)

It is nearly impossible to dive right into writing the learning intention if you have not spent some time digging into the content standards. Here is why: Nearly every standard we are provided as educators is deep, rich, and multifaceted. They are designed this way on purpose. The goal of the educational standards, as they were written, was to encourage students to engage in deep, thoughtful, and rigorous learning.

Expert Advice

Remember that when we deconstruct a standard, the goal is to take a large, broad, and multifaceted objective and break it into smaller, more manageable chunks of explicit learning targets. We want to know *what* the content standard requires students to know and be able to do, *not* how it will be assessed.

If, as an educator, we take a standard such as the following CCSS standard:

> RI 8.8—Delineate and evaluate the argument and specific claims in a text, assessing whether the reasoning is sound and the evidence is relevant and sufficient; recognize when irrelevant evidence is introduced.

Moreover, simplify it to this learning objective:

> I will read and evaluate Barack Obama's argument in *Statement by the President on the Shootings at Umpqua Community College, Roseburg, Oregon,* and assess whether the evidence is relevant and the reasoning is sound.

Then, when students complete the written product related to this learning and they believe that they have addressed the standard, they will be mistaken. This standard has many layers and levels. First, there are five specific and distinct verbs related to this standard, under-lined below:

> RI 8.8—<u>Delineate</u> and <u>evaluate</u> the argument and specific claims in a text, <u>assessing</u> whether the reasoning is sound and the evidence <u>is</u> relevant and sufficient; <u>recognize</u> when irrelevant evidence is introduced.

Next, the teacher must realize that each of these verbs has associated nouns to which these verbs are acting on, underlined below:

> RI 8.8—**Delineate** and **evaluate** the <u>argument</u> and specific <u>claims</u> in a text, **assessing** whether the <u>reasoning</u> is sound and the <u>evidence</u> **is** <u>relevant</u> and <u>sufficient</u>; recognize when irrelevant <u>evidence</u> is introduced.

Essentially, within this single standard, students should be able to show evidence of the following:

- Delineating an argument from a claim.
- Evaluating and argument.
- Evaluating a claim.
- Assessing the reasoning of an argument.
- Assessing the reasoning of a claim.
- Assessing if the evidence backing the argument or claim is relevant.
- Assessing if the evidence backing the argument or claim is sufficient.
- Recognizing when irrelevant evidence is introduced.

The complicated nature of this standard is not unique to this stan-dard. Quite the contrary; nearly every standard has many embedded learning objectives. The best and most effective way to ensure your learning intention is well written or that you have several learning intentions to meet a specific standard is to deconstruct the standards.

The following are the steps you can follow to deconstruct a standard. In addition, you will find a helpful blank template you can utilize when deconstructing your standards.

Step 1: Select the standard you wish to deconstruct.

- Underline all of the verbs in the standard.

- Circle all of the nouns in the standard.

Step 2: Look at each of the verbs.

- Determine if they are knowledge, reasoning, skill/product, or disposition related.

- Are there key targets, vocabulary, or understanding students need to know?

Step 3: Use the nouns with the verbs to write discrete targets.

Step 4: Use your deconstructed standard to write your learning targets.

Resource 3.1: SAMPLE Deconstructing the Standards: Teacher Template

Deconstructing Standards Template

STANDARD: Verbs are underlined and nouns are italicized
2NBT.B.9 <u>Explain</u> why *addition and subtraction strategies* work, <u>using</u> *place value* and the *properties of operations*.

NOUN	VERB
addition strategies, subtraction strategies, place value, properties of operations	explain, using
CONTENT	**SKILL**
<ul><li>addition and subtraction strategies</li><li>place value</li><li>operations properties</li></ul>	<ul><li>explain why they work</li><li>use</li></ul>

Deconstructed Concept	Deconstructed Skill	Level of Taxonomy	
		Blooms	**DOK**
addition and subtraction strategies<ul><li>place value</li><li>operations</li><li>properties</li></ul>	explain why they work, use	4	3

Resource 3.2: BLANK Deconstructing the Standards: Teacher Template

Deconstructing Standards Template

STANDARD:

NOUN	VERB
CONTENT	SKILL

Deconstructed Concept	Deconstructed Skill	Level of Taxonomy	
		Blooms	DOK

Step 2: Use Your Deconstructed Standards Template to Formulate Your Learning Intention

Once you have done the hard work of breaking down the standard into nouns, verbs, content, skill, and levels of rigor, you get to dive into the fun part, creating the students' learning intentions. Following are some tips for you:

- Make them SMART: use words to make each intention specific, measurable, attainable, relevant, and time bound.

- Consider using a student-friendly engaging tone.

- Make sure they are based on the deconstructed standard and match its rigor level.

- Use words associated with learning and your discipline language.

Typically, wording your learning intentions in terms of "I can" statements is most effective and student-friendly. For the example in Resource 3.2:

- I can use and explain why partial sums and partial differences work.

- I can use and explain why adjusting works.

- I can explain addition and subtraction using the properties of operations (commutative, associative, identity).

- I can explain why one can subtract by counting back or adding up.

In this example, you may give students two learning intentions at once or focus on a single learning intention and follow it to mastery before introducing the next learning intention.

Remember, in the words of John Hattie (2012).

> Good learning intentions are those that make clear to the students the type or level of performance they need to attain so that they understand where and when to invest energies, strategies, and thinking, and where they are positioned along the trajectory toward successful learning. In this way, they know when they

> have achieved the intended learning. . . . Learning intentions
> describe what we want students to learn, and clarity is at the
> heart of formative assessment. Unless teachers are clear about
> what they want students to learn (and what the outcome of this
> learning looks like), they are hardly likely to develop a good
> assessment of that learning. (p. 47)

In summary, learning intentions are what we expect a student should be able to know, do, or understand after our lesson or group of lessons. It helps to focus on what we want students to learn and not what we want them to be able to produce. Providing learning intentions to students at the onset of a lesson encourages students to begin engaging in metacognitive processes. There are many solid and research-based reasons why learning intentions strengthen a lesson and your overall efficacy as an educator.

Success Criteria: A Deeper Dive

In this section, we will dive deeper into success criteria, why they matter (what the research says about them), and provide specific steps for beginning implementation.

Unlike learning intentions focused on what a student is expected to know, do, or understand, student success criteria have a different purpose. Success criteria are designed to give students a clear and measurable understanding of "success" on a task. The overall goal of success criteria is for students to know what the teacher expects on a given task. Meeting this goal allows students to engage in self-assessment and determine if they have achieved the lesson objective.

Douglas Fisher, Nancy Frey, Olivia Amador Valerio, and Joseph Michael Assaf wrote *The Teacher Clarity Playbook* in 2018 and compared learning to flying a plane.

> Imagine getting into an airplane being flown by a pilot who did
> not know where he or she was headed. Rather, a control tower

would contact her at some unspecified time to let her know she had arrived, or worse, that she missed the mark entirely. That is a completely irrational way to fly a plane. (p. 20)

In essence, the analogy that they are making here is that if we do not provide students with a clear direction of not only *what* they are doing, but *how* they will be expected to show their knowledge at the end of a learning sequence, we are no different from the pilots and the control tower in this example. Our students need to know from the onset where we are going in a lesson, how we will get there, and what they will need to show to provide evidence of mastery.

Effective success criteria share several common characteristics, as follows:

- Show students how to demonstrate mastery successfully.

- Utilize precise and meaningful language.

- Allow for differentiation of products to increase student ownership and agency.

- Allow for flexibility, iteration, and refinement as the lesson progresses, and students' needs shift.

The Benefits of Success Criteria

In the most recent revision of his meta-analysis, John Hattie found that the use of success criteria on student learning is an effect size of .88. Since .4 is the equivalent of one year's growth in one year, this means that effective implementation of success criteria can catapult student performance and achievement.

In addition, success criteria have been shown to increase students' internal motivation. The more explicitly and precisely a student can see the goal, the more likely they will be motivated to meet it.

Success criteria are the logical next step after developing learning intentions because they work in concert with those learning intentions so that students know what success in the content area will look like. The reality is that when students know how to be successful and what that looks like, they are far more autonomous and engaged in their learning, and they can better assess their progress.

Creating Success Criteria: A Step-by-Step Guide

While creating learning intentions can be a rather time-intensive and laborious process until you get the hang of it, creating success criteria feels relatively natural and straightforward for most teachers. One of the main goals in creating success criteria is to be precise. You want to be specific and intentional about word choice and verb selection. This helps students see where these success criteria tie in with their learning.

The following are a few key steps you can follow when creating success criteria in your classroom and for your lessons.

Step 1: Use Precise Language

The importance of precise language choice in developing success criteria cannot be overstated. Remember, when you plan with the end in mind, you need to determine how students will show their learning and then be able to describe clear and concise success criteria. Teachers should work to engage their students throughout the entire learning sequence so that students have a clear understanding of what successful learning looks like. The careful and thoughtful development of these criteria enables teachers to focus their conversations with students, improve their assessment for learning, determine how students are responding to instruction, provide feedback to students, and develop assessment tasks and tools; when you create success criteria, it is essential to spend time to save time. As you think through the tasks your students will be able to know or do, make sure you are as explicit as possible.

Table 3.2 Ways to format success criteria for precision and impact.

Type	Description	Example
"I can" statements	Focus on explicit statements of future success levels.	I can use correct grammar so that my reader will understand my writing.
Statement of learning	These focus on specific and explicit statements of what has been learned.	My response explains the main idea and has evidence from the text that supports the main idea.
Layered success criteria	This is where there are multiple measurements of success within a single learning sequence.	I can identify the numerator and denominator. I can draw a model to represent fractions. I can use inequality symbols to compare fractions.

Success criteria are not telling students to "try hard or "do your best." They are also not tasks to be completed, such as "finish the art project" or "complete the writing assignment."

There are several ways to format your success criteria to be explicit and direct with your language, as described in Table 3.2.

While success criteria *can* include rubrics, rubrics alone are not success criteria. Success criteria can be used as the foundation of the rubric; then, the rubric is an indicator of the quality of a particular work. As with success criteria, rubrics must be written with descriptive and robust language so students can monitor their learning.

Step 2: Determine If the Skills Required Are Open or Closed

All skills we require of students in their success criteria can be classified as either open or closed. For a skill to be open, there are several ways a student may be able to demonstrate mastery. Examples of proficiency may include a menu of options a student can select to show mastery of the skill. Conversely, a closed skill would be one in which there is one correct answer and a limited number of strategies from which a student could select to demonstrate skill mastery. One example may be success criteria in a mathematical equation (closed skill). It might look like a list of the steps a student would follow to divide a fraction, as shown in Table 3.3.

In contrast, an open skill may have several methods by which a student could exemplify mastery, and they may be provided a choice board to determine how they would like to show their learning. See the success criteria menu in Table 3.4 on types of persuasion (open skill).

Table 3.3   Sample success criteria chart.

Steps to Divide a Fraction	Completed? Y/N
1. Invert or flip the second fraction to make it into its reciprocal.	Y
2. Multiply the first fraction by the reciprocal.	Y
3. Simply the fraction as needed.	Y

Table 3.4   Open-ended sample task menu with success criteria (persuasive techniques).

Menu item	Success criteria
Explore and describe figurative language in advertisements and create a digital shoe ad using these strategies.	• I can identify figurative language in advertisements. • I can identify persuasive devices in advertisements. • I can embed figurative language into my ad message.
Create a still-image advertisement to promote a product.	• I can identify the intended audience that my product, service, or message will appeal to. • I can determine if an emotional appeal, bandwagon pressuring (AKA bandwagon advertising), expert testimony, endorsements, or social proof is the most effective strategy for my audience.
Explore vocabulary choices in advertisements.	• I can create a persuasive ad using emotive language techniques. • I can find and identify when the author has used emotive language as a technique to pursue the reader. • I can explain how emotive language persuades audiences.

If you do not start by understanding the type of skill required, you will struggle with determining the most effective way to measure student progress on the skill.

Step 3: Wherever Possible, Involve Students in Creating Success Criteria

As teachers, it is easy for us to want to maintain all of the control when it comes to measuring student performance and mastery. In addition, on its face, it also seems to make the most sense. We know it is "us" who are responsible for ensuring students have achieved mastery, and our performance will be measured against how well we were able to get our students to that point.

While we recognize the inherent desire for teachers to "own" the measurement of mastery and the development of success criteria, we urge you to involve your students in this process. We believe that rather than having the teacher be the one who decides what quality work looks like, students can play an active role in this process as well.

This idea of working together with students in the development of creating success criteria is often referred to as "co-constructing success criteria."

There are a number of benefits to involving students in creating success criteria. First and foremost, involving students helps increase clarity. Sometimes, as teachers, we believe our expectations are explicit and clear. When students turned in their assignments, we soon learned we were not as straightforward as we thought. Involving students in creating success criteria also strengthens their ability to assess their work and their classmates' work. Finally, co-constructing success criteria allow teachers to make "in-the-moment" shifts based on student feedback. This improves a teacher's overall ability to plan his or her instruction.

It is important to note that "co-construction of success criteria" can take a variety of forms depending on the age of the students and the comfort level of the teacher. See Table 3.5.

Table 3.5   Various classroom methods for co-constructing success criteria.

	Teacher role	Student role
Teacher-driven	The teacher fully develops an assignment.	Students carefully examine success criteria.
Shared-responsibility	The teacher begins the assignment draft.	Students provide input and guidance for the assignment throughout its creation.
Student-directed	The teacher elicits student input before the assignment has been created.	Students weigh in on how they feel their learning would be best assessed.

By utilizing the model of co-constructing success criteria in your classroom, you can accelerate student learning at a more rapid pace. There are several key reasons for co-constructing success criteria to speed up the learning process. First and foremost, co-constructing success criteria put students in the driver's seat for their learning, agency is increased, and students "buy in" to their learning at a much higher level. Second, as a result of their increased agency, students become more deeply rooted and engaged in their learning. As we know from Hattie's (2015) work, student engagement has an effect size of .54, so it falls within the "zone of desired effects" and facilitates accelerated learning. Finally, and most importantly, the "co-construction" of success criteria profoundly engages students in metacognition. Students begin to analyze truly (often for the first time in their educational journeys) their thinking, learning expectations, anchor papers, and student samples. They then create mental comparisons of expected learning against these samples to discern what quality work looks like truly. It allows students to determine expectations, compare progress toward an expectation, and articulate the next steps needed to meet expectations.

How to Co-Construct Success Criteria with Your Students

As stated throughout this chapter, by co-constructing success criteria, you have created a shared understanding of what success looks like in a lesson, assignment, or unit. To make this a successful endeavor, students will need to be provided with exemplars, anchor papers, models, and examples so that they may actively engage in evaluating learning.

Resource 3.3: Steps to Co-Creating Success Criteria

Steps to co-creating success criteria.		
Step 1	Make yourself an expert first.	While it may be tempting to dive into this work alongside students, be sure you are well versed in the standards (deconstructed) and learning intentions within the curriculum. You can only guide students to develop the most meaningful measure of learning if you genuinely understand the rigor of the standard.
Step 2	Audit work samples.	Before beginning the process with your students, make sure you have reviewed previous work samples and collected or procured anchor papers so that you may use these to assist you in developing a solid shared understanding of quality work
Step 3	Introduce the concept to students.	The first time you work to co-construct with students it may feel unfamiliar to them. Over time, this will become a standard and welcome practice. For this step, make sure your students know what you are doing, "providing evidence that you have met the learning target," and why you are doing it: "to increase their involvement in assessing their learning." The first time you present this idea, you might want to spend an entire lesson reviewing the procedural steps in co-constructing success criteria. However, you can launch right into the process once this is a typical classroom practice.
Step 4	Provide students with work samples at various levels.	At this point, students understand the process, and now they need to dig into the work. You can lead this activity with the whole class or a small group. The first time you do this work, it may make sense to model it for the whole class, then use heterogeneous groups in subsequent sessions. Provide students with work samples, anchor papers, or materials to review. Ask them to determine the strengths and struggles of each work sample. Ask them to determine which of the following categories they would place the work into: meets learning intention, does not meet learning intention, exceeds learning intention.

Steps to co-creating success criteria.		
Step 5	Talk about it.	We are working to allow students to engage in the metacognitive process. Do *not* skip the opportunity for rigorous discourse with students about "how" and "why" they made the decisions that they made. This also gives you a glimpse into their thinking and allows you to clear up any misconceptions. This may be done in the whole class or in small groups with you circulating the classroom.
Step 6	Identify critical components.	It helps to provide documentation supplies or graphic organizers so that students may begin to create a list of components they deem as critical to meeting expectations.
Step 7	Share out.	At this point, bring students together and have them share out the critical components they discussed. Allow them to negotiate, and discuss as a group before generating a whole class agreed-upon list of success criteria.
Step 8	Nuance the wording.	As a class, decide how you want the success criteria stated. Will you use the "I can" statement, opt for specific descriptors or critical components, and create a visual in the classroom with the agreed-upon criteria?
Step 9	Throughout the learning, provide opportunities to self- and peer-assess.	Provide checkpoints throughout the learning whereby students can self-assess and peer-assess their work against anchor papers and exemplars.

How Learning Intentions and Success Criteria Differ

As mentioned already, learning intentions describe what students can learn and do; they are derived from the standards and guide lesson design. In contrast, success criteria are *derived from* the learning goals, but they give much more detail. Their goal is to explain precisely and explicitly what students will be able to say, make, do, or compose to demonstrate they have met the learning intention. In the following figures, you will see some graphic representations of how learning intentions and success criteria differ. In Figure 3.1, a Venn diagram lays out the differences between learning intentions and success criteria. Table 3.6 dives deep by giving a specific upper elementary/middle school example in the content area of science. Finally, the images making up Figure 3.2 delve into what these might look like in an elementary school classroom.

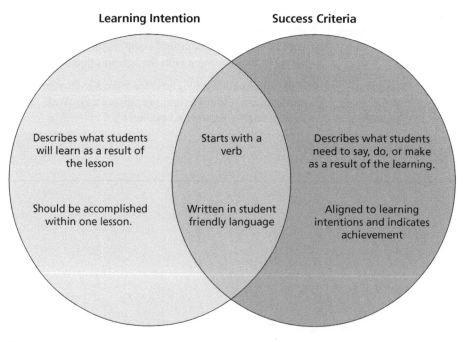

Figure 3.1   Learning intentions versus success criteria.

Table 3.6 Sample learning goals versus sample success criteria in science.

Learning goal	Success criteria
Understand the cellular structure related to a plant's cellular functions.	Define structure and function and create a diagram showing how chloroplast converts light energy via the photosynthetic process. Then discuss how chloroplasts also provide other diverse metabolic activities for plant cells, specifically those related to membrane lipids and fatty acids.
Use what you know about predicting, connecting, and clarifying to help you determine what a text says as you read.	Determine when clues context use is appropriate and how you used familiar words to determine the meaning of an unknown word in a story.
Represent and solve multiplication and division of fractions.	Explain and name each number in a fractional equation, describe the fractional part to whole units, and explain why numbers get small when multiplied in the division.

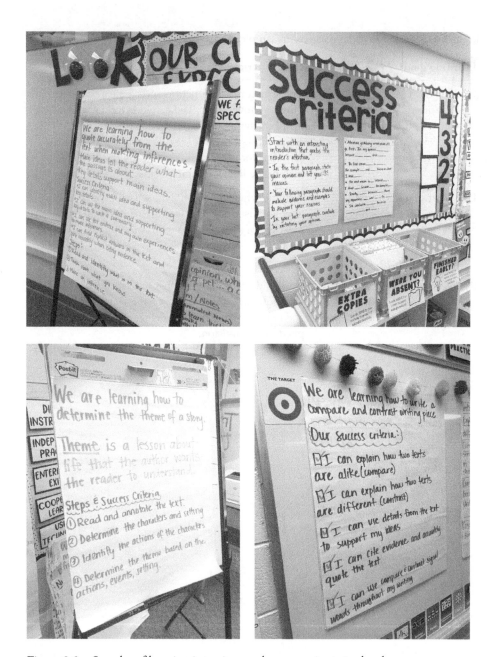

Figure 3.2   Samples of learning intentions and success criteria in the elementary classroom.

Summary

This chapter created a working definition of learning targets and success criteria. We defined learning targets as what teachers use to determine what they will teach the students *and* what the students will learn as a result of their instruction. We defined success criteria as the specific guidance and feedback provided directly to the student. We further distinguished between these two by explaining that teachers use learning targets to decide what successful mastery of knowledge and skills looks like and that teachers use success criteria so that students may know what success looks like for them and be more actively engaged in their learning and be able to measure their progress and assess their learning.

As we discussed both learning intentions and success criteria, we identified the clear benefits to the classroom by embedding these into our instruction. We also provided concise, step-by-step examples of how to work to provide and create these within your classroom, including specific details on deconstructing standards to truly home in on the key verbs of the standards presented. We ended by providing some photographic examples of effective learning targets and success criteria within the classroom.

Key Takeaways

- I set learning intentions with my students.
- I make sure the learning intention is clear and links to the purpose of the learning.
- I have worked to include "language of the discipline" into my learning intentions.
- I review learning intentions at the start of class each day, then revisit them throughout the lesson for emphasis and recall.

- I try to make my learning intentions SMART (specific, measurable, actionable, realistic, and time bound).
- I have a plan to begin engaging my students in co-constructing success criteria.
- I understand and can implement the steps of co-constructing success criteria with my students.

CHAPTER 4

Utilizing Pre-Assessments

When most people think of formative assessment, they think about those moments throughout a unit where they stop and check for understanding. While this is the most common use of formative assessment, the role of pre-assessment in the formative assessment process has yet to be utilized.

Many of us in education can recall our educational experiences in elementary school. Most of us likely had a teacher who utilized a practice such as the one described below:

> Students are about to begin a new unit in spelling or vocabulary. The classroom teacher hands out or orally delivers what she calls a "pretest." She tells students that this will help her to know what the students already know about this topic. Once the students complete their pre-test, they hand it in or trade papers and receive the results of what they do/do not have mastery of for the upcoming unit of study. From there, the teacher proceeds to assign the weekly homework and teach the lessons without attention to making changes to their instruction by utilizing the data from the pretest.

While pre-assessments *can* be hugely valuable to a teacher in helping them to set up effective classroom practices, teachers do not utilize the formative assessment pretest as a tool to guide instruction. This chapter will dive into what pre-assessment is within the context of formative assessment and how one can successfully employ formative assessment to create differentiated learning opportunities and resources for successfully implementing pre-assessments in the classroom.

What Is Pre-Assessment and Why Does it Matter?

For this chapter, pre-assessment will be defined as

> An assessment that occurs before instruction takes place, with the intent and purpose of gauging a student's understanding before instruction.

Pre-assessment is an excellent tool for teachers to gain insight and information about what students can do before receiving instruction. Pre-assessments can also help teachers gain additional information about students' interests, learning styles, and modalities. Pre-assessments often can serve as a "diagnostic tool" to help a teacher better understand students' strengths and weaknesses and the overall classroom knowledge profile prior to the onset of instruction. When used correctly and effectively, pre-assessments can guide our instruction and make us more effective and impactful teachers.

Table 4.1 lists the benefits of using pre-assessments in your classroom.

Table 4.1   Benefits of using pre-assessment in your classroom.

1. Pre-assessment allows the teacher to determine if what is going to be covered in an upcoming lesson or unit has been mastered already by some or all of the students in the class.

If all the students have shown mastery of specific content, the teacher can skip portions of an upcoming lesson and devote more time to areas of common challenge.	If only a few students are having problems with specific skill set, the teacher can individualize instruction to catch them up and bring them along with the rest of the class.

2. Pre-assessments help measure authentic learning. Teachers can compare pre-assessment data to summative assessment data to determine how much learning has taken place as a result of instruction. Since pre-assessment data exists, the summative will accurately measure growth.
3. Pre-assessments help provide clear expectations to students. This allows students to strategically target their focus as new learning is presented.
4. Finally, pre-assessments provide teachers with additional information about students' composite strengths and struggles. This allows teachers to utilize this information to determine content decisions for upcoming lessons.

Using Pre-Assessments to Create Differentiated Learning

The key aspect and most critical reason for conducting a pre-assessment, as a teacher, is to identify what students already know and what students need to learn so that you do not waste valuable classroom time on material the students have already mastered. In addition, completion of a pre-assessment will guide you in determining what teaching and instructional methods may be ineffective in reaching the predetermined learning goals.

These pre-assessments aim to determine students' knowledge base *prior to* the lesson or unit of study. These assessments will help drive the instructional sequence and provide the maximum benefit for each learner. The purpose of these assessments is to assist teachers in determining strengths and struggles and to guide the unit of study. These assessments should be completed before the instruction on a new topic and should *not* be assigned any grade. That said, recording this score can be very beneficial to assess knowledge acquired throughout a unit accurately.

There are two primary purposes of pre-assessments. The first is to determine students' learning styles and interests and assist in guiding the teacher in understanding their students' needs for the school year and lesson.

The second primary purpose, and the more often utilized purpose, is to identify students' understanding of upcoming content and materials. Identification of students' understanding can be completed through formal content-based pretests and several other pre-assessment types defined in this chapter's resource forms.

Each of these styles of pre-assessment helps the classroom teacher to determine where a student, or the entire class, may need additional support, enrichment, adjustments to learning style, or require a different interest-based approach. Utilizing the information garnered in a pre-assessment can assist a teacher in creating appropriate learning resources, developing enrichment materials, and creating timelines for upcoming projects and lessons.

Regarding differentiated learning, pre-assessment aims to provide the classroom teacher with the information needed to create small groups with differentiated and engaging tasks appropriately leveled at a student's zone of proximal development (ZPD). Lee Vygotsky defines ZPD as "the difference between what a learner can do without help and what he or she can achieve with guidance and encouragement from a skilled partner" (McLeod, 2023). In essence, as instructors the goal is always to provide sufficiently challenging learning without placing undue stress on students to the point where they become frustrated and shut down to new learning. *This is the art and the science of classroom teaching. The ability to maintain the appropriate equilibrium between what a student needs to be pushed to their ideal learning capacity without being overwhelmed to utter frustration.* By utilizing the results from a formal or informal pre-assessment, teachers can create instructional groupings driven by assessment data to create learning cohorts that best address student needs. When used correctly, a pre-assessment can lead to explicit, meaningful instruction, guiding each student toward appropriately challenging work.

Types of Pre-Assessment: Resources for Successful Implementation

Just as there are many types of formative assessments, there are also many types of pre-assessment. In this section, we will outline five key types of pre-assessment, describe each of them and when it may make the most sense to use this assessment type, and provide examples of each.

Pre-Assessment Type 1: Traditional Individual Student Pre-Assessments

A traditional pre-assessment is, just as it sounds, a fundamental beginning assessment of knowledge. These can be administered as a paper-and-pencil exam or given digitally with resources such as Google forms and various other online resources (many of which can save you much time on the grading side). Another time-saving strategy is to find the end-of-chapter or end-of-unit test and then create a shortened version of this, or even slightly adjust the questions and answer choices. As with any assessment, ensure your questions are squarely aligned with your learning targets within your unit of study.

One drawback to traditional pre-assessments conducted via paper and pencil is that it can be very laborious to code students' answers by standard and to use this information to create small instructional groupings. Furthermore, as we said before, if pre-assessment data is not utilized with the specific intent of guiding instruction and promoting student learning, there is no purpose in developing and administering pre-assessments. For this reason, we highly recommend using an online pre-assessment tool that can code and compile your student data, disaggregated by the question, so that you may utilize this data to determine your instructional groupings. To that end, we have added a simple, easy-to-use resource on creating digital pre-assessments in Google forms to assist teachers in creating traditional pre-assessments that will save them time and energy in terms of data collection and implementation.

Resource 4.1: How to Create a Pre-Assessment in Google Forms

Open a form in Google forms.

1. At the top of the form, click Settings.

2. Turn on "Make this a quiz."

   Optional: To collect email addresses, next to "Responses," click the down arrow and turn on Collect email addresses.

3. You can make this an answer key with any type of question (Short Answer, Multiple Choice, Checkboxes, Dropdown, and Grid). To make the answer key:

   i. To add a question, click "Add question" (plus mark).

   ii. Fill out your question and answers.

   iii. In the bottom left of the question, click "Answer key."

   iv. Choose the answer or answers that are correct.

   v. In the top right of the question, choose how many points the question is worth.

4. To add a written or YouTube video explanation to an answer, click "Add answer feedback."

Expert Advice

Choose what people see during and after quiz.

1.   Open a quiz in Google Forms
2.   At the top of the quiz, click Settings.
3.   Turn on "Make this a quiz."
4.   Under "Respondent settings," change settings as needed.

Pre-Assessment Type 2: Individual and Collective Student Response Systems

In this chapter, we have discussed the very traditional and targeted "pretest." While this can be a highly effective means of determining a student's individual needs, not all pre-assessments needs to be administered in a formalized pencil/paper or digital quiz. One way for teachers to keep their classes interesting and engaging, even when administering pre-assessment, is by incorporating variety into their pre-assessment routines. Depending on your specific goal within pre-assessment administration, you likely will select each of these at different times during your annual instruction based on specific goals and needs within your classroom. The goal of all pre-assessment is to gauge where your students are at so that you may better help them get to where they need to go. This section on student response systems will dive into specific individual student and collective whole class monitoring systems to determine student prerequisite knowledge.

Physical Movement: Pre-Assessment

Creating a physical moment game or activity is a fun and exciting way to keep your class moving and your pre-assessment targeted but also highly engaging. These games will allow students to show what they may already know regarding a specific topic or upcoming learning sequence. One bonus to getting students moving during the pre-assessment phase is that research has shown that physical activity amplifies learning and can have a powerful effect on student engagement (Merrill and Gonser, 2021).

4 Corners

One strategy for doing this is through a game called "4 Corners." The easiest way to create this game within your classroom is to create multiple-choice questions and have students move themselves to the "corner" of the classroom that associates with what they believe to be the correct answer to a pre-assessment question. You can create questions in an A, B, C, and D multiple-choice format, then assign each corner a letter. After you read the question (and post for visual learners), students can then move themselves to the corner they believe represents the correct answer to the pre-assessment question. Then, remind the students that since you have not yet instructed on this content, the purpose of your pre-assessment is to gauge (collectively) what level of background knowledge they bring to the table as a class.

Expert Advice

Organize the questions from least to most challenging so that you can understand the level of scaffolding necessary for student success. It is also helpful to begin with questions for which you would expect the students to have some prior knowledge. This will help you gauge how well your expectations of their previous exposure match their reality

Finally, while this is a collective class activity, designed in large part to give you an overall snapshot of where your entire class is beginning, it is also beneficial in identifying specific student needs. Suppose you strategically design the questions from the simplest to the most complex. In that case, you can begin taking anecdotal notes during the assessment to work on creating flexible groupings based on content knowledge and the required level of scaffolding and support.

Resource 4.2: 4 Corners

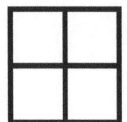

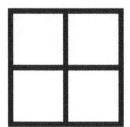

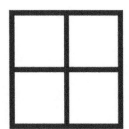

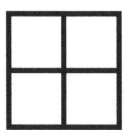

Front Board

Chat Log

Another strategy for getting students up and out of their seats is a pre-assessment activity called "chat log." The easiest way to create this game within your classroom is to create a chat log laminated card for each student (like the ones pictured below—but age appropriate to your student population). There are several ways that student pairings can be assigned (more on this later). When the teacher is administering a pre-assessment or any informal exchange of information between students, they can ask students to see their _____ Partner and share a specific answer to a question.

For example:

"Boys and girls, we are about to dive into a unit on space and the planets. Pull out your chat log and find your YouTube Partner. Once there, tell your partner everything you know about the planets in our solar system."

Then when they have completed this task, you can follow up with something like this:

"Boys and girls, now that you have met with your YouTube Partner, I want you to find your Minecraft Mate and discuss with them how you think the location of a planet may be related to its temperature."

While this can be a valuable assessment, if you do not add in some recording system for students to utilize in their partnership, you may not be able to get all of the pre-assessment feedback. An added modification to this chat log activity would be to have partner pairs record their answers and turn those on so that you have an idea from each grouping about their prerequisite knowledge.

One effective strategy in developing these "chat log" sample cards is to create a system for how students are partnered on their cards. For example, on a high school student's card, I may always assign their TikTok Partner as someone on the opposite academic spectrum they are on so I know that partnering can provide needed clarification for struggling students and the opportunity to model and teach successful students. I also may be sure to make their Facebook Friends as other students at similar academic achievement levels so that I can pose questions for which I want both students to feel brave in being equal contributors. Finally, I may make the Instagram Follower simply someone I know to be a trusted friend to them, so they may feel bold in sharing ideas or personal information.

Resource 4.3: Chat Log Sample Card Secondary

_____ 's Chat Log

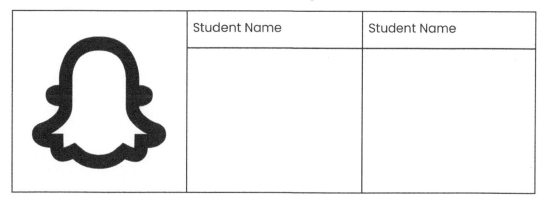

	Student Name	Student Name

_____ 's Chat Log

	Student Name	Student Name

_____ 's Chat Log

	Student Name	Student Name

Resource 4.4: Chat Log Sample Card Primary

_____ 's Chat Log

	Student Name	Student Name

_____ 's Chat Log

	Student Name	Student Name

_____ 's Chat Log

	Student Name	Student Name

Whiteboards

One of the easiest and most effective ways to gauge understanding on a pre-assessment is simply to utilize whiteboards within your classroom. Without diving into technology, whiteboards can give you a simple, easy way to check for student understanding and background knowledge on a specific concept or idea. You can ask students to write out a sentence, answer a True/False question, rate something on a scale, or even create a visual in response to a quick question.

Expert Advice

 Practice routines for handout and distribution of whiteboards so that students can seamlessly transition to utilizing these tools within the classroom with minimal disturbance to the classroom environment.

Digital Tools for Pre-Assessment (Plickers, Kahoots, Nearpod, and GimKit)

While whiteboards are a straightforward and effective way to complete pre-assessment, it can take a skilled teacher to keep track of each student's answers to refer back to them while looking to create differentiated flexible groupings. By utilizing one of the many online digital tools, you may find it easier to track student answers and their prerequisite learning to best differentiate your instruction. There are hundreds and hundreds of online resources to assist you in conducting formative assessments in your classroom. In Table 4.2, we outline four specific pre-assessment tools that we particularly appreciate.

Table 4.2 Four pre-assessment tools.

Plickers	
What is it?	Classroom polling app which lets teachers use a single mobile device to scan and collect data from student responses.
How can it be used for pre-assessment?	1—Add your class to the queue. 2—Open the "Now Playing" window. 3—Open the Plickers app and start your quiz (pre-assessment). 4—Enter the scanner. 5—Scan student answers. 6—View the results instantly.
Advantages	+ Plickers allows teachers to get on-the-spot pre-assessment data without needing to use paper and pencils. + Used by millions worldwide. + Works well in a classroom that is not technology rich because it does not require students to have a device. + For multiple-choice questions and data can be collected by individual student.
Disadvantages	– Requires each question to be entered one at a time. – Some significant time spent up front setting up the class or classes. – Limited to multiple-choice and true/false.
Cost	Free
Website	https://get.plickers.com/

Kahoots	
What is it?	Kahoots is a game-based classroom response system played in real time. The questions are projected on a whiteboard and students answer the questions with their smartphone, tablet, or computer. The questions are multiple-choice and timed to create a leaderboard.
How can it be used for pre-assessment?	1—Click on Kahoots at the top menu after creating an account. 2—On the quiz page, select the checkbox of the Kahoot you want to play and click play. 3—Have students enter the pin on the Kahoots mobile app and create a nickname. 4—Click start to begin. 5—Students will select the correct answer choice and a bar graph will come up with an overview of the leaderboard. 6—Results will be saved to an Excel spreadsheet.

Kahoots	
Advantages	+ Motivates students' learning and helps determine where students are at in their learning. + Allows the teacher to know where students are and to further differentiate instruction.
Disadvantages	− Requires all students to have a device. − No longer free for a full class.
Cost	Free (Basic account —10 players at a time) Then prices go up to $10, $20, and $30 per month)
Website	https://kahoot.com/

GimKit	
What is it?	This is a game-show platform in which students compete by answering questions on their laptops or smartphones. Students earn virtual money, which they can "invest" during the game to boost their score.
How can it be used for pre-assessment?	1—Sign up and find your school. 2—Click "Create a new kit" and add your questions. 3—Click "Finish kit" and choose a game mode and options. 4—Have students enter the code and play
Advantages	+ Highly Interactive + Motivating for students
Disadvantages	− Not fully free − Creates a competitive atmosphere
Cost	Free limited subscription allows five kits and one edit.
Website	https://www.gimkit.com/

Pre-Assessment Type 3: Show What You Know

This third type of assessment allows students to showcase all of their individual and collective learning on a particular upcoming topic. As we know, our students come to the classroom with various background knowledge and prerequisite skills, which can vary from one student to the next. The "show what you know" pre-assessment strategy allows a more open-ended brain dump of everything a student may know regarding a specific topic. These can be valuable because sometimes, as instructors, we would not know to ask about specific background knowledge and content.

Words and Wonders

The purpose of the word activity is to get a general idea of everything that students already bring to the table on the topic and everything they may want to know. Similar in theory to a KWL chart, the idea is to gain an understanding, as the classroom teacher, of the background knowledge your students have about a specific topic. The easiest way to do this in a primary classroom is to post a large Post-it note or piece of butcher paper on the wall and draw a line down the middle. On one half, have students write every word they can think of related to the topic. On the other side, have students write down everything they may wonder about this topic.

Gallery Walk

During a "show what you know" gallery walk, students can get up and move around the classroom. Throughout the classroom are various posters with words and topics. At each station, students are asked to write what they know about this topic on each poster. This can be used at the beginning of a more extended unit, such as a history unit. You may have students circulate a room and visit posters with various topics related to a unit. They may stop by posters with the words such as Boston Tea Party, Boston Massacre, Declaration of Independence, Loyalist, Patriot, and Revolutionary War. While students may not *yet* know how each of these is related, it can serve to begin to spark their interest and wonder in how these topics might be affiliated with one another.

At each station, students are asked to write what they know about this topic on each poster. Typically, students will write their thoughts and ideas directly on the poster or a sticky note that they then stick to the poster. Another variation of this activity would be to have students use Resource 4.5 to record their notes as they circulate to each station.

Resource 4.5: Show What You Know—Gallery Walk

Name: _____ Date: _____

Gallery Walk

Directions: Record your notes as you walk through each station.

	Station	I know...	I wonder...
1.			
2.			
3.			
4.			
5.			

ABC Brainstorm

The purpose of an ABC chart is to provide another way for students to show their prerequisite knowledge on a specific topic. These often work best with upper elementary and secondary students when used in relation to specific vocabulary surrounding a content area of topic. While it can be used highly effectively with science and social studies, we have seen this pre-assessment used successfully in various other subject areas too!

This can be a very effective strategy where students brainstorm ideas and summarize concepts through the written summary of an ABC list of learning. Students use the 26 letters of the alphabet as a guide to generate words or sentences to describe a concept or idea. This strategy can be effective because it provides students with an alternative when trying to access and recall previous content and concepts and encourages students to think critically.

Once complete, students also can be placed into partnerships or teams to share ideas and fill in any gaps in their learning.

Resource 4.6: Show What You Know—ABC Brainstorm

Name: _____ Date: _____

Directions: Generate words related to the topic, starting with each letter of the alphabet.

Topic:			
A		**N**	
B		**O**	
C		**P**	
D		**Q**	
E		**R**	
F		**S**	
G		**T**	
H		**U**	
I		**V**	
J		**W**	
K		**X**	
L		**Y**	
M		**Z**	

Resource 4.7: Show What You Know—ABC Brainstorm (Sample Completed)

Name: _____   Date: _____

Topic: The Water Cycle			
A	accumulation	**N**	
B		**O**	ocean
C	cumulus clouds	**P**	precipitation
D		**Q**	
E	evaporation	**R**	runoff water
F	fog	**S**	soil
G	groundwater	**T**	transportation
H	humidity	**U**	
I		**V**	
J		**W**	water table
K		**X**	
L		**Y**	
M		**Z**	zones of saturation

Pre-Assessment Type 4: Assessment One-Pagers

Finally, in this last pre-assessment type section, you will find several reasonably standard formative assessments that also can be utilized to conduct a pre-assessment with the students in your classroom. These are simple, straightforward, and common prep examples with corresponding resources.

Entry Tickets

Exit tickets can be provided at the beginning of a lesson or the beginning of a unit. Short prompts on half sheets or index cards help teachers take a quick mental diagnostic. Unlike a more traditional pretest, these will not provide extensive comprehensive feedback but can give you general pre-assessment information about students' readiness and understanding of the content you are about to introduce. These are more effective as pre-assessments on individual lessons vs. entire units of study.

Resource 4.8: Sample Entrance Ticket

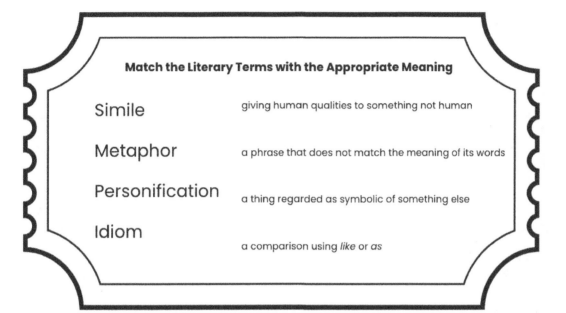

Match the Literary Terms with the Appropriate Meaning

Simile

Metaphor

Personification

Idiom

giving human qualities to something not human

a phrase that does not match the meaning of its words

a thing regarded as symbolic of something else

a comparison using *like* or *as*

**What is the main idea of the passage?
Use details from the text to explain your answer.**

Resource 4.9: Blank, Editable Sample Entrance Tickets

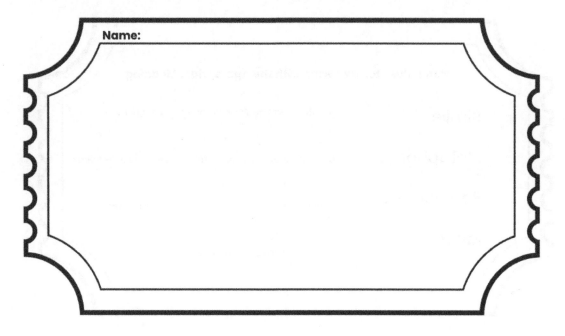

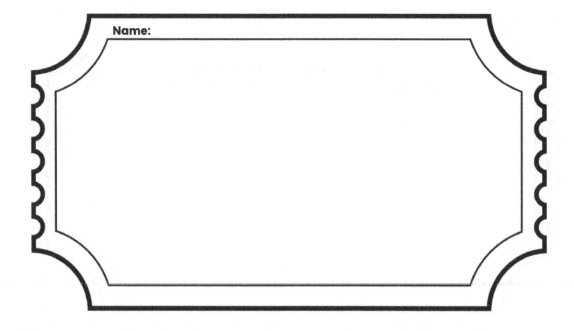

True/False Statements

An actual/false statement paper is a super quick test you can have students complete to determine their background knowledge on a discrete set of facts before delivering instruction. It is important to note that just as with any pre-assessment, if you do not use this information to guide what you are teaching and how you spend your time, you are not maximizing your impact. These can be administered via formalized sheets you create for your class or simple Post-it notes or index cards.

Anticipation Guides

An anticipation guide is designed to gauge student knowledge and understanding and simultaneously fuel students' interest in an upcoming topic of a unit of study. Measuring student knowledge before and after instruction can be a valuable tool for a teacher to utilize to measure the impact of her instruction. In addition, these guides teach students how to make predictions, verify predictions, and set expectations for learning in the upcoming unit. They also can guide students on what information in an upcoming unit is essential.

Resource 4.10: Animal Adaptations Anticipation Guide

Name: _____ Date: _____

Anticipation Guide: Animal Adaptations

Before Reading			After Reading	
Yes, I agree	**No, I disagree**		**Yes, I agree**	**No, I disagree**
		One animal adaptation is the noises they make		
		Adaptations in animals happen quickly		
		Animal adaptations can look different, depending on the animal's location		
		Reasons for adaptations include attracting mates, catching prey, and survival		
		The climate is unrelated to adaptations		

Resource 4.11: Blank, Editable Anticipation Guide

Name: _____ Date: _____

Anticipation Guide:

Before Reading			After Reading	
Yes, I agree	**No, I disagree**		**Yes, I agree**	**No, I disagree**

Summary

In this chapter, we created a working definition of pre-assessment in the classroom as a formative tool. We defined pre-assessment as *an assessment occurring before instruction takes place, with the intent and purpose of gauging a student's level of understanding before instruction*. There are many different types of pre-assessment that we discussed in this chapter. Each type of pre-assessment has specific strengths and weaknesses and can be utilized to assess students' prior knowledge. While some pre-assessments are very effective at giving specific feedback about individual student performance and creating targeted groupings, other pre-assessments give you a better picture of where your whole class is performing. This assessment helps you determine if need to adjust or scaffold your instruction based on the collective prerequisite knowledge of your student population. We tried to provide a variety of types of pre-assessment to help new and veteran teachers see that there are many ways to conduct pre-assessment within the classroom. We felt that devoting an entire chapter to this topic was critical because, as teachers, we often lose valuable instructional minutes in delivering lessons on content that students may have mastered already. By integrating some pre-assessment into all levels of your instruction, you will not only be able to create instructional groupings effectively, but you likely will be able to get back those critical instructional minutes in your classroom to increase your overall impact on student achievement.

Key Takeaways

- I use pre-assessments in my classroom on a regular basis.
- I use data from pre-assessments to determine my lesson pacing.
- I understand the differences in pre-assessments and which ones will provide me with a whole class snapshot versus which ones will tell me about specific student progress.

- I understand that each type of pre-assessment has specific strengths and weaknesses and can be utilized to assess students' prior knowledge and that some pre-assessments are very effective at giving specific feedback about individual student performance, while other pre-assessments give you a better picture of where your whole class is performing.

- I can identify each of these types of pre-assessments and how to utilize them to augment my instruction.

During Instruction: Effective "In-the-Moment" Formative Assessment Instructional Practices and Resources

Effective Formative Assessment Instructional Practices and Resources

In Part I of the book, we dove into many types of formative assessment that you, as the teacher, can use before you even begin to instruct students. In this second part of the book, we will share with you 20 "in-the-moment" formative strategies you can use *while* you are instructing students.

Remember, formative assessment is designed to provide us feedback during the instructional process while learning is occurring. When we refer to "in-the-moment" formative feedback, we are referring to feedback that you gather mid-lesson to measure student progress and assess your efficacy as an instructor. As an example, when teaching a new concept in your classroom you can determine your efficacy in a number of ways: through observation, by surveying students, or by having students hold up whiteboards. While these assessments are not graded, they can assist you in gauging a student's learning progress and determining how well you are reaching your students.

In this chapter, you will find strategies and resources that are meant to support your formative assessment during your instruction. Interweave these strategies into your lesson to ensure you can monitor your student's progress toward meeting the learning goal.

KWL Chart

Use a KWL chart as part of your lesson to get students to think about what they already know (K), what they want to learn (W), and what they have learned after participating in the lesson (L).

Here's how to implement a KWL chart:

1. Make sure students know the learning goal and success criteria and how this task is related to the learning goal.

2. Use Resource 5.1 and hand it out to students before you start your lesson.

3. Explain to students that they will use a KWL chart to write out what they already know (K) about the learning goal, what they are wondering or want to learn as it relates to the learning goal (W), and what they learned (L) when the lesson is over.

4. Start your lesson and state the learning goal. Ask students to use the K column for thoughts and ideas about what they already know.

5. You can have students put this off to the side as you continue the lesson, or you can have students share with an A/B partner and then with the whole group.

6. Ask students to then write down anything they're wondering about the learning goal or things they'd like to learn as it relates to the learning goal in the W column.

7. Again, you can have students share with a partner and then with the whole group.

8. Have students put their KWL chart to the side and continue your lesson.

9. At the end of the lesson, have students write down what they learned in the L column.

10. Have students share with A/B partners and then have students share out with the whole class.

11. Students can also go back to their K column and cross out misconceptions while revisiting the L column and answering the questions about the learning goal.

12. If students still have questions, they can highlight them and use them for the next lesson.

You can use a KWL chart to plan further instruction. You can use the K column to determine students' misconceptions about learning goals and determine what students know or think they might know. The W column can be used to determine future questions to help facilitate classroom discussions or future lessons. The L column can help you determine how students are feeling about their learning.

Resource 5.1: KWL Chart

Name: _____ Date: _____

K	W	L
What do you already know about the learning goal?	What are you wondering or what do you want to know as it relates to the learning goal?	What did you learn and why did you learn it?

One-Minute Essay

This is a quick formative assessment that allows you to gather information about student learning in *one* minute. This strategy gives students time to think and reflect on the learning without any restrictions on how they want to communicate the learning. The one-minute reflection should be free of anxiety for students. This is a place for them to write in an open format to literally just communicate what they have learned.

Here's how to implement it:

1. Make sure students know the learning goal and success criteria and how this task is related to the learning goal.

2. Pose a question to students that is related to the learning goal.

3. Set a timer for one minute.

4. Allow students to respond.

The one-minute essays can be used in a variety of ways for future instruction. Use it to determine what students know about the learning goal and what misconceptions students may still have. It is a great opportunity to have insight into what students are thinking about the learning goal. These essays will also give you a glimpse into how students structure their writing that also can help you inform different instructional goals for the future.

Resource 5.2: One-Minute Essay

Name: _____ Date: _____

One Minute Essay

Name: _____ Date: _____

One Minute Essay

Light Bulb Moments

This quick formative assessment allows you to gather information about student learning and how they feel about the learning goal and the lesson.

Here's how to implement it:

1. Make sure students know the learning goal and success criteria and how this task is related to the learning goal.

2. Give students a light bulb paper.

3. Have students think about their biggest takeaway or "light bulb" moment.

4. Tell students to write down their ideas in the light bulb.

5. You can also have students turn and share their light bulb moments with a partner.

Collect students "light bulb moments" papers and use them for planning future lessons and instructional goals. Students' light bulb moments can be used to spark classroom discussions, journal prompts, new lessons or units of study, and morning meeting questions. Light bulb moments also can help you determine misconceptions students might have about a topic.

Resource 5.3: Light Bulb Moments

Formative Classroom Mastery Desk Cards

This is a quick formative assessment that allows you to gather information about student learning during class instruction as you circulate the classroom. It is also a form of student self-assessment.

Here's how to implement it:

1. Make sure students know the learning goal and success criteria and how this task is related to the learning goal.

2. Print out the cards and cut them out.

3. Hole punch each card and put them together on a brass ring.

4. Give each student a set of cards.

5. Instruct students to use the cards during independent practice.

6. They can turn to the card that they feel best describes their level of understanding while doing their independent practice.

7. They can make sure the card is up on their desk so you as the teacher can see them as you quickly walk around the room.

8. You also can color code these cards by printing them on the colored paper of your choice.

When students use these cards, it can help you improve class culture by making students feel comfortable when sharing how they are feeling about the learning goals. The cards also can help build students' ability to understand where they are at in their learning progression toward meeting the learning goal.

Resource 5.4: Formative Classroom Mastery Deck Cards

I am having some trouble with this and I need help to understand.	I am having some trouble with this and I need help to understand.
I am having some trouble with this and I need help to understand.	I am having some trouble with this and I need help to understand.

I've got this and I can do it on my own!	I've got this and I can do it on my own!
I've got this and I can do it on my own!	I've got this and I can do it on my own!

I am still learning this and I may need help to do it on my own.	I am still learning this and I may need help to do it on my own.
I am still learning this and I may need help to do it on my own.	I am still learning this and I may need help to do it on my own.

I feel like I know this enough to help others in my class!	I feel like I know this enough to help others in my class!
I feel like I know this enough to help others in my class!	I feel like I know this enough to help others in my class!

Student Mastery Tracker

Student mastery tracker is a cumulative student self-assessment that students can keep at their desks and pull out on a daily or weekly basis to track their mastery toward a specific skill. It allows students to assess their mastery of a benchmark standard and evaluate their performance over time.

Here's how to implement it:

1. Make sure students know the learning goal and success criteria and how this task is related to the learning goal.

2. Provide students with the sheet or something similar to track daily mastery.

3. As you proceed through the content (such as a math chapter), allow students time to reflect on their level of mastery at the end of each daily lesson.

4. Monitor for growth over time.

When students use this level of mastery tracking, it increases their own self-assessment of learning. This has a high effect size and allows students to gauge their learning and take pride in the growth they are making as it is happening. It is good for student self-esteem and also their level of agency and connectedness to the content.

Resource 5.5: Student Mastery Tracker

Name: _____ Date: _____

Student Mastery Tracker

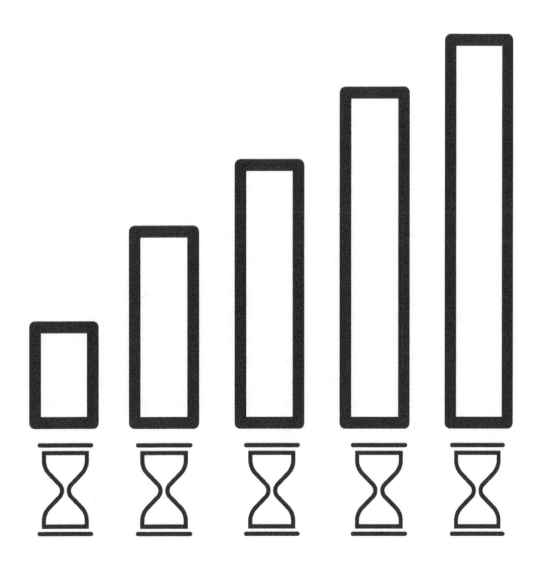

Clarify This!

This formative assessment helps students think about what misconceptions their peers might have and how they would explain those misconceptions to their peers. This can be done as students are learning to think about ways to explain the learning in their own words.

Here's how to implement it:

1. Make sure students know the learning goal and success criteria and how this task is related to the learning goal.

2. Have this handout ready to use during and after your lesson.

3. As students go through independent or guided practice, have them write down some misconceptions or what they think their classmates may be confused about.

4. If students are unsure about what their classmates might be confused about, have them think about three different ways they would teach it to their classmates instead.

5. After students have written down what they think the misconceptions might be, have students explain in the other column how they would clarify those conceptions.

Getting students' insight on how they would explain a concept is a helpful tool to have because it can help you plan for future lessons, small group re-teach, and have a different perspective on how to teach a skill. This information can help you plan how you will model another skill during a lesson. Having these misconceptions on paper also can help you determine how to teach new skills differently so these same misconceptions don't come up again.

Resource 5.6: Clarify This!

Name: _____ Date: _____

Clarify This!

Directions:
List three things you think a classmate may misunderstand about this topic, then let them know what it means by explaining it in your own words.

Something I think a classmate may misunderstand:	How I would explain or clarify this for them:

Think Pair Share (TPS)

This is a partner strategy that helps students share ideas with one another, but with structure and purpose.

Here's how to implement it:

1. Make sure students know the learning goal and success criteria and how this task is related to the learning goal.

2. Print out the template.

3. Have it ready to use during your lesson.

4. Assign students as A/B or TPS partners before your lesson starts. A/B or TPS partners are just two students paired together to share ideas. One student is "A" and the other is "B." If you choose to call them TPS partners, then make sure each student knows who needs to share first.

5. As you go through your lessons and ask your students questions, pause to give students time to TPS. They can use the handout to organize their ideas.

6. Ask the question, then have students think quietly about the answer first. As they think, they can jot down notes in the "Think" box.

7. Then, after students have a minute to think, they can turn to their A/B or TPS partner and share their ideas. They can use the share box on the template to write down their partner's thoughts.

8. They also can write their partner's name in the "pair" section of the template.

Collecting these after the lesson can be helpful because students' ideas and responses can be great classroom discussion topics. It is also an opportunity to clear up misconceptions, to come up with new lesson ideas, and to follow up with students on ideas or questions that they still may have about the topic.

Resource 5.7: Think-Pair-Share

Name: _____ Date: _____

Think, Pair, Share!

Directions:

In the spaces below, record your thoughts from the reading/notes/discussion in the think box. When asked by the teacher, pair up with a classmate near your desk and discuss your responses together, and decide what to share with others.

Think
Pair
Share

Questions for My Teacher

This strategy encourages students to come up with questions for the teacher and also explain why they want to know more or why they are asking that specific question.

Here's how to implement it:

1. Make sure students know the learning goal and success criteria and how this task is related to the learning goal.

2. Print out the template and have it ready to use for particular lessons.

3. Give each student the handout and have them write down their questions at the end of the lesson. Make sure students explain why they are asking the question.

4. You also can use this as a reflective tool at the end of the school day.

The questions students ask can be used to brainstorm future lesson planning. You can also use students' questions to check in with students about their learning, to plan class meetings, or to clear up misconceptions.

Resource 5.8: Questions for My Teacher

Name: _____ Date: _____

Questions for My Teacher

Directions:
Think about what we have learned. What are three questions that you have for me? Record them here:

Questions to Learn More	Why I Want to Know This

Learning Logs

A learning log is a journal that students can keep to record their thoughts, feelings, and ideas about their learning. Teachers can read students' log entries and leave comments and feedback.

Here's how to implement it:

1. Make sure students know the learning goal and success criteria and how this task is related to the learning goal.

2. Make copies of the daily learning log template.

3. Have a spot in your classroom that students can access to get a learning log at the end of the day.

4. Establish an end-of-day routine where students know it is time to get a learning log and reflect on their day.

5. Have students fill out the content area and learning goal(s) for that content, and rate their level of understanding.

6. You should encourage students to write down why they were learning what they were learning and reflect on their progress.

7. Collect the learning logs at the end of each day or week and monitor students' reflections.

Use learning logs to help students become self-reflective and to understand the purpose of what they're learning. You can also use learning logs to plan instruction, whether whole group or small group, based on students' reflections and level of understanding.

Resource 5.9: Learning Logs

Name: _____ Date: _____

Learning Log

Content Area	Learning Goal	Why Are We Learning This?
		Level of Understanding: 4 3 2 1
		Level of Understanding: 4 3 2 1
		Level of Understanding: 4 3 2 1
		Level of Understanding: 4 3 2 1

Anonymous No

Anonymous no is a simple question-and-answer activity you can do with your students to talk about misconceptions and mistakes. It is an effective way to get students to know it is okay to get answers wrong and it helps you as the classroom teacher clear up misconceptions.

Here's how to implement it:

1. Make sure students know the learning goal and success criteria and how this task is related to the learning goal.

2. Project or write a question on the board for students to answer that is based on a previous day's lesson.

3. Give students time, one to three minutes, to write down the question and answer.

4. Collect students' slips and go through them pulling out the ones with the wrong answers. Choose ones that you think will make an impact on students' learning and clear common misconceptions.

5. Make sure that you do not identify the students' names when you display the wrong answers.

6. Go through mistakes students may have made and clear misconceptions for students.

7. Fix the mistakes in front of the whole group and discuss why this mistake may have been made.

Seeing students' mistakes and misconceptions can you help plan further instruction by understanding how students are viewing and thinking about specific skills. This can impact your planning and instructional routines.

Resource 5.10: Anonymous No

Name: _____ Date: _____

Anonymous No

Question
Answer

Name: _____ Date: _____

Anonymous No

Question
Answer

Sheet Protector Boards

Similar to a mini whiteboard, sheet protector boards allow students to write answers and responses with a dry-erase marker that they can share with you in a whole group lesson. The only difference is that sheet protector boards can be made to hold specific papers and questions you want students to use while you're teaching a lesson.

Here's how to implement it:

1. Make sure students know the learning goal and success criteria and how this task is related to the learning goal.

2. Print out the papers you want to insert in the sheet protector. You can use the template.

3. You can also copy the paper on different colored computer paper. Use the different colors as a classroom management strategy when you are calling on groups of students to share their boards with their responses. For example, if you have green, blue, yellow, and orange papers, you can call on students with only green papers to show their responses. This will help you isolate groups of students and see fewer responses with more clarity.

4. Always have these ready to use during guided practice portions of your lesson. Students also can keep these at their desks to access them quickly and easily.

Sheet Protector Boards are a great way to change instruction in the moment. You can see students' answers and their work as they think about the question and you also are able to have conversations with students during instruction.

Resource 5.11: Sheet Protector Boards

Level of Understanding: **4   3   2   1**

Work and Thinking
Answer

What Are Your Wonderings?

This is an opportunity for students to think about the wonderings they have for a specific question or skill. Use this strategy after a concept has been taught to get students to think about their learning.

Here's how to implement it:

1. Make sure students know the learning goal and success criteria and how this task is related to the learning goal.

2. During the modeling or guided practice portion of your lesson, give students a question related to the learning goal.

3. Ask students to fill out the template before they answer the question you have given them.

4. The first prompt on the template is for students to write down what they notice. Give students about 45 seconds to write down things they notice about the question.

5. Then have students write down what they wonder about the question.

6. Next, have students think about any connections they can make to the question.

7. Finally, have students write down anything that they need clarified about the question.

8. You can pause after each of these sections on the template and add them to a class anchor chart, or you can have a class discussion about them. Students also can turn and discuss their answers with a partner.

9. After students have finished the template, have them answer the question.

This strategy can be used to determine students' misconceptions and questions they still have about a particular skill. These questions can inform how you will teach your next lesson or design small group instruction. These questions and wonderings also can help you create whole group discussion questions or opportunities for you to model metacognition.

Resource 5.12: What Are Your Wonderings?

Name: _____ Date: _____

What are Your Wonderings?

What do you notice?

What do you wonder?

What connections can you make?

What clarification do you need?

Learning Target Tickets

Learning target tickets are an opportunity for students to self-reflect and to assess their learning. Students rate their level of understanding after they know the learning goal of the lesson. After the teacher teaches the lesson, students rate their learning goal again and see if there was a shift in their level of understanding.

Here's how to implement it:

1. Make sure students know the learning goal and success criteria and how this task is related to the learning goal.

2. Print out the template and have the quarter sheets ready for your lessons.

3. Give students the tickets before you start your lesson.

4. State the learning goal of your lesson and ask students to rate their level of understanding before starting the lesson, based on the learning goal.

5. Have students put the tickets aside and teach your lesson.

6. At the end of your lesson, state the learning goal again and ask students to rate their level of understanding now that the lesson is over.

7. Students also can fill out the self-reflection on the ticket.

8. Students can staple the ticket to their independent practice or you can collect them as an exit ticket.

The tickets are helpful for further instruction because they help the classroom teacher understand how to differentiate future small group instruction and tasks. The reflection portion of the ticket also enables the teacher to understand their student's perspective of the lesson.

Resource 5.13: Learning Target Tickets

Name: _____ Date: _____

Learning Target Tickets

Learning Goal				
Before Lesson	4	3	2	1
After Lesson	4	3	2	1

Reflection	
• I feel _ • I learned _ • I wonder _ • In the end _	• At the beginning _ • The lesson was _ • Next time I will _ • I am still stuck on _

Quick Writes

This is a simple routine that can be done before, during, and after instruction. It gives students an opportunity to write their thoughts about their learning in a quick, concise manner. The purpose of this strategy is to give students an outlet through writing, without the pressure of conventions.

Here's how to implement it:

1. Make sure students know the learning goal and success criteria and how this task is related to the learning goal.

2. Keep copies of the template and have them ready to use during instruction.

3. Ask students to write down the learning goal of the lesson on the template.

4. You can decide if you want students to write their quick notes before, during, or after the lesson. Just make sure students circle it on the template.

5. Ask students to write down their thoughts and notes.

Quick writes can give you an insight on students' questions, notes, wonderings, and what they have learned. This can help you plan for future lessons, cooperative activities, and also schedule one-on-ones with students to clarify any misconceptions about skills.

Resource 5.14: Quick Writes

Name: _____ Date: _____

Quick Writes

Learning Goal	Before	During	After

Quick Write

Name: _____ Date: _____

Quick Writes

Learning Goal	Before	During	After

Quick Write

Doodle It

Draw your answer.

Here's how to implement it:

1. Hand out doodle it sheets and ask students open-ended questions. Instead of expecting them to write and record an answer to your question, allow them to doodle and create an image to assist them in remembering their learning.

What we know about how the brain works is that students make patterns and remember things visually. When they have engaged in developing a visual, they are more likely to recall their learning. This activity also assists teachers in learning about students' understanding and thinking and in considering what else they may need to do to bring learners along.

Resource 5.15: Doodle It!

Name: _____ Date: _____

Doodle It!

Name: _____ Date: _____

Doodle It!

Stoplight Cards: Red, Yellow, Green

These are square pieces of red, yellow, and green cards that students have at their desk that they use as a "stoplight" to let the teacher know how they're feeling about their work.

Here's how to implement it:

1. Make sure students know the learning goal and success criteria and how this task is related to the learning goal.

2. Print out the cards on green, yellow, and red paper. Use the directions on the top to determine which color paper to use with which directions.

3. Create a deck of cards for each student by hole punching one green, one yellow, and one red card and putting them together with a ring.

4. Give each student a deck of cards that they can use during independent work time.

5. Instruct students about the meaning of each card.

   a. Green: "Good to go!" means you can work without help and support and can finish the task independently.

   b. Yellow: "I need to slow down" means you can work independently, but have to stop to reread to clarify things for yourself.

   c. Red: "I had to stop" means you could not keep working independently and need support and help to finish the task.

6. As students are working, remind students to use their "stoplight" cards. Walk around the room and look at students' desks to see which card they have facing up while they are working.

If you see a lot of red cards on students' desks, this may indicate that the skill or task was too difficult for a majority of your class and that gives you the signal to change the way that skill was taught. This may mean doing a whole group re-teach of the skill. This strategy also helps to build students' ability to be vulnerable and open in sharing their level of understanding for completing a topic, which just increases a positive and safe classroom culture.

Resource 5.16: Red, Yellow, Green
Copy on green paper

Good to go!	Good to go!
Good to go!	Good to go!

Copy on yellow paper

I need to slow down.	I need to slow down.
I need to slow down.	I need to slow down.

Copy on red paper

I had to stop.	I had to stop.
I had to stop.	I had to stop.

Parking Lot

This is a system to get students' questions in one place that you can answer with more clarity and time. It also can be a place where students can go to look at their peers' questions to determine if they have similar wonderings.

Here's how to implement it:

1. Make sure students know the learning goal and success criteria and how this task is related to the learning goal.

2. Use the template as a model to create your chart.

3. Title a chart paper with "Parking Lot." You can laminate this chart paper for continued use so you can move it around your classroom. You also can just use space on your whiteboard and write "Parking Lot" on the board.

4. Make sure your students have a stack of sticky notes.

5. Have students take out their sticky notes so they are prepared for the lesson. They can use them to write down questions or wonderings while the lesson is going on.

6. Students can put their sticky notes on the chart paper with the understanding that the question will be answered after the lesson or during guided/independent practice.

7. When the time is right during your lesson, look at the sticky notes and determine which questions to answer and how to answer them.

8. Maybe the questions are more for individual conferences or maybe the questions can be addressed with the whole group.

The questions from the parking lot can be used to determine future lessons, clarify misconceptions, or as a starting point for class discussions. You also can use these questions to facilitate group work, research projects, and small group cooperative activities. The parking lot also can be used digitally through the use of a Jamboard or Google Docs using the template.

Resource 5.17: Parking Lot

Use sticky notes to write down questions you have about the lesson during the lesson and put the sticky notes on this chart paper.

Costa's Levels of Questioning

Costa's levels of questioning are a hierarchy of question levels that you can have students create to assess their level of understanding in the moment. This style of questioning is characterized by its depth, breadth, and specificity, as well as its ability to elicit thoughtful and insightful responses from the students.

The Costa's level of questioning typically involves asking open-ended questions that encourage students to provide detailed and nuanced answers, and to go beyond a simple yes or no responses. These questions often require students to reflect on their experiences, share their perspectives, and provide thoughtful insights and analysis.

Costa's level of questioning can be used as a formative assessment tool to help teachers gauge their students' understanding of a particular topic or concept. By asking open-ended, thought-provoking questions that require students to think critically and reflect on their learning, teachers can gain insight into their students' thought processes, reasoning, and knowledge gaps.

Using the Costas level of questioning in formative assessment also can help students develop higher-order thinking skills, such as analysis, evaluation, and synthesis, as they learn to engage with complex questions and provide well-reasoned responses.

Here's how to implement it:

1. Make sure students know the learning goal and success criteria and how this task is related to the learning goal.

2. Give students the template(s).

3. Ask students to generate questions at each level based on the topic they are learning about. They do not have to answer the questions.

4. Students can use the other template to write their questions, or they can write their questions in their notebooks, on sticky notes, or wherever you feel is best for their organization.

5. After each prompt, write a leveled question, then ask students to turn and talk to share what they came up with. They do not have to answer each other's questions unless you would like them to!

6. Have students create questions throughout the lesson, during guided practice, or as part of independent practice.

You can collect the sticky notes on anchor chart paper and leave the chart paper up for students to look through and wonder about. The questions also act as a great starting point for future class discussions, writing prompts, and group work lesson ideas. Reading students' questions also will give you an idea about their misconceptions and how they access the different levels of questions. You may find that students need more support with understanding the different levels and what they mean, which gives you a reason to have a lesson or teach about how to use the questions.

Resource 5.18: Levels of Questioning

Levels of Questioning

Level One	Level Two	Level Three
These questions can be answered with yes, no, or specific information found in the text. Someone could point to the information, read it, or see it.	These questions require you to expand on what you already know by using facts, details, or clues.	These questions require you to reflect upon your thinking and be able to respond with a personal opinion that is supported by facts.
define, repeat, name, list, recall, match, identify	compare, contrast, outline, analyze, infer, support, construct	prove your answer, value, decide, assess, summarize, give
• What happened _? • Locate in the story where _ • When did _ take place? • List the _ • Where did _ • Who was/were _ • What events led to _?	• What would happen to you if _? • What occurs when _? • Compare and contrast _ • Give me an example of _ • What is the author trying to explain when _ and _? • Make an inference about _	• Design a _ to show _ • Write a new ending to the story. • Describe the events that might occur if _ • Pretend you are _ and write _ • What do you think will happen to _? Why? • If you were there would you _? • Do you agree with _? Why or why not?

Anchor Charts

Anchor charts help to anchor learning in the classroom by creating a place that students can refer back to while progressing toward the learning goal. It is a great way to "anchor" the learning and be able to refer back to it while building previously learned skills.

Here is a list of different ways you can implement anchor charts in your classroom. Always be sure to have chart paper and markers ready to go so you always have the ability to make an anchor chart.

- Display the learning goal and success criteria.
- Steps to complete a skill, like adding fractions.
- Notes from a class discussion.
- Target responses, also known as writing exemplars.
- Student ideas from gallery walks.
- Two- or three-column charts to collect ideas.
- Language frames to support student writing.
- A parking lot for questions using sticky notes.
- "Around the World" questions (see cooperative group ideas).
- Student notes from Jigsaw activities (see cooperative group ideas).

The information from anchor charts can be used to help students understand skills that they have learned and refer back to previous learning. Anchor charts help students solidify their learning and contribute to the learning as well. The topics and details written on the anchor charts can be used to spark ideas for future lessons or think about topics for class discussions.

Resource 5.19: Anchor Charts

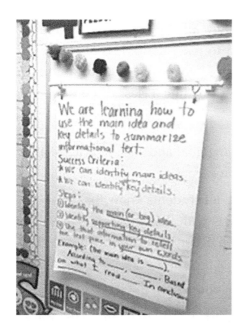

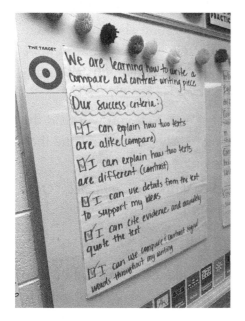

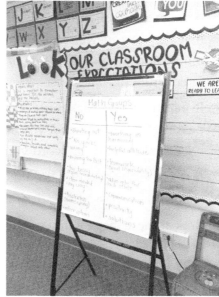

Shout Out the Word That I Leave Out

This is a read-aloud strategy that involves all students while also lowering anxiety when students are asked to read aloud. It is also a great way to listen to students as they read aloud, to ensure they stay on task, and to involve them in the reading while leading a class discussion.

Here's how to implement it:

1. Make sure students know the learning goal and success criteria and how this task is related to the learning goal.

2. Before reading aloud with students, let students know that you will be reading aloud in a variety of ways with the whole class or small group. Make sure students have a partner they can turn to, to discuss the reading.

3. Start by reading part of the passage yourself to the class.

4. Then ask students to read the next part silently to themselves. Make sure it is a smaller passage that students read independently.

5. After students read that passage, ask a question about the passage that they can answer with their partners. Give students one to three minutes to discuss. Use this time to walk around and listen to different students' answers.

6. Bring the group back and let students know that you will read the passage, but as you read, you are going to leave a word out and they have to shout out the word you leave out.

7. If students need to practice this, practice with a few sentences. Only choose short passages to do this part of the strategy.

8. Repeat these steps while you read the passage as a class.

This strategy can help you listen to students' voices, while also keeping students focused and on task during read-aloud. Listening to students share with each other while using this strategy can help you determine students' misconceptions.

Fist to Five

Students use this hand signal during instruction to let the teacher know how they are feeling about the learning goals on a scale from 0 to 5, with their fist representing "0," meaning that there is no understanding, and number 5 representing full understanding.

Here's how to implement it:

1. Make sure students know the learning goal and success criteria and how this task is related to the learning goal.

2. Display the posters in your classroom so students can refer to them during instruction.

3. Explain each of the hand signals to students and that you will refer to them during lessons and other classroom activities.

   a. Fist: 0, which means needing support and clarification.

   b. Index Finger: 1, which means little understanding.

   c. Two Fingers: 2, which means somewhat of an understanding.

   d. Three Fingers: 3, which means a pretty good understanding.

   e. Four Fingers: 4, which means a strong understanding.

   f. Five Fingers: 5, which means full understanding.

4. While you are teaching, ask students to show "fist to five" to show their level of understanding.

Use this as an opportunity to see how students feel about the instruction and to determine how you will group students when you are offering small group re-teaching times. Take note of students who show a full understanding so you can provide opportunities for extension based on the skill you're teaching.

Resource 5.20: Fist to Five

I don't understand.

I need help understanding.

I somewhat understand.

I understand.

I understand and can explain in my own words.

I understand and can teach it to others.

3-2-1

This is a simple template that enables students to summarize their learning in three different parts. You can use this at the end of lessons as an exit ticket, at the end of the day, or at the end of the week.

Here's how to implement it:

1. Make sure students know the learning goal and success criteria and how this task is related to the learning goal.

2. Print out the template and make sure you have enough to use throughout the day for lessons, or for whenever you choose to use them.

3. Have students quietly reflect on the lesson, day, or week.

4. The template will direct students to think of the following:

   a. 3 words to describe their thinking

   b. 2 questions they still have

   c. 1 goal they hope to accomplish

5. You also can use the template that has blank spaces to choose different phrases for students to complete. Here are a few examples:

   a. Wonderings you still have.

   b. Statements they can make.

   c. Discoveries that occurred.

   d. Things they still want to learn.

The information students provide on this exit ticket can help you plan future instruction, create discussion prompts for class discussions, and also see students' thinking about a topic which can help with daily check-ins and individual conversations.

Resource 5.21: 3-2-1

Name: _____ Date: _____

3 – 2 – 1

- Write 3 things you hope will happen this week.
- Write 2 things you want to learn about.
- Write 1 goal you have for the week.

3	
2	
1	

Visual Map

Visual maps are graphic organizers that help students organize their thinking during learning.

Here's how to implement it:

1. Make sure students know the learning goal and success criteria and how this task is related to the learning goal.

2. Choose which graphic organizer will be best for the lesson/activity.

3. Model using the graphic organizer for students.

4. Use metacognition during modeling so students understand how to process the information they are learning so they know how to organize it on their graphic organizer.

5. Have students practice using graphic organizers in pairs and independently so students can share ideas and organize what they are learning with more confidence.

Students can use the graphic organizers to help them with future tasks. Graphic organizers can be used for prewriting, getting students to think about previously learned skills to reactivate them before learning something new, and improving organizational skills.

Resource 5.22 Visual Maps

Name: _____ Date: _____

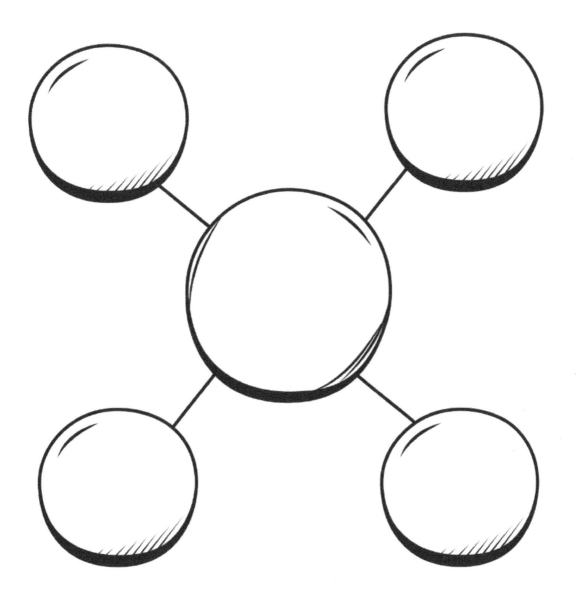

Name: _____ Date: _____

Name: _____ Date: _____

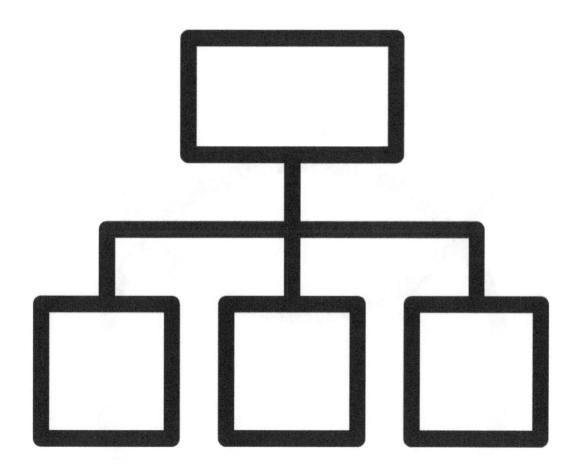

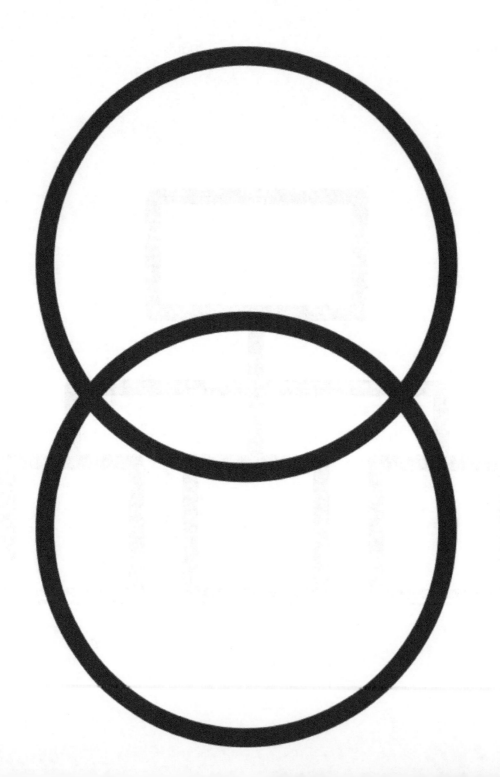

Picture Notes

Students draw a representation of their learning during instruction and share their ideas with their partners.

Here's how to implement it:

1. Make sure students know the learning goal and success criteria and how this task is related to the learning goal.

2. Have the template ready to use during instruction and make sure students are partnered up to complete the activity.

3. While teaching students a new skill, model how you draw a representation.

4. Ask students to do the same based on a question about the new skill their learning.

5. This also can be used while reading a new piece of information, after learning a new skill, or while listening to a presentation or video.

6. After students draw something based on what they're learning, reading, or listening, have them share their picture notes with a partner.

Use student picture notes to gather information about what students know and how they feel about the learning. You can use this information to create instructional groups, plan future lessons, and to also understand students' thinking.

Resource 5.23: Picture Notes

Name: _____ Date: _____

Picture Notes

Learning Goal
Picture Notes

Name: _____ Date: _____

Picture Notes

Learning Goal
Picture Notes

Error Analysis

This is an opportunity for students to analyze a problem and determine the mistake while also communicating the correct answer and why they think their answer is correct and why the error occurred.

Here's how to implement it:

1. Make sure students know the learning goal and success criteria and how this task is related to the learning goal.

2. Use the template and fill it in with questions and answers that are incorrect.

3. Make sure the questions you ask are related to the learning goal and success criteria and that it is a skill that students have learned or are learning.

4. Students will answer the questions on the template to complete the error analysis.

5. After students complete the questions on the template, have them share their thinking with a partner.

6. Once students have finished sharing, have students come together and talk about the error and correct answers as a whole group.

Error analysis is a great way to see how students analyze problems and determine errors, while also explaining their thinking. Using this activities for future instruction can help you determine if you need to model more metacognition with solving more of these problems and see how students think about errors and how to explain them.

Resource 5.24: Error Analysis

Name: _____ Date: _____

Error Analysis

Learning Goal	
Question	
Is the answer incorrect?	
How do you know?	
What is the correct answer?	
Explain your thinking.	

2- and 3-Column Charts

These are two different types of charts students can use to organize their thinking and learning during the lesson.

Here's how to implement it:

1. Make sure students know the learning goal and success criteria and how this task is related to the learning goal.

2. Print the templates to use during your lessons.

3. You also can use an anchor chart to create the same type of chart to use as a model and guide for students to follow.

4. Use the chart during the lesson to help students collect their thoughts. Label the chart with the appropriate information that students will need.

5. Here are some examples:

   a. Lesson notes

   b. Vocabulary instruction

   c. Math skill practice

   d. Levels of questions

   e. Summaries

   f. Error analysis and justification

   g. Main idea and details

   h. Character analysis

   i. Cause and effect

   j. Compare and contrast

Have students keep these notes so they can refer to them during future instruction. These notes will help students stay organized and make connections between previous and future skills they are learning.

Resource 5.25a: 2-Column Charts

Name: _____ Date: _____

2 – Column Chart

Resource 5.25b: 3-Column Charts

Name: _____ Date: _____

3 - Column Chart

Summary

There is no one way to complete formative assessments. Students may be given multiple opportunities and different methods to show their understanding of concepts. The key is that this formative assessment happens "in the moment." This allows the teacher to make adjustments to instruction in the moment to best meet student needs and understanding

Key Takeaways

- I have used a variety of formative assessments from this chapter.

- I use information that I gather from formative assessments to change my instruction *while* I am teaching the lesson.

- I use information that I gather from formative assessments to change my instruction *after* I have taught the lesson to make changes and prepare for upcoming lessons.

- I understand that each type of in-the-moment formative has a specific purpose and I work to match the information I hope to gather with the intent of the formative lesson.

CHAPTER 6

In-the-Moment Formative Instruction: Collaborative Routines

In the previous chapter, we offered a variety of resources to implement for in-the-moment formative assessment of students. In this chapter, we will share with you a number of "in-the-moment" formative collaborative routines that students can engage in with one another to process their learning as it is happening.

A *collaborative routine* for learning is a structured approach for students to work together in a group setting to achieve a common learning goal. This can include activities such as group discussions, problem-solving tasks, and peer-to-peer teaching.

Collaborative learning has been shown to have a number of benefits for students, including:

- **Increased motivation and engagement:** Working with others can make learning more enjoyable and interactive, which can lead to increased motivation and engagement.

- **Greater understanding of the material:** Collaborating with others can help students better understand and retain new information.

- **Development of social and communication skills:** Collaborative learning activities can help students develop important social and communication skills, such as teamwork and active listening.

- **Increased diversity of perspectives and ideas:** Collaborating with a diverse group of peers can expose students to a range of perspectives and ideas, which can broaden their understanding of the material and the world around them.

- **Improvement in problem-solving skills:** Collaborative learning activities often involve problem-solving tasks, which can help students develop critical-thinking and problem-solving skills.

In this chapter, you will find strategies and resources that are meant to support your collaborative routines as formative assessments during your instruction. Interweave these strategies into your lesson to ensure you can monitor your student's progress toward meeting the learning goal.

Jigsaw

This is a cooperative learning activity in which students work in collaborative groups and are able to teach each other. During this activity, students are each given a section or chunk of a larger assignment and become experts on their section. After every student has worked at becoming an expert, they then teach the rest of their group about their area of expertise, and when complete, the overall assignment has been covered and "jigsaw-ed" together. From our experiences, learning in this way promotes increased student motivation and agency and increases students' overall enjoyment of learning new content.

Here's how to implement it:

1. Make sure students know the learning goal and success criteria and how this task is related to the learning goal.

2. Break up students into smaller groups of four to six students per group, depending on the content size.

3. Assign one student to serve as the group leader or allow groups to self-select.

4. Make sure the assignment is divided up into segmented sections that equal the number of students per group.

5. Allow the group to break up the sections among themselves.

6. Set a timer and allow students to learn their part of the topic to become the "expert."

7. When the time has expired, allow students to join with the others in the class that reviewed the same topic to share ideas and make sure they did not miss any key points.

8. Have students join back with their original groups and share out the main points and key details from their section.

We have found Jigsaw to be most effective (and an excellent time-saver) in areas such as science and social studies, where there is a large amount of text and content and several key points and takeaways. This can allow for students to learn the essential information but also save instructional minutes and allow for collaboration

Resource 6.1: Jigsaw

Name: _____ Date: _____

Jigsaw

My Expert Information

Partner Information

Partner Information

Partner Information

Inside/Outside Circle

Inside/Outside Circle was initially developed as a strategy to assist English Language Learners in their language acquisition skills. Since its inception, this strategy has proven to be helpful in assisting all students to practice the sharing of ideas. It can be structured to build on ideas, review concepts, or share information.

Here's how to implement it:

1. Make sure students know the learning goal and success criteria and how this task is related to the learning goal.

2. Make sure you have plenty of space and have the students form two circles, one inside and one outside. Make sure there are an equal number of students in both circles.

3. Name one circle the inner circle and one circle the outer circle.

4. Establish a start and stop signal (bell, chime, music, etc.).

5. Present a question or prompt for the students to exchange ideas.

6. Begin with the inner circle responding to the question as the outer circle listens.

7. Use the sound signal to signify the communication exchange has been completed.

8. Now the outer circle may respond to the same prompt or question while the inner circle listens.

9. Use the sound signal to signify the communication exchange has been completed.

10. Now have everyone in the inner circle move one person to the left and have the new partners greet each other before continuing the activity with new prompts.

This strategy can be useful for many purposes within the classroom. After completing a section of reading, this can be a helpful way to share ideas or review concepts. It can also be used in content areas to review previously taught information.

Resource 6.2: Inside/Outside Circle

Inside Outside Circle Steps (this can be a poster for display in the classroom)

- The teacher will present a question or prompt for the students to exchange ideas.

- Students in the inner circle will respond first to the question as the outer circle listens.

- Wait for the sound signal. This will signify the communication exchange has been completed.

- Then, the outer circle will respond to the prompt or question while the inner circle listens.

- Wait for the sound signal. This will signify the communication exchange has been completed.

- Then, everyone in the inner circle will move one person to the left.

- New partners greet each other before continuing the activity with new prompts.

Structured Language Talk

This is a partner and group discussion routine that will ensure each student has a chance to read/listen to new information, share their ideas based on a question or prompt, and respond to others in their groups. This is structured in that students are using language functions (compare/contrast, cause/effect, time sequence, opinion, etc.) to communicate their ideas.

Here's how to implement it:

1. Make sure students know the learning goal and success criteria and how this task is related to the learning goal.

2. You will need to make sure you have the templates, reading material, or something students listen to, and questions for students to respond to ready to go. You also will need to make sure you have the language function you want students to practice:

    a. Cause/effect

    b. Compare/contrast

    c. Opinion

3. Set the activity for students by letting them know the question first, then have students read a passage that is connected to the question.

4. Have students think about their answer and write it down first.

5. Then have students share their answers with a prechosen partner.

While students are sharing and talking, walk around the room and listen to their conversations. You can use this as a time to make sure students understand the language function, the question you are asking, and the passage they are reading or listening to.

Resource 6.3: Structured Language Talk

Name: _____ Date: _____

Structured Language Talk

Opinion Language Frames
<ul><li>In my opinion _ because _.</li><li>I believe _ because _.</li><li>Based on what I read _and _.</li><li>I feel _ is _ because _.</li><li>I think _ because _.</li><li>I know _ is _ because _.</li></ul>
Compare and Contrast Language Frames
<ul><li>_ is similar to _ because _.</li><li>Based on what I read, _ and _ are similar because _.</li><li>Both texts share _ and _. For example _.</li><li>The difference between the two texts is _.</li><li>One difference between the two texts is _.</li><li>Based on what I read, _ and _ are different because _.</li></ul>
Cause and Effect Language Frames
<ul><li>As a result _.</li><li>One effect of the _ is that _.</li><li>There are several reasons _.</li><li>Because of this _.</li><li>One effect is _.</li><li>_ cause _ to _.</li><li>Because of _, then _.</li><li>Since _, then _.</li></ul>

Talking Sticks

Talking sticks are an idea derived from the Native American culture when tribe members used sticks during their tribal meetings to determine who had the right to speak at a given time. While one person held the stick, all others were asked to stay silent. As a teacher, you can use a similar strategy in your classroom to facilitate effective opportunities for sharing among classmates and to teach the concept of turn-taking,

Here's how to implement it:

1. Make sure students know the learning goal and success criteria and how this task is related to the learning goal.

2. Share with the class the history behind talking sticks.

3. Put students into pairs and give each pair a 6-inch wooden dowel to decorate.

4. Provide students with beads, leather cords, feathers, and other decorative materials.

5. Allow students to decorate their talking sticks, and each time your class completes the talking stick activity, select a different stick to use for the day's activities.

The talking stick strategy can be an effective way to facilitate complete group discussions, resolve conflicts, conduct class read-alouds, and even do creative storytelling.

Pass It On!

In this activity, students work in a group to process new learning. They do this by writing down their answer to a question and passing this on to another student to respond. Once this takes place, the team discusses the answers and reflects as a group.

Here's how to implement it:

1. Make sure students know the learning goal and success criteria and how this task is related to the learning goal and aligned with the questions they're answering for this task.

2. Use the template to facilitate this discussion.

3. Get students into groups of three to five.

4. Have a list of questions ready that could have possible answers.

5. Display the question for students or write it on the template.

6. Give each student a few minutes to answer the question.

7. Then have students pass their paper to the student to their right.

8. That student will read the previous student's answer and comment on it by writing on a piece of paper.

   a. They can comment if they agree, disagree, like, or have more to add and why they feel that way about the answer.

   b. Give students one to three minutes during this time to comment on it.

9. Then that student will pass the paper again to the student to their right.

10. This will continue until the paper gets back to the original person.

11. Let students discuss answers and ideas as a whole group and see if they can come to a consensus.

12. While students are working, walk around and listen to discussions and read what students are writing.

These writing sheets are good to use to clear up students' misconceptions about learning goals and to come up with topics for future class discussions. These groups also help students practice group norms and get used to having academic conversations about content

Resource 6.4: Pass It On!

Name: _____ Date: _____

Pass it on!

I agree with _ because _.   I disagree with _ because _.

I think the answer is _ because _.   Based on _, then _.

Question	
Teammate 1	
Teammate 2	
Teammate 3	
Teammate 4	

Think-Aloud

Think-aloud allows teachers to verbalize what is happening in their minds as they read a text. These verbalizations allow students access into someone's brain as they work to understand a text so they may begin to understand how good readers construct meaning. Over time, you can transition this strategy so students are engaging in a think-aloud themselves for you and/or their classmates.

Here's how to implement it:

1. Make sure students know the learning goal and success criteria and how this task is related to the learning goal.

2. First, model this strategy by telling the students what you are thinking as you read. Think about what concepts may be confusing or challenging to them.

3. Next, introduce an assigned text to students and provide them "stems to use" to guide their thinking:

   a. I think this section will be about . . .

   b. As I read this, I am visualizing . . .

   c. I think some people might get confused by . . .

   d. To me, the author means ____ when he says _____.

   e. This connects to what we have already learned because . . .

4. Have students pair up with a classmate and allow them to practice this technique while you circulate the classroom and provide structured feedback to student pairs.

As you work with students to grow their ability to comprehend and decode more challenging text, it can help to revisit this strategy with students in your class throughout the school year.

Resource 6.5: Think-Aloud

Cut these in half and give them to students to use as bookmarks.

Think Aloud

- What do I know about this topic?

- What do I think I will learn about this topic?

- Do I understand what I just read?

- Do I have a clear picture in my head about this information?

- What more can I do to understand this?

Think Aloud

- What do I know about this topic?

- What do I think I will learn about this topic?

- Do I understand what I just read?

- Do I have a clear picture in my head about this information?

- What more can I do to understand this?

Collaboration Board

This is an ideal way to elicit feedback from students, especially shy students, by allowing for digital collaboration to a posted prompt or learning idea.

Here's how to implement it:

1. Make sure students know the learning goal and success criteria and how this task is related to the learning goal.

2. Use an online platform such as Jamboard to create questions for students in your classes to allow them to share their thoughts on a topic or their ideas.

3. This digital bulletin board allows students to respond to questions with images, messages, and GIFS.

4. As students reply, teachers and classmates can "like" their responses or comment on other students' ideas.

We have found that at times, students who were uncomfortable sharing with the whole class were more open to participating in classroom questions via a digital forum. This allows for students with quieter voices to have a larger role in classroom conversations.

Resource 6.6: Collaboration Board

Google Jamboard is an online collaboration resource and whiteboard. It allowed for in-the-moment participation and feedback. It allows for learning both in a face-to-face and a virtual environment and allows for collaboration.

1. To begin go to: jambord.google.com or by clicking the "new" button in your Google Drive and hovering over the word "more.

2. There are several tools in the Jamboard to explore such as draw, eraser, select, choose sticky note, image, text box, laser, background, clear frame, frame bar, menu, and zoom.

3. Allow students to log in and collaborate or share their Jamboards from other sections of student groups with a shareable link.

4. There are many uses of Jamboard, including small group brain-storming, virtual learning and exchange of ideas, and generating feedback.

Goals and Steps

In this formative assessment activity, students talk together about creating their learning goal and then discuss the steps they will take to get to their goal (success criteria). These goals and steps are generated by the students so that they take ownership of their learning. By employing this strategy, you can make sure students understand the overall lesson goal, and they can tie this into the steps they need to complete to be successful. This also builds opportunities for self and peer evaluation.

Here's how to implement it:

1. Make sure students know the learning goal and success criteria and how this task is related to the learning goal.

2. Determine an assignment for the students to complete.

3. Have students work in small groups to develop the learning goal and the "steps" needed to achieve that goal.

4. Each student should have developed steps that need to be taken to reach the learning goal.

5. Make sure students share their ideas with each other while in the group and students collaborate on determining the steps.

Students can share their ideas with other groups and eventually be able to teach the skill to one another. Have students create posters, anchor charts, or layered activities that can be used for future activities and lessons.

Resource 6.7: Goals and Steps

Name: _____ Date: _____

Goals and Steps

Learning Goal

Steps

Reflection

Peer Feedback (Nonverbal Signals)

In this strategy, students share with the class one thing that they worked on in class that day (i.e., how to create a topic sentence). After the student has shared, the class responds with their level of mastery to the expected learning criteria.

Here's how to implement it:

1. Make sure students know the learning goal and success criteria and how this task is related to the learning goal.
2. The teacher calls on one student to review out loud a topic of the day's learning.
3. After the student has shared, classmates raise their hands to the level that they feel that they have met the learning criteria for the intended learning.
4. Raising hands all the way up = I got this; halfway up = I am okay or I am getting there but could use a little help; just above the desk = I'm going to need additional support on this topic.

As the classroom teacher, this is a simple way to get a snapshot of where the class is as a whole, and if you need to revisit a topic with the class at another time.

One-Minute Shares

This is a one-minute routine where students share ideas with each other based on skills they have already learned. Each partner has 30 seconds to share their idea with their partner and then they can write down their ideas on their recording sheet.

Here's how to implement it:

1. Make sure students know the learning goal and success criteria and how this task is related to the learning goal.

2. Pose a question to the class related to the learning goal (i.e., What is one strategy you can use to find the answer to 4 × 3?).

3. Give students one minute to share the answer with each other (30 seconds each).

4. Ask for volunteers to share their partner's ideas.

5. Then use one minute for students to write their ideas down on their recording sheet.

While this activity is happening, walk around and listen to students' ideas. As they are talking to each other, take note of what students are saying and either clarify misconceptions and/or acknowledge high-level thinking. Use their conversations to help drive future instruction and to determine extension activities.

Resource 6.8: One-Minute Shares

Name: _____ Date: _____

One Minute Shares

Teacher Question
My Answer

Name: _____ Date: _____

One Minute Shares

Teacher Question
My Answer

Lingering Questions (Like the Muddiest Points but It Is a Group Effort)

Completing the lingering questions with your students is relatively straightforward. However, it is very effective because it allows students to tell you where in the learning process they are confused and "why" it is confusing.

Here's how to implement it:

1. Make sure students know the learning goal and success criteria and how this task is related to the learning goal.

2. Decide precisely where you want group feedback. Is it with an entire unit, a lesson, or a segment? The more specific you are with your students, the more targeted and valuable the data will be.

3. Ensure ample time at the end of class for students to complete this activity thoroughly. If they rush out to race the bell, the data you get back will not be as valuable to you. It also helps to set time parameters. *"Scholars, I will be handing out a "muddiest points form" for today's lesson. You will have seven minutes to complete this; then, I will collect them before the bell rings."*

4. Do something with the data you collect. When we strategically carve out time before the summative assessment to determine areas for remediation, we *must* use these data to guide our next steps in the classroom. A "muddiest point" is not adequate if you are administering a summative the following day. Ideally, you want to give this out and have one or two lesson spaces for re-teach based on what you have learned before administering a summative assessment.

You begin with a prompt, asking student teams to name one area from the last lesson to overview their learning. Before administering a summative assessment, you will go through these and do two things as the teacher.

1. Search for common themes. Are there specific points and ideas with which many or most students share concerns? If so, spending a day on a re-teach lesson will assist you in better teaching to mastery.

2. Are there specific groups of students to pull and re-teach before the assessment so that you can provide clarification?

Resource 6.9: Lingering Questions

Name: _____ Date: _____

Lingering Questions

Directions: Name one concept or skill you learned this week. How did you learn it? Describe the process. Were any concepts unclear? How so? What goals do you have for your learning next week? If you could design an activity to help a classmate learn this activity or skill, what would you have them do?

Give One, Get One

The "give one, get one" formative assessment strategy is a technique where students exchange information with their peers in a structured and collaborative manner. This approach encourages active engagement, self-reflection, and peer-to-peer teaching.

Here's how to implement it:

1. Make sure students know the learning goal and success criteria and how this task is related to the learning goal.

2. Teachers should provide students with a list of key concepts or topics related to the material they are studying.

3. Students should then identify one concept or topic that they feel confident about and write it on a note card or piece of paper.

4. Students should then move around the classroom, finding a partner and sharing their concept or topic.

5. After sharing, each student should add one new concept or topic to their card, based on the information they received from their partner.

6. Students should continue to find new partners and share their knowledge, adding new concepts or topics to their cards after each exchange.

7. After several rounds of exchanging and adding information, students can review their cards and reflect on what they have learned.

Use this strategy so students have the opportunity to engage with their peers, reinforce their own knowledge, and gain new insights and perspectives on the material they are studying. This promotes collaborative learning that helps create a positive classroom environment where students can support and learn from each other.

Resource 6.10: Give One, Get One

Name: _____ Date: _____

Give One, Get One

TOPIC:	
Give One	**Get One**
1.	1.
2.	2.
3.	3.
4.	4.
5.	5.

Summary

In summary, collaborative routines is a structured approach to learning that involves small groups of students working together to achieve a common goal. These collaborative routines can take many forms such as think-pair-share, discussion opportunities, and jigsaw activities. The benefits of engaging in these activities are that students can engage actively with the material, share ideas and perspectives, learn from one another, and collaborate to develop the skills of teamwork and problem-solving.

Key Takeaways

- I have tried a variety of the collaborative routines shared in this chapter.

- I have determined which routines are most effective with which lessons.

- I can see how the use of these routines encourages higher levels of student engagement and autonomy.

Dialogic Teaching and Dialectic Synergy

Once upon a time in America, a noisy classroom was considered a poorly managed classroom. From the beginning of the American school system and well into the 1990s and beyond, administrators often judged the efficacy of a teacher based on how quiet their classroom was. Classrooms were set into rows, students responded to bells, and we were preparing a nation of future factory workers. As the tide has shifted and we have become a more globalized nation, our needs have changed and so too have our expectations within classrooms across the country. These shifts have given rise to a new philosophy in teaching called dialogic teaching.

While it is easy to provide resources and grab-and-go's on quick formative assessments that you can embed within your instruction, we would be remiss if we did not spend significant time touching upon a teaching method that we think, at its face, is true formative teaching. We believe that by embedding dialogic teaching into your instructional strategies, day in and day out, not only will you have an immediate handle on the pulse and learning in your classroom, but you will find your students are able to go far deeper into their learning and understanding than they would have via traditional in-the-moment formative assessments.

Dialogic Teaching

While the term dialogic teacher was first coined by Robin Alexander in the early 2000s to describe how teachers can engage students, expand on ideas, push high levels of reasoning, and stimulate deeper learning, its true roots go back to the Vygotskian Sociocultural Theory, which emphasized the role of dialogue in the process of teaching and learning. A teacher who employs this style of teaching in their classrooms is able to empower students to engage in the democratic process and inspire a lifelong love of learning. One hallmark characteristic of dialogic teaching is that it is not simply the question-and-answer routines that are typical in a traditional classroom, but instead, it is a classroom wherein the teacher acts as a facilitator to encourage children to engage in deeper learning, justify their thinking, and build upon one another's ideas.

What Does Dialogic Teaching Look Like in the Classroom?

Since dialogic teaching pushes students to higher levels of understanding and expands their thinking, it looks quite different from teaching in a "traditional" classroom. Dialogic teaching is not a "method" of teaching; it is more of an approach and a professional framework. Teachers who engage in dialogic teaching are less concerned with the techniques they employ and more concerned with the classroom relationships they foster. They eschew traditional techniques for a deeper understanding of the ways their students conceive of learning, and they eliminate the hierarchical classroom structure. These teachers work to provide high levels of thinking and talking time to students in their classrooms and they work to allow students to justify their thinking.

If you were to visit a truly dialogic classroom there are several things that you would see as commonalities in all of these classrooms. Many of these are outlined in Table 7.1. You will find that the pupils in these classrooms rarely complete recall-based exams. Instead, dialogic educators focus on students imagining, narrating, explaining, and justifying their thinking. You will find a large emphasis on the skill of listening and even see discrete lessons dedicated to the art of listening. You will see a high level of wait time and thinking time provided to students in these classrooms. In a dialogic classroom, students are encouraged to disagree

Table 7.1 Key components of dialogic teaching.

Component	What it looks like
Balanced talk time.	Students are talking more than 51% of the time.
Various levels of questioning.	Teachers ask various open-ended questions, employing the strategies of think time/wait time/process time and collaborative synthesis time so that students can feel confident in sharing out their ideas to rigorous questions.
Enables student agency.	Students are given the confidence and the opportunity, within a safe space, to ask questions, without fear of shame or judgment.
Allows for collaborative groups.	Time is defined for students to engage in group and partner sharing as a part of each lesson.
Asks open-ended questions.	Questions such as • How do you know that? • What is your justification? • How can you be sure? • Is there another way? • What do you think? • Why do you think that?
Built-in opportunities for student self-reflection.	The teacher builds in time for pause and reflection, both orally and in writing through a learning sequence to aid in the synthesis of ideas.
Common misconceptions addressed.	The teacher works to identify common misconceptions and address them via class (student-led) discussions.
Think-aloud.	The teacher *and* students model the metacognitive process.

in a respectful manner, and to defend opposing viewpoints. These classrooms often have walls that are print rich with samples of "sentence stems," "accountable talk," "scaffolded language," or conversation entry points. When students speak in a dialogic classroom, instead of seeing a teacher call on a student and then move on to the next student's ideas, you are more likely to hear the teacher say things like

- "Tell me more about why you feel that way."

- "Help me understand how you came to that conclusion."

- "I wonder if any of your classmates may want to build upon this great idea."

- "Can you take that to the next level or dig a little deeper into that idea for us?

If you are unsure if what you are seeing is an example of dialogic teaching (or if you are engaging in dialogic teaching), use this quick and easy checklist to determine if you're on track.

Dialogic Instruction Checklist

My instruction is

- Purposeful (is planned and structured with specific learning goals in mind).

- Collective (allows for teamwork to address an essential question or the problem).

- Supportive (allows for students to express ideas freely in a safe space without anxiety about being "wrong").

- Reciprocal (allows for the exchange of ideas, active listening, and the space to consider alternative viewpoints).

- Cumulative (allows students to build on one another's ideas and string those together with their own ideas in an effort to deepen understanding.

Benefits of Dialogic Teaching

There are many great reasons to make dialogic teaching a regular part of your instructional routine. First and foremost, dialogic teaching increases student agency, thus increasing student engagement. It assists students in creating meaning and in achieving higher mental functions, which aid in cognitive development. Dialogic teaching helps to move classrooms away from the idea of content being "transmitted" from teacher to student and instead focuses on students engaging in dialogue to construct their knowledge and understanding. Dialogic teaching encourages students to think and question ideas as well as construct knowledge, engage in dialogue, and explore alternate perspectives.

Various studies have supported the idea that dialogic teaching lends itself to increases in academic achievement. In one study from 2017, Alexander conducted a randomized clinical trial with the purpose of examining the benefits of classroom talk by teachers who had been trained in dialogic teaching methods. The data indicated that after 20 weeks in the study, students whose teachers had been trained in dialogic teaching showed two months greater growth than those not placed in these classrooms (Alexander, 2017). Another study, from 2012, uncovered that the use of dialogic teaching in classrooms led to more inclusive environments as students were able to increase their level of participation (Lyle, et al., 2012). Essentially, dialogic teaching enables deeper thinking, more connected students, improved peer and teacher relationships, a redefinition of teacher–student relationships, and an increase in democratic values within the classroom. It is also important to note, when speaking about the benefits of this type of instruction, that while it positively impacts all children, it has the highest level of impact on lower-achieving students or those students who have demonstrated gaps in opportunity and achievement.

Steps to Begin Implementing Dialogic Teaching in Your Classroom

As a teacher, you play a crucial role in shaping the minds of the next generation. By implementing dialogic teaching in your classroom, you can create a more engaging and interactive learning environment that promotes critical thinking and collaboration among your students.

Here are the four steps you can take to begin implementing dialogic teaching in your classroom:

1. Start by understanding what dialogic teaching is and why it is important. Dialogic teaching is a teaching approach that prioritizes dialogue and collaboration among students. It is based on the idea that learning is a social process and that students learn best when they are actively engaged in discussions and debates with their peers.

2. Plan and structure your lessons to promote dialogue and collaboration. Dialogic teaching is not just about having students talk to each other, it is about creating opportunities for students to engage in meaningful discussions and debates about the material being taught. This means planning lessons that include activities such as group discussions, debates, and collaborative problem-solving tasks.

3. Use questioning techniques to facilitate student-led discussions. As a teacher, you can help facilitate dialogic teaching by asking open-ended questions that encourage students to think critically and engage with the material in a deeper way. Avoid asking leading questions that give away the answer or shut down the conversation.

4. Provide support and guidance as needed. Dialogic teaching can be challenging for both students and teachers, especially at first. It is important to provide support and guidance as needed to help students feel comfortable participating in discussions and collaborating

with their peers. This may include modeling good dialogue and collaboration skills, providing feedback on their participation, and offering support to students who may be struggling.

By taking these steps and continuing to adapt and evolve your teaching approach, you can create a classroom environment that promotes dialogue and collaboration among your students, fostering critical thinking and a love of learning.

Resources for Implementing Dialogic Teaching

Table 7.2 describes resources to help you begin implementing dialogic teaching in your classroom.

Table 7.2   Resources for implementing dialogic teaching.

Resource	Description
Developing Conversation Ground Rules Activity	Resource 7.1 is designed to assist student teams in developing plans for the sharing of thoughts and ideas in a respectful manner.
Classroom Stems Poster	Resource 7.2 provides students within the classroom with approved entry points to the class conversation that tie to learning goals and move the conversation forward.
Dialogic Classroom Stems Student Bookmarks (Grades 3–10)	Resource 7.3 provides individual students within the classroom with approved entry points to the class conversation that tie to learning goals and move the conversation forward.
Analysis of Classroom Rules for Discussion	Resource 7.4 provides an opportunity for whole-class feedback on the rules and norms that may be developed for the class along with opportunities for student input.
Peer Thinking Analysis/ Observational Tool	Resource 7.5 allows students to provide feedback to one another and rate the contributions of thought partners and teammates.

Resource 7.1: Developing Conversation Ground Rules

Name: _____ Date: _____

Developing Conversation Ground Rules

Directions:
Review the list of ground rules and select the ones that best apply for your group.

1. We will encourage contributions from everyone.

2. We will justify our thinking.

3. Listen respectfully without interrupting.

4. Listen actively to try and understand alternate perspectives.

5. Criticize ideas, not people.

6. Avoid heated language.

7. Allow everyone to be heard.

8. Try to learn, but not argue.

9. Be patient and do not interrupt.

Our Conversation Ground Rules in Order of Importance

Resource 7.2: Classroom Stems Poster

Classroom Discussion Stems

State an Opinion • I think/believe that… • In my opinion… • Based on … it seems that … • After reading this section I would say…	**Agree/Disagree** • I agree with (name) because… • I disagree with (name) because… • That answer makes sense because… • I came to a different conclusion because…
Build on Ideas • I'd like to build upon what (name) said… • I'd like to rephrase that point • Could we go back to the point {name} made • To add to what (name) said… • This reminds me of…	**Evaluate** • So what you are saying is… • I noticed that… • So what you are thinking is… • If I understand you correctly, your main point is…
Compare/Contrast • What would happen if….? • Is there another example of…? • How is this similar/different to…? • This reminds me of…	**Clarify** • Would you explain that again? • Could you clarify the point about…?
Paraphrase • So, what you are saying is…? • I noticed that… • So what you are thinking is…? • If I understand you correctly, your main point is…	**Reflect** • Today's discussion was effective because… • Today's lesson made me rethink… • My most valuable contribution to today was…

Resource 7.3: Dialogic Classroom Stems Bookmarks (Grades 3–10)

Print then fold at the line. Laminate for a two-sided bookmark to provide each student when engaging in dialogic discussions.

Classroom Discussion Engagement Bookmark	Classroom Discussion Engagement Bookmark
State an Opinion • I think/believe that… • In my opinion… • Based on … it seems that … • After reading this section I would say…	**Agree/Disagree** • I agree with (name) because… • I disagree with (name) because… • That answer makes sense because… • I came to a different conclusion because…
Build on Ideas • I'd like to build upon what (name) said… • I'd like to rephrase that point • Could we go back to the point {name} made • To add to what (name) said… • This reminds me of…	**Evaluate** • So what you are saying is… • I noticed that… • So what you are thinking is… • If I understand you correctly, your main point is…
Compare/Contrast • What would happen if….? • Is there another example of…? • How is this similar/different to…? • This reminds me of…	**Clarify** • Would you explain that again? • Could you clarify the point about…?
Paraphrase • So, what you are saying is…? • I noticed that… • So what you are thinking is…? • If I understand you correctly, your main point is…	**Reflect** • Today's discussion was effective because… • Today's lesson made me rethink… • My most valuable contribution to today was…

Resource 7.4: Analysis of Classroom Rules for Discussion

Analysis of Classroom Rules for Discussion

Directions:

Read the following possible rules and indicate whether you agree these rules are helpful for our class discussions and provide justification for why or why not.

Rules	Y/N	Justification
Ask for feedback from everyone in the group.		
Ask for justification or evidence.		
Talking takes too much time, write it all down first.		
If someone is wrong, make sure to point the blame on them.		
If someone has a better idea than you, it's okay to change your mind.		
Keep your ideas to yourself so that no one steals them.		
Speak loudly if you want to convince people of your ideas.		
If people challenge your ideas, provide evidence of your reasoning.		
It's okay to be critical of an idea; it's not okay to be critical of a person.		
Listen for alternate viewpoints with an open mind.		
Try and work on group consensus when you can.		
If someone likes to talk, they should speak the most.		
Respect other ideas.		
Agreeing with others is the polite thing to do, even if they are wrong.		
Look at and listen to the person speaking.		
It's okay to disagree as long as you are respectful about it.		
It's okay to dominate the conversation if you have the best ideas.		

Resource 7.5: Peer Thinking Analysis/Observational Tool

Peer Thinking Analysis/Observational Tool

Talk Partners/Team	Asked A Good Question	Made An Interesting Challenge	Justified Reasoning	Engaged In Active Listening	Made A Good Suggestion	Reached Consensus

Reflection

Dialectic Synergy

To understand the term dialectic synergy, we must begin by understanding the meaning of the words that make up this concept. The word "dialectic" comes from ancient Greek philosophy and refers to the process of logical and rational discourse or debate, typically involving the exchange of ideas and arguments between two or more people to arrive at a deeper understanding or truth. This concept is often associated with great philosophers. The term synergy typically is used to refer to the idea of two or more elements working together in a way that is greater than the sum of their individual parts. In the context of dialectic, synergy refers to the idea that different perspectives or ideas can come together in a mutually beneficial way to create a solution or understanding that is more powerful than any single perspective or idea would be on its own. In essence, it means that by bringing together different perspectives, we can, in essence, create a more robust conversation and set of solutions than can be developed by a single viewpoint.

In the context of education and teaching and learning, a classroom where the teacher engages in dialogic teaching *can* bring a classroom to the point of dialectic synergy. There is a difference in the look and feel of a classroom that is engaged in collaborative routines of answering teacher questions, and one truly engaged in dialectic synergy.

More often than not, school classrooms across America look like this: The teacher is standing somewhere in the classroom (usually the front) and poses a question to the classroom. The students raise their hands and are called on, or students call out an answer. Like a game of catch, the teacher takes that response and responds to it. Then another question is volleyed out, like a ball, for a student response. And like a game of volleyball the cadence of the classroom continues in this fashion: teacher question, student response, teacher response, and new question, student response.

While there is nothing inherently *wrong* with this model, it increases the overall amount of talk and control held by the classroom teacher and limits the opportunity for high amounts of student input and engagement throughout the process. Compare that to the following model of a classroom engaged in dialectic synergy.

The class session begins with the teacher posing an open-ended question to the class. One student calls out their potential thoughts and ideas. Rather than the teacher reacting or providing feedback, another student shares a different perspective on the topic, a third requests clarification of evidence and justification, while a fourth offers up an alternative interpretation and viewpoint while citing evidence for their findings. As the class period progresses, students work as a team to clarify and work through the questions posed while the teacher takes some anecdotal notes for her grade book about levels of participation and engagement. If the conversation begins to lose steam or focus, the teacher may throw in an "I wonder" statement to get things back on track. But the idea of a classroom looking like a volleyball game between teachers and students is nonexistent in this classroom as students become passionately engaged and active in the learning process.

The truth is that there may be times in your teaching when the first model makes more sense for your ultimate classroom goal. With that said, we would argue that every classroom, regardless of level, also should have some degree of dialectic synergy happening between students each day. Like dialogic teaching, which prioritizes collaboration among student groups, dialectic synergy allows for the entire class to be engaged in thoughtful, collaborative dialogue to engage them and drive their classroom thinking forward.

Top Five Signs Your Classroom Is Actively Engaged in Dialectic Synergy

There are several signs that can indicate that your students are engaged in dialectic synergy. Here are some possible ways to tell:

1. **Active participation:** Engaged students tend to actively participate in the discussion, offering their own ideas and insights, responding to the ideas of others, and asking questions without prompting or high levels of involvement by the teacher.

2. **Thoughtful responses:** Students who are engaged in dialectic synergy often will provide thoughtful, well-developed responses to questions or prompts and will take the time to explain their reasoning, usually citing evidence for their reasoning.

3. **Collaborative problem-solving:** When engaged in dialectic synergy, students may work collaboratively to solve problems or develop solutions to complex issues. They may build on each other's ideas and challenge each other to think more deeply about the topic at hand.

4. **Respectful communication:** Engaged students tend to communicate with each other in a respectful and constructive manner, even when they disagree or have different perspectives. They may ask clarifying questions or offer additional information to help build understanding.

5. **High-level thinking skills:** During oral conversations, students engaged in dialectic synergy will be highly engaged and may demonstrate higher-level thinking skills such as analysis, synthesis, and evaluation. They may compare and contrast different ideas or arguments, make connections between different concepts, and provide evidence to support their claims.

Overall, when students are highly engaged in dialectic synergy, they likely are to use a range of critical thinking skills, and the classroom environment is likely to be lively, collaborative, and intellectually stimulating. There is little to no involvement from the teacher and the conversations among students volley seamlessly, respectfully, and naturally. Dialectic synergy is the ultimate by-product of dialogic teaching and is among the most effective ways for students within a classroom to exchange ideas, grow, learn from one another, and develop highly attuned collaboration skills needed to succeed beyond the walls of the school.

Summary

Dialogic teaching was first coined by Robin Alexander in the early 2000s to describe how teachers can engage students, expand on ideas, push high levels of reasoning, and stimulate deeper learning. This approach empowers students to engage in the democratic process and inspires a lifelong love of learning. Dialogic teaching is not a method but a professional framework that focuses on classroom relationships, encourages higher levels of thinking and talking time and the use of language to justify students' thinking. The hallmarks of dialogic classrooms include an emphasis on listening, a high level of wait time, and thinking time provided to students. Students are encouraged to disagree respectfully and defend opposing viewpoints. This method is purposeful, collective, supportive, reciprocal, and cumulative. Dialogic teaching increases student agency, creates meaning, and helps achieve higher mental functions that aid cognitive development. It moves classrooms away from the idea of content being "transmitted" from teacher to student, instead focusing on students engaging in dialogue to construct their knowledge and understanding. Studies have shown that dialogic teaching leads to increases in academic achievement and fosters a more inclusive environment in classrooms. The natural by-product of dialogic teaching can be referred to as dialectic synergy. This is the synergy that exists within a classroom when the entire student population is engaged in a free-flowing, rigorous exchange of ideas, free from excessive teacher involvement. The synergy that exists within the walls of a classroom engaged in this level of rigorous thinking and idea exchange is nothing short of amazing.

Key Takeaways

- I can describe the elements of dialogic teaching.

- I have utilized the provided resources to begin the implementation of dialogic instruction in my classroom.

- I understand the benefits to student learning and engagement when dialogic teaching is happening.

- My students engage in discussions where student talk happens 51% or more of the time.

- My students engage in dialectic synergy where they are able to sustain rigorous classroom conversations with little to no input from me as they collectively tackle problems and debate new ideas.

Common Formative Assessments and Your PLC

If your school is like most schools in the United States, chances are that your school teams operate in PLCs (professional learning communities). As you work diligently to implement formative assessment in your classroom, it is absolutely critical that you know the tremendous role that an effective, well-trained, and dynamic PLC can have in the success of your implementation and next steps with formative assessment.

As educators, we understand that we are stronger together. The work of education can be tiring, relentless, and multifaceted. If you can harness your team together and integrate formative assessment into your PLC planning process, you can truly impact education and learning in your classroom and beyond your classroom walls.

The History of Professional Learning Communities in Education

Before we dive into the steps of utilizing your PLC in the formative assessment process, we wanted to take a moment (for those new to education or the terminology) to overview what a PLC is and where this idea originated.

The professional learning community origins date back to the 1960s, but it was not until the late 1980s that the term PLC was coined by Shirley M. Hord in a white paper she published in 1997 called

"Professional Learning Communities: Communities of Continuous Inquiry and Improvement." About a year later, DuFour and Eaker popularized the term with their first book titled *Professional Learning Communities at Work.*

No matter who the researcher is, all the studies looked at success in schools and found several key components that were shared by the most successful schools. By and large, the most successful schools share the following key characteristics:

- Shared norms, beliefs, and goals

- Supportive and collegial relationships

- Reflective teaching practices

- Collaborative practices and collective responsibility

- Ongoing learning and professional growth

- A relentless focus on maintaining continuous improvement and results

The importance of a thriving and successful PLC within the context of formative assessment cannot be overstated. If you are lucky enough to join a school team where the PLC is in place and functioning successfully, chances are you will feel supported, nurtured, and successful. The antithesis can also be true. If you join a school team with a nonexistent or toxic PLC, you may feel isolated, overwhelmed, and frustrated.

Before we dive into the specifics of how to leverage your PLC to build a comprehensive formative assessment rollout at your school, let us first spend some time understanding the rudimentary steps to formulate a cohesive and effective PLC.

Step 1: Develop Shared Norms, Beliefs, and Goals and Develop Shared Collegial Relationships

For any team to function successfully, it is essential that the group begin by creating a shared vision and set of norms. Nearly all successful PLCs begin with this initial step and often revisit it throughout their time together and whenever a new team member joins them.

A critical step in developing an effective PLC that can truly pave the way for formative assessment to thrive on campus is the development of supportive and collegial relationships. It is important to note that team dynamics and relationships ebb and flow. You cannot assume if your team shifts that the dynamics will remain the same. It is essential to revisit your shared beliefs every time you add new members to your PLC team and periodically throughout your school year together. Teachers must develop a trusting culture within their PLC. This type of culture allows people to take risks and make mistakes without fear of blame or judgment. One way of developing shared commitments is developing a shared set of beliefs about teaching and learning rather than creating team commitments. When a PLC is working at its highest level, the team members become dependent upon one another to collectively improve learning across the grade level by focusing on student learning through their lesson planning and rigorous goals and expectations. It is shocking how impactful collective goal-setting can be on both a team and a campus culture. When teachers see their colleagues as partners in the journey of education, it reduces the feeling of isolation, which can often accompany the profession.

Resource 8.1: Developing Team Commitments

Helpful PLC questions to guide shared beliefs and goals	
Who do we teach?	
Why are we teaching them?	
What strengths, skills, and attributes do they bring to the table?	
What struggles, challenges, and hurdles do they still have to overcome?	
What impact can we have on this group of students individually?	
What impact can we have on this group of students collectively?	
What commitments can I make to this team to assist us in getting our students where we want them to go?	
How will we measure success with our students?	
How will we celebrate it?	

Team commitments based on our beliefs

In addition to creating shared goals and beliefs, it is also critical for PLCs to come together and develop a shared set of norms. The development of shared norms is essential in facilitating an effective, safe, and inviting workspace that honors all voices in the room. In addition, shared norms serve to increase team productivity, allow for healthy disagreement, and allow for diverse viewpoints. There are *many* ways to develop norms for a team; Table 8.1 is a list of important areas for consideration when thinking about norm development.

While many PLCS try to skip past this first step, it tends to be a mistake that they regret down the road. By working alongside one another to create a shared vision, goals, beliefs, and norms, team members create clarity among their group about their mission, and they develop collective ownership of their goals. In Table 8.1, you will find a guide to creating norms via guiding questions. We find these questions valuable for PLCs to use as they begin the process of working as a team.

Once the team has developed norms, it is helpful to review those norms and make sure everyone is willing and able to commit to them. Once a commitment has been established, make sure to revisit the norms at the beginning of each meeting and when new members are added to the team.

Table 8.1   Team norm guiding questions.

Time	When will the meetings take place, and how long will they last? Do we have specific rules regarding how many attendees need to be present to meet?
Decision-making	What will decision-making look like? Will we use a consensus model? What happens when we don't have a consensus?
Participation/ voice	In what ways will we honor diverse perspectives? What will happen if we disagree? What will happen if we experience conflict?
Team agreements	What do we commit to each other? What do we expect of each other?
Listening	How will we work to listen to one another's ideas and add our ideas?

Resource 8.2: Team Norm Development Activity

"At the heart of team interaction lies a commitment-building process. The team establishes a social contract among its members that relates to their purpose, and guides and obligates how they must work together. At its core, team accountability is about the promises we make to ourselves and others, promises that underpin two critical aspects of teams: commitment and trust."

— Katzenbach & Smith, *The Wisdom of Teams*

Creating the High-Performance Organization (2003)

Purpose: This activity will assist your PLC/Grade Level/Department Team in creating an environment where all members can express their ideas freely.

Reminder: Norms exist within groups to provide a safe place for a free exchange of ideas in an environment that honors the needs of every member of the group or team and to increase productivity and progress toward agreed-upon goals.

Supplies:

Index cards	Standardized pens or pencils for anonymity
Large sticky notes	

Steps:

1. Give each member of your team five to seven index cards and a writing utensil.

2. Have each team member write and record ideal "group behaviors" with one idea on each card.

3. Shuffle all the cards together.

4. Review each card one at a time. Spend a few moments discussing each key idea and combine similar ideas together as necessary.

5. When ideas have been combined, select the five to seven most salient and important ideas presented by the group and record them on a sticky note or poster board.

6. Review the norms with the group one final time. Gain consensual agreement from all members of the group.

Team norm development—guiding questions		Proposed norm
Time	When will the meetings take place? How long will they last? Do we have specific rules regarding how many attendees need to be present to meet?	
Decision-making	What will decision-making look like? Will we use a consensus model? What happens when we don't have a consensus?	
Participation/voice	In what ways will we honor diverse perspectives? What will happen if we disagree? What will happen if we experience conflict?	
Team agreements	What do we commit to each other? What do we expect of each other?	
Listening	How will we work to listen to one another's ideas and add our ideas?	

Final Norms (record here):

1.

2.

3.

4.

5.

Step 2: Planning Your Common Formative Assessments

Throughout this book, we have spoken about a variety of formative assessments. Many of these assessments are conducted within the moment, in your classroom, in a nonstructured and nonformalized manner. These formatives guide you on the effectiveness of your instruction and where to re-teach on a daily basis. These are incredibly valuable tools for you as a teacher. Another type of formative assessment is called the CFA (common formative assessment). A common formative assessment is one that your PLC team compiles together. The goal is that each team member has an agreed-upon idea of what is being taught, what is being assessed, and what is critical to student understanding and success.

The common formative assessment process within the PLC begins with team members determining "what" is being assessed. This involves the team coming together to carefully consider all of the learning targets and which of these targets are critical to assess to help your team determine if students have reached mastery. The team should begin by thinking about what the essential standards are. They also should determine which components of the learning are prerequisite skills for future learning. Finally, it is important for the PLC team to take into account common misconceptions and areas of struggle or challenge for students during the previous in-the-moment, in-class formative assessments. These questions will assist your PLC team in drilling down to the most critical information to assess student learning.

As you will see in Resource 8.3, the first step in planning a formative assessment is to determine what will be assessed. You can do this with your PLC team by considering all of the learning targets that you have found as you deconstructed the standards. Once you have determined the deconstructed standards, it is important to describe which of these targets you and your team agree are vital to assess. It is important to keep in mind that you cannot and should not plan to assess every learning target. It is helpful to think about which targets are most critical to build for upcoming new learning (prerequisite skills), which targets tend to be challenging for students, or for which there have been common misconceptions. Finally, make sure that your team is able to come to an agreement on which of these standards is most critical to student learning and achievement.

Once your PLC team has determined which standards they plan to assess, it is a good time to decide *how* to assess each of these standards. There are two main parts of this decision. One is simply determining the type of assessment. As we know, students can be assessed with a variety of assessments, including T/F, multiple-choice response, short- and long-constructed response, and via a performance assessment. Each of these has positives and negatives. Table 8.2 reviews assessment types, best uses, and associated pros and cons of each type of assessment.

Table 8.2 Types of assessments.

Assessment type	Description	Pros	Cons
Multiple choice/ true-false	Gives students 2–5 options to determine the best answer to a predetermined closed-ended question.	Easy to develop. Cost effective. Easy to grade. Can cover a wide range of content.	Difficult to get to higher levels of depth of knowledge (DOK). Limited ability to provide feedback. Sometimes tests test-taking more than actual learning.
How to make these as effective as possible: Try to match questions to standards for quick opportunities to re-teach and collaborate with your PLC (using a second and third set of eyes) to make sure you are assessing what you are hoping to assess.			
Essay	Allows for students to show various levels of knowledge by responding to an open-ended long-constructed response on teacher determining learning goals.	Allows for higher depth of knowledge. Does not limit students' ability to show what they know. Easy to create.	Difficult and time-consuming to grade. Subjective. May not cover the full breadth of content.

(Continued)

Table 8.2   (Continued)

Assessment type	Description	Pros	Cons
How to make these as effective as possible: Calibrate scoring with your PLC, develop a rubric, and provide students with clear success criteria.			
Constructed response/ performance tasks	A variety of interdisciplinary opportunities for students to tap into various streams of learning and combine them to problem solve.	Learning occurs while working. Activates high-level critical thinking skills. Is interdisciplinary.	Takes a long time to grade. Not easily quantifiable. Limited breadth.
How to make these as effective as possible: Create success criteria, rubrics, and calibrate grading practices and allow for an extended time as needed.			

Resource 8.3: Formative Assessment in the PLC

Step 1: Decide What to Assess

Consider all the learning targets you have found during the unwrapping process that is being taught during this part of the unit. Describe which of these targets to assess. Remember, you do not have to assess every learning target.

- Which targets are most likely to cause certain students the most difficulty?

- Which targets are important or prerequisite skills for information to come?

- Which targets are absolutely necessary for students to know?

Step 2: Decide How to Assess

For each target, make sure the PLC team agrees on the level of thinking required for mastery of that target. Choose the most appropriate assessment method: selective response, constructed response, or performance assessment. Make sure the thinking level you are expecting can be assessed.

Step 3: Develop the Assessment Plan

Complete the assessment plan. Decide what type of items and how many items. Consider how long the assessment will take to administer.

Step 4: Determine the Timeline

Decide the date or range of dates for administering the assessment and the date for the next meeting to discuss results. Consider how long it will take to score.

Step 5: Write the Assessment
Use guidelines to create a quality assessment where the level of rigor of the questions matches the level of rigor of the standards.

Step 6: Review Before Administration and Set Proficiency Criteria
Determine when you will all administer the assessment and review one last time for accuracy, then determine the collective expectations for mastery.

Once the team has determined what is being assessed, they work to determine how to assess student learning and mastery. While some learning may be effectively assessed with a multiple-choice exam, other learning is more effectively assessed with constructed responses or performance assessments. During this phase of PLC planning, it is important for the PLC team to determine the level of rigor at which they wish to conduct the assessment. We often advise PLC teams to look closely at the verbs within the standard and use these verbs to determine the level of rigor to be assessed. The tool we feel is most effective in making this determination is Webb's Depth of Knowledge (DOK) Wheel. This wheel asks your PLC team to look at the verb and then offers activities for assessment of learning based on the rigor of the verb. We have included images of these resources for your PLC team to review and utilize during this phase of your common formative assessment planning.

As shown in Figure 8.1, Webb's DOK Wheel can be a valuable resource to use with your PLC team to determine if you are varying your level of questioning with students and are pushing your students to think at higher levels. This resource is critical in reviewing both assessment questions and your overall instruction and levels of questioning. It can help to have a peer observe your classroom and tally how many questions you ask at each level. In Table 8.3, you will see additional activities tied to the levels of DOK that you can incorporate into activities so you and your PLC team are creating work where the level of rigor is aligned across the grade level.

By utilizing these two resources, your PLC team can begin to complete the work of planning the common formative assessment.

Once your team has completed the planning as it relates to how you will assess student mastery, it is time to decide what type of items and how many items. Consider how long the assessment will take to administer. Remember, that longer is not always better when creating an assessment. Think back to what your team determined was the key

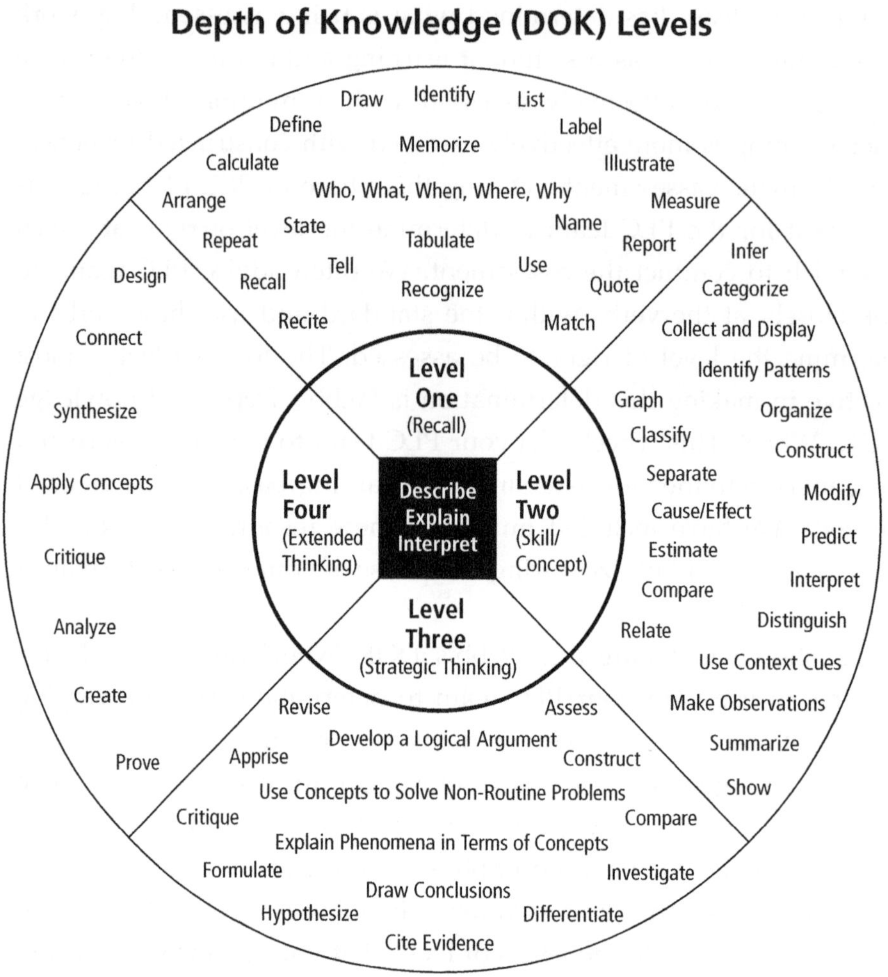

Depth of Knowledge (DOK) Levels

Figure 8.1   Webb's DOK Wheel.
Source: https://www.windham-schools.org/docs/DOK Wheel Slide for Teachers-0.pdf.

information you wanted to assess and focus your attention on in this area. As you will see later in this chapter, the key to effective common formative assessment comes when you see what you do with the student data once it has been collected. You do not want to overwhelm yourself with such a massive data set that you have too much information to

Table 8.3   Webb's DOK levels corresponding activities.

Level 1 activities	Level 2 activities	Level 3 activities	Level 4 activities
• Recall elements and details of story structure, such as sequence of events, character, plot, and setting. • Conduct basic mathematical calculations. • Label locations on a map. • Represent in words or diagrams a scientific concept or relationship. • Perform routine procedures like measuring length or using production marks correctly. • Describe the features of a place or people.	• Identify and summarize the major events in a narrative. • Use content clues to identify the meaning of unfamiliar words. • Solve routine multiple-step problems. • Describe the cause/ effect of a particular event. • Identify patterns in events or behavior. • Formulate a routine problem given data and conditions. • Organize, represent, and interpret data.	• Support ideas with details and examples. • Use voice appropriate to the purpose and audience. • Identify research questions and design investigations for a scientific problem. • Develop a scientific model for a complex situation. • Determine the author's purpose and describe how it affects the interpretation of a reading selection. • Apply a concept in other contexts.	• Conduct a project that requires specifying a problem, designing and conducting an experiment, analyzing its data, and reporting results/solutions. • Apply mathematical model to illuminate a problem or situation. • Analyze and synthesize information from multiple sources. • Describe and illustrate how common themes are found across texts from different cultures. • Design a mathematical model to inform and solve a practical or abstract situation.

Source: https://www.windham-schools.org/docs/DOK Wheel Slide for Teachers-0.pdf.

determine effectively your next steps as a PLC. When you create the common formative, continue to seek ways to pare down your questions to the most critical information to determine mastery.

Step 3: Maintain a Relentless Focus on Continuous Improvement and Results

It isn't enough for a PLC to meet regularly, plan assessments, and review assessment data. Effective PLCs need to encompass deep, thoughtful, and collaborative conversations among the members. These deep conversations lead to connectedness and vulnerability, which is essential for the true success of a PLC. In addition, the sharing of knowledge and information needs to be a reciprocal process with no one team member dominating the group. The tremendous research on collective teacher efficacy has shown time and again that while teachers may have limited confidence in their abilities to impact student achievement while working in isolation, they can collectively have a much stronger level of confidence in their effectiveness.

Resource 8.4: PLC Common Formative Protocol, Shortened Protocol

This protocol is designed to help PLC teams quickly and efficiently discuss common formative assessments. Each teacher should review their own assessment data prior to the team meeting when the formative results will be reviewed and the team will collaboratively complete this reflection.

PLC team:	PLC meeting date:

1. What standard(s) did your formative assess?

2. Which specific students did not demonstrate mastery of which specific standards (or question/task complexity levels)? Respond by the student and by the standard.

3. Which instructional practices proved to be most effective?

4. What patterns can we identify from student mistakes/apparent misconceptions?

5. How can our team improve this assessment?

6. What interventions are needed to provide students who did not perform well the additional support necessary for success on the next formative or the unit summative? How will we provide these interventions?

Resource 8.5: PLC Common Formative Protocol, Detailed Protocol

(*Italic* = complete before the meeting)   (**Bold** = complete during the meeting)

PLC team:	PLC meeting date:

1. *What were the intended learning outcomes (deconstructed standards)?*

2. On which three questions/standards did your students show the **greatest strength**? Note the questions/standards in the grid below and discuss with your team what might account for any differences (Did you teach the concept differently? Did you use different resources? Did you spend more time teaching that concept? etc.).

   Record your data below:

Teacher:			
Question #, Standard, %:			
Question #, Standard, %:			
Question #, Standard, %:			

Common student area of strength:	

3. On which questions/standards did your students demonstrate the **greatest need** for growth? Did your students show a unique area of weakness? Discuss with your team what might account for any differences (Did you teach the concept differently? Did you use different resources? Did you spend more time teaching that concept? etc.). What can you specifically do to address your students' **greatest area of need**?

Record your data below:

Teacher:			
Question #, Standard, %:			
Question #, Standard, %:			
Question #, Standard, %:			

Common student area of strength:	

Teacher			
What strategies, methods, and groupings have I already used to address this standard? [Each teacher completes]			
My plan to address during class time: [Each teacher completes]			

4. **Reflection: As a CIP team, what were the three greatest common areas of need for your students? Why do you think your students struggled in these areas? Please review the test and consider teaching strategies, resources, rigor (DoK), terminology, test construction, calendar/pacing, background knowledge, etc. What is your specific plan of action as a PLC to address these areas of need?**

Reflections for the next unit:

_____
_____
_____
_____
_____
_____
_____
_____
_____
_____
_____
_____

Our PLC Does Not Do Common Formatives— Should We?

Many teachers wonder if it is worth their time, energy, and effort to collectively work to create common formative assessments, when it might be easier to create their classroom assessments in isolation. We would argue that there are tremendous benefits to working with your collaborative group to build these assessments. We decided to look at the research to see if it backed up our opinion.

In their article "The Case for Common Formative Assessment," Dufour, Dufour, and Eaker (2007) make a solid argument for the immense benefits of common formative assessments in the PLCs. They share six critical reasons why assessments created by a PLC team are superior to the formal assessments developed by a teacher working in isolation. We have outlined their assertions here and will spend some time in this section reviewing each of these topics in a bit more detail:

- Team-developed common formative assessments are more efficient.

- Team-developed common formative assessments are more equitable.

- Team-developed common formative assessments are more effective at determining student learning and progress.

- Team-developed common formative assessments can inform and improve the practice of both individual teachers and teams of teachers.

- Team-developed common formative assessments can build the capacity of the team to achieve at higher levels.

- Team-developed common formative assessments are essential to systematic interventions when students do not learn.

As they shared in their article, DuFour, DuFour, and Eaker found that it just makes the most sense to work on these assessments within a team. First and foremost, each member of the team is responsible for providing students access to the same course material and ensuring all students achieve mastery. As a result, it just makes sense that teachers come together so they have a common language and understanding of what mastery will look like. Working in isolation would mean working harder, but not working smarter. In addition, they found that by creating consistent assessments, students are assessed, regardless of their teacher, on the same level of rigor and judged against the same success criteria. While we may want to believe that we all have a common understanding of what success looks like, it is not until we work to develop these assessments collectively that we truly ensure fairness in our assessments. DuFour, DuFour, and Eaker also found that there were several bodies of research to support the idea that common formative assessments developed within the PLC are one of the most powerful ways teachers can work collectively to improve student achievement within their school.

Another key benefit to common formative assessments is that teachers can make more well-informed decisions with common formative assessments because they are able to compare their data against that of their colleagues and use that information to determine if there is a more effective way to instruct on a concept. A PLC allows for collaboration and ongoing feedback not only on how your students are doing but also on how *all* students are progressing. When a teacher has evidence that their students are not becoming proficient in the skills their PLC team deemed as critical, and this is evidenced by an assessment that they co-created, they can become more reflective. If they are then able to see that the students within their teammates' classes have been successful, they can begin to do the true work of a PLC and actually look to change and improve their practice. Each of the ideas presented gets us one step closer to the concept of teacher collective efficacy (Hattie's effect size 1.34). Essentially, the school shifts from single teacher's isolated successes and celebrations to learning from one another and developing a mindset that each member of the school PLC team has an impact on student achievement. Finally, the team developed a common formative assessment to allow team members to come together and create answers to the essential question of what happens when our students have not learned what we taught.

Summary

PLCs (professional learning communities) are groups of teachers who work together to improve their teaching practices and achieve better outcomes for their students. One way that PLCs can assist teacher teams in developing effective common formative assessments is by providing a collaborative space for teachers to share ideas and resources for creating and implementing these assessments. PLCs also can provide support and guidance for teachers as they analyze and interpret the data from the assessments, use it to inform their instruction, and make adjustments as needed to better support student learning. Professional learning communities can use data from formative assessments and other sources to improve teacher effectiveness and student achievement in a number of ways. For example, PLCs can use data to identify areas where students are struggling and where teachers may need additional support or professional development. PLCs also can use data to track student progress over time and identify effective teaching strategies that lead to improved student outcomes. By analyzing and interpreting data on a regular basis, PLCs can provide teachers with valuable feedback and support that can help them improve their teaching practices and better support student learning.

Key Takeaways

- I have worked with my PLC to develop team commitments.
- I have worked with my PLC to develop guiding questions and norms.
- We use a common formative protocol tool to reflect on the celebrations and struggles of our students and develop next steps.

Formative Assessment After Instruction

CHAPTER 9

Formative Assessment Resources in Practice: Student Self-Assessment

As we know, formative assessment involves the teacher using the assessment data to inform instruction, but it also involves students being self-aware about and reflective of their learning. Once the learning sequence has been completed, it is critical for students to engage in thinking about their learning.

In comes student self-assessment.

But what exactly does student self-assessment mean, and how can it be implemented in your classroom?

Student self-assessment is the process by which students reflect on their own learning and performance and evaluate their own understanding and skills. Research has shown that student self-assessment can be an effective tool for improving student learning and motivation.

Student self-assessment can be implemented in various ways. When we think about self-assessment, we need to outline how our students can become agents in their own learning and evaluate the extent to which they've learned a skill. This can be through self-reflection, self-grading, self-questioning, using success criteria, and creating teacher clarity in the classroom.

Let's take a look at John Hattie's MetaX visible learning research, where he outlines the effect size of student self-assessment in various capacities (see Table 9.1).

233

Table 9.1   Effect sizes of student self-assessment according to MetaX.

Strategy	Description	Effect size
Peer and self-grading	Peer grading is a method of evaluating student work in which students are responsible for assessing the work of their classmates. Self-grading is a method of evaluating student work in which students are responsible for assessing their own work.	.42
Positive self-concept	Positive self-concept refers to an individual's overall perception and evaluation of themselves, including their abilities, characteristics, and worth as a person.	.46
Self-efficacy	First theorized in educational contexts by Albert Bandura, self-efficacy is an individual's belief in their ability to successfully execute a specific task or accomplish a goal. It refers to the confidence an individual has in their ability to perform well and achieve their desired outcomes. Self-efficacy beliefs can vary across different situations and tasks and can change over time depending on an individual's experiences and perceptions.	.65
Self-reported grades	A practice where students assess the quality of their work or their level of mastery of a subject. It is often evaluated by comparing a student's "self-reported" grade with that provided by an instructor.	1.33
Self-questioning/ verbalization	Self-verbalization (talking to oneself about a problematic intellectual task) and self-questioning (interrogating oneself about the information one encounters) are cognitive tools associated with higher levels of understanding.	.59
Success criteria	Success criteria are the standards by which a project or learning episode will be judged to determine mastery. At times, they are created in collaboration with those being assessed.	.88
Teacher clarity	Teacher clarity relates to organization, explanation, examples and guided practice, and assessment of student learning. It can involve communicating the intentions of the lessons and the success criteria. Clear learning intentions describe the skills, knowledge, attitudes, and values the student needs to learn.	.84

There are multiple ways for students to utilize self-assessment, and it can be overwhelming to determine how or what to implement to help your students be successful.

To make this easier to understand, Table 9.2 gives examples of self-assessments that fit into each of these strategies. (Table 9.1 defines each of these terms for you as well.)

Table 9.2 Strategies aligned to student self-assessment.

Strategy	Example
Peer and self-grading	Target responses and rubrics Reaching consensus groups Reciprocal teaching Peer writing conferences Peer goal-setting
Positive self-concept	Student-of-the-day notes Daily check-ins Student/teacher relationships Classroom climate Open communication
Self-efficacy	Daily mindfulness Student/teacher relationships Classroom climate Open communication Daily check-ins
Self-reported grades	Leveled turn-in bins Self-assessment tickets Target response and rubrics Success criteria Modeling steps
Self-questioning/verbalization	Self-assessment reflection Question stems Monitoring system Modeling metacognition Activating prior knowledge
Success criteria	Co-constructed success criteria Target responses and rubrics Modeling and guided practice Graphic organizers "I can" statements
Teacher clarity	Clear examples Guided practice Metacognition Learning goals Success criteria

Activating Prior Knowledge

Activating prior knowledge is a teaching and learning strategy that involves engaging students in activities that help them connect new information to their existing knowledge and experiences. This approach is based on the idea that students are more likely to understand and retain new information if they can relate it to what they already know. It can take many different forms, depending on the content being taught and the learning goals. For example, teachers may ask students to brainstorm and discuss what they already know about a topic, or to create a mind map that shows the connections between new information and their existing knowledge. Teachers also may use prompts, questions, or other types of prompts to help students reflect on their prior knowledge and make connections to the new information.

Activating prior knowledge can be an effective way to engage students and get them interested in a topic. By involving students in the learning process and making connections to their own experiences, teachers can help students see the relevance and importance of the material they are learning. This can motivate students to pay attention, participate, and take an active role in their own learning. It can also support student understanding and retention of new information. By connecting new information to what students already know, teachers can help students make sense of the material and build a deeper understanding of the content. This can help students organize and store new information in their long-term memory, which can support their ability to recall and use the information in the future.

Clear Examples

This simply means providing students with clearly worked examples of what is expected of them to use as a model for their instruction.

Co-Constructing Success Criteria

Co-constructing success criteria refer to the process of involving students in the creation of the criteria or standards by which their learning will be evaluated. This can be a powerful tool in formative assessment.

One of the key benefits of co-constructing success criteria is that it helps ensure the criteria are clear, relevant, and attainable. When students are involved in the process of creating the criteria, they have a better understanding of what is expected of them, and they are more likely to be motivated to meet those expectations. This can help increase their engagement in the learning process, which can ultimately lead to improved student achievement.

Another benefit of co-constructing success criteria is that it promotes a sense of ownership and responsibility among students. When students are involved in creating the criteria, they are more likely to feel invested in their own learning and more motivated to take ownership of their learning goals. This can help foster a growth mindset, where students believe that their abilities can be developed through effort and practice.

In addition, co-constructing success criteria can help promote collaboration and a sense of community in the classroom. When students are involved in the process of creating the criteria, they are able to share their perspectives and ideas and work together to come up with criteria that are fair and achievable. This can help create a supportive learning environment where students feel valued and respected.

Overall, co-constructing success criteria can be a valuable tool in formative assessment, helping to ensure the criteria are clear, relevant, and attainable, promoting student ownership and responsibility, and fostering collaboration and a sense of community.

Daily Check-Ins

Daily check-ins refers to taking time each day to assess student learning and growth toward mastery. This helps teachers to determine when re-teaching is appropriate for students.

Daily Mindfulness

Daily mindfulness, or the practice of being present and aware at the moment, can play a powerful role in the classroom and in relation to formative assessment. In the classroom, daily mindfulness can help promote a positive learning environment where students are better able to focus, concentrate, and learn. By teaching students mindfulness techniques, such as deep breathing and paying attention to the present moment, teachers can help students reduce stress, increase self-awareness, and improve their overall well-being.

In terms of formative assessment, daily mindfulness can help students better understand their own learning process and take a more active role in their own learning. By practicing mindfulness, students can develop a better understanding of their own thoughts, feelings, and behaviors, which can help them identify areas of strength and areas for improvement. This self-awareness can be a valuable tool in formative assessment, as it can help students to set realistic and achievable learning goals and to monitor their own progress toward those goals.

Graphic Organizers

Graphic organizers are visual tools that can assist teachers in effectively administering formative assessment. These tools can help teachers organize and present information in a clear and concise manner, making it easier for students to understand and process the information.

One way that graphic organizers can assist teachers in formative assessment is by providing a visual representation of key concepts or ideas. For example, a teacher might use a Venn diagram to compare and contrast two different concepts, or a flowchart to show the steps in a process. By presenting the information visually, teachers can help students better understand the material and to see the connections between different ideas.

Graphic organizers also can be used to help students organize their own thoughts and ideas. For example, a teacher might use a mind map to help students brainstorm ideas for a writing assignment or a concept map to help students organize their thoughts on a particular topic. By providing a visual structure for students to follow, graphic organizers can help students to better organize their ideas and to develop more coherent and well-reasoned arguments.

Guided Practice

Guided practice is a type of instructional strategy that is commonly used in formative assessment. It involves providing students with support and guidance as they practice a new skill or concept, with the goal of helping them develop their understanding and mastery of the material.

One of the key roles of guided practice in formative assessment is to provide students with the opportunity to apply what they have learned in a safe and supportive environment. By providing students with guidance and support as they practice a new skill or concept, teachers can help students develop their understanding of it and gain confidence in their abilities. This can be especially important for students who may be struggling with a particular concept, as it can help them overcome any challenges and make progress in their learning.

Another role of guided practice in formative assessment is to provide teachers with the opportunity to monitor student learning and to provide feedback. As students practice a new skill or concept, teachers can observe their progress and provide feedback to help them improve. This feedback can be critical in formative assessment, as it can help students to understand their strengths and areas for improvement and to adjust their learning strategies accordingly.

"I Can" Statements

"I can" statements are learning objectives or goals that are written in a student-friendly language and focus on what students will be able to do or understand by the end of a lesson or unit. They often are used in the classroom to align instruction with state and national standards and to make learning goals clear and measurable for both students and teachers.

"I can" statements typically start with the phrase "I can" or "I will be able to" and are written in a way that is easy for students to understand. They often are written in present tense and are specific, measurable, and align with the standards.

For example

- "I can explain the main idea of a text."
- "I will be able to use multiplication facts to solve word problems."
- "I can identify the different parts of a plant and their functions."

"I can" statements can be used to communicate what students will be learning and what they will be able to do as a result of the lesson or unit. They serve as a guide for instruction, assessment, and student self-evaluation. They help students understand what they are learning and give them a sense of ownership over their own learning. They also provide a clear and measurable way for teachers to evaluate student progress and understanding.

Learning Goals

Learning goals are important to the formative assessment process because they provide a clear and specific target for student learning. By setting learning goals, teachers can help students understand what is expected of them and develop a plan for achieving those expectations. This can be especially important in formative assessment, as it can help students understand the purpose of their learning and take a more active role in their own learning.

Another reason why learning goals are important to formative assessment is that they provide a basis for evaluating student learning. By setting specific and measurable learning goals, teachers can create criteria for evaluating student progress and achievement. This can help teachers monitor student learning and provide appropriate feedback and support to help students achieve their goals.

In addition, learning goals can help foster a growth mindset among students. By setting challenging but achievable learning goals, teachers can help students believe that their abilities can be developed through effort and practice. This can motivate students to persevere and strive for improvement, even in the face of challenges or setbacks.

Leveled Turn-In Bins

These turn-in bins can be used for more than just turning in work. You can use them for Self-Assessment Turn-In Bins to encourage your students to choose their Level of Understanding when completing their work. This will help get your students to turn in their work and acknowledge their level of understanding. This will also help get you into the routine of using turn-in bins as a formative assessment. Whether it is an independent practice page or a quick assessment, students can turn in their work according to their level of understanding. You can use four different bins and label them with each Level of Understanding. Here's an example of how you can label your bins:

- 4 – I understand and can teach my peers.
- 3 – I almost have it, but I may need a little more practice.
- 2 – I am a little confused and need some clarification.
- 1 – I am lost. Please re-teach me.

Metacognition

Metacognition, or the ability to think about one's own thinking, plays a crucial role in formative assessment. In formative assessment, metacognition can help students better understand their own learning process and take a more active role in their own learning.

One way that metacognition can support formative assessment is by helping students develop a better understanding of their own learning strengths and weaknesses. By being more aware of their own thinking processes, students can identify areas where they are struggling and develop strategies for addressing those challenges. This can help them become more independent learners who are better able to monitor their own progress and identify areas for improvement. Metacognition also can support formative assessment by promoting reflection and self-evaluation. By encouraging students to think about their own learning, teachers can help students become more reflective about their own progress and evaluate their own learning against specific criteria or standards. This can help students develop a more accurate and nuanced understanding of their own learning and identify areas where they can improve.

Modeling and Guided Practice

Modeling and guided practice are the processes of making sure, as the teacher, that with each lesson you teach, you take the time to thoroughly model for the students how to complete an activity and then provide them time to practice and to work toward mastery.

Monitoring System

A monitoring system in education is a tool or process used to track and evaluate student progress as well as the effectiveness of educational programs and policies. The goal of a monitoring system is to provide accurate and timely data on student performance, teacher effectiveness, and school or district performance.

Open Communication

Open communication in the classroom refers to the process of creating an environment where students feel comfortable sharing their thoughts and ideas, and where teachers actively listen and respond to student needs. This kind of communication helps establish a positive and collaborative learning environment, where students feel valued and respected and where they can be active and engaged learners.

Peer Goal-Setting

Peer goal-setting is a process in which students work together to set goals for their own learning and progress. This process allows students to set clear and measurable goals for themselves and to develop a plan to achieve them. It also allows students to work together to provide support and encouragement for one another, as well as to hold each other accountable for their progress.

Peer goal-setting can take many forms, such as these:

- Students working in small groups to set and share their goals with one another.

- Students providing feedback and support to one another as they work toward their goals.

- Students working together to develop strategies to achieve their goals.

- Students tracking their own progress and sharing their progress with their peers.

- Students using peer goal-setting as a way to build accountability and motivation for each other.

Peer goal-setting can be beneficial for students in a number of ways. It can increase students' motivation and engagement, as well as their sense of ownership over their own learning. It can also help promote a positive learning environment where students feel comfortable taking risks, making mistakes, and learning from them. Additionally, peer goal-setting can help build collaboration and teamwork, which are essential skills for students to be successful in their future lives.

Peer Writing Conferences

Peer writing conferences are a form of collaborative learning in which students work together to provide feedback and support for one another's writing. They typically involve small groups of students who meet to share and discuss their writing with their peers, with the goal of improving their writing skills.

During a peer writing conference, students take turns sharing their writing with the group and receiving feedback from their peers. This feedback can include constructive criticism, suggestions for improvement, and praise for what is working well. The conference is typically led by the teacher, who may provide guidance and prompts to help students focus their feedback on specific aspects of the writing, such as organization, grammar, or style.

Question Stems

Question stems are phrases or sentences that are used to create a specific type of question. They are used to help students focus their thinking, generate critical thinking and inquiry, and promote deeper learning.

Question stems can be used in a variety of ways, such as:

- To guide students in constructing their own questions.

- To help students understand the different types of questions that can be asked.

- To help students focus their thinking on a specific aspect of the material.

- To help students understand the purpose of a question.

Question stems can be used in different levels of Bloom's taxonomy; for example, lower-level question stems may focus on recall and comprehension, while higher-level question stems may focus on analysis, synthesis, and evaluation.

Reaching Consensus Groups

Reaching consensus groups are groups where students come together to discuss and make decisions on a specific issue or problem. The goal of these groups is to reach a consensus, or agreement, on a course of action or a solution to the problem at hand.

In reaching consensus groups, students are encouraged to express their opinions and perspectives, and to actively listen to and consider the views of others. The group works together to evaluate different options and to identify the most viable solution. Through discussion, negotiation, and compromise, the group aims to reach a decision that is supported by all members.

Reciprocal Teaching

Reciprocal teaching is a strategy that helps students to improve their comprehension of text by teaching them four specific skills: summarizing, questioning, clarifying, and predicting. The strategy is based on the idea that effective readers use these skills to actively engage with the text and construct meaning.

During reciprocal teaching, the teacher guides the students through the process of using these four skills to analyze a text. The teacher models the use of each skill, and then the students take turns leading the discussion and using the skills themselves. The teacher provides feedback and support as needed.

The details of the four skills of reciprocal teaching are:

- **Summarizing:** This skill involves identifying the main idea and key details of a text.

- **Questioning:** This skill involves generating questions about the text to deepen understanding and promote critical thinking.

- **Clarifying:** This skill involves identifying and resolving confusion or misunderstanding about the text.

- **Predicting:** This skill involves making inferences about what may happen next in the text.

Research has shown that reciprocal teaching can improve students' reading comprehension and critical thinking skills and also can increase their motivation to read.

Self-Assessment Reflection

A self-assessment reflection is a process in which an individual thinks about and evaluates their own learning, performance, or behavior. It is an opportunity for the individual to reflect on their own strengths and weaknesses, identify areas for improvement, and set goals for future growth.

Self-Assessment Tickets

A self-assessment ticket is a tool used in education to help students reflect on their own learning and progress. It is typically a small slip of paper or a form that students fill out to evaluate their own understanding and skills related to a specific topic or task. The form usually contains prompts or questions that guide the student in thinking about their own performance and also may include a space for the student to set goals for future learning. You can use self-assessment tickets in many ways, including the following:

- At the end of a lesson, to help students reflect on what they have learned and identify areas where they need further support.

- After completing a project or assignment, to help students evaluate their own work and set goals for improvement.

- As part of formative assessment, to help teachers understand how well students are progressing and where they need further support.

Self-assessment tickets are a way for students to take ownership of their own learning and also promote metacognition.

Student–Teacher Relationships

The relationship between a student and a teacher is an important factor in a student's academic and personal development. A positive and supportive relationship can help students feel safe and valued, which in turn can lead to better engagement and academic performance.

Student-of-the-Day Notes

Student-of-the-day notes are a form of recognition given to students who have exhibited positive behavior, strong work ethic, or academic achievement. They are typically in the form of a written note or certificate that is given to the student by the teacher or administrator. The student-of-the-day note serves as an acknowledgment of the student's positive contributions to the class or school community, and it also can serve as a positive reinforcement for the student to continue the positive behavior.

Success Criteria

Success criteria are specific, measurable, and clear statements that describe what students should be able to do or understand by the end of a lesson or unit. They are used to set clear expectations for student performance, and to help students understand what they are expected to learn and be able to do. Success criteria are often aligned with learning objectives or standards, and they provide a clear and measurable way for teachers to evaluate student progress and understanding.

Success criteria usually are shared with students in advance of an assignment so they understand the expectations and can work to meet them. They can take different forms, such as "I can" statements, checklists, or bullet points. They can be used to evaluate student work and provide feedback. They also help students self-evaluate their own work and set goals for improvement.

Target Response and Rubrics

Target response and rubrics are two tools that are used to evaluate student work and provide feedback.

A target response is a detailed description of what a student should be able to do or produce to demonstrate mastery of a specific skill or concept. It is a clear and measurable statement of what is expected and serves as a guide for both the student and the teacher when evaluating student work. Target responses can be used to set expectations for student performance, guide student learning, and assess student progress.

A rubric is a tool that is used to evaluate student work based on a set of criteria. Rubrics typically include a list of criteria that are used to evaluate student work, along with a scale or points system that is used to assign a grade or score. Rubrics can be used to evaluate a wide range of student work, including writing, research, presentations, and projects. Rubrics are a way to provide clear, consistent, and objective feedback to students on their performance.

Rubrics provide a clear, objective, and consistent way to evaluate student work and provide feedback. They serve as a guide for both the student and the teacher when evaluating student work and can be used to set expectations for student performance, guide student learning, and assess student progress. They also can be shared with students in advance of an assignment so they understand the expectations and can work to meet them.

Benefits of Self-Assessment

Student self-assessment is a valuable tool that can help improve student achievement by empowering students to take ownership of their learning and set goals for their own development. Self-assessment allows students to reflect on their own progress and identify areas where they need to improve, which can motivate them to take action and make positive changes in their learning.

Self-assessment also helps students develop important skills and competencies, such as critical thinking, problem-solving, and metacognition. By engaging in self-assessment, students learn how to evaluate their own work and identify areas for improvement, which can help them become more independent and self-directed learners.

In addition, self-assessment can help students develop a growth mindset, which is the belief that intelligence and abilities are not fixed but can be developed through effort and practice. By engaging in self-assessment, students can learn to see their mistakes and challenges as opportunities for growth and learning, which can foster a positive attitude toward learning and improve their overall achievement.

Furthermore, self-assessment can support effective teaching and learning by providing teachers with valuable feedback on student progress and needs. By involving students in the assessment process, teachers can gain insights into what students are learning and where they may need additional support. This information can help teachers tailor their instruction to better meet the needs of individual students and support their learning.

Overall, student self-assessment is a powerful tool that can support student achievement by empowering students to take ownership of their learning and develop the skills and mindsets needed to succeed. By involving students in the assessment process and using the information gained from self-assessment to inform instruction, teachers can help students achieve their full potential and reach their academic goals.

The following are the main benefits to student self-assessment:

- Increased intrinsic motivation in students.
- Enhanced classroom community.
- Highly developed trust and teacher–student relationship.
- Provides teacher clarity.
- Gives students the "why" and meaning behind their learning.
- Increase student academic performance.

Resource 9.1a: Student Self-Assessment Checklist (Primary)

Name: _____ Date: _____

Student Self-Assessment Checklist

Self Assessment	Yes	Not Yet
I am a good listener.	•	•
I follow directions from my teacher.	•	•
I keep my hands and feet to myself.	•	•
I use kind words.	•	•
I always treat my friends nicely.	•	•
I share classroom materials.	•	•
I say please and thank you.	•	•
I stay focused on my work.	•	•

Resource 9.1b: Student Self-Assessment Checklist (Upper Elementary)

Name: _____ Date: _____

Student Self-Assessment Checklist

Self Assessment	Great	Okay	Needs Work
Following directions	•	•	•
Having a positive attitude	•	•	•
Bringing all materials	•	•	•
Controlling off-task talking	•	•	•
Turning in work	•	•	•
Cooperating	•	•	•
Giving my best effort	•	•	•

Summary

As we shared in this chapter, student self-assessment is the process by which students reflect on their own learning and performance and evaluate their own understanding and skills. Research by Hattie and others has shown that student self-assessment can be an effective tool for improving student learning and motivation.

One of the main benefits of student self-assessment is that it can increase student motivation and engagement. When students are able to evaluate their own understanding and skills, they are more likely to take responsibility for their own learning and to set goals for improvement. This can lead to increased motivation and engagement in the learning process.

Student self-assessment also can improve student learning. When students are able to evaluate their own understanding and skills, they are better able to identify areas where they need further support and to set goals for improvement. This can help promote deeper learning and understanding. Additionally, self-assessment can help students develop metacognitive skills, such as self-regulation, self-reflection, and self-evaluation, that are essential for their future learning and development.

Research also suggests that student self-assessment can be an effective tool for formative assessment, it can provide teachers with valuable feedback on student understanding and progress, and it can be used to inform instruction and support differentiated learning. Teachers can use the information from student self-assessment to adapt their instruction to meet the needs of individual students.

Overall, student self-assessment is an important tool for improving student learning and motivation. It allows students to take ownership of their own learning, to set goals for improvement, and to evaluate their own understanding and skills. This can lead to increased motivation and engagement, deeper learning, and improved academic performance.

Key Takeaways

- I understand the research behind student self-assessment.

- I look to incorporate a variety of the strategies of student self-assessment into my daily instruction.

- I have built in time after each lesson for students to self-assess their learning.

- I understand the benefits of student self-assessment to teaching and learning.

CHAPTER 10

Formative Assessment After Instruction

By this point in the book, we hope that we have laid a basic foundation for *why* formative assessment matters before instruction happens (pre-assessment). We also hope we have provided sound reasoning for why formative assessment matters while instruction is happening ("in-the-moment" formatives).

The final type of formative assessment we will discuss is a formative assessment that happens *after* instruction (lesson, chapter, unit) has taken place before a summative assessment.

Even with your best-laid plans and your most diligent efforts to provide in-the-moment formative assessment, there are still times when you may believe that your students have achieved mastery, only to be let down when you administer the summative assessment. Before administering a summative assessment, you must know that you have provided multiple opportunities for re-teaching and remediation for struggling student groups.

Therefore, it is critical to determine student mastery before administering a summative assessment. As a teacher, this is the last opportunity you will have to determine if your class is ready to take the assessment and "show what they know."

This chapter will provide a variety of post-instruction formative assessments for teachers to administer after an instructional sequence.

These formatives can help teachers adjust their timelines, create remediation groups, and determine re-teaching opportunities before administering a summative assessment.

In addition to the ideas presented above, formative assessments conducted at the end of a learning sequence provide these additional benefits:

- **Provides teachers the ability to determine commonly held misconceptions:** As teachers, we often think we know where students may become tripped up in their thinking, but without some formative assessment, we cannot catch every commonly held misconception. If teachers administer an end-of-lesson formative, they can identify these misconceptions and provide whole class re-teaching before administering a summative assessment.

- **Helps teachers plan for future units:** By completing a post-assessment, moving forward, teachers can see if similar lessons may require more or less time based on students' ability to achieve mastery of instructed material.

- **Get a better gauge of student understanding:** When students can explain their thinking, as often happens in formative assessment, teachers can better understand why students struggle with mastery. As a result, the teacher can dive deeper when re-teaching.

- **Intervention before summative assessment:** Most importantly, students are not sent into a summative assessment without opportunities for re-teach and remediation.

Exit Tickets

An exit ticket is a question or series of questions given to all students after instruction. Often, these questions are posed before the end of a class period of the lesson. Students spend a few minutes recording their answers on a sheet provided by the teacher or on their own paper. Teachers then utilize these sheets as a formative assessment technique before moving on to the next lesson or administering a summative assessment. For this chapter, we will provide an overview of four basic types of exit tickets, create a working definition for each, and then provide a sample of each type of exit ticket.

What Is an Exit Ticket?

The first type of exit ticket is a general catch-all exit ticket we refer to as "basic knowledge." These exit tickets are typically the most basic and generic and often can be used interchangeably across content areas, classes, and types of lessons. At the same time, they serve to provide a general overview of student learning and understanding of a specific lesson; however, they do not always provide the specific information teachers made need to assess mastery.

This type of exit ticket is often helpful at the beginning of a new unit, where you provide a broad content overview and want to assess how much of the instruction was internalized by students. It also can provide critical insight to you as to where students' interest lies on a specific topic.

Table 10.1 describes all types of exit tickets.

Table 10.1 Types of exit tickets.

Types of exit ticket	Overview	Example	When to use	Advantages
Basic exit ticket	Focused on student's ability to give an overview of their learning at a high level, along with additional information about what they may still wish to learn better.	3 things you learned. 2 things you want to learn. 1 thing you still need help with.	After a unit introduction lesson. When you want a general idea of student learning and understanding.	Provides a broad-strokes picture of student learning. Allows students to share where they feel they need more support.

(Continued)

Table 10.1 (Continued)

Types of exit ticket	Overview	Example	When to use	Advantages
Procedural knowledge exit ticket	Focused on students' ability to recount the steps they need to take within a process to show they can "do" and show mastery of a specific learning sequence.	Record the three steps to divide fractions and when you would use them.	For learning that requires steps. For process-oriented learning.	Helps teachers understand if students can apply their learning.
Declarative knowledge exit ticket	Focused on students' ability to recount facts they have learned.	Recounting the six key causes of the American Revolution.	For factual recall. For recounting specific information.	Helps teachers know if students have specific content mastery.
Metacognative practices exit ticket	Allows students to think about their thinking and process information.	How might you re-teach this lesson to a classmate so it is more apparent? Asking the student to engage in a think-aloud.	Allows students to engage in and connect to their learning. Provides students with autonomy and agency.	Allows students to engage in thinking about how they think as a model for future learning.

Resource 10.1: Formative Post-Instruction, Basic Exit Tickets 3-2-1

Name: _____ Date: _____

3 things I learned today:
2 things I want to learn more about:
1 question I have after today's lesson:

Resource 10.2: Formative Post-Instruction, Procedural Exit Tickets, Strategy

Name: _____ Date: _____

Identify one strategy you learned today:
Show an example of how to use it:

Name: _____ Date: _____

Identify one strategy you learned today:
Show an example of how to use it:

Resource 10.3: Formative Post-Instruction, Declarative Exit Ticket, Message in a Bottle

Message in a Bottle

Name: _____ Date: _____

Directions: Write a message in a bottle to a friend about today's lesson.

Resource 10.4: Formative Post-Instruction, Metacognitive Exit Ticket, Thinking Head

Muddiest Points and Misconceptions Check

Name: _____ Date: _____

- Summarize: Describe our lesson in one sentence
- Connect: I can connect this to my life because...
- Clarify: One thing I would like clarification on is...
- Prioritize: For me, the most important part of today's learning was...

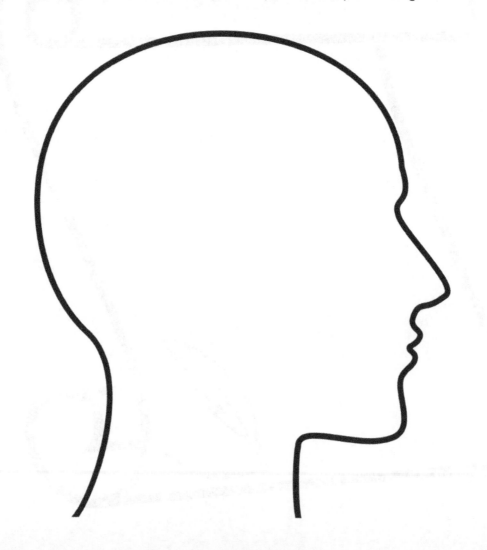

Muddiest Points and Misconception Checks

Exit tickets can provide teachers with individual and collective overviews of student learning. On the other hand, the strategy referred to as "muddiest points" by Angelo and Cross (1993) in *Classroom Assessment Techniques: A Handbook for College Teachers* combines strategies of students' self-assessment and provides the teacher with specific, actionable feedback about student learning and areas within the learning where points of clarification are needed.

Steps to Administer Muddiest Points

1. Decide precisely where you want student feedback. Is it with an entire unit, a lesson, or a segment? The more specific you are with your students, the more targeted and valuable the data will be.

2. Ensure ample time at the end of class for students to complete this activity thoroughly. If they rush out to race the bell, the data you get back will not be as valuable to you. It also helps to set time parameters. *"Scholars, I will be handing out a 'muddiest points form' for today's lesson. You will have seven minutes to complete this; then, I will collect them before the bell rings."*

3. Do something with the data you collect. When we carve out time strategically before the summative assessment to determine areas for remediation, we *must* use this data to guide our next steps in the classroom. A "muddiest point" is not adequate if you are administering a summative the following day. Ideally, you want to give this out and have 1 or 2 lesson spaces for re-teach based on what you have learned before administering a summative assessment.

To complete the muddiest points with your students is relatively straightforward. However, it is very effective because it allows students to tell you where in the learning process they are confused and why it is confusing.

You begin with a prompt, asking students to name the one area from the least clear, or muddiest, lesson. Before administering a summative assessment, you will go through these and do two things as the teacher.

- Search for common themes. Are there specific points and ideas with which many or most students share concerns? If so, spending a day on a re-teach lesson will assist you in better teaching to mastery.

- Are there specific individual students to pull and re-teach before the assessment so that you can provide clarification?

Reflections

Reflection formative assessments allow a deeper dive into metacognition. Metacognition, the act of thinking about our thinking, is critical to our students' success. By doing these, we allow our students to become aware of their learning experiences and how they align with their academic growth path. This reflection time allows students a more significant opportunity to process and apply their learning and connect it to the larger world and analyze its role in their lives.

Resource 10.5: Formative Post-Instruction, Reflection

Reflection

Name: _____ Date: _____

Directions: Name one concept or skill you learned this week. How did you learn it? Describe the process. Were any concepts unclear? How so? What goals do you have for your learning next week? If you could design an activity to help a classmate learn this activity or skill, what would you have them do?

3 Times Summary

Another simple, fun, and different way to conduct a formative assessment after instruction is to have students complete a 3 Times Summary. What we like about the 3 times summary is that it allows students to process the information multiple times and calls on them to prioritize what they believe to be the most critical and salient information.

Frequently, as teachers, we believe that we have been thoughtful in emphasizing the most key and important ideas. This is a great way to test that theory and to see if the ideas that we hoped students would pull from the lesson as the most important actually are the ones they extracted.

It is a straightforward process where we ask students to write three different summaries of their learning. The first summary requires students to use 75 to 100 words to summarize their learning; the second asks them to take the summary down to 30 to 50 words.

Resource 10.6: Formative Post Instruction—
3 Times Summary

3 Times Summary

Name: _____ Date: _____

#1 Recount your learning in 75-100 words:
 # 2 Recount your learning in 30-50 words:
 # 3 Recount your learning in 10-15 words:

Summary

In this chapter, we provided an overview of formative assessment after instruction. We shared four types of post-instruction formative assessment. These were exit tickets, muddiest points, reflections, and 3 times summary.

We shared that there are four types of exit tickets, and each has a specific purpose, specific advantages, and the best times to utilize each. While some exit tickets give you general information about broad student understanding, others help you determine how well students can apply learned processes or recount specific facts and details. Understanding each of these, along with their strengths and best uses, will help you make the most of your formative assessment practices.

While some teachers may feel that if they have assessed students before their learning and during their learning, that is sufficient, we argue that this final opportunity to assess students prior to moving on to the next lesson or administering summative assessments is critical in determining student learning and intervening before it is too late.

Key Takeaways

- I use exit tickets with my students.
- I can identify the types of exit tickets and when to use each one.
- I have tried a variety of exit tickets and post-instructional formatives and used them to guide my re-teaching.

CHAPTER 11

Concluding Thoughts

In conclusion, this book has provided a comprehensive overview of formative assessment and its significance in promoting student learning. We began the book by establishing a common language around formative assessment and differentiating it from summative assessment. We then delved into the research supporting formative assessment and the benefits of embedding it strategically throughout the learning sequence.

We also focused on learning targets and success criteria, providing working definitions and illustrating their significance in the classroom. We highlighted the benefits of embedding these into instruction and provided step-by-step examples of how to utilize them in the classroom.

It is our hope that as you walk away from this book, you see it as a resource you can refer to time and again during your education career. The research is clear that intentionally embedding formative assessment throughout the learning cycle will have immense impacts on your students' educational outcomes. We hope through this book that we have demonstrated how formative assessment can be a powerful tool for teachers to enhance student learning and for students to measure their progress and take control of their own learning. We also hope that you now feel empowered to begin strategically embedding formative assessment, to provide timely and relevant feedback that can help students identify their strengths and weaknesses, adjust their learning strategies, and work toward proficiency.

References

Altman, J.R., Lazarus, S.S., Quenemoen, R.F., et al. (2010). 2009 survey of states: Accomplishments and new issues at the end of a decade of change. University of Minnesota, National Center on Educational Outcomes

Angelo, T.A. and Cross, P.K. (1993). *Classroom Assessment Techniques: A Handbook for College Teachers*. San Francisco: Jossey Bass.

Black, P.J. and Wiliam, D. (1998). Inside the black box: Raising standards through classroom assessment. *Phi Delta Kappan* 80: 139–48.

CERI. (n.d.). The Centre for Educational Research and Innovation. OECD.org. https://www.oecd.org/education/ceri/.

DuFour, R., & Eaker, R. (2007). The Case for Common Formative Assessments (20 August). https://www.allthingsplc.info/blog/view/17/the-case-for-common-formative-assessments.

DuFour, R., & Eaker, R. (1998). Professional Learning Communities at Work: Best Practices for Enhancing Student Achievement. Bloomington, IN: National Educational Service.

Fisher, D., Frey, N., Amador Valerio, O., and Assof, J.M. (2018). *The Teacher Clarity Handbook*. Thousand Oaks, CA: Corwin.

Freibrun, M. (2021). *Getting Started with Teacher Clarity: Ready-to-Use Research-Based Strategies to Develop Learning Intentions, Foster Student Autonomy, and Engage Students*. Berkeley, CA: Ulysses Press.

Goertz, M.E., Olah, L.N., and Riggan, M. (2009). Can interim assessments be used for instructional change? CPRE (December).

Hattie, J. (2012). *Visible Learning for Teachers: Maximizing Learning*. London: Routledge,

Hattie, J. (2015). The applicability of Visible Learning to higher education. *Scholarship of Teaching and Learning in Psychology* 1 (1): 79–91. https://doi.org/10.1037/stl0000021.

Hord, S.M. (1997). Professional learning communities: Communities of continuous inquiry and improvement.

Katzenbach, J.R., & Smith, D.K. (2015). *The wisdom of teams: Creating the high-performance organization*. Boston, MA: Harvard Business Review Press.

Lyle, S., & Thomas-Williams, J. (2012). Dialogic practice in primary schools: how primary head teachers plan to embed philosophy for children into the whole school. *Educational Studies*, 38(1), 1–12.

Marzano, R. (2010). *Formative Assessment & Standards-Based Grading*. Centennial, CO: Marzano Research Laboratory.

McLeod, S. (2023). Vygotsky's zone of proximal development and scaffolding. Simply Psychology (14 May). https://www.simplypsychology.org/Zone-of-Proximal-Development.html.

Merrill, S. and Gonser, S. (2021). More than a dozen ways to build movement into learning. Edutopia (8 October). https://www.edutopia.org/article/more-dozen-ways-build-movement-learning.

OECD. (2005). Formative assessment: Improving learning in secondary classrooms. Oecd.org (1 November). https://www.oecd.org/education/ceri/35661078.pdf.

Sadler, D.R. (1989). Formative assessment and the design of instructional systems. *Instructional Science* 18: 119–140.

Stiggins, R.J. (2005). *Student-Involved Assessment for Learning*, 4th ed. Upper Saddle River, NJ: Merrill Prentice Hall.

Stiggins, R.J., Arter, J.A., Chappuis, J., and Chappuis, S. (2012). *Classroom Assessment for Learning, Doing It Right, Using It Well*. Upper Saddle River, NJ: Pearson Education Inc.

Wiggins, G.P. and McTighe, J. (2005). *Understanding by Design*, 2nd ed. Alexandria, VA: Association for Supervision and Curriculum Development.

Bibliography

Alexander, R.J., Hardman, F.C., and Hardman, J. (2017). Changing talk, changing thinking: Interim report from the in-house evaluation of the CPRT/UoY Dialogic Teaching Project. University of York.

Brunet, S., Fractor, C., and Freibrun, M. (2022). *Leading with Administrator Clarity School-Wide Strategies for Cultivating Communication, Fostering a Responsive Culture, and Inspiring Intentional Leadership*. Berkeley, CA: Ulysses Press.

Things PLC (13 September). https://www.allthingsplc.info/blog/view/17/the-case-for-common-formative-assessments.

Gonzalez, J. (2021). Build it together: Co-constructing success criteria with students. Cult of Pedagogy (19 August). https://www.cultofpedagogy.com/co-constructing-success-criteria/.

Hattie, J. (2009). *Visible Learning – A Synthesis of over 800 Meta-Analyses Relating to Achievement*. London: Routledge.

Hattie, J. and Timperely, H. (2007). The power of feedback. *Review of Educational Research* 77: 81–112.

Lui, A.M. and Andrade, H.L. (2022). The *next black box* of formative assessment: A model of the internal mechanisms of feedback processing. Frontiers in Education (15 February). https://www.frontiersin.org/articles/10.3389/feduc.2022.751548/full.

Mercer, N. and Howe, C. (2012). Explaining the dialogic processes of teaching and learning: The value and potential of sociocultural theory. Learning, Culture and Social Interaction 1 (1): 12–21. https://doi.org/10.1016/j.lcsi.2012.03.001.

Poth, R.D. (2019). Metacognition and why it matters in education. Getting Smart (6 October). https://www.gettingsmart.com/2019/10/06/metacognition-and-why-it-matters-in-education/.

Van der Kleij, J.J. and Cumming, A. (2018). Looney policy expectations and support for teacher formative assessment in Australian education reform. *Assessment in Education: Principles, Policy & Practice* 25: 620–637

Webb, N.L. (2005). Web Alignment Tool. Wisconsin Center of Educational Research. University of Wisconsin–Madison.

Index

2-column charts, 169, 170
    implementation process, 169
3-2-1 template, 146–147
    implementation process, 146
    printing, 146
3-column charts, 169, 171
    implementation process, 169
4 Corners (pre-assessment), 64–65
    diagram, 66

A
ABC brainstorm, 77–79
A/B partner
    assigning, 108
    sharing, 92–93
Academic achievement (increase),
        dialogic teaching (impact), 193
Accountable talk, 192
Achievement gains, 6
Active engagement, encouragement, 185
Active participation (dialectic
        synergy sign), 203
Anchor charts, 136–137
    implementation process, 136
    responses, targeting (writing
        exemplars), 136
Anonymous No, 114–115
    implementation process, 114

mistakes, repair, 114
    questions, projection/writing, 114
Anticipation guides, 83
    animal adaptations anticipation
        guide, 84
    blank, editable anticipation guide, 85
Assessment one-pagers, 80
Assessments
    administration, preview, 218
    content, decision, 217
    plan, development, 217
    process, decision, 217
    team determination, 219
    timeline, determination, 217
    types, 215t–216t
    writing, 218
Assignment
    determination, 177
    sections, division, 163

B
Basic exit tickets, 259
Behavior expectations
    posting, 25
    setting, 24–25
        advice, 24t
    teaching, 25
Blank spaces, phrases (selection), 146

C

"Can Interim Assessments be Used for Instructional Change?," 7

Cause and effect, 168
  chart labeling, example, 169

Character analysis, chart labeling (example), 169

Character traits, contribution, 30

Chat log
  pre-assessment type, 67–68
  sample card primary, 70
  sample card secondary, 69

Clarifying (reciprocal teaching skill), 246

Clarify This!, 106–107
  implementation process, 106
  student misconceptions, 106
  task, learning goal (relationship), 106

Class discussion, notes (usage), 136

Classroom
  collaborative work, 18
  community, enhancement, 250
  democratic values, increase, 193
  dialogic classroom stems, bookmarks, 198
  dialogic teaching, appearance, 190–192
  engagement, signs, 202–204
  formative assessment
    benefits, 9–12
    presence/absence, 10t–11t
  formative classroom mastery desk cards, 100–103
  hierarchical classroom structure, elimination, 190
  library, 20
  management strategy, colors (usage), 116
  methods, 48t
  organization, 18–23
  perspective, 189
  pre-assessment usage, benefits, 58t
  relationships, focus, 190
  rules, analysis/discussion, 199
  setup, 17
  stems, poster (usage), 197

Classroom Assessment Techniques (Angelo/Cross), 263

Clear examples, usage, 236

Closed skills, determination, 45–47

Collaboration board, 175–176
  implementation process, 175–176

Collaboration, promotion, 194, 237

Collaborative learning, 161
  peer writing conferences, relationship, 244

Collaborative practices, 208

Collaborative problem-solving dialectic synergy sign, 203

Collaborative problem-solving tasks usage, 194

Collaborative routines, 161

Collaborative work, 18

Collective responsibility, 208

Collegial relationships, development, 208–213

Common formative assessments (CFAs), 207
  benefits, 227–229
  planning, 214–221
  team-developed CFAs, benefits, 227

Common formative protocol, 223–226

Common language, creation, 3–5, 31

Communication
  exchange (signifying), sound signal (usage), 165
  open communication, usage, 243
  respectful communication (dialectic synergy sign), 203
  skills, development, 161

Compare and contrast, 168
  chart labeling, example, 169

Concept, student addition, 185

Content
  area, student completion, 112
  learning intention clarity, 33

Continuous improvement/results, focus
    (maintenance), 208, 221–226
Conversation
    entry points, 192
    ground rules, development, 196
    impact, 221–222
Cooperative group ideas, 136
Costa's level of questioning, 133–135
    implementation process, 133–134
    leveled question, writing, 134
    questioning levels, 135
    questions, student creation, 134
    template, supply, 133

D
Daily check-ins, usage, 238
Daily mindfulness, usage, 238
Data-based instruction, 12
Data collection, 182
Debates, 201
    usage, 194
Deck of cards, creation, 126
Declarative exit tickets, 261
Deconstructed standards template,
    usage, 41–42
Democratic values, increase, 193
Depth of Knowledge (DOK) Wheel
    (Webb), 219, 220f
    levels, corresponding activities, 221t
Dialectic synergy, 189, 201–202
    classroom engagement signs,
        202–204
Dialogic classroom stems, bookmarks, 198
Dialogic instruction checklist, 192
Dialogic teaching, 189
    appearance, 190–192
    benefits, 193
    classrooms, commonalities, 190–191
    components, 191t
    engagement, 201
    implementation

resources, 195–200, 195t
    steps, 194–195
    understanding, 194
Dialogue, promotion, 194
Differentiated learning (creation),
        pre-assessments (usage), 59–71
Differentiation, effectiveness (increase), 12
Digital bulletin boards, usage, 175
Disposition (learning intention type), 35
District benchmark testing, 4
District, formative assessment (benefits), 9–12
Doodle it, 124–125
    implementation process, 124

E
Education, PLC history, 207–208
Elementary classroom
    learning intentions, sample, 54f
    success criteria, sample, 54f
End-of-course exams, 4
End-of-day routine, establishment, 112
End-of-lesson formative, administration, 256
End-of-the-school-year statewide exams, 4
Engagement, increase, 161
Entrance tickets
    blank, editable sample entrance tickets, 82
    sample, 81
Entry tickets, 80
Error analysis, 167–168
    chart labeling example, 167
    implementation analysis, 167
    template, usage, 167
Events, character traits (contribution), 30
Exit tickets, 256–262
    declarative exit tickets, 261
    defining, 257
    formative post-instruction,
        relationship, 259–262
    metacognitive exit ticket, 262
    procedural exit tickets, 260
    types, 257t–258t

F

Face-to-face environment, learning
    capacity, 176
Feedback
    allowance, 176
    formative assessment, relationship, 12
    formative feedback, 4
    group feedback, location, 182
    loop, formative assessment (relation-
        ship), 13–14
    opportunities, 11
    peer feedback (nonverbal signals), 179
    providing, 248–249
    receiving, 7
Fingers (usage), fist to five
    (relationship), 139
Fist to five, 139–145
    I don't understand, 140
    implementation process, 139
    I need help understanding, 141
    I somewhat understand, 142
    I understand, 143
    I understand and can explain in
        my own words, 144
    I understand and can teach it
        to others, 145
Formative assessments, 3. *See also* Common
        formative assessments
    benefits, 9–12
    commonness, 8–9
    feedback
        loop, relationship, 13–14
        relationship, 12
    give one, get one formative assessment
        strategy, 185
    guided practice, role, 239–240
    implementation, classroom setup, 17
    instructional practices/resources, 91
    in-the-moment formative
        assessment, 4, 255
    learning goals, importance, 241

post-instruction formative
    assessment, 255
professional learning communities
    (PLCs), relationship, 207
reflection formative assessments, 264
research support, 5–9
resources, 233
support, metacognition (impact), 242
*Formative Assessment & Standards-Based
    Grading* (Marzano), 8
Formative classroom mastery desk
    cards, 100–103
    color coding, 99
    hole punching, 99
    implementation, 99
    usage, student instruction, 99
Formative feedback, 4
Formative post-instruction
    exit tickets, relationship, 259–262
    reflection, 265
    three times summary, 267
Future units, teacher planning, 256

G

Gallery walk, 74–75
    student ideas, 136
GimKit, 71–85, 73t
Give one, get one, 185–186
    implementation process, 185
Goals
    creation, 17–18
    peer goal-setting, process, 243–244
Goals and steps, 177–178
    implementation process, 176
Google Drive, usage, 176
Google Forms, usage, 62
Grab-and-go, providing (ease), 189
Graphic organizers, usage, 238–239
    student practice, 148
Group discussions, usage, 194
Group feedback, location, 182

Growth mindset, development, 249–250

Guided practice, 116, 239–240, 242–243

H

Handouts, usage, 106

Hand signals, explanation, 140–145

Hands, raising, 179

Hattie, John, 233

Hierarchical classroom structure, elimination, 190

Higher-order thinking skills, student development, 133

High-level thinking skills (dialectic synergy sign), 203

High-performance organization, creation, 212

Hord, Shirley M., 207–208

I

"I can" statements, 45t, 240

Ideas

diversity, increase, 162

partners, sharing, 179

student brainstorming, 239

writing, 180

Individualized instruction, small group rotations (usage), 9

Information

reading, 165

usage, 4

Inner circle, naming, 165

Inside/outside circle, 165–167

implementation process, 165

steps, 167

"Inside the Black Box," 6–7

Instructional improvement cycle, 7

Instructional planning, 25

Instructional routine, dialogic teaching (inclusion), 193

In-the-moment formative assessment, 4, 255

In-the-moment formative instruction, collaborative routines, 161

In-the-moment participation, allowance, 176

J

Jamboard, usage, 175, 176

Jigsaw

activities, student notes (usage), 136

cooperative learning activity, 162–164

implementation process, 162–163

timer, setting, 163

topics, sharing, 163

Justification, chart labeling (example), 169

K

Kahoots, 71–85, 72t–73t

Knowledge

learning intention type, 35

prior knowledge, activation, 236

Knowledge, display, 73–79

ABC brainstorm, 78–79

Gallery Walk, 76

Know Want Learn (KWL) chart, 92–94

usage, 74

L

Language frames, usage, 136

Layered success criteria, 45t

Learning

assessment, 4–5

objective, simplification, 36

social process, 194

statement, 45t

targets, 35–38, 279

common language, creation, 31

selection, 29

Learning goals, 26, 241

Clarify This! task, relationship, 106

learning logs, relationship, 112

Questions for My Teacher, relationship, 110

Learning goals (*Continued*)
sample, 53t
statement, 120
student knowledge, 122
Learning intentions, 31–32
benefits, 32–33
creation, step-by-step guide, 25–38
formulation, deconstructed standards
template (usage), 41–42
sample, 35, 54f
standard, deconstruction, 35–38
sample, 39
teach template, 40
success criteria, differences,
52–54, 52f
types, 34–35, 34t–35t
Learning logs, 112–113
collection, 112
end-of-day routine, establishment, 112
implementation process, 112
learning goals, relationship, 112
templates, copies, 112
Learning target tickets, 120–121
implementation process, 120
learning goal, statement, 120
quarter sheets, readiness, 120
student supply, 120
template, printing, 120
Lesson, introduction
appearance, 29
comparison, 30
Lesson notes, chart labeling
(example), 169
Leveled question, writing, 129
Leveled turn-in bins, 241–242
Level of Understanding, student selection
(encouragement), 241–242
Light bulb moments, 97–98
Lingering questions, 182–184
implementation process, 182
Long-constructed responses, 215

M
Main idea/details, chart labeling
(example), 169
Marzano, Robert, 8
Material, understanding (increase), 161
Math skill practice, chart labeling
(example), 169
McTighe, Jay, 7
Message in a bottle, 261
Metacognition
importance, 242
usage, 148
Metacognitive exit ticket, 262
MetaX visible learning research
(Hattie), 233, 234t
Misconceptions
checks, 263–264
Misconceptions, teacher determination
ability, 256
Mistakes, repair, 114
Modeling, 242–243
Monitoring system, usage, 243
Motivation, increase, 161
Muddiest points, 182–184, 263–264
administration, steps, 263
Multiple-choice responses, 215
Multi-tiered Systems of Support
(MTSS), 9

N
Nearpod, 71–85
Nonverbal signals (peer feedback), 179
Norms, shared set (PLC development), 211
Notes, student writings, 122

O
One-minute essays, 95–96
One-minute shares, 179–181
implementation process, 180
Ongoing learning, presence, 208

Online platforms, usage, 175

Open communication, usage, 243

Open-ended questions

    teacher, posing, 202

    usage, 194

Open-ended sample task menu, success

        criteria (inclusion), 46t

Open skills, determination, 45–47

Opinion, 168

Opposing viewpoints, student

        defense, 192

Outer circle, naming, 165

P

Parking lot, 131–132

    chart, creation, 131

    guided/independent practice, 131

    implementation process, 131

    sticky notes, student usage, 131

Pass it on!, 170–172

    implementation process, 171

Peer feedback (nonverbal signals), 179

Peer goal-setting, process, 243–244

Peer thinking analysis/

        observational tool, 200

Peer-to-peer teaching, encouragement, 185

Peer writing conferences, collaborative

        learning (relationship), 244

Performance assessment, 215

Perspectives, diversity (increase), 162

Persuasive technique, 46t

Physical movement, pre-assessment, 64

Physical space, 20

Picture notes, 165–166

    implementation process, 165

    template, readiness, 165

Plickers, 71–85, 72t

Post-instruction formative assessment, 255

Pre-assessments

    creation, Google Forms (usage), 62

defining, 58

digital tools, 71–85

implementation, resources, 60

importance, 58

tools, 72t–73t

type 1, 61

type 2, 63–65

type 3, 73–79

type 4, 80–85

types, 60–85

usage, 57, 59–71

    benefits, 58t

Precise language, usage, 44–45

Predicting (reciprocal teaching skill), 246

Pretest, usage, 57

Prior knowledge, activation, 236

Problem-solving skills, improvement, 162

Procedural exit tickets, 260

Professional development (PD), 5

Professional growth, presence, 208

Professional learning communities (PLCs)

    common formative protocol

        detailed protocol, 224–226

        shortened protocol, 223

    common formatives, execution

        (question), 227–229

    formative assessments

        relationship, 207

        usage, 217–221

    history, 207–208

    team, impact, 228–229

Professional Learning Communities at Work

        (DuFour/Eaker), 208

Proficiency criteria, setting, 218

Q

Quarter sheets, readiness, 120

Questioning

    reciprocal teaching skill, 246

    techniques, usage, 194

Questions
  answer, writing, 170
  lingering questions, 182–184
  posing, 180
  projection/writing, 114
  stems, phrases/sentences, 245
  student creation, 129
  student wondering, 118
  teacher, posing, 201
Questions for My Teacher, 110–111
  implementation process, 110
  task, learning goals (relationship), 110
  template, printing, 110
Quick writes, 122–123
  implementation process, 122
  template copies, holding, 122
  thoughts/notes, student writing, 122

R
Reaching consensus groups, 245
Reasoning (learning intention type), 35
Recall-based exams, completion
      (rarity), 191
Reciprocal teaching, strategy, 246
Recording sheet, ideas (writing), 180
Reflection formative assessments, 264
Reflective teaching practices, 208
Resources, providing (ease), 189
Respectful communication (dialectic
      synergy sign), 203
Response to Intervention (RTI), 9
Re-teaching, 214
Rubrics, usage, 248–249

S
Scaffolded language, 192
Scaffolding, effectiveness (increase), 12
Schools, success (characteristics), 208
Science, learning goals/success criteria
      (sample), 53t

Self-assessment, 25–26
  benefits, 249–250
  intention, 26
  learning goals, 26
  reflection, 246
  student self-assessment, 99, 233
  tickets, 25–26, 247
  turn-in bins, 241–242
Self-reflection, encouragement, 185
Sentence stems, 192
Shared collegial relationships,
      development, 208–213
Shared norms/beliefs/goals, 208
  development, 208–213
Sheet protector boards, 116–117
  copying, 116
  implementation process, 116
  papers, printing, 116
Short-constructed responses, 215
Shout out the word that I leave out, 138
  implementation process, 138
Silent reading, 138
Skills
  completion steps, 136
  determination, 45–47
  new skills, teaching, 165
Skills/products (learning intention type), 35
Small group rotations, 20–23
  usage, 9
Social skills, development, 161
Sound signal, usage, 165
Standard end-of-unit tests, 4
Statement of learning, 45t
Stems to use, providing, 173
Sticky notes, student usage, 136
Stoplight cards: red, yellow, green, 126–127
  card meaning, student instruction, 126
  deck of cards, creation, 126
  green paper copy, 128
  implementation process, 126

red cards, impact, 127
red paper copy, 130
yellow paper copy, 129
Structured language talk, 168–169
implementation process, 168
Student-of-the-day notes, 247
Student performance
expectations, 11
improvement, 11–12
Students
academic performance, increase, 250
achievement
improvement, 228
PLC team, impact, 228–229
agency, 9
increase, 12
assignment, determination, 177
daily mindfulness, usage, 238
engagement, increase, 12, 194
groups, forming, 171
growth mindset, development,
249–250
growth, monitoring, 101
guided/independent practice, 131
intrinsic motivation, increase, 250
learning intention clarity, 32–33
leveled question, writing, 129
mastery, determination, 255
mastery level, reflection, 101
mastery tracker, 104–105
implementation process, 104
new skills, instruction, 165
performance, 8
respectful disagreements,
encouragement, 191–192
response, allowance, 95
slips, collection, 114
student-led discussions (facilitation),
questioning techniques (usage), 194
support/guidance, providing, 194–195

understanding, gauging, 256
work, target response/rubrics (usage),
248–249
writing (support), language frames
(usage), 136
Students, self-assessment, 99, 233
benefits, 250
checklist
primary, 251
upper elementary, 252
effect sizes, 234t
strategies, alignment, 235t
Student-teacher relationships, 247
Success criteria, 248
benefits, 43–44
chart, sample, 46t
co-construction, 237
classroom methods, 48t
steps, 50–51
students, involvement, 49
common language, creation, 31
creation
step-by-step guide, 44–49
students, involvement, 47–48
development, 29
examination, 42–43
formatting methods, 45t
inclusion, 46t
learning intentions, differences, 52–54, 52f
sample, 53t, 54f
student knowledge, 92
Summaries, chart labeling (example), 169
Summarizing (reciprocal teaching
skill), 246
Summative assessment, 4
administering, 182
intervention, 256
Supportive/collegial relationships,
presence, 208
Synergy, term (usage), 201

T

Talking sticks, 170

Target response, tool, 248–249

Teachers

    clarity, providing, 250

    dialogic instruction checklist, 192

    dialogic teaching, engagement, 201

    learning intention clarity, 32

    open-ended question, posing, 202

    question, posing, 201

    student-teacher relationships, 247

    teacher-student relationships,

        redefinition, 193

    trusting culture, development, 209

Team commitments, development, 210

Team-developed common formative

    assessments, benefits, 227

Team norm

    development activity, 212–213

    guiding questions, 211t

Team productivity, increase, 211

Template, student completion, 118

Themes, search, 183

Think-aloud, 173–174

Thinking head, 262

Think Pair Share (TPS), 108–109

    implementation process, 108

    partner, communication, 108

    template, printing, 108

Thoughtful responses (dialectic synergy

    sign), 203

Thoughts, student writings, 122

Three times summary, 267

Tickets. *See* Learning target tickets

Time sequence, 168

Topics

    perspective, sharing, 202

    student addition, 185

    student thoughts, sharing, 175

TPS. *See* Think Pair Share (TPS)

Traditional individual student

    pre-assessments, 61

Triple summary, 265–266

True/false assessment, 215

True/false statements, 83

Trust, development, 250

Trusting culture, teacher development, 209

Turn-in bins, 18–20, 19f

    leveled turn-in bins, 241–242

Turn-taking, concept (teaching), 170

U

Understanding by Design (Wiggins), 7–8

V

Verbalizations, 173

Virtual environment, learning capacity, 176

Visual map, 148–164

    implementation process, 148

Vocabulary instruction, chart labeling

    (example), 169

W

Weekly homework, assigning, 57

What Are Your Wonderings?, 118–119

    implementation process, 118

    question, student answering, 118

    template, prompt, 118

Whiteboards, pre-assessment type, 71

Wiggins, Grant, 7

Word activity, 74

Writing

    assignment, ideas (student

        brainstorming), 239

    exemplars, 136

    self-assessment rubric, 30

Z

Zone of desired effects, 6

Printed and bound by CPI Group (UK) Ltd, Croydon, CR0 4YY

16/11/2023

08189992-0001

Cross the TOEIC® Bridge

Lynn Stafford-Yilmaz

Cross the TOEIC® Bridge, 1st edition
International Edition 2004

Published by McGraw-Hill/Contemporary, a business unit of The McGraw-Hill
Companies, Inc., 1221 Avenue of the Americas, New York, NY 10020.

10   09   08   07   06   05   04   03   02
20   09   08   07   06   05
CTF   SLP

ISBN 007-111012-7

Editorial director: Tina B. Carver
Senior sponsoring editor: Thomas Healy
Developmental editor: Susan Johnson
Editorial assistant: Kasey Williamson
Director of international sales and marketing: Kate Oakes
Cover Design: A Good Thing
Interior design and production services: Design Plus

When ordering this title, use ISBN 007-123620-1

Printed in Singapore

www.mhcontemporary.com

CONTENTS

Introduction

Welcome to *Cross the TOEIC® Bridge* v
Note to Users vii

SECTION 1: LISTENING COMPREHENSION

PART I   Photographs 3
Vocabulary Power!
Test Hints 1-12
Part I Practice Test 23

PART II   Stimulus-Response 27
Vocabulary Power!
Test Hints 13-23
Part II Practice Test 38

PART III   Short Conversations and Short Talks 39
Vocabulary Power!
Test Hints 24-34
Part III Practice Test 57

SECTION 2: READING

PART IV   Incomplete Sentences   61
             Vocabulary Power!
             Test Hints 35-50
             Part IV Practice Test   111

PART V   Reading Comprehension   113
             Vocabulary Power!
             Test Hints 51-58
             Part V Practice Test   145

SECTION 3: PRACTICE TESTS

Practice Test 1   157

Practice Test 2   181

ANSWER KEY AND AUDIO SCRIPT

Part I Answer Key and Audio Script   207
Part II Answer Key and Audio Script   211
Part III Answer Key and Audio Script   219
Part IV Answer Key   227
Part V Answer Key   239
Practice Test 1: Answer Key   244
Practice Test 2: Answer Key and Audio Script   257

Welcome to *Cross the TOEIC® Bridge*

This book is for English learners who will take the TOEIC Bridge. This book can be used as a classroom text. It can also be used as a self-study guide.

The TOEIC Bridge is a test of English language ability. It measures listening and reading skills. The TOEIC Bridge is for beginning to intermediate level students. It is often used as a "preparatory test." It helps students prepare for the TOEIC test. "TOEIC" stands for Test of English for International Communication.

The TOEIC Bridge has 100 questions and takes about one hour. It has five parts.

Format of the TOEIC Bridge

Part	Type of Question	Number of Questions	Time
Part I	Photographs	15 questions	25 minutes for parts I-III (Listening)
Part II	Stimulus-Response	20 questions	
Part III	Short Talks and Short Announcements	15 questions	
Part IV	Incomplete Sentences	30 questions	35 minutes for parts IV-V (Reading)
Part V	Reading Comprehension	20 questions	

TOEIC Bridge Information

Purpose　　Measures English language ability in listening and reading

Format　　100 questions (50 listening, 50 reading)

Time　　One hour

Difficulty Level　　Beginning to Intermediate

Contents　　Everyday English (shopping, transportation, weather, entertainment, health, simple business)

Test-Takers　　Workers, teachers, immigrants, and students from elementary school through adulthood.

Score	20-180 points (90 points each for Listening and Reading). Bridge-takers scoring over 160 may be ready for the TOEIC test.
Other Area Grades	Test-takers are graded in five areas: Functions, Listening Strategies, Grammar, Vocabulary, and Reading Strategies. Scores range from one to three: one is low, three is high. Information helps learners gauge their strengths and weaknesses.
Taking the Test	To learn your country's TOEIC Bridge schedule, contact your local TOEIC office. A complete listing of offices is available on the Web: http://www.toeic.com.
TOEIC	The TOEIC test is more difficult than the TOEIC Bridge. It is by comparison longer than the Bridge. It has 200 questions and takes 2.5 hours.
Web Site	http://www.toeic.com/2_2_4bridge.htm

Note to Users

This section contains important information about using this book. It is helpful for both teachers and self-study users.

Introduction

This text contains approximately 50 hours of instructional material. Your time depends on student level and class size. The following chart gives a rough timeline for study.

Approximate Study Time Guideline

Section 1 Listening Comprehension	15-20 hours
Section 2 Reading	20-25 hours
Section 3 Practice Tests	5-8 hours
Total Book	**40-53 hours**

Language Level

Every explanatory sentence in this book is short: 12 or fewer words. In this way, all users can easily understand this book.

Test Hints

This book is organized around 58 test hints. These test hints may be taught in the order that they are presented. Or you can "jump around" among hints in this book. Each hint stands independently. For a longer study period, try varying the types of hints that you study. Choose a few from the listening section of the test. Choose a few from reading. Variety will add interest to your study.

You should aim to finish any given test hint in one sitting. Avoid starting a hint during one sitting and completing it in another. Go through each test hint from start to finish. Check your answers as soon as the directions tell you to. Completing one test hint takes about eight to 30 minutes.

Listening Practice

For all listening work, you should listen to the audio while studying. You should not read the audio script. Reading the audio script changes the purpose of a listening exercise. The audio script is printed only for reference after completing a practice.

For all listening practices, you may listen to the audio multiple times. Repeated listenings give additional listening practice. For the sample tests, however, you may only listen once. This prepares students for real testing conditions.

Vocabulary Power

Vocabulary is the most important single factor to improving your Bridge score. For this reason, *Cross the TOEIC® Bridge* emphasizes vocabulary development.

Each part of this book begins with a section called "Vocabulary Power." These opening Vocabulary Powers teach high-frequency TOEIC Bridge vocabulary. These Vocabulary Power words occur several times in the book. After all, learning a new word requires many exposures to the word. *Cross the TOEIC® Bridge* provides that exposure. This is a unique opportunity to increase vocabulary.

Throughout each chapter, you will find additional Vocabulary Powers. These may teach additional, specific vocabulary items. Some Vocabulary Powers present word roots, suffixes, and prefixes. Others give specific suggestions on how to build and retain vocabulary.

Grammar Review

This book contains a complete review of beginning to intermediate grammar points. For example, one grammar point is the simple past tense. Another is non-count nouns. Each grammar point is followed by six to ten practice test questions.

The grammar review prepares you for TOEIC Bridge Part IV. About 15 questions on the TOEIC Bridge directly test grammar. In other words, 15% of the TOEIC Bridge directly tests grammar. Studying grammar in proportion to its importance on the test makes good sense. Remember that grammar is only one part of the TOEIC Bridge. In the same way, it is only one part of learning English.

Practice Tests

Cross the TOEIC® Bridge has two, full-length practice tests. Each test takes one hour. Each test is followed by an audio script and explanatory answers.

The practice tests and part tests are authentic. That is, they are like *real* TOEIC Bridge tests. The tests mirror the actual test in length, style, content, and difficulty. The practice tests use actual TOEIC Bridge test directions. Authentic answer sheets are included for every test.

You may use the practice tests according to your needs. Here are some ways to use them:
- Use the practice tests for practice at the end of your study.
- Take one test as a pre-test and one as a post-test.
- Divide the tests in half. Take the listening half on one day. Take the reading on another.

As soon as possible after taking a test, examine the correct answers.

TOEIC Preparation

This book can be used for beginning to intermediate TOEIC takers.

This book was initially written for takers of the TOEIC Bridge. During its piloting, users became thrilled about its usefulness for TOEIC takers. After all, the TOEIC test and TOEIC Bridge are very similar tests. The level of this book is perfect for lower level TOEIC takers.

The TOEIC test has one question type that is not on the Bridge. TOEIC Part VI is Error Recognition. In this part, a sentence has four underlined parts. Test takers must identify which underlined part contains an error. The grammar review in this book helps students prepare for Error Recognition.

ACKNOWLEDGMENTS

Many devoted educators supported the creation of this textbook, sharing expertise, personal experience, and student resources. Thank you to Sudie Allen-Henn, University of Washington; Sally Cocco, Bellevue Community College; Paul Hackshaw, Kyoto Institute of Technology; and Jan Peterson, Edmonds Community College. Also, thanks to KimMarie Cole, Richard Firsten, Garnet Templin-Imel, Julie Vorholt, and Barbara Wright, for their valuable feedback.

From its inception to its completion, this textbook grew from the dynamic suggestions of several talented publishing professionals. Thanks to my acquisitions editor, Thomas Healy. My editor, Susan Johnson, helped create the highly navigable organizational structure for this text. Sharing his market knowledge and agility in shaping test materials, KC Kang went beyond the call of duty.

Among the hundreds of students who piloted materials in this text, three arose with a keen willingness to provide additional feedback and insight. Thanks to Kenichi Fukuzawa, Yumiko Ota, and Fion Shen, for their rigorous input on this work.

Over time, several individuals have inspired my work in language education. My highest regards go to Dr. Lin Lougheed, who has modeled for me professionalism and attention to detail in writing test prep materials. Thank you to the Monterey Institute of International Studies, in particular to Dr. Kathi Bailey and Dr. Jean Turner. Also, let me recognize the inspiration and support of Marcelino Aguilar, Linda Bennett, Colleen Butler, Cara Kennedy, Kazuhiro Katagiri, Tom Lampkin, Nozomi Miyashita, Kayoko Sasaki, Yukiko Sato, Shannon Stafford, Garnet Templin-Imel, Isao Yaguchi, and Mustafa Yilmaz.

Photographer credits

TH = Test Hint: PT = Part Test: ST = Full-length Practice Test

Joe Budne: PT #8, FT2 #1, #12; Colleen Butler: Author's photograph, back cover; Jake Cook: FT2 #5; Hilary Gibson: TH4 #3; Scott Guthrie and Guthrie's Images: TH2, TH5 #3, TH7 #1, TH12 #2, PT #13, #6, FT1 #12; Jasmin Hagen: FT2 #2; Jessica Flagler: PT #4, #17; Alison Hershberger: PT #1; Craig Huber: TH1 #4, TH3 #2, TH7 #6, TH8 #1,

TH9 #4, FT1 #6, FT2 #6, #15; Soo-Ryeon Kim: TH4 #1; Debby Nixon: TH12 #4, FT1 #1, #8, #13, FT2 #14; Anne Ogawa: TH3 Ex., #4, TH7 Ex., TH 10 #3, FT1 #4, #11, #15, FT2 #4, #8, #11; Beth Porterfield: TH5 #4, FT2 #7; Julia Sharpe: TH5 Ex.; TH12 #3; University of Washington Mary Levin TH1 #6, FT1 #10; Karen Orders: TH8 #3, TH10 Ex.; Kathy Sauber FT2 #10; University of Washington Media Relations TH4 Vocab Power; Joanie Komura TH1 #2, TH9 #1; Bruce Terami FT2 #3

Model credits

Bryona Anastassopoulos, Midori Barmi, Kendall Bates, Claudia E. Bishop, Andrea Boag, Addie Gearhart, Taylor Gearhart, Zoey Gearhart, Kirk Graves, Megan Hartsig, Miho Hasegawa, Misa Hasegawa, David Herrman, Eriko Hyodo, Cathy M. Jochen, Tamiyo Kasaki, Jae-Chun Kim, Sandra Kim, Yuko Kobayashi, Ally Love, Bradley Lewis, Ninyel Masterjohn, Debra Morris, Phil Nixon, Bill Noble, Nancy Noble, Lauren Perinchief, Trisha Ruis, Fion Shen, Jane Stafford, Hiroshi Uno, Tsui-Ping Yamamoto, Ertugrul Yilmaz, Lawrence J. Zwier

Section 1

LISTENING COMPREHENSION

Test Summary

Part I of the TOEIC Bridge tests your understanding of spoken English. It has 15 questions. Each question is based on a photograph. The photographs show people, things, animals, activities, and places. You will hear statements about each photograph. The statements are short. They use simple grammar. They are spoken slowly.

Sample Question

You will hear:

> Look at the picture marked number 1 in your test book.
>
> (A) The player is kicking the ball.
> (B) She's standing in the goal.
> (C) There's a play at the theater.
> (D) She's throwing the soccer ball.

In your test book, you will see: Ⓐ Ⓑ Ⓒ Ⓓ

Statement (A), "The player is kicking the ball," best describes the picture. Therefore, you should choose answer (A).

Taking the Test

You will hear four statements about each photograph. The statements are not printed in your test book. You will see only the letters (A), (B), (C), and (D). Each letter corresponds to one statement. One of the statements is true. Three are false. You must choose the true statement.

On the TOEIC Bridge, all correct answers help your score. Incorrect answers do not count against you. Therefore, answer every question, even if you aren't sure.

Timing

The listening comprehension section is 25 minutes in total. Part I takes about 7 minutes. The timing is set by the audio recording. You must work as fast as the recording goes.

Learn these important words for Part I of the test. These words occur several times in this book.

Family

1. **be/get married** *v.*
   They are <u>getting married</u>.
2. **pregnant** *n.*
   Several women are <u>pregnant</u>.

Home and Apartment Life

3. **build** *v.*   They're <u>building</u> new bookshelves.
4. **garbage** *n.*   The <u>garbage</u> is full.
   There's <u>garbage</u> on the floor.
5. **mirror** *n.*   They took the <u>mirror</u> off the wall.

Nature

6. **fire** *n.*   A <u>fire</u> is burning in the West.
7. **fog** *n.*   There's <u>fog</u> in the East.
8. **forest** *n.*   The fire is in the <u>forest</u>.
9. **snow** *v./n.*   It's <u>snowing</u> in Chicago.

Physical

10. **ambulance** *n.*
    They're putting the man in the <u>ambulance</u>.
11. **dentist** *n.*
    The <u>dentist</u> is pulling the man's teeth.

Restaurants

12. **meal** *n.*   The <u>meal</u> looks delicious.

School

13. graduate *v./n.* Mary <u>graduated</u> in June. She was a proud <u>graduate</u>.

Shopping

14. button *v./n.* Sachi <u>buttoned</u> her sweater. It had lots of <u>buttons</u>.

Transportation

15. ride/rode *v.* Many people are <u>riding</u> on the train.

16. seat *n.* There are no <u>seats</u>.

17. track *n.* Workers are working on the <u>tracks</u>.

Travel

18. luggage *n.* They have a lot of <u>luggage</u>.

19. passenger *n.* The <u>passengers</u> are waiting to check in.

Work

20. paint *v./n.* The painter is <u>painting</u> a picture. He has <u>paint</u> on his shirt. <u>Painters are painting</u> the house.

Test Hint 1

Mark an answer that seems correct *while* you listen to the audio. Mark it lightly. If you change the answer, you can erase the mark. If you keep the answer, remember to darken the mark. Work quickly. There are seven seconds between questions.

Practice

Directions   Look at the photographs. Listen to the statements. *While* you listen, mark the answer that seems correct. Mark it lightly and quickly.

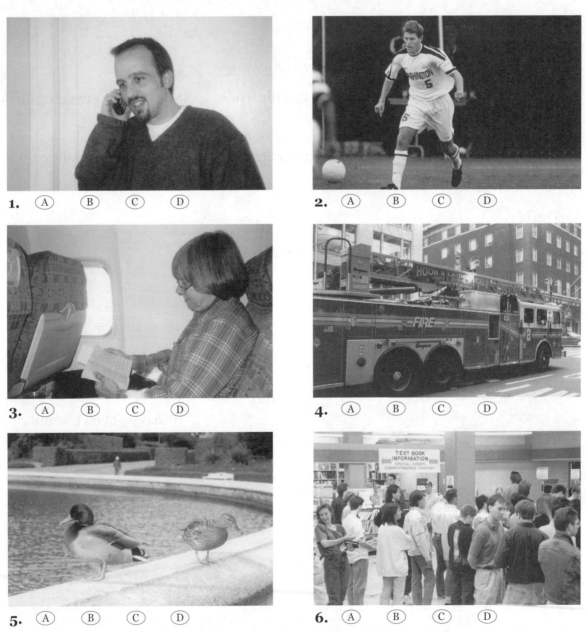

1. (A)   (B)   (C)   (D)

2. (A)   (B)   (C)   (D)

3. (A)   (B)   (C)   (D)

4. (A)   (B)   (C)   (D)

5. (A)   (B)   (C)   (D)

6. (A)   (B)   (C)   (D)

Check your answers on page 8.

Test Hint 2

Recognize the kind of information that is given. Photograph statements usually focus on one type of information. This may be actions, animals, clothing, feelings, people, places, quantities, or things.

Type of Information	Examples
actions	skiing, reading, eating
animals	horses, dogs, fish
clothing/physical	tall, coat, glasses, blue jeans
feelings	excited, tired, angry
people	woman, dentist, runners
places	library, classroom, park
quantities	one, a few, many
things	chairs, trains, present

Practice One

Directions   Look at the picture. Look at the list next to it and study the true statements. Note the *type* of information that each statement gives. Then, cover up the list on the right. For each statement, name the type of information it gives.

True Statements	Type of Information
(A) They are looking at some papers.	action
(B) One woman is wearing glasses.	clothing/ physical
(C) They are serious.	feelings
(D) A mother is holding her son.	people
(E) They are holding some papers.	things
(F) They're in a doctor's office.	place
(G) There are three people.	quantities
(H) There aren't any dogs.	animals

Practice Two

Directions   Look at Test Hint 1 again and study the photographs. Next, read the audio script for Test Hint 1 that is printed below. For each photograph, read the answer that is marked as correct. Then, write down the focus of the correct statement in the blank. Select the focus from the following list.

Focus of Information

Actions	People
Animals	Places
Clothing/Physical	Quantities
Feelings	Things

1.   (A) He's buying a cell phone.
     (B) He's applying for a loan.
  √ (C) He's talking on his cell phone.   *action*
     (D) He's dialing the number.

2.   (A) He's a tennis player.
     (B) He's a runner.
  √ (C) He's a soccer player.
     (D) He's a coach.

3.   (A) The lady has an aisle seat.
     (B) A drink spilled on the center seat.
     (C) The lady is pregnant.
  √ (D) She has a window seat.

4.   (A) It's a fire.
     (B) It's an ambulance.
     (C) It's a police car.
  √ (D) It's a fire truck.

5.   (A) There is just one duck.
  √ (B) There are two ducks.
     (C) There is just one dog.
     (D) There are two dogs.

6. √ (A) The shoppers are waiting in line.
     (B) The shoppers are trying on clothes.
     (C) The shoppers are paying by credit card.
     (D) The shoppers are looking at textbooks.

Check your answers on page 207.

Test Hint 3

Understand prepositions of location. TOEIC Bridge photographs often show where someone or something is. Bridge questions test location from *your* viewpoint. "What is on the left?" means "What is on *your* left?" "Where is the table?" means "Where is it *from your point of view*?"

Vocabulary Power!

Look at the photograph. Read the sentences and look at the underlined prepositions.

Prepositions of Location

The man is <u>at</u> the table.

His legs are <u>under</u> the table.

A wall is <u>behind</u> the man.

The man is <u>between</u> the wall and the table.

The teacup is <u>in</u> his hand.

The man's finger is <u>through</u> the teacup handle.

The saucer is <u>on</u> the table.

The towel is <u>to the left</u> of the saucer.

An empty chair is <u>across from</u> the man.

His necktie is <u>around</u> his neck.

Two empty chairs are <u>next to</u> each other.

Practice One

Directions   Look at the photographs. Listen to the audio. Listen for words that tell "where." Choose the correct statement for each photograph.

1. Ⓐ   Ⓑ   Ⓒ   Ⓓ

2. Ⓐ   Ⓑ   Ⓒ   Ⓓ

3. Ⓐ   Ⓑ   Ⓒ   Ⓓ

4. Ⓐ   Ⓑ   Ⓒ   Ⓓ

Check your answers on page 207.

Practice Two

Directions   Study the prepositions of location in the chart below. Then look at the photographs in Practice One again. Listen to the Practice One audio again. Listen for the prepositions in the chart. Each time you hear one, check it in the box.

Prepositions	Question 1	Question 2	Question 3	Question 4
above				
behind				
between				
in	√			
in front of				
next to	√			
on	√			
to the left of				
under	√			
up				

Check your answers on page 207.

Test Hint 4

Photo questions often test numbers and quantities. Listen for words that tell _how much_ or _how many_.

Vocabulary Power!

Look at the photograph. Read the sentences, and look at the underlined words that show quantity.

Quantity Words

There are <u>nine</u> women.

They're <u>all</u> sitting down.

<u>A few</u> of them are wearing sunglasses.

<u>A couple</u> of them aren't wearing hats.

The boat is <u>full</u>.

<u>Most</u> of them are wearing hats.

<u>None</u> of them is swimming.

<u>One</u> of them is looking to her right.

Practice

<u>*Directions*</u>   Look at the photographs. Listen to the audio. Listen for the words that tell amount. Choose the true statement.

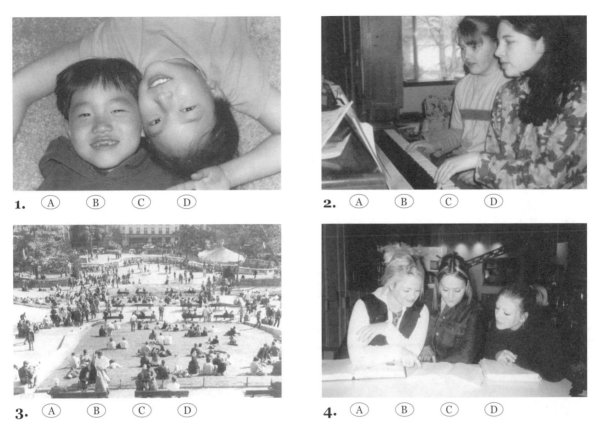

1. (A) (B) (C) (D)

2. (A) (B) (C) (D)

3. (A) (B) (C) (D)

4. (A) (B) (C) (D)

Check your answers on page 207.

Test Hint 5

Some photo questions test just one word. These questions are often short but difficult. Each statement is the same except for one word or phrase. The type of word tested varies. It may be a noun, verb, adjective, adverb, or preposition. Focus on the word that changes.

Example *Four Statements with One Word that Differs*

(A) It's a dog.
(B) It's a cat.
(C) It's a mouse.
(D) It's a lion.

Practice

Directions   Look at the photographs. Listen to the audio. Listen for the word that changes. Choose the true statement.

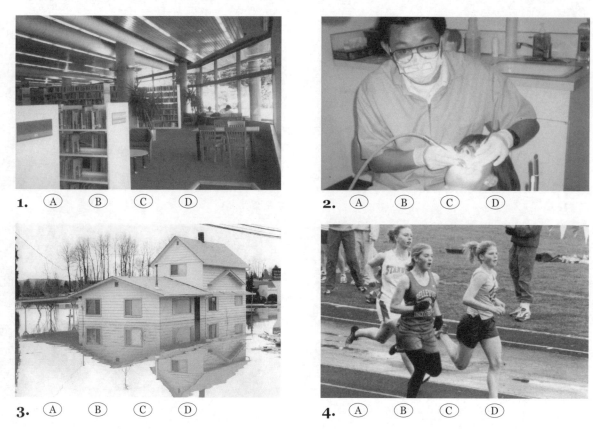

1. Ⓐ   Ⓑ   Ⓒ   Ⓓ   **2.** Ⓐ   Ⓑ   Ⓒ   Ⓓ

3. Ⓐ   Ⓑ   Ⓒ   Ⓓ   **4.** Ⓐ   Ⓑ   Ⓒ   Ⓓ

Do NOT check your answers yet.

Test Hint 6

Increase your chances of answering correctly by guessing. Always note statements that are _not_ true. (Write the letters of the false statements in your test book. This way you will not forget them. Or, you may lightly cross out statements that are not true. However, you must later erase these marks.) Then, guess from only those statements that may be true. The fewer possible answers, the higher chance you have of guessing correctly. Remember to answer every question, even if you are not sure.

Practice

Directions   Look at the photographs in Test Hint 5. Listen to the audio. Note any statements that are _not_ true. Choose the best answer from the remaining statements.

1. Ⓐ   Ⓑ   Ⓒ   Ⓓ   **3.** Ⓐ   Ⓑ   Ⓒ   Ⓓ

2. Ⓐ   Ⓑ   Ⓒ   Ⓓ   **4.** Ⓐ   Ⓑ   Ⓒ   Ⓓ

Check your answers on page 208. Compare your answers to the questions in Test Hints 5 and 6. Did you answer more questions correctly in Test Hint 6 or 5?

Vocabulary Power!

Use photographs to build your vocabulary. Look at the photographs in Test Hint 5. Find two or three things whose English word you don't know. Ask a classmate for the English word. Or, look it up in the dictionary. Talk about the photographs. Practice using your new words.

Test Hint 7

Understand the present progressive. This verb tense is often used in Part I to describe photos. Photos show scenes that are happening *right now*. The present progressive talks about present actions. It is difficult for photos to show the past or the future. (See the Present Progressive, page 98.)

Example *Statements in the Present Progressive*

(A) They're riding the train.
(B) The mother is dressing her son.
(C) The boy is carrying the boxes.
(D) They're playing on the floor.

Statement (D), "They're playing on the floor," best describes the picture.

Practice One

Directions Look at the photographs. Listen to the audio. Listen for the words that correctly describe the action in the photograph. Choose the true statement for each photo.

1. Ⓐ   Ⓑ   Ⓒ   Ⓓ

2. Ⓐ   Ⓑ   Ⓒ   Ⓓ

3. Ⓐ   Ⓑ   Ⓒ   Ⓓ   **4.** Ⓐ   Ⓑ   Ⓒ   Ⓓ

5. Ⓐ   Ⓑ   Ⓒ   Ⓓ   **6.** Ⓐ   Ⓑ   Ⓒ   Ⓓ

Do NOT check your answers yet.

Practice Two

Directions   Look at the photographs in Practice One again. Read the following audio script. Underline the words in the present progressive.

1.   (A)   The worker <u>is painting</u> the walkway.
      (B)   Water <u>is pouring</u> into the hole.
      (C)   The man <u>is riding</u> in the truck.
      (D)   The man <u>is digging</u> in the hole.

2.   (A)   The students are graduating.
      (B)   The graduates are singing.
      (C)   Every desk is occupied.
      (D)   They are all wearing raincoats.

3.   (A)   The woman is washing his hair.
      (B)   The man is getting a haircut.
      (C)   The hare is sitting quietly.
      (D)   The man is riding a horse.

4.   (A)   They're building a new wall.
      (B)   They're unloading wood from the truck.
      (C)   They're looking at the forest.
      (D)   They're both standing on ladders.

5.   (A)   They're chatting on the sofa.
      (B)   The man is pushing a button.
      (C)   They're playing with a remote control car.
      (D)   They are getting haircuts.

6.   (A)   The man is building a fence around the driveway.
      (B)   The man is carrying heavy luggage.
      (C)   The man is walking into the garage.
      (D)   The man is moving the garbage cans.

Check your answers on page 208.

There are many true statements you can make about a photograph. There are also many false ones. Listen carefully to tell a true statement from a false one.

Example *Several True and False Statements for Each Picture*

True Statements	False Statements
He is smiling.	He is wearing a hat.
He is cooking corn.	He is working in a restaurant.
He is standing outside.	His shirt is buttoned.

Practice One

<u>Directions</u>   Look at the photographs. Listen to the audio. Separate true and false statements. Write T for true statements. Write F for false statements.

1. a. _T_ b. _T_ c. _____
    d. _____ e. _____ f. _____

2. a. _____ b. _____ c. _____
    d. _____ e. _____ f. _____

3. a. _____ b. _____ c. _____
    d. _____ e. _____ f. _____

4. a. _____ b. _____ c. _____
    d. _____ e. _____ f. _____

Practice Two

Directions   Look at the photographs in Practice One again. This time, read the sentences.
Write T for true sentences. Write F for false sentences. Compare your answers in this
practice to your answers in Practice One. Circle any words that were difficult for you. For
more listening practice with those words, listen to the audio again.

1.   _____ a. The woman is looking in the mirror.
       _____ b. The woman is wearing a necklace.
       _____ c. She is combing her hair.
       _____ d. She is standing outside.
       _____ e. She is looking at herself.
       _____ f. The woman is building a closet.

2.   _____ a. He's riding in an elevator.
       _____ b. He's throwing something in the garbage.
       _____ c. He's wearing glasses.
       _____ d. He's pressing the button.
       _____ e. He's using a calculator.
       _____ f. He's erasing his paper.

3.   _____ a. They're playing volleyball.
       _____ b. They're playing badminton.
       _____ c. They're on a track.
       _____ d. Each team has two players.
       _____ e. They're all wearing long pants.
       _____ f. He's about to hit the shuttlecock.

4.   _____ a. They're taking food.
       _____ b. A mirror is hanging on the wall.
       _____ c. One woman is smiling.
       _____ d. The man is looking at the food.
       _____ e. They're all wearing glasses.
       _____ f. They're holding plates.

Check your answers on page 208.

Test Hint 9

Focus on listening. Look quickly at the photograph. Then, concentrate on what you hear. The
TOEIC Bridge tests your English listening ability. It does not test your ability to examine
photographs in detail. It does not test your ability to memorize four answer choices. After one
question is finished, go immediately to the next picture. Look at it. Think about it. Be ready to
listen.

Practice One

Directions   Look at the photo once. Then, cover it with a piece of paper while you listen.
Do not look at the photo again. Listen carefully. Choose the true statement. *Note: This is
only an exercise. We do not recommend this practice during the actual test.*

1. Ⓐ   Ⓑ   Ⓒ   Ⓓ   2. Ⓐ   Ⓑ   Ⓒ   Ⓓ

3. Ⓐ   Ⓑ   Ⓒ   Ⓓ   4. Ⓐ   Ⓑ   Ⓒ   Ⓓ

Do NOT check your answers yet.

Vocabulary Power!

Use photographs to build your vocabulary. Look at the photographs in Test Hint 9.
For each, find one main thing whose English word you don't know. Ask a classmate the
meaning of the English word. Or, look it up in the dictionary. Write your new words on
the lines below. Take two minutes to memorize these four words. Talk about the
photographs. Practice using your new vocabulary.

1. _____*uniform*_____   3. _____
2. _____   4. _____

Practice Two

Directions   Look at the photographs in Practice One again. Do not cover them. Listen to
the audio again. Choose the true statement.

1. Ⓐ   Ⓑ   Ⓒ   Ⓓ   3. Ⓐ   Ⓑ   Ⓒ   Ⓓ
2. Ⓐ   Ⓑ   Ⓒ   Ⓓ   4. Ⓐ   Ⓑ   Ⓒ   Ⓓ

Check your answers on page 209.

Test Hint 10

Answer choices often *name things* that are in the photo. They may name objects, activities, people, situations, or emotions. Don't choose an answer just because it names something in the photo. Instead, listen for the actual meaning of the statement. Only one statement correctly describes the picture.

Example *Answer Choices that Name Things in the Photograph*

Statements	Things Named in the Photograph
(A) The man is in the water.	man: water
(B) The pool is full of swimmers.	pool: swimmers
√ (C) The man is diving.	man: dive (correct answer)
(D) The diver is jumping into the ocean.	diver: jump

Practice

Directions Look at the photographs. Listen to the audio. Choose the true statement for each photo.

1. Ⓐ   Ⓑ   Ⓒ   Ⓓ   **2.** Ⓐ   Ⓑ   Ⓒ   Ⓓ

3. Ⓐ   Ⓑ   Ⓒ   Ⓓ   4. Ⓐ   Ⓑ   Ⓒ   Ⓓ

Check your answers on page 209.

Test Hint 11

Incorrect answers often *sound similar* to words that describe the picture. They may have the same vowel sound. They may have the same first letter. They may rhyme. Don't choose an answer because of words that sound similar. Instead, listen for the actual meaning of the statement. Remember: Only one statement correctly describes the picture.

Example *Words that Sound Similar to Words that Describe the Picture*

Words that Sound Similar

√ (A) He's <u>walking</u> in the <u>rain</u>.
(B) He's <u>talking</u> on the <u>train</u>.

"talking" sounds like "walking":
  "train" sounds like "rain"

(C) He's <u>waiting</u> in the rain.
(D) He's walking into the <u>plane</u>.

"waiting" sounds like "walking"
"plane" sounds like "rain"

Practice

<u>Directions</u>   Look at the photographs for the previous hint, Test Hint 10. Listen to the new audio that goes with those photographs. Choose the true statement for each photo.

1. Ⓐ   Ⓑ   Ⓒ   Ⓓ   3. Ⓐ   Ⓑ   Ⓒ   Ⓓ
2. Ⓐ   Ⓑ   Ⓒ   Ⓓ   4. Ⓐ   Ⓑ   Ⓒ   Ⓓ

Check your answers on page 209.

Answer choices may use words *related to* the photo topic. Don't choose an answer just because it has related words. Learn to identify false answers with related words.

Example *Statements with Words Related to the Photo*

	Statements	Words Related to the Photo
	(A) Passengers are waiting for the airplane.	passenger: wait: airplane
√	(B) The airplane is at the airport.	airplane: airport
	(C) The pilots are in the terminal.	pilots: terminal
	(D) The jet is flying below the clouds.	jet: fly: clouds

Practice One

Directions   Look at the photographs. Listen to the audio. Choose the correct statement for each photo.

1. Ⓐ Ⓑ Ⓒ Ⓓ

2. Ⓐ Ⓑ Ⓒ Ⓓ

3. Ⓐ Ⓑ Ⓒ Ⓓ

4. Ⓐ Ⓑ Ⓒ Ⓓ

Check your answers in Practice Two.

Practice Two

Directions   Look at the photographs in Practice One again. Then, read the following audio script. Look for words that are related to the photo. Underline them.

1.   √ (A) The women are airplane passengers.
        (B) The passengers are waiting for take-off.
        (C) All the seats are empty.
        (D) They're riding motorcycles.

2.   (A) The woman is holding the baby.
        (B) The woman is a graduate.
        (C) The woman is in an ambulance.
    √ (D) The woman is pregnant.

3.   (A) They built a snowman.
    √ (B) It's cold and snowing.
        (C) The skiers are in the house.
        (D) Fog has settled in.

4.   (A) His hands are dirty.
    √ (B) He's throwing away garbage.
        (C) He's storing things in a bin.
        (D) He's throwing rocks in the lake.

Check your answers on page 209.

Practice Test

Directions   You will see a picture in your test book. You will hear four short statements. Choose the statement that best describes the picture.

1.

Ⓐ   Ⓑ   Ⓒ   Ⓓ

2.

Ⓐ   Ⓑ   Ⓒ   Ⓓ

3.

Ⓐ   Ⓑ   Ⓒ   Ⓓ

4.

Ⓐ   Ⓑ   Ⓒ   Ⓓ

5.

Ⓐ   Ⓑ   Ⓒ   Ⓓ

6.

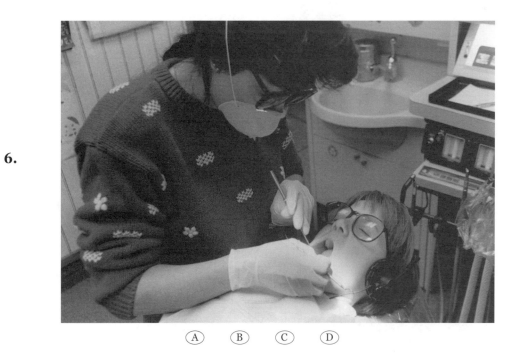

Ⓐ   Ⓑ   Ⓒ   Ⓓ

7.

   Ⓐ   Ⓑ   Ⓒ   Ⓓ

8.

   Ⓐ   Ⓑ   Ⓒ   Ⓓ

Check your answers on page 210.

Test Summary

Part II of the TOEIC Bridge tests spoken English. It tests your ability to answer simple questions. It also tests your ability to respond to simple statements. There are 20 questions. They use short, simple grammar. They are spoken slowly.

Part II of the TOEIC Bridge tests listening only. You will hear the questions or statements and the responses. They are not printed in your test book.

Sample Question

You will hear: Where did you buy your sweater?

Then you will hear: (A) At the mall.
                          (B) Size large.
                          (C) Last week.

In your test book, you will see: Ⓐ Ⓑ Ⓒ

The best response to the question, "Where did you buy your sweater?" is choice (A), "At the mall." You should choose answer (A).

Taking the Test

First you will hear a question or statement. Then you will hear three possible responses. You must choose the best response: (A), (B), or (C). You will hear each question and the responses only one time. You must listen carefully.

On the TOEIC Bridge, all correct answers help your score. Incorrect answers do not count against you. Therefore, answer every question, even if you aren't sure.

Timing

The listening comprehension section is 25 minutes in total. Part II takes about 7 minutes. The timing is set by the audio recording. You must work as fast as the recording goes.

Learn these important words for Part II of the test. These words occur several times in this book.

Family

1. grandparents *n.*
Tommy's <u>grandparents</u> played golf.

2. husband *n.*
Each team had a <u>husband</u> and a <u>wife</u>.

3. wife *n.*

Physical

4. haircut/get a haircut *n./v.*
One woman is <u>getting a haircut</u>.

5. hurt *v.*
The hairdresser <u>hurt</u> her foot.

6. stomach *n.*
The little girl is showing her <u>stomach</u>.

7. weigh *v.* **weight** *n.*
The man doesn't <u>weigh</u> much. What is his <u>weight</u>?

Restaurants

8. bill *n.* The men need to pay their <u>bill</u>.

9. favorite *adj.* The girl got her <u>favorite</u> dessert.

10. full *adj.* After lunch, the men were <u>full</u>.

11. hungry *adj.* The boy was very <u>hungry</u> at lunchtime.

12. order *v./n.* He <u>ordered</u> a big lunch.

13. snack *n./v.* His mom just ordered a <u>snack</u>.

School

14. forget/forgot *v.*

One student <u>forgot</u> about the test.

15. memorize *v.*

Other students are <u>memorizing</u> the words.

16. professor *n.*

The <u>professor</u> has a lot of books.

17. remember *v.*

One student didn't <u>remember</u> his pens and pencils.

Shopping

18. buy/bought *v.*   She is <u>buying</u> groceries.

19. cash/cashier *n./n.*

The <u>cashier</u> is weighing the mushrooms.

20. change *n.*

One shopper is taking her <u>change</u>.

21. credit card *n.*

The woman wants to pay with her <u>credit card</u>.

22. expensive *adj.*

The mushrooms are <u>expensive</u>.

Travel

23. find/found *v.*

The travelers <u>found</u> their luggage in the lobby.

Sports

24. catch/caught *v.*

The right fielder <u>caught</u> the ball.

25. lose/lost *v.*

The Flames <u>lost</u> the baseball game.

26. win/won *v.*

The Moons <u>won</u> the game.

Test Hint 13

As you listen to the responses, mark the answer that seems correct. Mark it lightly. If you change the answer, you can easily erase the mark. If you keep the answer, remember to darken it. Answer quickly. There are only eight seconds between questions.

Practice

Directions   You will hear a question or statement. Then you will hear three responses. You will hear each question and the possible responses only once. Listen carefully. Choose the best response.

1. (A)   (B)   (C)   5. (A)   (B)   (C)
2. (A)   (B)   (C)   6. (A)   (B)   (C)
3. (A)   (B)   (C)   7. (A)   (B)   (C)
4. (A)   (B)   (C)   8. (A)   (B)   (C)

Check your answers on page 211.

Test Hint 14

Most questions in Part II are information questions. They ask *who, what, when, where, why, how, which,* or *whose.* Understand the kind of information that is asked for. Understand the kind of information that is given. Make sure that the answer answers the question that was asked. If the question asks "where," the correct response must tell *where.*

Example *Information Question and Answer Choices*

Where did you buy your boots?   **where**

  (A) Thirty dollars.   how much
  (B) Just last week.   when
  (C) At the mall.   where (Correct response answers "where?")

Only (C) answers the question "where." The other choices answer different information questions.

Example Questions	Example Answers
Who paid the bill?	My wife paid it.
What is that?	It's a huge butterfly.
What color is his hair?	His hair is gray.
What time does the movie end?	It ends at 9:15.
What kind of street do you live on?	It's very quiet.
When will the bus arrive?	In a few minutes.
Where do you live?	We live in Sapporo.
Why is the office closed?	It's closed for the holiday.
How are you?	Fine, thank you.
How old is this milk?	Marla bought it a couple weeks ago.
How far is it to the bus stop?	It's about 500 meters.
How much were the tickets?	Ten thousand yen each.
Which color do you prefer?	I like the red.
Whose chair is this?	It's mine.

Practice

Directions   You will hear a question. Then you will hear three responses. Choose the best response.

1. (A)   (B)   (C)   5. (A)   (B)   (C)
2. (A)   (B)   (C)   6. (A)   (B)   (C)
3. (A)   (B)   (C)   7. (A)   (B)   (C)
4. (A)   (B)   (C)   8. (A)   (B)   (C)

Check your answers on page 211.

Test Hint 15

Part II has many Yes-No questions. A Yes-No question can be answered by "yes" or "no." Yes-No questions often have short answers. Short answers have three parts.

1. "yes" or "no"
2. a pronoun (I/you/he)
3. a helping verb (do/be/can). This verb repeats from the question.

Yes-No Questions	Examples of Short Answers	
Do you fly on Asia Air?	Yes, I do.	No, I don't.
Did you take your passport?	Yes, I did.	No, I didn't.
Are you bringing any carry-on bags?	Yes, I am.	No, I'm not.
Were you late for your flight?	Yes, I was.	No, I wasn't.
Will we board soon?	Yes, you will.	No, you won't.
Can I use the restroom?	Yes, you can.	No, you can't.

Practice 🎧

Directions   You will hear a question. Then you will hear three responses. Choose the best response.

1. (A)   (B)   (C)   5. (A)   (B)   (C)
2. (A)   (B)   (C)   6. (A)   (B)   (C)
3. (A)   (B)   (C)   7. (A)   (B)   (C)
4. (A)   (B)   (C)   8. (A)   (B)   (C)

Check your answers on page 212.

Test Hint 16

A few Part II dialogs begin with a statement. They do not begin with a question. For these, you must choose the best response to the statement.

Example   *Statement-Response Dialog*

I'm hungry.
  (A) Me, too. Let's stop at the cafeteria.
  (B) Steak and potatoes for dinner.
  (C) In the kitchen.

In the example, "I'm hungry" is a statement. It is not a question. The best response to "I'm hungry" is "Me, too. Let's stop at the cafeteria." You should choose (A).

Practice 🎧

Directions   You will hear a question. Then you will hear three responses. Choose the best response.

1. (A)   (B)   (C)   4. (A)   (B)   (C)
2. (A)   (B)   (C)   5. (A)   (B)   (C)
3. (A)   (B)   (C)   6. (A)   (B)   (C)

Do NOT check your answers yet. Go on to Test Hint 17.

Test Hint 17

Increase your chances of finding the correct answer. Note incorrect choices. This will increase your chance of finding the correct answer choice. Answer every question, even if you aren't sure of the correct response.

Example *Increase Your Chances of Finding the Correct Answer*

(woman) The door has been open all day long.
(man) (A) The store is closed.
        (B) This house needs fresh air.
        (C) Room 722.

Choice (B) explains why the door has been open all day. You may not know that (B) is the correct response. However, you may understand that choice (C) is not a reasonable answer. Cross (C) out very lightly. If you do not know the correct answer, guess. There are now only two choices remaining. You have a 50-50 chance of guessing correctly.

Practice

Directions   Listen to the talks in Test Hint 16 again. While you listen, note incorrect answers. (If you cross out incorrect answers, cross lightly and erase afterwards.) If you are not sure of the correct answer, guess.

1. Ⓐ Ⓑ Ⓒ   4. Ⓐ Ⓑ Ⓒ
2. Ⓐ Ⓑ Ⓒ   5. Ⓐ Ⓑ Ⓒ
3. Ⓐ Ⓑ Ⓒ   6. Ⓐ Ⓑ Ⓒ

Check your answers on page 212.

Test Hint 18

Listen for indirect answers. Answers in Part II often give information that answers the question indirectly. They do not directly answer the question.

Example *Indirect Answer to a Question*

What's your favorite city?
    (A) The address is 1015 9th Street.
    (B) In a big city.
    (C) Actually, I prefer small towns.

Choice (C) answers the question indirectly. The person doesn't have a favorite city. In fact, the person doesn't even like big cities. The person likes small towns. Choice (C) answers the question indirectly.

Practice One

Directions   You will hear a question. Then you will hear three responses. Choose the best response.

1. Ⓐ Ⓑ Ⓒ   5. Ⓐ Ⓑ Ⓒ
2. Ⓐ Ⓑ Ⓒ   6. Ⓐ Ⓑ Ⓒ
3. Ⓐ Ⓑ Ⓒ   7. Ⓐ Ⓑ Ⓒ
4. Ⓐ Ⓑ Ⓒ   8. Ⓐ Ⓑ Ⓒ

Check your answers on page 213.

Practice Two

Directions   In the chart below, read the questions from Practice One. Then read some possible direct answers to the questions. Match each question to a direct answer.

Questions	Direct Answers
1. When will the talk start?	a. It's my brush, but everybody uses it.
2. How many chairs do we need?	b. No, I can't.
3. Which color would you like, the gold or the red?	c. At 2:00.
4. Can I use your pen?	d. It's raining outside.
5. Whose brush is this?	e. Whichever one is cheaper.
6. Could you please hold my umbrella?	f. No, you can't.
7. Did you get your change?	g. Yes, I got my change.
8. Why is your hair wet?	h. We need at least 60.

Which type of answer is easier to identify, direct or indirect?

Check your answers on page 213.

Test Hint 19

You will see questions on the TOEIC Bridge that give a choice. Make sure that the answer addresses the choice.

Example *Questions that Give a Choice*

Would you rather play tennis or take a walk?
    (A) Yes, that sounds nice.
    (B) Thirty minutes or so.
    (C) I really like walking.

Practice

Directions   You will hear a question. Then you will hear three responses. Choose the best response.

1. Ⓐ Ⓑ Ⓒ   4. Ⓐ Ⓑ Ⓒ
2. Ⓐ Ⓑ Ⓒ   5. Ⓐ Ⓑ Ⓒ
3. Ⓐ Ⓑ Ⓒ   6. Ⓐ Ⓑ Ⓒ

Check your answers on page 213.

Test Hint 20

Some answers repeat the first word or two of the question. The answers may then seem to address the question. Do not choose an answer because it starts like a correct answer. Always listen for the real meaning.

Example A *Answers Whose First Word(s) Seem to Address the Question*

Can she use your pen?

(A) Yes, we can.
(B) No, she did not.
(C) Sure, it's in my purse.

Yes-No questions often have Yes-No answers. Answer choices (A) and (B) begin with "yes" or "no." However, they don't answer the question. Choice (C) is the correct answer. "It" refers to "pen." "In my purse" tells where the pen is. "Sure" means "yes."

Example B *Answers Whose First Word(s) Seem to Address the Question*

Why didn't you say "hi" when you saw me?

Answer Words

(A) Because they were in a box.
(B) So the banker could see.
(C) You were all the way across the street.

Why . . . Because
Why . . . So

The question "why" asks for a reason. Reasons are often introduced with the words "because" or "so." Answer choices (A) and (B) give reasons. They use the words "because" and "so." However, they do not answer the question. Choice (C) answers the question, "Why didn't you say "hi"? The person did not say "hi" because he was far away.

Practice

Directions You will hear a question. Then you will hear three responses. Choose the best response.

1. Ⓐ   Ⓑ   Ⓒ   5. Ⓐ   Ⓑ   Ⓒ
2. Ⓐ   Ⓑ   Ⓒ   6. Ⓐ   Ⓑ   Ⓒ
3. Ⓐ   Ⓑ   Ⓒ   7. Ⓐ   Ⓑ   Ⓒ
4. Ⓐ   Ⓑ   Ⓒ   8. Ⓐ   Ⓑ   Ⓒ

Check your answers on page 214.

Some answer choices repeat question words. However, these answers may take your attention from the correct answer. Don't choose an answer because of one or two repeated words. Always listen for the real meaning.

Example *Answers that Repeat Words from the Question*

	Words that Repeat in Question and Answer

Who is driving to the concert?
   (A) They like concerts.   concert
   (B) My sister is.
   (C) I'm taking driving lessons.   driving

Choice (B) answers the question, "Who is driving to the concert?" It does not repeat any words from the question. Nevertheless, it answers the question.

Practice

Directions   You will hear a question. Then you will hear three responses. Choose the best response.

1. (A)	(B)	(C)		**5.** (A)	(B)	(C)	
2. (A)	(B)	(C)		**6.** (A)	(B)	(C)	
3. (A)	(B)	(C)		**7.** (A)	(B)	(C)	
4. (A)	(B)	(C)		**8.** (A)	(B)	(C)	

Check your answers on page 215.

Some answers have words that sound similar to words in the question. These answers may then seem correct. However, they may only take your attention from the correct answer. Don't choose an answer because of similar-sounding words. Always listen for the real meaning.

Example *Answers with Words that Sound Similar to Words in the Question*

	Words that Sound Similar

Have you met my parents?
   (A) I'd like a pair, thank you.   pair/parents
   (B) It's a brand new mitt.   mitt/met
   (C) Yes, when they were here last year.

Choice (C) answers the question, "Have you met my parents." The speaker did meet the parents. They met last year when the parents were here.

Practice

Directions   You will hear a question. Then you will hear three responses. You will hear each question and the possible responses only once. Listen carefully. Choose the best response.

1. Ⓐ   Ⓑ   Ⓒ   5. Ⓐ   Ⓑ   Ⓒ
2. Ⓐ   Ⓑ   Ⓒ   6. Ⓐ   Ⓑ   Ⓒ
3. Ⓐ   Ⓑ   Ⓒ   7. Ⓐ   Ⓑ   Ⓒ
4. Ⓐ   Ⓑ   Ⓒ   8. Ⓐ   Ⓑ   Ⓒ

Check your answers on page 215.

Test Hint 23

Some answer choices have words that relate to words in the question. These answers may then seem correct. However, they may only take your attention away from the correct answer. Don't choose an answer because of one or two related words. Always listen for the real meaning.

Example *Words that Relate to Words in the Question*

	Words that Relate
Who wants to <u>play</u> <u>volleyball</u>?	
(A) She's wearing a hair <u>net</u>.	"Net" relates to "volleyball."
(B) I do.	
(C) They're in the <u>theater</u>.	"Theater" relates to "play."

Choice (B) answers the question, "Who wants to play volleyball." It is a simple Yes-No question with a simple Yes-No answer.

Practice

Directions   You will hear a question. Then you will hear three responses. Choose the best response.

1. Ⓐ   Ⓑ   Ⓒ   4. Ⓐ   Ⓑ   Ⓒ
2. Ⓐ   Ⓑ   Ⓒ   5. Ⓐ   Ⓑ   Ⓒ
3. Ⓐ   Ⓑ   Ⓒ   6. Ⓐ   Ⓑ   Ⓒ

Check your answers on page 216.

Practice Test

Directions   You will hear a question or statement. Then you will hear three responses.
You will hear each question and the possible responses only once. Listen carefully.
Choose the best response.

1. (A) (B) (C)
2. (A) (B) (C)
3. (A) (B) (C)
4. (A) (B) (C)
5. (A) (B) (C)

6. (A) (B) (C)
7. (A) (B) (C)
8. (A) (B) (C)
9. (A) (B) (C)
10. (A) (B) (C)

Check your answers on page 217.

PART III — Short Conversations and Short Talks

Test Summary

Part III of the TOEIC Bridge tests your understanding of spoken English. It tests both listening and reading skills. There are 15 questions. Each question is based on a short conversation or short talk.

The conversations are between two people. The question and the possible answers are printed in your test book.

The talks are announcements. The announcements are one person speaking to a group. They are usually under 60 words long. They are more formal than the conversations.

The conversations and talks are mixed together in the test. (This book uses the word "talk" to refer to conversations and talks.)

Sample Question: Short Conversation

You will hear:

(man)	Do you have any grandchildren?
(woman)	Yes, we have twelve.
(man)	Twelve! We have three sons, but none of them have children yet.

Then you will read:

How many grandchildren does the woman have?

(A) None.
(B) Three.
(C) Twelve.
(D) Twenty.

The correct response to the question, "How many grandchildren does the woman have?" is choice (C), "Twelve." You should choose answer (C).

Sample Question: Short Talk

You will hear:

(man) It is now five o'clock and the beach is closed. All swimmers must get out of the water. It is five o'clock. The lifeguards are now off duty. All swimmers must get out of the water. Thank you.

Then you will read:

Why do swimmers have to stop swimming?

    (A) They need to rest for five minutes.
    (B) The water is too cold.
    (C) The lifeguards are leaving.
    (D) The water is dirty.

The best response to the question, "Why do swimmers have to stop swimming?" is choice (C), "The lifeguards are leaving." You should choose answer (C).

Taking the Test

You will read a question about a conversation or a talk. You will hear a conversation or talk (see examples). You will read four possible answers. You must choose the best answer: (A), (B), (C), or (D).

On the TOEIC Bridge, all correct answers help your score. Incorrect answers do not count against you. Therefore, answer every question, even if you aren't sure.

Timing

The listening comprehension section is 25 minutes in total. Part III takes about 7 minutes. The timing is set by the audio recording. You must work as fast as the recording goes.

Learn these important words for Part III of the test. These words occur several times in this book.

Family

1. **daughter** *n.*
   Her <u>daughter</u> is a nurse.
2. **grandchildren** *n.*
   She has many <u>grandchildren</u>.
3. **son** *n.*
   Her <u>son</u> has four children.

Physical

4. **appointment** *n.*
   make an appointment *v.*
   She's <u>making an appointment</u> with the doctor.
   Her <u>appointment</u> is on Tuesday.

Restaurants

5. **reservations** *n.*
   make reservations *v.*
   Somebody is <u>making reservations</u> for dinner.
6. **tip** *n.*
   There's a <u>tip</u> on the table.

School

7. **homework** *n.*
   The student is doing his <u>homework</u>.
8. **quarter** *n.*
   It must be winter <u>quarter</u>.
9. **register** *v.*
   They are waiting to <u>register</u>.

Shopping

10. be in style *v.* One lady's dress <u>is in style</u>.
11. cheap *adj.* One lady is looking at a <u>cheap</u> shirt.
12. customer *n.* One <u>customer</u> is paying.
13. department *n.* They're in the women's <u>department</u>.
14. try on *v.* One woman is <u>trying on</u> a jacket.

Sports

15. exercise *v./n.* The runners are <u>exercising</u>.
16. gym *n.* They're in the <u>gym</u>.
17. practice *v./n.*
The volleyball players are <u>practicing</u> their serves. Basketball <u>practice</u> is outside today.

Transportation

18. arrive *v.*
Passengers <u>arrive</u> two hours before their flight.
19. be cancelled *v.* Some flights <u>are cancelled</u>.
20. depart *v.* One airplane is <u>departing</u>.

Travel

21. announcement *n.*
There are lots of <u>announcements</u> about parking.
22. check in *v.* **check-in** *n.*
Passengers are waiting to <u>check in</u>.

II. Focusing on Correct Responses

Test Hint 24

Listen carefully to the whole talk. Do not mark your final answer while the speakers are talking. You might miss important information. If you think an answer is correct, mark it lightly. Do not stop listening. If you change your answer later, you can erase your first mark. Work quickly. There are 9 seconds between questions.

Practice

Directions   Read the question. Listen to the talk. Read the four possible answers. Choose the best answer.

1. Ⓐ   Ⓑ   Ⓒ   Ⓓ   4. Ⓐ   Ⓑ   Ⓒ   Ⓓ
2. Ⓐ   Ⓑ   Ⓒ   Ⓓ   5. Ⓐ   Ⓑ   Ⓒ   Ⓓ
3. Ⓐ   Ⓑ   Ⓒ   Ⓓ   6. Ⓐ   Ⓑ   Ⓒ   Ⓓ

1. What does the man want to do?

   (A) Make dinner reservations.
   (B) Get his house cleaned.
   (C) Talk to the police about the trouble.
   (D) See a dentist.

2. How much does it cost to send the letter?

   (A) One dollar.
   (B) Two dollars.
   (C) Two dollars and fifteen cents.
   (D) Three dollars and fifty cents.

3. Where is the speaker?

   (A) In an airport.
   (B) In a train station.
   (C) In a hospital.
   (D) At a school.

4. When does the sale start?

   (A) In two days.
   (B) On Tuesday.
   (C) In three days.
   (D) On the thirtieth.

5. Why was the flight canceled?

   (A) Mechanical failure.
   (B) There was no pilot.
   (C) Bad weather.
   (D) There was an airline strike.

6. What is the speaker talking about?

   (A) Trees.
   (B) The temperature.
   (C) A basketball game.
   (D) Baskets.

Check your answers on page 219.

Read the question before you hear the talk. Then listen to the talk. This is important. It will focus your listening. Then, you can listen for the answer to the question. You won't have to memorize information that isn't related to the answer.

Practice

Directions   Read the question. Listen to the talk. Read the four possible answers. Choose the best answer.

Note: Before each short talk, you will hear a reminder. It advises you to read the question before listening to the talk. The reminders help you to develop a good habit: reading the question first. On the real Bridge test, there are no reminders.

1.	Ⓐ	Ⓑ	Ⓒ	Ⓓ
2.	Ⓐ	Ⓑ	Ⓒ	Ⓓ
3.	Ⓐ	Ⓑ	Ⓒ	Ⓓ

4.	Ⓐ	Ⓑ	Ⓒ	Ⓓ
5.	Ⓐ	Ⓑ	Ⓒ	Ⓓ
6.	Ⓐ	Ⓑ	Ⓒ	Ⓓ

1. **What does the man want to do now?**

   (A) Swim.
   (B) Drink some water.
   (C) Try on watches.
   (D) Learn the time.

2. **Whose uniform is it?**

   (A) The woman's.
   (B) The woman's son's.
   (C) The man's.
   (D) The man's son's.

3. **Where does the daughter go to school?**

   (A) An elementary school.
   (B) A middle school.
   (C) A high school.
   (D) A university.

4. **Why doesn't the woman try on the boots?**

   (A) Because the man will buy them.
   (B) Because they're not her size.
   (C) Because they're out of style.
   (D) Because they're too expensive.

5. **Who is playing the guitar?**

   (A) The man.
   (B) The woman's daughter.
   (C) The daughter's teacher.
   (D) A professional.

6. **How will the woman make her appointment?**

   (A) On the Web.
   (B) By phone.
   (C) By mail.
   (D) In person.

Check your answers on page 219.

The answer to a question is mentioned many times in a talk. You may hear several references to the correct answer. You do not need to memorize details. The correct answer is rarely found in a single detail.

Example *Announcement with Several References to the Correct Answer*

You will hear:
Ticket windows one, two, and three are now open. Stand on the blue line, the red line, or the yellow line. Three cashiers are now open. Moviegoers are asked to wait in three separate lines. If you are planning to see an R-rated movie, have your ID ready.

Where is the announcement being heard?

    (A) In a paint store.
    (B) In a train station.
    (C) At a subway station.
    (D) At a movie theater.

Choice (D) is the correct response. The talk refers to movie theaters many times. The references include ticket window, cashier, moviegoer, R-rated, movie.

Practice

Directions Read the question. Listen to the talk. Read the four possible answers. Choose the best answer.

1. (A) (B) (C) (D)   4. (A) (B) (C) (D)
2. (A) (B) (C) (D)   5. (A) (B) (C) (D)
3. (A) (B) (C) (D)   6. (A) (B) (C) (D)

1. Who is talking?

    (A) A student.
    (B) A high school teacher.
    (C) An author.
    (D) A sports coach.

2. Where is the wedding ring now?

    (A) In the restroom.
    (B) At a jewelry store.
    (C) At a police station.
    (D) In the lost and found.

3. What should listeners do?

    (A) Get on the bus.
    (B) Take the elevator.
    (C) Use caution.
    (D) Take off their shoes.

4. Where would you hear this talk?

    (A) At a hospital.
    (B) At a bank.
    (C) At a school.
    (D) At a store.

5. Why should people go to their seats?

    (A) The show will begin.

    (B) The plane is landing.

    (C) Five passengers are missing.

    (D) The trip has ended.

6. What is the topic of the announcement?

    (A) Airport safety.

    (B) The location of the check-in.

    (C) Smoking.

    (D) A canceled flight.

Check your answers on page 220.

Test Hint 27

Create a mental picture of the speakers and the setting. Imagine real people talking in a real place. See the speakers in your mind. Imagine their faces. See them as your family and friends. Imagine the place: a store, a bus, a theater. See them in the place. See the clothes they are wearing. See the weather. This will make their conversations real for you. It will be easier to remember who said what.

You must create your mental picture as fast as you can. The talks are short.

Note: Many test-takers feel that Part III is the most difficult. It is difficult if you can't remember what was said. Do not think of two unknown English-speakers talking on an audio recording. If you do, naturally you may not remember their conversation.

Example *Making Speakers and Places Real*

    (W) No running on the pool deck.

    (M) I wasn't running; I was walking fast.

    (W) The decks are wet and running is dangerous.

	General	**Specific Example**
Where are they?	A pool	Smith Pool
Who is the woman?	A lifeguard	My swimming teacher, Sally
Who is the man?	A swimmer	My brother, John

What do you think the lifeguard is wearing?	A swimsuit.
How do you think the man feels?	He is probably embarrassed.

Practice

Directions   Read the question. Listen to the talk. Read the four possible answers. Choose the best answer.

1. (A) (B) (C) (D)

2. (A) (B) (C) (D)

3. (A) (B) (C) (D)

4. (A) (B) (C) (D)

5. (A) (B) (C) (D)

6. (A) (B) (C) (D)

1. Why can't they see?

   (A) The stage is too far away.
   (B) Everyone is standing.
   (C) Their seats are bad.
   (D) It's too dark.

2. What is the man looking for?

   (A) Fruit.
   (B) A CD.
   (C) A magazine.
   (D) A drink.

3. What does the man want?

   (A) A dog.
   (B) A snack.
   (C) Her homework.
   (D) A meeting time.

4. Where will they go?

   (A) To a restaurant.
   (B) To a movie.
   (C) To work.
   (D) To a park.

5. What does the woman want?

   (A) Stamps.
   (B) To go jogging.
   (C) The man's umbrella.
   (D) A new watch.

6. Where will they meet?

   (A) Four o'clock.
   (B) The library.
   (C) At work.
   (D) At school.

Check your answers on page 220.

Test Hint 28

Focus on the words that you know in a talk. You will not understand every word. This is common. Work from the words you do know. Do not let unfamiliar terms stop you. Keep going.

Example *Focusing on Known Words in an Announcement*

Attention, <u>shoppers</u>. For security reasons, <u>backpacks</u>, <u>large bags</u>, and merchandise from <u>other stores</u> are <u>not allowed</u> in the <u>store</u>. <u>Please check</u> your belongings <u>at</u> the security <u>desk</u> <u>before you shop</u>. <u>Backpacks, bags</u>, and purchases <u>from other stores</u> are prohibited inside Marvin's. <u>These</u> items <u>must be left in your car</u>. In addition, <u>free</u>, guarded <u>lockers are</u> <u>available</u> at the security <u>center by the main entry</u>. <u>Thank you</u>.

What is the purpose of the talk?
   (A) To announce that the store is closing.
   (B) To tell shoppers about a sale on backpacks.
   (C) To encourage shoppers to use their own bags.
   (D) To keep some things out of the store.

The correct answer is (D). The announcement tells shoppers they can't bring certain things into the store. The things include backpacks, large bags, and merchandise.

Practice

Directions   Read the question. Listen to the talk. Read the four possible answers.
Choose the best answer.

1. When does the man want to meet his professor?

   (A) This week.
   (B) Next week.
   (C) On Friday.
   (D) Next quarter.

2. Where is this announcement being heard?

   (A) At an airport.
   (B) In a post office.
   (C) On the radio
   (D) In a restaurant.

3. What do the women do together?

   (A) Practice the piano.
   (B) Exercise.
   (C) Work.
   (D) Ride horses.

4. Where are the uniforms?

   (A) In the store.
   (B) In the locker room.
   (C) In his office.
   (D) In the sports bag.

Check your answers on page 221.

Test Hint 29

Understand information questions. These questions asks who, what, when, where, why, how, whose, and which. Information questions are in every part of the TOEIC Bridge Test.

Practice

Directions   Read the question. Listen to the talk. Read the four possible answers. Choose the best answer.

1.	Ⓐ	Ⓑ	Ⓒ	Ⓓ		5.	Ⓐ	Ⓑ	Ⓒ	Ⓓ
2.	Ⓐ	Ⓑ	Ⓒ	Ⓓ		6.	Ⓐ	Ⓑ	Ⓒ	Ⓓ
3.	Ⓐ	Ⓑ	Ⓒ	Ⓓ		7.	Ⓐ	Ⓑ	Ⓒ	Ⓓ
4.	Ⓐ	Ⓑ	Ⓒ	Ⓓ		8.	Ⓐ	Ⓑ	Ⓒ	Ⓓ

1. What are they discussing?

   (A) A hair style.

   (B) A belt.

   (C) A hat.

   (D) A model.

2. Why can't the man join the tour?

   (A) He arrived late.

   (B) He doesn't have enough money.

   (C) The tour was cancelled.

   (D) His son is too young.

3. What time does the woman want her reservation?

   (A) 6:00.

   (B) 6:30.

   (C) 7:00.

   (D) 7:30.

4. How often does the woman clean her house?

   (A) Every day.

   (B) Rarely.

   (C) Saturdays and Sundays.

   (D) Once a week.

5. How do you start the timer?

   (A) Click on "start."

   (B) Pull the knob.

   (C) Push the button.

   (D) Turn the handle.

6. Where are the speakers?

   (A) In the gym.

   (B) On the first floor.

   (C) In the basement.

   (D) On the second floor.

7. What's wrong with the uniform?

   (A) It turned pink.

   (B) It's torn.

   (C) It's too small.

   (D) It's missing.

8. Why do they like Disneyland for their grandchildren?

   (A) The weather is good.

   (B) There's a lot to do.

   (C) It's cheap.

   (D) It's safe.

Check your answers on page 221.

Listen for keys to the speaker and the location of a talk. Three common questions about short talks are 1. *Who is speaking?* 2.*Where is the announcement being heard?* and 3. *Where is the speaker?* Knowing the location can tell you the speaker. Knowing the speaker can tell you the location. Listen for the key words that answer these questions.

Example *Announcement with Keys to Speaker and Location*

If you are here for mail pick-up *only*, I can help you. Pick-up only is at window one. I can't sell stamps or weigh packages here. Mail pick-up at window one.

Who is speaking?
    (A) A doctor.
    (B) A postal worker.
    (C) A taxi driver.
    (D) A beautician.

Choice (B) answers the question, "Who is speaking?" Several words in the talk indicate that this announcement is in a post office: *mail, pick-up, stamps, weigh packages, window.*

Practice One

Directions   For each announcement, one of the three questions will be asked: *Who is speaking? Where is the announcement being heard?* or *Where is the speaker?* First, read the question. Then listen to the audio. Choose the best answer.

1. (A) (B) (C) (D)   5. (A) (B) (C) (D)
2. (A) (B) (C) (D)   6. (A) (B) (C) (D)
3. (A) (B) (C) (D)   7. (A) (B) (C) (D)
4. (A) (B) (C) (D)   8. (A) (B) (C) (D)

1. Where is the announcement being heard?

    (A) Hospital.
    (B) Sports event.
    (C) Radio station.
    (D) Beach/pool.

2. Where is the announcement being heard?

    (A) At a swimming pool.
    (B) In a theater.
    (C) On an airplane.
    (D) At a museum.

3. Where is the speaker?

    (A) In an airport.
    (B) In a restaurant.
    (C) In a furniture store.
    (D) At a party.

4. Where is the speaker?

    (A) In an airport.
    (B) In a post office.
    (C) At a sports event.
    (D) In a luggage store.

5. Where is the announcement being heard?

   (A) In a theater.
   (B) In an office.
   (C) In a train station.
   (D) At a sports event.

6. Where is the speaker?

   (A) In a museum.
   (B) In a bus station.
   (C) In a jewelry store.
   (D) At a beach.

7. Who is speaking?

   (A) A bus driver.
   (B) A secretary.
   (C) A dentist.
   (D) A lifeguard.

8. Where is the announcement being heard?

   (A) On the radio.
   (B) At the airport.
   (C) In a department store.
   (D) At a museum.

Check your answers in the following practice.

Practice Two

Directions Read the audio script for each announcement in Practice One. Circle the words that tell you about the speaker and the location.

1. (C) You're listening to KBIQ Light Jazz at 1040 on your AM dial. Stay tuned for sports, news and weather, coming up after this commercial announcement.

2. (C) Ladies and Gentlemen, the captain has turned on the seat belt sign. Please return to your seats and fasten your seat belts. Thank you.

3. (B) Leslie Hatsfield. Party of four. Leslie Hatsfield. Your table is ready. The hostess is now seating the Hatsfield party of four. Last call. Thank you.

4. (A) Many bags look alike. Please take a moment to ensure that the bag you claim is yours by matching the claim check with the tag on your luggage.

5. (D) Fifteen–love, Louise Ellen serving. From where I'm sitting, that looks like a net ball. Net. This is her second serve. Tracy returns it. And Louise Ellen comes to net. What a rally this is. It's deep left, and she pushes Tracy all the way into the alley. Return . . . and it's out. Thirty–love.

6. (A) The show just opened in June, and we've already had over 30,000 visitors. One reason this art is so popular is that it's famous: Everybody knows the word Impressionism. Another reason is that this art is timeless. Now, let's start with this Picasso and talk about why it has been around for so many years.

7. (B) Mark Hanson, you have a call waiting on line three. Mark Hanson, caller holding on line 3.

8. (C) Shoppers: Remember: Only six items are allowed in the changing rooms. If you would like to try on more than six items, please ask the clerk to store your extra items outside of your changing room. Only six items are allowed in at one time.

Check your answers on page 222.

Test Hint 31

Announcements on the TOEIC Bridge usually occur in the same places. Learn the words that signal each of these locations.

Common Places for Announcements			
airport	*bus*	*museum*	*post office*
radio	*school*	*theater*	*TV*
beach/pool	*store*	*office*	
restaurant	*sports event*	*train station*	

Practice

<u>Directions</u>   Study the word lists. Choose a place name from the box above. Write it on the line.

1. *train station*

track	arrive	depart	seat
ticket	no-smoking car		

2. _____

art/artist	sculpture	painting
portrait	show	

3. _____

news	weather	lightning	storm
thunder	local/national/world	channel	cable
advertisement			

4. _____

principal	class	gym	homework
teacher	club		

5. _____

reservations	party of 4	table	order
menu	server	tip	bill

6. _____

line	fax machine	computer	copy
e-mail	letter	envelope	manager
secretary	schedule		

7. _____

mail	stamp	package	send
weigh	first-class		

8. _____

AM/FM	be tuned to	song	rock 'n' roll
jazz	news	weather	traffic

9. _____

bus stop	break	seat	driver
stand	fare	tour guide	

10. _____

player	ball	court	net
field	score	point	win
lose	basket	goal	team

11. _____

check-in	check-out	luggage	bags
carry-on	gate	passenger	flight
canceled	delayed	snack	meal
board	take-off	land	captain

12. _____

lifeguard	water	beach	swimmer
shower	deck	diving board	deep
shallow			

13. _____

department	floor	sale	elevator
customer service	clothing	jewelry	try on
coupon	clerk	shoppers	

14. _____

tickets	stage	seat	aisle
row	curtain	intermission	movie
play	actor/actress	audience	

Check your answers on page 222.

Test Hint 32

Answer choices may purposely include words to distract your attention. They may repeat or sound similar to question or topic words. They may relate to the topic. The answers may then seem to be correct. Don't choose answers only because of repeating, similar, or related words. Listen for meaning. Choose the answer that makes sense.

Example *Answers with Words that Repeat, Sound Similar, or Relate to Words in the Question*

    (W) Is this sweater in style?
    (M) Oh, yes. Mid-length sleeves are really fashionable this year.
    (W) Then I'll buy it in red.

What is the woman buying?	**Words that Repeat, Sound the Same, or Relate**
√ (A) A sweater.	"Sweater" repeats: "Sweater" relates to "sleeves."
(B) A fashion magazine.	"Fashion" repeats: "Magazines" relate to "style."
(C) Bread.	"Bread" sounds similar to "red."
(D) A red skirt.	"Red" repeats.

Practice

Directions   Read the question. Listen to the talk. Read the four possible answers. Choose the best answer.

1. Where do they work?

    (A) In an apartment.
    (B) In a department store.
    (C) In a school.
    (D) In a theater.

2. What sport will they play?

    (A) Badminton.
    (B) Basketball.
    (C) Tennis.
    (D) Pool.

3. What did the woman do last night?

    (A) She took a class.
    (B) She registered.
    (C) She posted his Web page.
    (D) She paid her tuition.

4. Where would you hear this reminder?

    (A) In a flower shop.
    (B) In a hotel room.
    (C) At a cashier's aisle.
    (D) In a department store.

5. When will the bus arrive?

    (A) In thirteen minutes.
    (B) In thirty minutes.
    (C) In an hour.
    (D) In two hours.

6. How much tip will they leave?

    (A) Five percent.
    (B) Fifteen percent.
    (C) Twenty percent.
    (D) Twenty-five percent.

7. What is for sale?

   (A) Tickets.

   (B) Food.

   (C) Drinks.

   (D) Ice.

8. Why does the woman need to practice a lot?

   (A) To be a good athlete.

   (B) To play faster.

   (C) To have a healthy heart.

   (D) To learn the song by memory.

Check your answers on page 223.

Check your answers on page 223.

Test Hint 33

The speakers in the talks are a man and a woman. Pay attention to who says what. The correct answer may depend on it.

Example *Distinguishing Man and Woman Speakers*

(W) Do you exercise every day?

(M) I don't have time. I jog three or four days a week.

(W) Every other day—that's a lot. I only exercise once a week.

How often does the **man** exercise?

   (A) Never.

   (B) Every day.

   (C) Every other day.

   (D) Once a week.

How often does the **woman** exercise?

   (A) Never.

   (B) Every day.

   (C) Every other day.

   (D) Once a week.

The man exercises three or four days a week. You should choose answer (C) for the first question. The woman exercises only once a week. You should choose answer (D) for the second question.

Practice One

Directions   Read the question. Listen to the talk. Read the four possible answers. Choose the best answer.

1. (A) (B) (C) (D)
2. (A) (B) (C) (D)
3. (A) (B) (C) (D)

4. (A) (B) (C) (D)
5. (A) (B) (C) (D)
6. (A) (B) (C) (D)

1. Where does the woman live?

   (A) In a city.

   (B) In the countryside.

   (C) On a farm.

   (D) At a university.

2. What will the woman do?

   (A) She'll make restaurant reservations.

   (B) She'll pick up the car.

   (C) She'll eat meat.

   (D) She'll call her husband.

3. What has the man been doing?

    (A) Changing his clothes.
    (B) Doing his homework.
    (C) Waiting.
    (D) Cleaning.

4. Why is the woman returning her chicken?

    (A) It's cold.
    (B) It's strange.
    (C) It isn't cooked.
    (D) It's too salty.

5. Who did the man give his tickets to?

    (A) His secretary.
    (B) His brother.
    (C) The woman.
    (D) His older son.

6. What does the man need to do now?

    (A) Talk to a customer.
    (B) Go to a meeting.
    (C) Talk to the woman.
    (D) Solve a problem.

Do NOT check your answers yet. Go on to Practice Two.

Practice Two

Directions   Listen to the audio for Practice One again. Read the new questions to go with the audio. Choose the best answer.

1. (A) (B) (C) (D)
2. (A) (B) (C) (D)
3. (A) (B) (C) (D)

4. (A) (B) (C) (D)
5. (A) (B) (C) (D)
6. (A) (B) (C) (D)

1. Where does the man live?

    (A) In a city.
    (B) In the countryside.
    (C) On a farm.
    (D) At a university.

2. What will the man do?

    (A) He'll make restaurant reservations.
    (B) He'll pick up the car.
    (C) He'll eat meat.
    (D) He'll call his wife.

3. What has the woman been doing?

    (A) Changing her clothes.
    (B) Doing her homework.
    (C) Waiting.
    (D) Cleaning.

4. Why is the man returning his chicken?

    (A) It's cold.
    (B) It's strange.
    (C) It isn't cooked.
    (D) It's too salty.

5. Who did the woman give her tickets to?

    (A) Her secretary.
    (B) Her brother.
    (C) The man.
    (D) Her older son.

6. What does the woman need to do now?

    (A) Talk to a customer.
    (B) Go to a meeting.
    (C) Talk to the man.
    (D) Solve a problem.

Check your answers on page 223.

Practice Test

Directions Read the question. Listen to the talk. Read the four possible answers.
Choose the best answer.

1. (A) (B) (C)   5. (A) (B) (C)
2. (A) (B) (C)   6. (A) (B) (C)
3. (A) (B) (C)   7. (A) (B) (C)
4. (A) (B) (C)   8. (A) (B) (C)

1. What time do they need to be at the airport?

   (A) One o'clock.
   (B) Two o'clock.
   (C) Three o'clock.
   (D) Four o'clock.

2. What's the problem?

   (A) The woman didn't pay.
   (B) The woman wants to return something.
   (C) The man doesn't have any more money.
   (D) The man counted the change wrong.

3. What did Yolanda win?

   (A) Tickets to a baseball game.
   (B) A vacation.
   (C) A telephone.
   (D) An automobile.

4. What does the man like in his ice cream?

   (A) A chocolate swirl.
   (B) Nuts.
   (C) Real berries.
   (D) Marshmallows.

5. What is the announcement about?

   (A) A sale.
   (B) Store hours.
   (C) A new department.
   (D) The store's return policy.

6. What did the man do?

   (A) He returned her earring.
   (B) He bought her some jewelry.
   (C) He pushed in her chair.
   (D) He lost his hearing aid.

7. What was the test about?

   (A) Presidents.
   (B) Mathematics.
   (C) Spelling.
   (D) Russian.

8. Where would you hear this announcement?

   (A) At a restaurant.
   (B) At a school.
   (C) At a dock.
   (D) At a pool.

Check your answers on page 225.

Section 2

READING

PART IV — Incomplete Sentences

Test Summary

Part IV of the TOEIC Bridge tests your ability to read English. Part IV has 30 grammar and vocabulary questions. These are mixed together. The questions are incomplete sentences. The sentences are short and use simple grammar.

Sample Questions

Grammar   Her favorite color ------- green.

      (A) is
      (B) are
      (C) be
      (D) being

The sentence should read, "Her favorite color is green." You should choose answer (A).

Vocabulary   An ------- drove through the red light without stopping.

      (A) accident
      (B) ambulance
      (C) antenna
      (D) apartment

The sentence should read, "An ambulance drove through the red light without stopping." You should choose answer (B).

Taking the Test

You will read an incomplete sentence. There are four possible answer choices: (A), (B), (C), or (D). You must choose the best word or phrase to complete the sentence.

On the TOEIC Bridge, all correct answers help your score. Incorrect answers do not count against you. Therefore, answer every question, even if you aren't sure.

Timing

You will have 35 minutes to complete Parts IV and V of the test.

Index of Grammar Points

I. Vocabulary Power!   64

II. Sentence Formation   67

Parts of a Sentence   67
Types of Sentences   67

III. Nouns & Pronouns   70

Count Nouns   70
Non-Count Nouns   73
Verbals: Gerunds and Infinitives   76
Pronouns   77

IV. Adjectives   81

Ordinal Numbers   81
Comparatives   81
Superlatives   83
Irregular Adjectives   83
Equivalents (as . . . as)   84
Possessive Adjectives and Nouns   85
Participles as Adjectives   86

V. Prepositions   88

Prepositions of Locations   88
Prepositions with Indirect Objects   89
Prepositions in Two-Word Verbs   90

VI. Conjunctions   91

Coordinating and Correlative Conjunctions   91

VII. Verbs   93

    Verb "to have"   93
    Verb "to be"   94
    Simple Present   96
    Present Progressive   98
    Simple Past   99
    Past Progressive   101
    Future with "will"   102
    Future with "be going to"   104
    Helping Verbs   104
    Passive   106
    Present Perfect   107
    Verb Tense Review   108

VIII. Adverbs   109

    Adverbs of Frequency   109

IX. Part IV Practice Test   111

X. Part IV Answer Key   227

I. Vocabulary Power!

Learn these important words for Part IV of the test. These words occur several times in this book.

Entertainment and Hobbies

1. **collect** *v.* **collection** *n.*
   My sister <u>collects</u> colored beach glass.
   She picked up the old bottles to add to her <u>collection.</u>

Family

2. **be/get divorced** *v.*
   Chuck and Louisa just <u>got divorced</u>.
3. **invite** *v.* **invitation** *n.*
   The lady is writing <u>invitations</u>.
   She wants to <u>invite</u> Chuck and Louisa.

Home and Apartment Life

4. **be broken** *v.*
   The door <u>is broken</u>.
5. **fix** *v.*
   The repairman is <u>fixing</u> it.
6. **own** *v.* **owner** *n.*
   The woman is the <u>owner</u> of the apartment building. She has <u>owned</u> the building for 7 years.

School

7. **dormitory** *n.*
   They live in the <u>dormitory</u>.
8. **grade** *v./n.*
   He got a bad <u>grade</u> on his homework.
9. **miss class** *v.*
   One student is <u>missing class</u>.
10. **semester** *n.*
    It's the end of the <u>semester</u>.

11. accident *n.*

The driver had an <u>accident</u>.

12. ID (identification) *n.*

She is giving the officer her school <u>ID</u>.

13. license *n.*

The police officer wants to see her driver's <u>license</u>.

Work

14. boss *n.*

The <u>boss</u> looks angry.

15. employee *n.*

Some <u>employees</u> are working.

16. employer *n.*

Their <u>employer</u> is Pabble Copy Center.

17. Internet *n.*

One worker is surfing the <u>Internet</u>.

18. job *n.*

He may lose his <u>job</u>.

19. schedule *n.*

The work <u>schedule</u> is posted on the wall.

Practice timing. Spend no more than 13 minutes on Part IV. This is about 30 seconds per question. Work quickly to have enough time for Part V. (Save at least 22 minutes for Part V.)

Practice

Directions This part of the test has incomplete sentences. After each sentence, you will see four words or phrases. These are marked (A), (B), (C), or (D). You must choose the best way to complete the sentence. Mark your answer on your answer sheet.

1. (A) (B) (C) (D)   5. (A) (B) (C) (D)
2. (A) (B) (C) (D)   6. (A) (B) (C) (D)
3. (A) (B) (C) (D)   7. (A) (B) (C) (D)
4. (A) (B) (C) (D)   8. (A) (B) (C) (D)

1. The students were early ------- the teacher was, too.

    (A) too
    (B) both
    (C) and
    (D) either

2. My glasses ------- broken.

    (A) is
    (B) are
    (C) be
    (D) will

3. I start work ------- 7:30 on Tuesdays.

    (A) at
    (B) on
    (C) in
    (D) for

4. My snack was ------- than my lunch.

    (A) big
    (B) bigger
    (C) biggest
    (D) bigger than

5. Yesterday, we ------- my friend move into his new apartment.

    (A) help
    (B) helped
    (C) will help
    (D) had helped

6. We are planning ------- a birdhouse for that tree.

    (A) build
    (B) building
    (C) to build
    (D) built

7. The painter isn't painting this area -------.

    (A) still
    (B) already
    (C) anymore
    (D) somewhat

8. Last weekend, we went ------- on Lake Michigan.

    (A) sail
    (B) sailed
    (C) sails
    (D) sailing

Check your answers on page 227.

Three types of English sentences are common in the TOEIC Bridge. These are simple, compound, and complex. A simple sentence has one main idea. A compound sentence has two main ideas. A complex sentence has a main idea with a subordinated point.

Parts of a Sentence

Sentences are made of parts: subjects, objects, complements, modifiers. The parts included depend on the idea expressed. In turn, parts of a sentence are made of parts of speech.

Parts of a sentence	Parts of speech
subject	noun (including pronouns, noun clauses, verbal nouns)
verb	verb (may require an object or complement)
helping verb (auxiliary)	helping verb (be, have, do, modals)
object	noun
complement (for subject)	adjective (describes subject)
	noun (renames subject)
modifier*	adjectives
	adverbs (including clauses and phrases modifying sentence parts)
	determiners (a, the, my, every)
coordinating conjunction*	conjunctions (and, for, nor, or, so, yet, but)

*This chart lists some parts of speech as sentence parts for convenience.

Model   Sample Sentence and Sentence Parts

subject						verb	complement	conjunction	subject	verb	modifier
det	adjective	noun	prep	det	noun	verb	adjective	conjunction	pronoun	verb	adverb
The	green	grapes	at	the	market	were	cheap,	and	they	sold out	quickly.

Types of Sentences

A sentence must have at least one independent clause. An independent clause has a subject and a verb, at least. An independent clause must make sense. It can stand alone.

A. Simple Sentences

Model   Subject + Verb

subject (pronoun)	verb
I	swim.

Model   Subject + Verb + Object

subject (noun)	verb (helping verb + adverb + verb)	indirect object (det + noun)	direct object (det + noun)
Miss Kong	didn't show	the students	the pictures.

B. Compound Sentences

Independent clauses can be combined to make a compound sentence. They are joined with a coordinating conjunction. (See Conjunctions on page 91.)

Model   Compound Sentence

Independent Clause Number 1				Independent Clause Number 2			
subject (noun)	verb	complement (adjective)	coordinate conjunction	subject (noun)	verb	modifier (adverb)	complement (adjective)
January	was	cold,	but	February	was	even	colder.

C. Complex Sentences

A complex sentence has one independent clause. It also has one or more subordinate clauses. A subordinate clause has a subject and verb. The clause begins with a subordinate conjunction. A subordinate clause does not make sense when it stands alone. It must be joined to an independent clause. It may come before or after an independent clause.

Model   Subordinate Clause

Subordinate Clause			
subordinate conjunction	subject (noun)	verb	direct object (article + noun)
After	I	make	the bed,

Model   Complex Sentence

Subordinate Clause	Independent Clause	Subordinate Clause
After I make the bed,	I will wash the towels	that you used.

D. Questions

Questions are sentences. Questions also have a subject and verb. Word order for questions is different from word order for statements.

Model   Yes-No Question

helping verb	subject	main verb	other (direct object)
Do	the Smiths	have	a dog?

Model   Yes-No Question

helping verb	subject	main verb	other (adverb)
Should	Ann	visit	Venezuela?

Model   Information Word Question

question word as object	helping verb	subject	main verb	object
What	will	you	give	her?

Model   Information Question

question word as subject	verb	other
Who	made	the announcement?

E. Negative Sentences

Make a negative verb form by putting "not" after an auxiliary verb.

Model   Negative Sentence

subject	aux	adv	verb	object	conj	subject	aux + adv	verb	object
I	did	not	forget	you,	but	I	can't	remember	your name.

Nouns

Nouns tell who and what. They name people, places, and things.

Count Nouns

Model

> The sign is about movie tickets. (one sign)
> Tickets are on sale now. (many tickets)
> Yesterday I bought tickets for my friend and me. (many tickets)
> Today I'll buy a ticket for my sister. (one ticket)

Use

Some nouns are called count nouns. These nouns have both a singular and a plural form: *one pan, five cities, twenty-three oranges.* Most nouns are count nouns. Numbers and certain determiners may be used with count nouns.

1. My boss gave me two ------- to read during the break.
   (A) book
   (B) books
   (C) of books
   (D) a book

Form

There are two ways to make a count noun plural.

Add -s or -es to the noun

singular (one)	plural (more than one)
cat	three cats
horse	six horses
match	matches

Change the spelling of the noun

singular (one)	plural (more than one)
child	many children
man	a lot of men
woman	a few women
foot	two feet
tooth	36 teeth

2. There are two ------- on your desk.
- (A) fax
- (B) faxing
- (C) faxes
- (D) faxed

3. The dentist had to pull her four front -------.
- (A) tooth
- (B) teeth
- (C) teething
- (D) tooth's

Test Hint 35

Nouns can act as subjects of sentences. A subject must agree with its verb in number. Use plural verb forms with plural count nouns. Use singular verb forms with singular count nouns.

4. These CDs ------- on sale today.
- (A) is
- (B) am
- (C) are
- (D) be

5. Nine of the students ------- late to class.
- (A) is
- (B) was
- (C) am
- (D) were

Determiners before Count Nouns

Model

> That dog chased my cat up the tree.

Use

A determiner comes at the beginning of a noun phrase. A determiner helps to identify things. A determiner may tell how much, how many, which, or whose. For example, "a" means "one." It shows that the noun is general. The noun can be any one of a group. "The" shows that the noun is specific. There is only one.

1. My new sweater has ------- large green button at the top.
- (A) any
- (B) those
- (C) a
- (D) these

2. Did you see ------- horse that fell in the river?
- (A) a
- (B) the
- (C) these
- (D) two

Test Hint 36

The TOEIC Bridge often tests count nouns by testing the determiners before them.

3. Eriko missed ------- questions on the math test.
   (A) a
   (B) one
   (C) six
   (D) any

Vocabulary Power!

There are many determiners. Watch for them in this book. Practice reading the following sentences with determiners from the correct list below.

(singular) _____ customer will see the advertisement.

(plural) _____ customers will see the advertisement.

Determiners before singular count nouns

close/far	this, that
amount	a, the, no, neither, one, each, either, every
whose	my, your, his, her, its, your, our, their

Determiners before plural count nouns

close/far	these, those
amount	the, no, both, a few, fewer, enough, some, several, more, most, a lot of, many/how many, all, any (usually used in questions and negative statements), two, three, four, and so forth
whose	my, your, his, her, its, our, your, their

4. Martin made ------- field goals during the second half.
   (A) each
   (B) every
   (C) one
   (D) several

5. ------- contact lenses fell on the floor.
   (A) One
   (B) Either
   (C) Each
   (D) Both

Test Hint 37

One of the most difficult determiners to use correctly is "any." It may be used with plural count nouns. It is usually used in questions and in negative statements. You will surely see it on the Bridge.

6. We didn't buy ------- erasers because they were sold out.
   (A) some
   (B) no
   (C) every
   (D) any

7. Are there ------- cookies in the kitchen?
   (A) a
   (B) most
   (C) any
   (D) all

Non-Count Nouns

Model

> I'd like two cheeseburgers and some <u>ketchup</u>.

Use

Some nouns are called non-count nouns. Some common non-count nouns are "ketchup," "money," and "rain." Non-count nouns have only a singular form. Certain determiners may be used with non-count nouns.

1. The taxi driver had to stop to put ------- in his cab.
   (A) gas
   (B) darkness
   (C) traffic
   (D) health

Form

Many different grammar rules affect the use of non-count nouns.
- Non-count nouns do not have a plural form. (No final "-s" is added.)
- Noun-count nouns always take a singular verb.
- Non-count nouns are never immediately preceded by "a/an" or a specific number.

2. The tea ------- boiling on the stove.
   (A) will
   (B) is
   (C) are
   (D) that

3. She packed ------- jewelry in her suitcase.
   (A) a
   (B) four
   (C) any
   (D) some

Vocabulary Power!

Certain things are often non-count nouns. Memorize the list below. Learn what kind of thing is non-count, and remember the examples.

Common Non-Count Nouns

Category	Non-count nouns
Things that are too small to count	hair, corn
Foods that are usually measured, not counted	sugar, bread, salt, rice
Abstract things	information, music, work, education, health, help, love, time, news
Groups of things made up of many parts	furniture, fruit, jewelry, mail, money, traffic
Liquids	oil, coffee, milk, soup, tea, water, gas
Weather and nature	weather, fog, lightning, rain, snow, thunder, wind, darkness, light, sunshine

Some nouns can be either count or non-count. "Mixed nouns" are not tested on the Bridge. However, you will need to know them for the TOEIC.

Examples
Mika has black hair.   (non-count)

There is a hair in my soup!   (count)

4. There ------- snow on the ground and we could hardly walk.
- (A) are
- (B) were
- (C) was
- (D) fell

Vocabulary Power!

Non-count nouns, like count nouns, use determiners. Some non-count determiners are the same as count determiners. Some are different. Look up the difficult ones in a dictionary. Watch for determiners in this book. Practice reading the sample sentences with determiners from below.

We spilled _____ milk on the floor.

The children spent _____ time at the park.

Determiners before non-count nouns

close/far	this, that
amount	no, not much, how much, much, a little, some, more, less, a lot of, the, any (usually used in questions and negative statements)
whose	my, your, his, her, its, your, our, their

5. How ------- money is in the piggy bank?
- (A) much
- (B) many
- (C) lot
- (D) big

6. We ate ------- rice at lunchtime.
- (A) a
- (B) many
- (C) a lot of
- (D) any

The determiner "any" can also be used with non-count nouns. It is usually used in questions and in negative statements. You will surely see this on the Bridge.

7. There wasn't ------- lightning at the airport at 2 P.M.
   (A) some
   (B) any
   (C) the
   (D) many

8. ------- information about the election.
   (A) There are
   (B) There is no
   (C) There is any
   (D) There are some

Verbals: Gerunds and Infinitives

Gerunds

Model

> The teacher enjoys <u>asking</u> questions to the students.

Use and Form

Gerunds are verbals. Verbals are nouns made from verbs. A gerund plays many roles in a sentence:

a. Subject   <u>Swimming</u> is great exercise.
b. Object of some verbs   I love <u>dancing</u>.
c. Object of a preposition   She makes extra money <u>by fixing</u> jewelry.

You can make any verb into a gerund. Add "-ing" to the base form of a verb.

1. ------- in the dormitories saves students time and money.
   (A) Live
   (B) Lives
   (C) Living
   (D) Having living

2. He quit ------- so that he could focus on his education.
   (A) works
   (B) worked
   (C) working
   (D) to works

3. They paid for the new sign by ------- money from all the club members.
   (A) collect
   (B) collection
   (C) to collect
   (D) collecting

Vocabulary Power!

Nouns are often created by adding an ending to a word. One common noun ending is "-tion." In this section on gerunds, there are three nouns ending in "-tion." Circle them. Practice making sentences with these nouns. Think of three more nouns that end with "-tion." Write them here.

a. _____

b. _____

c. _____

Infinitives

Model

> My husband learned how <u>to play</u> the guitar in high school.

Use and Form

Infinitives are the "to" form of a verb. All verbs have an infinitive form. Infinitives can play similar roles to gerunds in a sentence:

a. Subject	<u>To collect</u> stamps requires time and money.
b. Object of some verbs	My assistant would like <u>to grade</u> these papers.
c. To show purpose	He bought a hammer <u>to fix</u> the roof. (This is really a short form of "in order to." It is very common. "He bought a hammer <u>in order to fix</u> the roof.")

1. ------- all these papers by 5:00 will be almost impossible.
(A) Grade
(B) To grade
(C) Graded
(D) For grading

2. The younger children seem ------- school more often than the older students.
(A) miss
(B) to miss
(C) missing
(D) of missing

3. We're going to stay in Barcelona ------- my sister-in-law.
(A) visit
(B) visiting
(C) to visit
(D) for to visit

Vocabulary Power!

Certain verbs can be followed by either a gerund or an infinitive. You need to memorize these verbs. For example, *enjoy, finish,* and *practice* may be followed by a gerund. They may not be followed by an infinitive. Other verbs may be followed by an infinitive: *ask, choose, need, want.*

Pronouns

Use and Form

Pronouns are used in place of nouns. In sentences, they are divided into four types. These are subjective, objective, possessive, and reflexive.

Subjective	Objective	Possessive	Reflexive
I	me	my, mine	myself
you	you	your, yours	yourself
he	him	his, his	himself
she	her	her, hers	herself
it	it	its, its	itself
we	us	our, ours	ourselves
they	them	their, theirs	themselves

Subject Pronouns

Model

> We planted flowers in the spring.
> I showed our garden to my friends, and they liked it.

Use

A subject pronoun is the subject of a sentence or clause.

1. ------- waited in line for over an hour.
(A) They
(B) Themselves
(C) Them
(D) Theirs

2. She listens to music when ------- takes a shower.
(A) Her
(B) Hers
(C) Herself
(D) She

Object Pronouns

Model

> We mailed her the tickets, and she paid us for them when she saw us at the show.
>   indirect   indirect   object   direct
>   object   object   of preposition   object

Use

Object pronouns may be objects of prepositions or objects of verbs. As objects of verbs, they may be either direct or indirect objects.

1. John gave ------- the letter.
(A) we
(B) ourselves
(C) us
(D) ours

2. Please come to ------- if you have any problems.
(A) I
(B) me
(C) mine
(D) myself

3. We took the dogs for a walk and fed
------- .
(A) them
(B) him
(C) you
(D) me

4. We talked to Mark at the party, but
neither of us liked ------- very much.
(A) them
(B) him
(C) us
(D) me

Model

> The hostess explained <u>it</u> <u>to the passengers</u>.
>   direct   indirect
>   object   object

Form

When pronouns are direct objects, they usually come before indirect objects. The indirect object then usually takes a preposition "to" or "for." (See Direct and Indirect Objects on page 67. Also, see Prepositions with Indirect Objects on page 89.)

5. The professor ------- .
(A) told to the students it
(B) to the students told it
(C) told it the students
(D) told it to the students

6. My grandmother used to sing -------
when I was younger.
(A) to me the song
(B) it me
(C) the song me
(D) it to me

Possessive Pronouns

Model

> The green glass is <u>mine</u> and the blue one is <u>yours</u>.

Use

Possessive pronouns tell whose. They can take the place of nouns. In this case, a possessive pronoun stands in for the possessive noun. The noun must be clear in the context. (For more practice with Possessive Pronouns, see page 85).

1. Your apartment is bigger than ------- .
(A) me
(B) my
(C) I
(D) mine

2. This is ------- basketball, but the soccer
ball is ours.
(A) she
(B) us
(C) her
(D) hers

Reflexive Pronouns

Model

> The boy taught <u>himself</u> to read. He did it <u>himself</u>, all by <u>himself</u>.

Use

Reflexive pronouns have three general uses:

a. Show the receiver of the action is the doer of the action

b. Emphasize a noun or another pronoun

c. Act in some cases as the object of a preposition

1. Marcus cut ------- while he was grating the carrot.
(A) myself
(B) himself
(C) itself
(D) yourself

2. I dumped my boyfriend because he talked only about -------.
(A) himself
(B) myself
(C) itself
(D) yourself

Vocabulary Power!

A reflexive pronoun can come with the preposition "by" ("by myself/yourself"). In this case, it means "alone, without help."

3. Jessica prefers to go jogging by ------- because she can set her own pace.
(A) alone
(B) self
(C) one
(D) herself

4. My husband wants to paint the house ------- himself.
(A) with
(B) by
(C) to
(D) on

IV. Adjectives

An adjective describes a noun or a pronoun. An adjective answers these questions: *Which? What kind? How many?*

Ordinal Numbers

Model

> My birthday is January <u>fourth</u>.
> Our soccer team took <u>first</u> place.

Use

Ordinal numbers are often used as adjectives. They show degree, quality, or position in a series. They are often used in dates.

1. This semester begins on September
   -------.
   (A) seven
   (B) seventh
   (C) number seven
   (D) one-seventh

2. My granddaughter is in the ------- grade.
   (A) five
   (B) fifth
   (C) number five
   (D) fiftieth

Form

Generally, add "-th" to the cardinal number. For multiples of ten, add "-ieth." Exceptions are one, two, and three. (Spelling changes occur with numbers ending in "e," "ve," and "y.")

Cardinal numbers	Ordinal numbers	Cardinal numbers	Ordinal numbers
one	first	nine	ninth
two	second	ten	tenth
three	third	eleven	eleventh
four	fourth	twelve	twelfth
five	fifth	thirteen	thirteenth
six	sixth	twenty	twentieth
seven	seventh	twenty-five	twenty-fifth
eight	eighth	thirty-nine	thirty-ninth

Comparatives

Model

> Los Angeles is <u>bigger than</u> San Francisco.
> A truck is <u>more expensive</u> than a car.

Use

Comparative adjectives compare two nouns.

1. Our uniforms are ------- than theirs.
- (A) warm
- (B) warmly
- (C) warmer
- (D) more warmth

2. Her employer is ------- than her boss.
- (A) relaxed
- (B) very relaxed
- (C) so relaxed
- (D) more relaxed

Form

Add the endings "-er/-r" to short adjectives of one or two syllables. For longer adjectives, add the comparative word "more" or "less." Do not use "more" or "less" with "-er."

Adjective	Comparative
big	bigger
soft	softer
nice	nicer
casual	more casual
tired	less tired

Model

> There are <u>more part-time workers</u> in the factory <u>than full-time workers</u>.
> The assembly workers work <u>more quickly</u> now <u>than they did in May</u>.

Use and Form

"More" and "less" are also used with nouns and adverbs. If a noun is a count noun, "fewer" is used instead of "less." (See Count Nouns on page 70.)

3. There were ------- this year than last year.
- (A) many graduates
- (B) more graduates
- (C) too many graduates
- (D) very many graduates

5. We sold ------- bicycles this year than last year.
- (A) less
- (B) least
- (C) few
- (D) fewer

4. Your daughter works ------- than other children in the class.
- (A) slow
- (B) slowly
- (C) more slowly
- (D) most slowly

Superlatives

Model

> Anne's grandfather is <u>the tallest</u> man in town.
> He's <u>the most popular</u> man, too.

Use

Superlative adjectives compare three or more nouns.

1. The apple is small, the lemon is smaller, and the apricot is the -------.
   (A) small
   (B) smaller
   (C) smallest
   (D) smallness

2. This is the ------- coffee I've ever had.
   (A) sweet
   (B) sweeter
   (C) sweetest
   (D) sweetly

Form

Add the ending "-est" to most short adjectives. Generally, for longer adjectives, add the superlative "most" instead of "-est."

Adjective	Superlative
tall	the tallest
smart	the smartest
creative	the most creative

3. Driving an automobile is one of the ------- dangerous things we do in life.
   (A) most
   (B) more
   (C) too
   (D) so

4. That was the ------- candy I've ever seen in my life.
   (A) most
   (B) more
   (C) very
   (D) most amount of

Vocabulary Power!

Some comparative and superlative forms of adjectives are irregular.

Irregular adjectives

Adjective	Comparative	Superlative
good	better than	the best
bad	worse than	the worst
far	farther than	the farthest

5. Last night, I saw the ------- movie that I've ever seen.
(A) good
(B) better
(C) more good
(D) best

6. Six hundred miles is the ------- that I've driven in one day.
(A) far
(B) farther
(C) more far
(D) farthest

Equivalents (as . . . as)

Model

Julie is <u>as tall as</u> Susan, but she can't run <u>as fast as</u> Susan can.

Use and Form

"As _____ as" compares two things. It shows that they are the same. To form the equivalent, place the quality compared between "as" and "as." "As _____ as" may be used to compare adjectives or adverbs. (See the Adverb Review on page 109.)

1. His Japanese is ------- good as a native speaker's.
(A) the
(B) a
(C) as
(D) more

2. Sleeping is ------- natural as eating.
(A) than
(B) as
(C) of
(D) more

Vocabulary Power!

"Nat-" means "to be born." In this section, there are two words that use this root. Can you find them? Write them on the following lines. You can guess the meaning from the context. Write a new sentence for each word.

a. _____

b. _____

3. My mother's ------- is Canadian because she was born in Quebec.
(A) net
(B) north
(C) nylon
(D) nationality

4. We like to go hiking because we enjoy -------.
(A) nature
(B) numbers
(C) niece
(D) nurse

Possessive Adjectives and Nouns

Model

> <u>Her</u> brother lost <u>our</u> luggage at the airport.

Use

Possessive adjectives and nouns show ownership.

1. ------- car is parked on the street.
   (A) My
   (B) Me
   (C) It
   (D) Myself

Form

Possessive adjectives are the possessive form of pronouns. In a sentence, they play the role of a determiner. (See pages 71-72 and page 74 for Determiners.)

<u>Subject pronoun</u>	<u>Possessive adjective</u>
I	my
you	your
he	his
she	her
it	its
we	our
they	their

2. My husband drove over ------- bicycle in the driveway by accident.
   (A) he
   (B) he's
   (C) him
   (D) his

3. ------- seats are in aisle 17, row 4.
   (A) We
   (B) We're
   (C) Our
   (D) Ours

Model

> Most <u>workers'</u> offices are small, but <u>Mika's</u> office is by far the smallest.

Form

To show possession, add an "-s" and an apostrophe to many nouns. In this way, nouns act as adjectives.

Mika + 's   = Mika's   (Mika is one person)
children + 's   = children's   (children are many people: "children" doesn't end in "s")
workers + s'   = workers'   (workers are many people: "workers" ends in "s")

4. By accident, the badminton ------- racket was left in the car.
  (A) play
  (B) player
  (C) players
  (D) player's

5. All ------- haircuts are 10% off, even if you pay by credit card.
  (A) man
  (B) men
  (C) man's
  (D) men's

Vocabulary Power!

This section has three common expressions using the preposition "by." Can you find them? Reread the section. Circle the expressions. Try to guess their meaning. Write sentences using these words.

a. _____

b. _____

c. _____

Participles as Adjectives

Model

My suitcase is <u>new</u>.	(adjective)
The wheels are <u>lost</u>.	(past participle adj.)
The <u>broken</u> handle fell off.	(past participle adj.)
It is <u>surprising</u>.	(present participle adj.)

Use and Form

Participles are often used as adjectives. The may come before a noun. Or, they may come after with "be" or "get." Participles are a form of verbs. (See pages 76 and 107 for the participle forms of verbs.)

1. My sister is going to get ------- in July.
  (A) marry
  (B) marriage
  (C) marrying
  (D) married

2. My ex-boyfriend has a ------- heart.
  (A) broken
  (B) broke
  (C) break
  (D) was broken

Vocabulary Power!

Here are common expressions with "be" and/or "get" + past participles. Memorize the prepositions that follow these words. "Get" is like "become." It shows a change in a condition or situation. "Be" means that a condition exists.

Common participles used as adjectives

be/get bored (with)   be/get interested (in)
be/get broken   be/get lost
be closed   be made of
be/get divorced (from)   be/get married
be done (with)   be/get scared
be/get excited (about)   be/get tired (of)
be finished (with)   be/get used (to)
be/get hurt

3. I am used ------- riding this broken
   bicycle, and it's not for sale.
   (A) with
   (B) be
   (C) of
   (D) to

4. The students are done ------- the
   assignment.
   (A) with
   (B) be
   (C) of
   (D) to

Prepositions have many purposes. One important purpose is showing location. Some prepositions are used much more than others. These include *at, by, for, from, in, of, on, to,* and *with*. Prepositions often answer the question: Where is it?

Prepositions of Locations

Model

> She took her keys <u>off</u> the table and put them <u>in</u> her pocket.

Use

Prepositions of location tell physical location.

1. The truck driver left his license -------the police station.
   (A) at
   (B) across
   (C) among
   (D) up

Form

A preposition is followed by a noun or pronoun. Together, they form a "prepositional phrase."

2. The children played -------.
   (A) the lake next to
   (B) the next to lake
   (C) next to lake
   (D) next to the lake

Vocabulary Power!

Learn these common prepositions. Study the chart. Write "L" next to those prepositions that can show location. (To review other prepositions of location, see page 9.)

Prepositions

about	below	next to
above	beside	of
according to	by	through
across	except	toward
around	for	up
at	from	with

Grammatically, most prepositions of location work the same way. Therefore, the TOEIC Bridge often tests their meaning, but not their grammar.

3. She rents an apartment ------- the edge of town.
(A) on
(B) like
(C) without
(D) according to

5. The criminal had used fake ID, ------- the newspaper.
(A) by
(B) until
(C) with
(D) according to

4. ------- the first quarter, tuition always goes up.
(A) Of
(B) Across
(C) After
(D) Except

Prepositions with Indirect Objects

Model

> She gave <u>Mary</u> <u>the dishes</u>, but she gave <u>the piano</u> <u>to John</u>.
>   indirect   direct   direct   indirect
>   object   object   object   object

Use

An indirect object may come after a direct object. In this case, the indirect object needs the preposition "to" or "for." (See Objects on page 67. Also, see Object Pronouns on page 78.)

1. They gave a T-shirt ------- at the concert.
(A) everyone
(B) to everyone
(C) for everyone
(D) everyone to

2. Mrs. Cameron taught the song -------.
(A) the students
(B) to the students
(C) at the students
(D) the students to

Sometimes a preposition is not expressed for an indirect object. This can happen when the indirect object comes before a direct object.

3. The store gave all ------- a 4% raise.
    (A) workers
    (B) to workers
    (C) for workers
    (D) them workers

4. The new manager sent ------- a letter.
    (A) all employees
    (B) to all employees
    (C) all to employees
    (D) for all employees

Model

> They bought candy <u>for the boys</u> and they gave balloons <u>to the girls</u>.

Form

A few verbs usually take an indirect object with the preposition "for." Memorize these.

<u>Verb + "for" + indirect object</u>

buy (for)   get (for)
make (for)   play (for)

5. We made a birdhouse ------- my brother.
    (A) to
    (B) for
    (C) into
    (D) at

6. We made ------- a birdhouse.
    (A) my brother
    (B) to my brother
    (C) for my brother
    (D) at my brother

Prepositions in Two-Word Verbs

Model

> We <u>ran into</u> Mr. Coleman at the graduation ceremony.

Use

Two-word verbs are made of a verb + a preposition. In this case, the preposition is part of the verb. It may lose its meaning as a preposition. (See Two-Word Verbs on page 102.)

1. We looked ------- the word in the dictionary.
    (A) in
    (B) up
    (C) on
    (D) with

Conjunctions link words, phrases, or clauses.

Coordinating and Correlative Conjunctions

Model

> <u>Both</u> Regina <u>and</u> Sylvia were born in Brazil, <u>yet</u> they can <u>neither</u> read <u>nor</u> speak Portuguese.

Use

Coordinating conjunctions link words, phrases, or clauses of equal importance. They may connect two or more nouns, verbs, or main clauses. In the model, "yet" is a coordinating conjunction. Other coordinating conjunctions are *and, but, nor, or, for,* and *so.*

1. Carl read the report, ------- his boss read it too.
   (A) too
   (B) and
   (C) or
   (D) either

2. They will graduate not in June, ------- in December.
   (A) and
   (B) but
   (C) for
   (D) so

Use

Some conjunctions pair with other words to create "correlative conjunctions." In the model sentence, "both . . . and," and "neither . . . nor" are correlative conjunctions.

Vocabulary Power!

Learn these three common correlative conjunctions:
both . . . and . . .
either . . . or . . .
neither . . . nor . . .

3. Most students would support ------- a ball field or a tennis court.
   (A) so
   (B) both
   (C) either
   (D) neither

4. Our company will ------- export nor import shoes.
   (A) and
   (B) both
   (C) either
   (D) neither

5. ------- the airport and the seaport were closed because of fog.

   (A) And

   (B) Nor

   (C) Too

   (D) Both

See Subordinate Conjunctions on page 68.

Vocabulary Power!

"Port-" means "carry." In this section, there are six words that use this root. Can you find them? Write them on the following lines. You can guess the meanings from the context. Write a new sentence for each word.

a. _____

b. _____

c. _____

d. _____

e. _____

f. _____

6. The ship will arrive in the ------- at 4 P.M.

   (A) pearl

   (B) pear

   (C) pail

   (D) port

7. Tea is ------- from China, but it's quite expensive here.

   (A) decided

   (B) departed

   (C) reported

   (D) imported

Verbs express actions, happenings, or states of being. For example, "run," "fall," and "be" are verbs.

Verb "to have"

Model

> She <u>has</u> a license, but they don't <u>have</u> a car yet.
> Mr. Lee <u>has</u> brown hair and blue eyes.

Use
"Have" has several meanings: own, hold, experience, be identified by.

1. I don't ------- my schedule with me.
   (A) has
   (B) have
   (C) to have
   (D) having

Form
The simple present of "have" has two forms: "have" and "has."

I/We/You/They	*have/don't have*	a bicycle.
He/She/It	*has/doesn't have*	a bicycle.

2. She ------- enough money for the bus and for lunch.
   (A) has
   (B) have
   (C) to have
   (D) having

3. ------- luggage for your trip?
   (A) Do you
   (B) You have
   (C) Does you have
   (D) Do you have

Form
The past tense of "have" is "had."

4. The electronics department ------- many customers yesterday.
   (A) has
   (B) have
   (C) had
   (D) would have

The verb "to have" plays an important role in English. Alone, it has meaning. However, it is also used to form some verb tenses. (See Present Perfect on page 107.) You will see this verb often on the TOEIC Bridge.

Verb "to be"

Model

I _am_ very hungry, she _isn't_ very hungry, and they _are_ completely full.

Use

"Be" gives a state of being. It is commonly used in contractions ("I'm," "he's").

1. I ------- on the volleyball team because I'm so tall.
(A) am
(B) is
(C) are
(D) be

Form

The present tense of "be" has three forms: "am," "is," and "are."

I	*am*	(not)	a student.
You	*are*	(not)	a student.
He/She/It	*is*	(not)	a student.
We/You/They	*are*	(not)	students.

2. What ------- your excuse for being late?
(A) has
(B) is
(C) are
(D) say

3. Police ------- looking into the cause of the accident.
(A) am
(B) is
(C) are
(D) to

Form

In a contraction, an apostrophe replaces one or more letters.

I + am = I'm
you + are = you're
he + is = he's
she + is= she's
it + is = it's   he/she/it + is + not = he/she/it isn't

we + are = we're
you + are= you're   we/you/they + are + not= we/you/they aren't
they + are = they're

4. ------- going to wash the dishes, aren't you?
   (A) You
   (B) Your
   (C) You're
   (D) Yours

Model

> My mother <u>was</u> a doctor.

Form

The past tense of "be" has two forms: "was" and "were."

I	*was*	(not)	a student.
You	*were*	(not)	a student.
He/She/It	*was*	(not)	a student.
We/You/They	*were*	(not)	students.

5. She ------- so sick yesterday that she stayed home from school.
   (A) is
   (B) was
   (C) were
   (D) had

Model

> <u>Are you</u> from Taiwan?

Form

In a question, the verb "be" comes before the subject. It needs no auxiliary.

6. ------- ready to leave for their dance class?
    (A) Are the girls
    (B) Do the girls
    (C) Do the girls be
    (D) Do the girls are

Vocabulary Power!

"Cause-" means "reason/cause." In this section, there are three words that use this root. Can you find them? (Hint: Roots may change slightly in use. Two words in this section spell this root as "cuse.") Write them on the lines. You can guess the meanings from the context. Write a new sentence for each word.

a. _____

b. _____

c. _____

7. The car stopped running ------- we were out of gas.
    (A) for
    (B) that
    (C) because
    (D) so

8. ------- me, is the manager available?
    (A) Cause
    (B) Excuse
    (C) Accuse
    (D) Because

Test Hint 42

The verb "to be" also plays an important role in English. Alone, it states that a condition exists. However, it is also used to form some verb tenses. (See Progressive Tenses on pages 98 and 101.) You will see this verb on the TOEIC Bridge.

Simple Present

Model

> I <u>sing</u> and my brother <u>dances</u>.

Use

Simple present shows daily habits, usual activities, and general facts.

1. Kayoko is in trouble because she ------- class every Thursday.
   (A) miss
   (B) misses
   (C) to miss
   (D) missing

2. They ------- two houses in Korea.
   (A) is owning
   (B) owns
   (C) going to own
   (D) own

Form

For regular verbs, add an "-s" or "-es" for third person singular. Otherwise, use the base form of the verb.

| I/We/You/They | *play/don't play* | the guitar. |
| He/She/It | *plays/doesn't play* | the guitar. |

See irregular present forms for "have" (page 113) and "be" (page 94).

3. I ------- in the computer science department.
   (A) works
   (B) are working
   (C) don't work
   (D) doesn't work

4. ------- you remember if the party is in the afternoon or in the evening?
   (A) Does
   (B) Is
   (C) Are
   (D) Do

Vocabulary Power!

In this section, there are examples of four different uses of "in." Find them. Circle them. Write your own sentences using the "in" expressions that follow.

Expressions with "in"
in + the morning/evening
in + month or year ("in June" or "in 2008")
in + language
in + a department
in + country
in + clothing ("in a skirt")
in front of
in trouble
in a hurry

5. The fire ------- the men's department cost the store millions.
   (A) on
   (B) of
   (C) to
   (D) in

6. At least they don't yell ------- front of their children.
   (A) at
   (B) of
   (C) to
   (D) in

Practice for the Bridge by writing test questions and answers. For example, here is part of a test question. Try to complete it. Make sure that there is only one correct answer. Ask a friend or classmate to answer your question.

7. My grandson always ------- when he runs downhill.
(A) falls
(B)
(C)
(D)

Present Progressive

Model

> The men <u>are cutting</u> the fruit.
> Unfortunately, they <u>aren't washing</u> it first.
> The next time, <u>I'm washing</u> the fruit.

Use

a. Present progressive shows something that is happening now. It probably started in the past. It will probably continue in the future. But that is not important. It is now.

Past   Now   Future

b. The present progressive can also show future time.

1. The art teacher ------- students' photographs now.
(A) grading
(B) had graded
(C) is grading
(D) graded

2. The police officer ------- at a driver's ID whenever he stops a car.
(A) looks
(B) is look
(C) not looking
(D) isn't looking

Form

The present progressive is formed with "be" + "-ing verb."

3. Are you ------- on the soccer team this spring?
(A) play
(B) played
(C) will play
(D) playing

4. He's ------- for his student visa next week.
(A) applying
(B) will apply
(C) apply
(D) to apply

Simple Past

Model

> Mary <u>played</u> the song for her friends.

Use
Simple past shows something that began and ended in the past.

Past	Now	Future

1. Hiroshi ------- his cousin this morning on his cell phone.
   (A) call
   (B) calls
   (C) called
   (D) was calling

2. The airport ------- next week on Friday.
   (A) open
   (B) opened
   (C) has opened
   (D) will open

Form
To form the past tense, most verbs add "-ed." Some verbs are irregular.

<u>Regular Past</u>		<u>Irregular Past</u>	
act	acted	begin	began
collect	collected	eat	ate
play	played	go	went
travel	traveled	speak	spoke

3. He ------- the test on time.
   (A) finish
   (B) finished
   (C) finishing
   (D) finish

Test Hint 44

The TOEIC Bridge doesn't use "unreal" or incorrect English. For example, you will never have to choose between "spoke" and "speaked." This is because "speaked" isn't a correct form of the verb.

4. We ------- about the accident on the radio.
   (A) hear
   (B) hearing
   (C) heard
   (D) to hear

Vocabulary Power!

In this section, there are examples of five different uses of "on." Find them. Circle them. Write your own sentences using the following "on" expressions.

Preposition "on"

on + date (on May 3rd)
on + musical instrument (on the piano)
on the phone
on purpose
on the radio
on sale
on schedule
on time
on a trip
on vacation

a. _____

b. _____

c. _____

d. _____

e. _____

5. How many postcards did you write while you were ------- vacation?

   (A) on

   (B) in

   (C) with

   (D) to

"Used To"

Model

> Martin <u>used to</u> collect shells, but he doesn't anymore.

Use

"Used to" shows a past situation that no longer exists. The past situation was either a long-lasting situation or habitual.

Form

Use "used to" + a verb in base form.

6. Our company used to ------- water pipes, but now we only sell new ones.

   (A) fix

   (B) fixing

   (C) fixed

   (D) was fixing

Past Progressive

Model

> At 4:30, my roommate <u>was putting away</u> her winter clothes.

Use

Past progressive describes a past action in progress. The action was in progress at a specific time.

begin   end

Past   Now   Future

1. That employee wasn't ------- on this computer at 4:00.
   (A) work
   (B) to work
   (C) worked
   (D) working

Form

Form the past progressive with a past form of "be" + "-ing verb."

2. She ------- getting off the bus when the man approached her.
   (A) has
   (B) was
   (C) did
   (D) were

Model

> I <u>was filling in</u> your form when the baby woke up.
> Did he figure out problem while he <u>was changing</u> the oil?

Use

The past progressive can describe two past actions. One action is simple and short in length. The other action is longer. The past progressive is used to describe the long action.

Form

A clause with "while" often states the past progressive action. The main clause is in the simple past.

3. While she ------- the new word, she found the other word that we didn't know.
   (A) looked up
   (B) had looked up
   (C) was looking up
   (D) had been looking up

4. Was it pouring rain when you ------- your husband from work?
   (A) were picking up
   (B) picking up
   (C) pick up
   (D) picked up

Vocabulary Power!

This section on the past progressive has seven two-word verbs. Find them. Circle them. Try to guess their meanings from the context. Learn all of the two-word verbs in the chart. Think of another verb with a similar meaning. Write it in the chart.

Two-Word Verbs

fill in	*write*	look up	
figure out	*answer*	pick up	
get back (from)		put away	*organize*
get off		put on	
get in		take off	
get on		throw away	
get out	*go*	try on	
give up		turn off	
grow up		turn on	*start*
hand in		wake up	

5. You should always ------- the light before you leave the house.
(A) turn off
(B) fill in
(C) make up
(D) try on

6. He tried ------- his tuxedo, but it was much too tight.
(A) in
(B) off
(C) up
(D) on

Test Hint 45

Compare the simple past (see page 99) and the past progressive (see page 101). They are similar, but different. They will be tested on the TOEIC Bridge.

7. Our records show that he ------- for his glasses with a credit card.
(A) pay
(B) paid
(C) paying
(D) be paying

Future with "will"

Model

> She <u>will take</u> the test soon, or she <u>will not go</u> to college.

Use

"Will" states future time.

1. We will ------- careful when we cross the street.
   (A) be
   (B) are
   (C) being
   (D) to be

Form
Use "will" + the simple form of the verb.

2. The fog ------- lift by mid-afternoon.
   (A) be
   (B) will
   (C) will be
   (D) is

Form
In a contraction, an apostrophe replaces one or more letters.

I + will = I'll
he + will = he'll
will + not = won't

3. You ------- be able to graduate this semester if you don't take the test.
   (A) not
   (B) are not
   (C) don't
   (D) won't

Vocabulary Power!
This section, Future with "will," has three future time expressions. Find them. Circle them. Write new sentences using these expressions.

Expressions of the future
Learn the future expressions in the list that follows. Imagine that it is now Monday morning. Number the time expression below in order of occurrence, 1 through 12. The first to occur is "1." The last to occur to "12." (Note: Some of these time expressions are unclear. For those, you can decide the order yourself.)

ASAP (as soon as possible) *2*	soon	
by Thursday	ten years from now	
immediately (right away) *1*	the day after tomorrow	
in a minute	this afternoon	
later on	tomorrow evening	
next month	tonight	

Future with "be going to"

Model

> Some of the third-grade students <u>are going to visit</u> their teacher in the hospital.

Use

"Be going to" shows future time.

1. I ------- to take my visor to the baseball game tonight.
   (A) am
   (B) am going
   (C) will
   (D) will be

2. The students ------- their student IDs last Tuesday.
   (A) got
   (B) were getting
   (C) are getting
   (D) are going to get

Form

The future with "be going to" is made of "be going" + infinitive.

3. Are the tourists going ------- a visa to enter Morocco?
   (A) need
   (B) to need
   (C) needing
   (D) be needing

Vocabulary Power!

"Vis-" means "see." In this section, there are three words that use this root. Can you find them? Write them on the lines below. You can guess the meaning from the context. Write a new sentence for each word.

a. _____

b. _____

c. _____

Helping Verbs (Auxiliary Verbs)

Model

> I <u>can</u> speak Russian and I <u>should</u> learn to write it, too.

Use

Helping verbs are verbs. They add meaning to another verb. They show conditions and possibilities regarding the action. (Sometimes "helping verbs" are called "auxiliary verbs.")

1. You ------- smoke in the lobby because it's against the law.

(A) may

(B) should

(C) mustn't

(D) don't have to

Form

Helping verbs are followed by another verb. The other verb is in its base form.

2. Can they ------- badminton on Wednesday?

(A) play

(B) to play

(C) playing

(D) will play

Vocabulary Power!

Helping Verb	Meaning	Sample Sentences
can/could	ability	She can apply for the job.
	permission	You can eat those cookies.
	possibility	You could invite your secretary.
may/might	permission	You may turn on the TV.
	possibility	It might snow tomorrow.
should/ought*/had better	advice	You should watch your step.
	obligation	The store ought to refund you.
have*/have got*/must	necessity	We have to study hard.
		We've got to get ready for the test.
		We must pass this time.
do not have*	lack of necessity	You don't have to come if you don't want to.
must not	prohibition	The model mustn't gain weight.
would you/could you/ will you/can you	polite request	Would you please wash this lettuce?
		Could you wash your hands, first?
		Can you chop it, too?
would rather	preference	I'd rather go to a play.

* Three common helping verbs are followed by the infinitive. (They are not followed by the base form of a verb.) These may be tested in two ways. One way is for the order of the words. Another way is for inclusion of the word "to":

have

have got

ought

3. If her purse was stolen, she ------- call the police.
   (A) has
   (B) has got
   (C) has got to
   (D) has to got to

Test Hint 46

Grammatically, helping verbs usually work the same way. The Bridge often tests their meaning, but not their grammar.

4. ------- you please wait for me in the lobby?
   (A) Might
   (B) Would
   (C) Should
   (D) Had better

6. We ------- meet you for coffee than for lunch.
   (A) should
   (B) rather
   (C) would rather
   (D) can

5. You ------- dry your hair before we take the photograph.
   (A) would
   (B) rather
   (C) have to
   (D) ought

Passive

Model

> **passive:** Jane's boss <u>was invited</u> to her wedding (by Jane).
> **active:** Jane <u>invited</u> her boss to the wedding.

Use and Form
A passive sentence has three features:
a. The subject of a passive sentence does not do the action. (Example: Jane's boss did not do an action.)
b. The object of an active sentence becomes the subject. (Example: "Boss" is the object in the active sentence. In the passive, "boss" becomes the subject.)
c. The subject of an active sentence may become a "by phrase." (Example: Jane is the subject of the active sentence. In the passive this becomes "by Jane.")

1. The employee was ------- a raise.
   (A) give
   (B) gave
   (C) to give
   (D) given

2. Was the history class taught ------- the mathematics professor?
   (A) by
   (B) from
   (C) of
   (D) as

Test Hint 47

The Bridge will test passive voice. Usually the questions are in simple past tense.

Form

Use the past tense of the verb "be" + past participle. A passive sentence may have a "by" phrase. The "by" tells who did the action.

Verb (base form)	Simple past	Past participle
bake	baked	baked
collect	collected	collected
give	gave	given
go	went	gone
see	saw	seen
take	took	taken

3. My photo has already been -------.
   (A) take
   (B) took
   (C) taken
   (D) taking

Present Perfect

Model

My boss <u>has eaten</u> her lunch already.

Use

Present perfect has three main uses:

a. A recent past event at an unclear past time. (often with "already" or "yet")

b. A repeated past event at unclear past times. The event is likely to happen again in the future.

c. A past event that continues in the present. (often with "since" or "for")

1. These employees ------- in this dormitory since May.
- (A) live
- (B) lived
- (C) was living
- (D) have lived

Form

Use the present tense of "have" + past participle. (See page 93 for the verb "have.")

2. She ------- seen that movie seven times.
- (A) was
- (B) did
- (C) has
- (D) have

3. My secretary has already ------- to an office supply store to look for those covers.
- (A) go
- (B) gone
- (C) going
- (D) went

Verb Tense Review of Seven Basic Tenses

Test Hint 48

The TOEIC Bridge will test your understanding of seven verb tenses. These seven tenses are different from each other. Their times are different, and their grammar is different. You need to understand them all.

Seven common verb tenses
Simple present
Present progressive
Simple past
Past progressive
Future with "will"
Future with "be going to"
Present perfect

1. At 3:00 tomorrow, Beth ------- a haircut.
- (A) is
- (B) got
- (C) will get
- (D) had gotten

2. She can't join us for coffee because she ------- a haircut right now.
- (A) gets
- (B) got
- (C) is getting
- (D) had gotten

3. Actually, she ------- her hair cut twice yesterday!
- (A) gets
- (B) got
- (C) will get
- (D) has gotten

4. When she ------- her first haircut, there was an earthquake.
- (A) got
- (B) gets
- (C) had gotten
- (D) was getting

An adverb describes a verb, an adjective, or other adverbs. Some example of adverbs are "gently," "quietly," and "very." Adverbs answer these questions: When? Where? How? Why? Under what conditions? To what degree?

Adverbs of Frequency

Model

> I rarely visit my grandfather.

Use

Adverbs of frequency tell how often or when.

1. She worries about her weight so she ------- exercises.
  (A) often
  (B) seldom
  (C) rarely
  (D) never

2. They both hate to cook so they ------- eat out.
  (A) never
  (B) seldom
  (C) occasionally
  (D) always

Test Hint 49

Adverbs of frequency are often tested for their place in a sentence.

Form

Some frequency adverbs can be placed in three locations. These are the beginning, middle, or end of a sentence. Others must be placed according to rules.

1. Adverbs that can be placed in the middle, beginning, or end of sentence

finally	occasionally	sometimes
frequently	often	usually
generally	probably	

2. Adverbs that are placed mid-sentence, according to the following rules

always	not ever
ever	rarely
just	seldom
never	

Rules for placing some adverbs of frequency

a. Place the adverb after the first helping verb.

Example: *We can always hear the ambulances at night.*

b. Place the adverb before a main verb, unless the verb is "be."

Example: *Our club never collects dues from members.*

c. Place the adverb after "be" if "be" is the main verb.

Example: *She is generally a very good student.*

3. ------- because of the cholesterol.

(A) We can eat rarely eggs

(B) We rarely can eat eggs

(C) We can eat eggs rarely

(D) We can rarely eat eggs

4. The sale clothes ------- of the store.

(A) are never in the front

(B) never are in the front

(C) are in never the front

(D) are in the front never

Directions   This practice test has 15 incomplete sentences. After each sentence, you will see four words or phrases, marked (A), (B), (C), or (D). You must choose the best way to complete the sentence. Mark your answer on your answer sheet.

1. (A)   (B)   (C)   (D)
2. (A)   (B)   (C)   (D)
3. (A)   (B)   (C)   (D)
4. (A)   (B)   (C)   (D)
5. (A)   (B)   (C)   (D)
6. (A)   (B)   (C)   (D)
7. (A)   (B)   (C)   (D)
8. (A)   (B)   (C)   (D)

9. (A)   (B)   (C)   (D)
10. (A)   (B)   (C)   (D)
11. (A)   (B)   (C)   (D)
12. (A)   (B)   (C)   (D)
13. (A)   (B)   (C)   (D)
14. (A)   (B)   (C)   (D)
15. (A)   (B)   (C)   (D)

1. My brother has a pet snake, but my father is ------- of it.
   (A) scare
   (B) scary
   (C) scared
   (D) scaring

2. These ------- were picked from the tree by my grandparents.
   (A) cherries
   (B) chairs
   (C) charts
   (D) chips

3. She wrapped her jewelry in tissue and put ------- in her purse.
   (A) them
   (B) themselves
   (C) it
   (D) to

4. All of the sports ------- is stored in the gym.
   (A) elevator
   (B) entrance
   (C) equipment
   (D) element

5. The tour guide ------- several passengers slipped on the ice.
   (A) too
   (B) and
   (C) also
   (D) so

6. They didn't bake any cookies because everyone was -------.
   (A) failed
   (B) full
   (C) funny
   (D) fast

7. The tickets in her wallet ------- for the play tonight.
   (A) is
   (B) will
   (C) are
   (D) have

8. Visibility was low because of the -------.
   (A) can
   (B) fog
   (C) ring
   (D) top

9. In their home, they speak ------- German.
   (A) at
   (B) on
   (C) with
   (D) in

10. I can't help you right now because I ------- this pudding.
    (A) cook
    (B) cooking
    (C) am cooking
    (D) was cooking

11. Did you ------- the announcement about the sale?
    (A) hear
    (B) heard
    (C) hearing
    (D) to hear

12. ------- the new company ID cards?
    (A) When did they issue
    (B) When they did issue
    (C) Did they issue when
    (D) When they issued

13. My grandson ------- ride his scooter.
    (A) is
    (B) is going
    (C) is going to
    (D) is going to be

14. Makiko ------- already talked to her math teacher about the book.
    (A) has
    (B) have
    (C) will
    (D) did

15. Professors must turn in their grades promptly after the end of the -------.
    (A) career
    (B) graduate
    (C) license
    (D) quarter

Check your answers on page 237.

PART V — Reading Comprehension

Test Summary

Part V of the TOEIC Bridge tests your ability to read English. Part V has 20 reading comprehension questions. The questions are based on short passages. These include notices, letters, newspaper articles, and advertisements. The readings are ten to 100 words. They use simple grammar.

Sample Question

> ## Please see pool attendant on duty for help with lockers.

1. Where would you see this sign?
   (A) A bank
   (B) A police car
   (C) A swimming center
   (D) A lock store

2. Who will help with the lockers?
   (A) A police officer
   (B) A locksmith
   (C) A guard
   (D) A worker

The sign says that you should see a pool attendant. For question 1, you should choose answer (C). The sign says that a pool attendant will help with the lockers. For question 2, you should choose (D).

Taking the Test

In your test book, you will see a short passage. Each passage is followed by two or three questions. Each question has four possible answers: (A), (B), (C), or (D). You must choose the best answer.

On the TOEIC Bridge, all correct answers help your score. Incorrect answers do not count against you. Therefore, answer every question, even if you aren't sure.

Timing

You will have 35 minutes to complete Parts IV and V of the test.

Learn these important words for Part V of the test. These words occur several times in this book.

Entertainment and Hobbies

1. **admission** *n.*
   Admission fees are listed above the ticket booth.
2. **subscribe** *v.* **subscription** *n.*
   The boy subscribes to Science magazine.
3. **article** *n.*
   He's reading an article about the moon.

Government

4. **president** *n.*
   She wants to be the president again.
5. **vote** *v./n.*   She voted for herself.
6. **government** *n.*
   The people want an honest government.

Home and Apartment Life

7. **rent** *n./v.*   The house is for rent.
   The couple wants to rent it.

Shopping

8. **advertisement** *n.*
   The advertisements are for sale goods.
9. **receipt** *n.*   The man has his receipt.
10. **refund** *n.*   The cashier is giving him a refund.
11. **return** *v./n.* He is returning some shoes.

<u>*Sports*</u>

12. rule *n.*

The pool <u>rules</u> are posted next to the pool.

<u>*Transportation*</u>

13. cautious *adj.* **caution** *n.*

The new driver is <u>cautious</u>.

14. permit *v./n.*

She is not <u>permitted</u> to drive alone.

<u>*Work*</u>

15. schedule *v./n.*

The executive keeps her <u>schedule</u> on her desk.

Test Hint 50

Save at least 22 minutes to do Part V. (Remember: You have 35 minutes to do both Parts IV and V.) This gives you about 1 minute per passage. This includes reading the passage and answering its questions. If a question is difficult for you, answer it anyway. Then make a mark next to it. If you have time, return to it later.

Practice

Directions   Each question is based on a reading passage. For each question, read the passage and choose the best answer. Spend about 9 minutes on this practice.

1. (A) (B) (C) (D)   5. (A) (B) (C) (D)
2. (A) (B) (C) (D)   6. (A) (B) (C) (D)
3. (A) (B) (C) (D)   7. (A) (B) (C) (D)
4. (A) (B) (C) (D)

Questions 1—2 refer to the following notice.

ADMISSION TICKET

Dear Ms. Saito,

You are registered for the NGAT test on November 3, 2005 at the University of California, Stanton Hall, Room 316.
Registration begins at 9:00 A.M. and the test starts at 10:00 A.M.
No one will be allowed in after the test starts.
Bring this admission ticket as proof of registration, a photo ID (passport or license), and number 2 pencils with erasers.

---

1. What will happen if you arrive after 10:00?
   (A) Your score will not count.
   (B) You will miss the test.
   (C) You must wait until the break.
   (D) You will be registered for the next test.

2. What do you NOT need to bring to the test?
   (A) Proof of registration
   (B) Identification
   (C) Pencils
   (D) Your payment

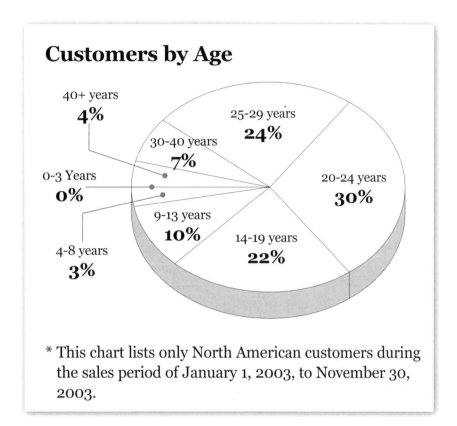

Customers by Age

40+ years
4%

30-40 years
7%

25-29 years
24%

0-3 Years
0%

20-24 years
30%

9-13 years
10%

14-19 years
22%

4-8 years
3%

* This chart lists only North American customers during the sales period of January 1, 2003, to November 30, 2003.

3. Who are most of their North American customers?
   (A) Children
   (B) Teens
   (C) Young Adults
   (D) Seniors

4. How many months of sales does this chart show?
   (A) 10
   (B) 11
   (C) 12
   (D) 23

Questions 5—7 refer to the following article.

Angel Mountain Bows to Snowboarders

The gondola sails above the roofs of hotels and condos. Riders see a new sight in the powder below: wide snake patterns in the snow below them.

For the first season ever, Angel Mountain is open to snowboarders. This historic skiers' heaven has long rejected snowboarders. "They're wild, young, out of control," complains long-time Angel skier Maxwell Thurston.

Snowboarders see it differently. "These older skiers aren't open to change," says Dylan White.

The fastest growing snow sport in America, snowboarding is permitted at major resorts across the country. Now, the Angel can see where boarders fly, too.

5. What has Angel Mountain started to do?
(A) Allow snowboarding
(B) Forbid skiing
(C) Open a history museum
(D) Give airplane rides

6. According to Dylan White, why don't skiers like the new plan?
(A) They're greedy.
(B) They're close-minded.
(C) They're wild and young.
(D) They're selfish.

7. What can you see in the snow as you go up the mountain?
(A) Snowboard tracks
(B) Angel shapes
(C) Snakes
(D) Advertisements for hotels and condos

Check your answers on page 239.

Vocabulary Power!

Look at question 5 again. It has the words "allow" and "forbid." "Allow" and "forbid" have opposite meanings. These words often occur on the test. A related word is "permit." "Permit" and "allow" have the same meaning.

Test Hint 51

Read with purpose. Focus your reading to save time.
1. First, look at the reading quickly. Try to get an idea of the topic. Do not read the whole passage.
2. Read the questions.
3. Read the passage. Try to find the answers to the questions. Read quickly. Look only for the answers to the questions.
4. Answer the questions.
5. If you aren't sure of the correct answer, answer anyway. First, identify the wrong answers. Then, choose the answer that sounds the best from the remaining answers. (If you guess, mark the question in your test book. Then, you can return to it later.)

Practice

Directions   The questions are based on a reading passage. For each question, choose the best answer.

1. Ⓐ   Ⓑ   Ⓒ   Ⓓ   4. Ⓐ   Ⓑ   Ⓒ   Ⓓ
2. Ⓐ   Ⓑ   Ⓒ   Ⓓ   5. Ⓐ   Ⓑ   Ⓒ   Ⓓ
3. Ⓐ   Ⓑ   Ⓒ   Ⓓ   6. Ⓐ   Ⓑ   Ⓒ   Ⓓ

Questions 1—2 refer to the following notice.

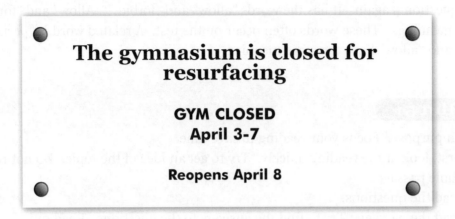

The gymnasium is closed for resurfacing

GYM CLOSED
April 3-7

Reopens April 8

1. Why is the gym closed?
   (A) For a sports event
   (B) To redo the surface
   (C) For the April holiday
   (D) To park service equipment

2. When will the gym open?
   (A) April 3
   (B) April 7
   (C) April 8
   (D) April 18

Questions 3—4 refer to the following notice.

■ **RETURN POLICY** ■

Full refund available on all returns within 30 days of purchase. Original receipt required.

3. If you return something within 30 days and with the receipt, what can you get?
   (A) All of your money back
   (B) Some of your money back
   (C) An in-store credit
   (D) An original receipt

4. What do you need to show when you return something?
   (A) ID
   (B) This policy
   (C) A problem with the purchase
   (D) The cash register receipt

Questions 5—6 refer to the following article.

City Gets Excellent Recycling Rating

The City of Trenton has earned a five-star rating for its recycling program. The program, started in 1991, includes curbside pickup for all residential and business solid waste customers. Eighty percent of Trenton customers recycle regularly. Another six percent recycle occasionally. Trenton recycling pickup currently takes newspapers, cardboard, glass, and aluminum. Starting next October, they will add plastics to their list.

5. What is the topic of the article?
  (A) A recycling score
  (B) Solid waste
  (C) Customers' problems
  (D) A change in recycling plans

6. When can Trenton residents recycle plastics?
  (A) Starting in 1991
  (B) In five days
  (C) In the fall
  (D) Immediately

Check your answers on page 239.

Vocabulary Power!

The prefix "re-" means "again." A prefix is placed at the beginning of a word. It adds to the meaning of the word. In the Test Hint 51 questions, many words use the prefix "re-." Five of them use "re-" to mean "again." Find them and write them on the lines below. You can guess the meanings from the context. Write a new sentence for each word.

a. _resurfacing_ _____

b. _____

c. _____

d. _____

e. _____

Look at the word "resurface" in question 1. Can you guess its meaning? This gives you the correct answer, (B).

Test Hint 52

Certain types of readings are common on the TOEIC Bridge. Pay attention to the types of reading passages on the test. Before each reading, there is a description of the reading. For example: *Questions 1-2 refer to the following ticket.* From this, you know that you will read a ticket. This information can help you answer questions.

Vocabulary Power!

Learn these words for typical types of readings.

notice	newspaper article
advertisement	questionnaire
coupon	rule
instructions/directions	road sign
form	schedule
graphs and chart	subscription
letter	ticket
magazine article	warning/label
menu	

Practice One

Directions   Look at the sentence *before* each reading. (They are marked with a ➤➤). Find the word that tells what kind of reading it is. Circle it. Write the word on the line. *Do not read the passages yet.* Then, answer questions 1, 3, 5, and 7. Just answer those four questions. (Do not try to answer 2, 4, 6, or 8 yet.)

Type of Reading for Questions 1 and 2   _____*rules*_____

1. Ⓐ   Ⓑ   Ⓒ   Ⓓ

Type of Reading for Questions 3 and 4   _____

3. Ⓐ   Ⓑ   Ⓒ   Ⓓ

Type of Reading for Questions 5 and 6   _____

5. Ⓐ   Ⓑ   Ⓒ   Ⓓ

Type of Reading for Questions 7 and 8   _____

7. Ⓐ   Ⓑ   Ⓒ   Ⓓ

Check your answers on page 240.

 Questions 1–2 refer to the following rules.

> ## Pool Safety
>
> ☛ No running, jumping, pushing, or rough-housing.
> ☛ No food, drink, glass containers, or gum chewing.
> ☛ Children under seven must be accompanied by an adult.
> ☛ Appropriate swimwear required at all times. No shorts or shirts.

1. What is the purpose of the sign?
   (A) To tell the price
   (B) To explain the rules
   (C) To caution swimmers
   (D) To sell swimwear

2. Where would you see this sign?
   (A) A pool
   (B) A school
   (C) A restaurant
   (D) A park

<u>**Questions 3—4**</u> refer to the following subscription.

> ☑ Yes, please start my subscription to The City
> Union Times at 50% off for the first 12 weeks.
>
> ▮ ____ 7 days a week for only $5.15 per week
> ▮ ✔ Every Sunday for only $2.65 per week
> ▮ ____ Monday through Friday for only $2.50 per
>   week
>
> ▮ Name <u>Mariana Perka</u>
> ▮ Address _____
> ▮ Phone _____
>
> ▮ Credit Card Number _____
> ▮ Check Number _____

3. What is the purpose of this form?
   (A) To sell clocks
   (B) To get a newspaper subscription
   (C) To get a patient's information
   (D) To charge a fine

4. Who is Mariana Perka?
   (A) A writer
   (B) A reader
   (C) A mailer
   (D) A patient

	A	**B**	**C**
Transit Center	4:10 P.M.	4:25 P.M.	4:50 P.M. **W**
4th and Main	4:21 P.M.	4:36 P.M.	5:01 P.M. **W**
I-5 Park & Ride	4:30 P.M.	4:45 P.M.	5:10 P.M. **W**
250th and James	4:44 P.M.	4:59 P.M.	5:24 P.M. **W**
Cherry and 3rd	4:56 P.M.	5:11 P.M.	5:38 P.M. **W**

W = wheelchair accessible

5. What is the purpose of the reading?
   (A) To give bus times
   (B) To explain wheelchair access
   (C) To describe the city map
   (D) To give class times

6. Who would look at this schedule?
   (A) An athlete
   (B) A housewife
   (C) A bus rider
   (D) A pedestrian

Questions 7—8 refer to the following road sign.

> # Caution
> Roadway slippery when wet.
> Reduce speed.
> Do not change lanes.

7. What is the purpose of the sign?
 (A) To close the roadway
 (B) To warn drivers
 (C) To post the speed limit
 (D) To give directions

8. What should a driver do if the road is wet?
 (A) Drive slower
 (B) Stop driving
 (C) Change lanes
 (D) Stay in the right lane

Practice Two

Directions   Look at the readings in Practice One. First, note the type of reading. Then, look at the reading quickly. Read the questions. Read the whole reading passage. Then, for each question, choose the best answer.

1.	Ⓐ	Ⓑ	Ⓒ	Ⓓ	**5.**	Ⓐ	Ⓑ	Ⓒ	Ⓓ
2.	Ⓐ	Ⓑ	Ⓒ	Ⓓ	**6.**	Ⓐ	Ⓑ	Ⓒ	Ⓓ
3.	Ⓐ	Ⓑ	Ⓒ	Ⓓ	**7.**	Ⓐ	Ⓑ	Ⓒ	Ⓓ
4.	Ⓐ	Ⓑ	Ⓒ	Ⓓ	**8.**	Ⓐ	Ⓑ	Ⓒ	Ⓓ

Check your answers on page 240. Note your answers for questions 1, 3, 5, and 7. Compare them for Practice One and Two.

Test Hint 53

Pay attention to the main ideas in a reading passage. Main ideas often contain answers to questions. To find main ideas, look for:

- Capital letters (BIG LETTERS)
- Different fonts (includes bolding and italics)
- The first few words in the reading
- Repeated words or thoughts

- Bigger typeface
- Titles (of articles)
- The first sentence in each paragraph

Example *Focusing on Main Ideas*

Questions 1—3 refer to the following magazine article.

Prime Time for Birdwatching

W inter is a good time to watch birds because many species fly south during the colder months. "It's a real interesting time to see birds you don't normally see," says Lea Barker of the National Bird Society. Winter birdwatching can be done on foot, by car, or even in your own backyard.

Ms. Barker leads an annual winter birdwatching trip to Hawaii called "Birding on the Islands." She says, "Hawaii is a great winter destination for birdwatchers."
If you're a beginning bird watcher, you might start locally. For tips, check out the NBS Web site at www.NBS.org.

1. What is the topic of the article?
   (A) Watching birds
   (B) A trip to Hawaii
   (C) Sick birds
   (D) The National Bird Society

2. When is a good time to see birds?
   (A) Spring
   (B) Summer
   (C) Winter
   (D) Fall

3. Where does the National Bird Society watch birds each year?
   (A) In the company yard
   (B) In Hawaii
   (C) At the North Pole
   (D) Locally

Reading only the first sentence in each paragraph, you can answer questions 1-3. The answers are 1. (A), 2. (C), and 3. (B).

Practice

Directions Look at the reading quickly. Identify the main ideas. For each question, choose the best answer. Finally, read the entire passage to check your answers.

1. Ⓐ Ⓑ Ⓒ Ⓓ   4. Ⓐ Ⓑ Ⓒ Ⓓ
2. Ⓐ Ⓑ Ⓒ Ⓓ   5. Ⓐ Ⓑ Ⓒ Ⓓ
3. Ⓐ Ⓑ Ⓒ Ⓓ   6. Ⓐ Ⓑ Ⓒ Ⓓ

Check your answers on page 240-241.

Questions 1—2 refer to the following advertisement.

The Fashion Alley's
24-Hour SALE

Come see our exciting new spring fashions
at FASHION ALLEY'S ANNUAL, ALL-DAY SALE EVENT.

Get **big discounts** on men's and women's clothing,
children's fashions, jewelry, shoes, accessories, and more!
The FULL DAY AFFAIR runs from 12:01 A.M. to 11:59
P.M., **with non-stop discounts** for everyone in the
family.

JOIN US for the BIGGEST SALE OF THE YEAR and the
BIGGEST DISCOUNTS AROUND!!!!

1. What event is being advertised?
   (A) A store opening
   (B) A fashion show
   (C) A sale
   (D) A store closure

2. How long is the event?
   (A) Just two minutes
   (B) Two to four hours
   (C) From 9 to 5 on Friday
   (D) All day

Questions 3—4 refer to the following ticket.

THE PERFORMATA THEATER

Proudly presents
Three Days to Take-Off

Admit: One Adult   Admission Fee: $28.50 + tax

Date: Friday, November 4   Time: 7:30 P.M.

NO REFUNDS   **NO REFUNDS**

3. What is the ticket for?
(A) A flight
(B) A play
(C) A bus
(D) A lecture

4. How is the ticket limited?
(A) It can't be returned.
(B) It must be paid for in cash.
(C) The user must show photo ID.
(D) Late arrivals may not use the ticket.

Questions 5—6 refer to the following directions.

Welcome to the Department of Animal Control

To minimize your wait, follow these directions:
▸ Take a number.
▸ Have a seat.
▸ Listen for your number.
▸ When you hear your number, go to any available agent.

5. Where would you see this sign?
(A) At a government office
(B) At a restaurant
(C) In a pet store
(D) At the zoo

6. What is the purpose of the directions?
(A) To entertain late people
(B) To shorten the wait
(C) To explain how to drive
(D) To tell how to get a license

Check your answers on page 240.

You can understand a passage without knowing every word. You can still answer questions correctly. Read the whole passage but skip unfamiliar words. Do not give up because of words you do not know. Focus on words that you know.

Example *Continue Reading Through Unknown Words*

Photography 3: Lighting
This advanced-level class will ~~stress multiple lighting techniques~~ You will learn lighting with different light ~~temperatures~~ We will ~~combine ambient~~ and ~~flash techniques, plus bounce flash techniques, to achieve~~ a more professional-~~quality product~~.

1. What does the class teach?
   (A) Light in painting
   (B) Martial arts techniques
   (C) How to run a business
   (D) Photography

2. Who is the class for?
   (A) Beginning students
   (B) Experienced students
   (C) Professional advertisers
   (D) Publishers

The information describes a photography class. Therefore, you should choose answer (D) for question 1. The class is "advanced level." Therefore, you should choose answer (B) for question 2.

Practice One

<u>Directions</u>   The questions are based on a reading passage. For each question, choose the best answer.

1. (A) (B) (C) (D)
2. (A) (B) (C) (D)
3. (A) (B) (C) (D)
4. (A) (B) (C) (D)

5. (A) (B) (C) (D)
6. (A) (B) (C) (D)
7. (A) (B) (C) (D)

Questions 1–2 refer to the following questionnaire.

Health History

Patient Name: <u>Nancy Blackstock</u>   Date: <u>12/12/04</u>

Do you have a family history of the following?

_____	anemia	_____	mental problems
_____	diabetes	**XX**	migraine headaches
_____	glaucoma	_____	chronic pain
XX	heart disease	_____	tremors
_____	kidney problems	_____	urinary tract infections

1. What is the purpose of this form?
   (A) To gather health information
   (B) To diagnose an illness
   (C) To get a patient's contact information
   (D) To give a patient medicine

2. What health problems are in the patient's history?
   (A) Diabetes and blood diseases
   (B) Vision problems
   (C) Mental problems
   (D) Headaches and heart problems

DANGER

Contents under pressure.
Open away from people, animals,
and objects.
Point away from eyes.
Do not shake.

3. What does this warning tell you?
   (A) How to open something
   (B) Who should use this item
   (C) What the contents are
   (D) Where to store it

4. Where would you see this warning?
   (A) On a loaf of bread
   (B) On a carbonated drink
   (C) On an automobile
   (D) On a computer

TransLux Airlines

Mr. Guillermo Soriano
McKan Industries
12189 146th Ave. S.E.
Claygo, IL 87888

Dear Mr. Soriano,

We enclose a bonus upgrade to thank you for collecting 60,000 miles. Now you can upgrade your next TransLux flight to business class. If you have two vouchers, you can upgrade to first class. You can also use this voucher to treat any friend, family member, or acquaintance traveling in your company.

Thank you for participating in TransLux Airlines' Miles Plus program.

Yours sincerely,

Karsten Konig

5. Why did Mr. Soriano receive this letter?
   (A) He lost his upgrade voucher.
   (B) He flew over 60,000 miles.
   (C) He often travels with family or friends.
   (D) He doesn't participate in the airline's program.

7. Who can use the voucher?
   (A) Mr. Soriano or anyone he travels with
   (B) Only Mr. Soriano
   (C) Any employee of McKan Industries
   (D) Karsten Konig

Check your answers on page 241.

6. What can a person do with bonus upgrades?
   (A) Fly for free
   (B) Bring a traveling companion for free
   (C) Get a discount on tickets
   (D) Sit in a better seat

Practice Two

Directions   Look at the reading passages in Practice One. Count the number of words in each passage that you know. Count your number of correct answers. Write them in the chart below.

	Total No. of Words	No. of Words You Know	No. of Questions	Your No. of Correct Answers
Questions 1 and 2, Questionnaire	44		2	
Questions 3 and 4, Warning	18		2	
Questions 5, 6, and 7, Letter	83		3	

Vocabulary Power!

Keep a vocabulary notebook. Write down new words that you see or hear. Write the word in a sentence. It is easier to learn words in context than in lists.

Test Hint 55

Answer choices may repeat words in the reading. Don't choose an answer just because it repeats words in the passage. Listen for the real meaning.

Practice One

Directions   The questions are based on a reading passage. For each question, choose the best answer.

1. (A)   (B)   (C)   (D)   4. (A)   (B)   (C)   (D)
2. (A)   (B)   (C)   (D)   5. (A)   (B)   (C)   (D)
3. (A)   (B)   (C)   (D)   6. (A)   (B)   (C)   (D)

Questions 1—2 refer to the following instructions.

❖ Insert and remove key card.
❖ Wait for light.
❖ Turn handle to open.

1. What is the purpose of these instructions?
   (A) To explain the light
   (B) To sell keys
   (C) To describe the handle
   (D) To explain how to open a door

2. When should you turn the handle?
   (A) Before inserting the card
   (B) Before removing the card
   (C) After the light comes on
   (D) After the door opens

Questions 3—4 refer to the following biographical information.

Jessica Taylor...

is an international photojournalist and writer now based

in New York. She has a BA in International Relations

from the University of Wisconsin and earned her

Masters of Fine Arts from the University of Hawaii,

where she also taught several classes. Jessica has

produced many documentary photography projects on

El Salvador. To learn more about her work, go to her

Web site at *www.jessicataylor.com.*

3. What is Ms. Taylor's job?
   (A) She's an international relations
       specialist.
   (B) She teaches art.
   (C) She is a photographer and journalist.
   (D) She is a Web designer.

4. Where does she live now?
   (A) New York
   (B) Wisconsin
   (C) Hawaii
   (D) El Salvador

Questions 5—6 refer to the following invitation.

The Green Chemistry Program
invites you to
a public lecture by the
American Chemical Society

May 16th, 4:00-5:00 P.M.
155 Lawrence Hall
followed by an open house
and reception in their new laboratory.

5. What is the invitation for?
  (A) To attend a lecture
  (B) To tour the American Chemical
       Society
  (C) To enroll in the Green Chemistry
       Program
  (D) To use the new laboratory

6. Where is the event?
  (A) At the Green Chemistry Company
  (B) At the American Chemical Society
  (C) In Lawrence Hall
  (D) In somebody's house

Check your answers on page 241.

Vocabulary Power!

Read a lot. One of the best ways to improve your vocabulary is through reading. Read anything that you can find in English. Read newspapers, magazines, Web pages, and books. Read hotel registration forms and train schedules. Read everything!

Test Hint 56

Answer choices may include related words. The words may relate to the topic of the reading. They may relate to other words in the reading. Do not choose an answer just because of related words. Listen for the meaning.

Practice

Directions   The questions are based on a reading passage. For each question, choose the best answer.

1. (A)   (B)   (C)   (D)   4. (A)   (B)   (C)   (D)
2. (A)   (B)   (C)   (D)   5. (A)   (B)   (C)   (D)
3. (A)   (B)   (C)   (D)   6. (A)   (B)   (C)   (D)

Questions 1—3 refer to the following article.

Mustafa Kemal Ataturk, the father of the Turkish Republic and its first president, is one of the great leaders of the 20th Century. Few leaders have done so much in such a short time. Ataturk was an officer in World War I. He took apart the Ottoman dynasty. He created the Republic of Turkey in 1923. His nation had full independence. It was a model of democracy.

1. Who was Mustafa Kemal Ataturk?
   (A) A sultan
   (B) A U.S. president
   (C) The founder of Turkey
   (D) A model in the early 1900s

2. What did he do?
   (A) Fought in WWII
   (B) Created an independent nation
   (C) Led 20th Century fashion trends
   (D) Fathered many children

3. How can we describe his country after 1923?
   (A) It was a monarchy.
   (B) It was a democracy.
   (C) It was a dictatorship.
   (D) It was a communist state.

Questions 4–6 refer to the following form.

Application for Employment, The Roxell Company

General Health   Excellent   (Good)   Fair   Poor
Disability Code (see attached page)   _C_

Education (circle last completed)
10 11 12   College (1 2) 3 4   Graduate 1 2

Other training
CPR, D-class driver's license, crane operator

Applicant's Name   Chan Luk Lo

4. Who would complete this form?
   (A) A job hunter
   (B) A doctor
   (C) A student
   (D) An employee

5. What is the last year of school that Chan Luk Lo finished?
   (A) Freshman year in high school
   (B) Senior year in college
   (C) Sophomore year in college
   (D) Second grade in elementary school

6. What other skills does Chan Luk Lo have?
   (A) He can type fast.
   (B) He works well with disabled people.
   (C) He works as a phone operator.
   (D) He knows cardiopulmonary resuscitation.

Check your answers on page 242.

Vocabulary Power!

Look at question 6 again. "Disabled" means "not able." "Dis-" means "not." For example, a person in a wheelchair has a disability. Another word for disability is "handicap."

Test Hint 57

Do the shorter readings first. This will increase your chances of finishing the test. It will help you get a better score.

Practice

Directions   Complete these 5 questions in 2 minutes. First, look at the two readings. Decide which is shorter. Do it first. Then, do the next reading. For each question, choose the best answer.

1. Ⓐ   Ⓑ   Ⓒ   Ⓓ   4. Ⓐ   Ⓑ   Ⓒ   Ⓓ
2. Ⓐ   Ⓑ   Ⓒ   Ⓓ   5. Ⓐ   Ⓑ   Ⓒ   Ⓓ
3. Ⓐ   Ⓑ   Ⓒ   Ⓓ

Questions 1—2 refer to the following ID.

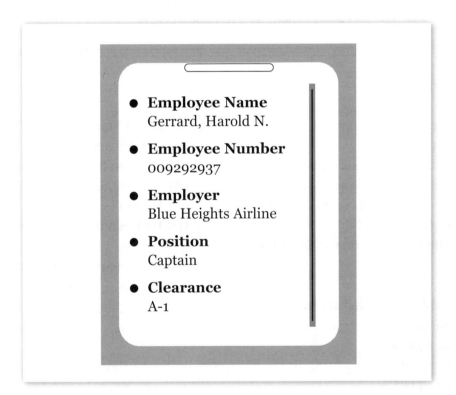

ID Card:
- **Employee Name**
  Gerrard, Harold N.
- **Employee Number**
  009292937
- **Employer**
  Blue Heights Airline
- **Position**
  Captain
- **Clearance**
  A-1

1. Who is Harold Gerrard?
   (A) An employer
   (B) A passenger
   (C) An attendant
   (D) A pilot

2. What company does he work for?
   (A) Gerrard, Harold N., Inc.
   (B) Blue Heights Airline
   (C) Captain
   (D) A-1

Questions 3—5 refer to the following article.

Students in Capital Know Fewer States

Elementary school students living in Washington, D.C. know fewer state capitals than students on the West Coast. A recent study shows that the average D.C. student, age 8 to 11, can name only 22 states and 4 state capitals.

By comparison, students of the same age in California remember, on average, 29 states and 13 capitals.

According to Jeffrey Klingham, a California 10-year-old, he had to memorize all 50 states and their capitals for a test. He got 96% on the test, even though he can only recall 35 states and 29 capital cities.

Martin Anderson, a D.C. third-grader, says that he has a bad memory in general. He can't remember state names, he can't remember his mother's birthday, and he can't even remember what day today is.

3. Which group of students can name the most capital cities?
   (A) Elementary school students
   (B) Californian grade schoolers
   (C) Kids from 8 to 11 years of age in Washington, D.C.
   (D) Young students on the East Coast

4. Why did Jeffrey Klingham learn the state names?
   (A) For a game
   (B) For a test
   (C) For a play
   (D) For a study

5. Why can't Martin Anderson remember more states and capitals?
   (A) He's too busy.
   (B) His mother doesn't help him study.
   (C) He can't even read yet.
   (D) He has a poor memory.

Check your answers on page 242.

Vocabulary Power!

In the two previous readings, two words use the root "cap." Find them. Write them on the lines. "Cap" itself is a word. Do you know what it means? Try to figure out the meaning.

a. _____

b. _____

"Mem-" means "remember." Look at the article in Test Hint 57, "Students in Capital Know Fewer States." There are three words that use the root "mem-." Find them. Write them on the lines. If you don't know the meanings, try to guess from the context. Write a new sentence for each word.

a. _____

b. _____

c. _____

Test Hint 58

If you have no time to read a passage, read the question. Read only the question. Do not read the passage. Guess at the answer. Remember: Answer every question on this test. Do not leave any questions unanswered.

Practice

Directions   The questions are based on a reading passage. Read only the questions. Do not read the reading passages. Choose the best answer. Spend about 30 seconds on this Practice.

1. Ⓐ   Ⓑ   Ⓒ   Ⓓ   2. Ⓐ   Ⓑ   Ⓒ   Ⓓ

3. Ⓐ   Ⓑ   Ⓒ   Ⓓ

Close Vote Has No Winner

There's no mayor, yet.

Yesterday's election was so close that no clear winner has been named. At eight o'clock last night, when polls closed, over 96,000 voters had voted. Some local television stations reported on the 11:00 news that Conrad Mosher was ahead, with 32,000 votes. However, as the count continued, the numbers got closer. At 3 A.M., the first unofficial count was given: Mosher 47,222; Cottonwood, 48,778. The numbers were too close to declare a winner, according to Roxanne Haldey, the city's public relations officer.

City government will continue operating as normal. The new mayor must be named by midnight this Thursday.

1. What is the topic of the article?
   (A) The weather
   (B) An election
   (C) A sporting event
   (D) A new drug

2. What happened yesterday?
   (A) There was a vote.
   (B) There was an accident.
   (C) A famous person visited the city.
   (D) A hospital had a problem.

3. Who reported that the numbers were very close?
   (A) Mosher
   (B) Cottonwood
   (C) A police officer
   (D) A public relations worker

Check your answers on page 242.

Directions   The questions are based on a reading. For each question, choose the best answer. Spend about 22 minutes on this sample test.

1. (A) (B) (C) (D)
2. (A) (B) (C) (D)
3. (A) (B) (C) (D)
4. (A) (B) (C) (D)
5. (A) (B) (C) (D)

6. (A) (B) (C) (D)
7. (A) (B) (C) (D)
8. (A) (B) (C) (D)
9. (A) (B) (C) (D)
10. (A) (B) (C) (D)

Questions 1—2 refer to the following warning.

CAUTION!

This truck stops and backs frequently.
Please follow safely.
Prepare to stop.

1. Where would you see this sign?
   (A) On a train track
   (B) On a truck
   (C) On a crane
   (D) On a wheelchair

2. How often do stopping and backing happen?
   (A) Never
   (B) Rarely
   (C) Occasionally
   (D) Often

Questions 3—4 refer to the following notice.

Access www.was.gov/dol for information on

- Driver Licenses and Identification Cards
- Office Locations
- Changing Your Address
- Intermediate (Teen) Driver License
- Motorcycle Endorsement
- Commercial Driver License
- Vehicle Registration

3. What agency is this Web site for?
   (A) Elections and Voter Registration
   (B) National Tax Agency
   (C) The Department of Licensing
   (D) The Department of Housing

4. When would you go to this Web site?
   (A) When you have a baby
   (B) When you move
   (C) When you get a new job
   (D) When you enter high school

Mushrooms and Heart Disease

Mushrooms can help your heart. As well, they may have benefits that the health community is just starting to understand.

Researchers are looking at mushrooms for various medicinal purposes. In Japan, for example, health practitioners use the maitake mushroom to treat high blood pressure. It also may lower cholesterol. The maitake is considered by many a benefit in the fight against cancer.

Mushrooms alone can't make you healthy. In addition, you need a healthy lifestyle. Exercise, a balanced diet, and reducing stress can all lead to a happier heart.

5. How can mushrooms help your health?
   (A) They have "good cholesterol."
   (B) They may lower blood pressure.
   (C) They help fight liver disorders.
   (D) They produce blood.

6. How do health professionals view mushrooms?
   (A) They agree on their health benefits.
   (B) They think mushrooms are most effective in treating skin disorders.
   (C) They have known about their benefits for a long time.
   (D) They are just starting to recognize their value.

Questions 7—8 refer to the following advertisement.

7. What is the purpose of this advertisement?
   (A) To describe an apartment that is for rent
   (B) To describe a renter who needs an apartment
   (C) To sell an apartment building
   (D) To find a roommate for an occupied apartment

8. What is a benefit of this apartment unit?
   (A) It has a dishwasher.
   (B) It has a washer and dryer in it.
   (C) It has no damage yet.
   (D) It is near shops.

Questions 9—10 refer to the following notice.

Vote for Student Body Government

President
* Jane Heartfield
* Samuel Finn

Secretary
* Mark Toffler
* Vivian Fairchild

Vice President
* Ann Bauer
* Barry Holden

Treasurer
* Rebecca Stanton
* Shane O'Reilly

You may vote for one candidate for each office.
Mark your ballot clearly! Thank you for voting!

9. What is the purpose of this form?
   (A) To give admission into the student body
   (B) To choose the student government
   (C) To explain the candidates' positions
   (D) To apply for the student body government

10. How many students will be elected?
    (A) One
    (B) Two
    (C) Four
    (D) Eight

Check your answers on page 243.

Section 3

PRACTICE TESTS

Practice Tests

There are two, full-length practice TOEIC Bridge tests in this section. These tests are the same as the actual TOEIC Bridge test. Their length is the same—100 questions. The style of the questions is the same. The topics and the vocabulary are the same. The difficulty level is the same. The audio speed and delivery is the same.
The answer key and audio script follow each test.

Taking the Practice Tests

These tests give excellent practice for the actual TOEIC Bridge. When you take a test, try to create realistic test conditions. Prepare yourself mentally. This will help you prepare for the actual test day.

Create Realistic Test Conditions

1. Spend one hour on the test. Time yourself.
2. Work in a quiet study area. Music, food, and drinks are not allowed at test centers.
3. Work independently. Do not look at the answer key or audio script. Dictionaries are not allowed at test centers.
4. Mark your answers on your answer sheet. Each test has its own answer sheet. Remove the answer sheet from this book. Use it to mark your answers.
5. Fill in each answer space completely. Use black-lead pencils. Keep a good eraser on your desktop. Erase unwanted marks completely.
6. Make sure you are marking your answer in the correct place. Match the numbers in your answer sheet and in your test book.
7. Take only one test at a time. Do not try to take two tests in a row. This will tire you.

Prepare Yourself Mentally

1. Relax. Breathe deeply. Do not stress yourself. It will not help your score.
2. Be comfortable. Have a sweater ready, in case you feel cool.
3. Work at a steady pace. In the Listening Comprehension section, you must follow the audio. In the Reading section, you must set your own time. For Part IV and Part V, you have 35 minutes.
4. Check your answers. If you have extra time, review your Reading section answers.
5. Answer every question, even if you aren't sure. Eliminate incorrect answers. Guess if you have to.
6. Enjoy your completion of each test. You are helping yourself by preparing for this test. Be happy about your hard work.

You will see the following set of general directions in your test book.

TOEIC® Bridge

General Directions

This is a test of how well you can use the English language. The total time for the test is about one hour. The test is divided into five parts.

You should answer every question. Your score will be based on the number of questions that you answer correctly. Do not mark your answers in this test book. **You must put all of your answers on the separate answer sheet.**

When you answer a question, fill in the answer space corresponding to the letter of your choice. Fill in the space as in the example below.

Mr. Jones ------- to his accountant yesterday.

(A) talk
(B) talking
(C) talked
(D) to talk

Sample Answer

The sentence should read, "Mr. Jones talked to his accountant yesterday." Therefore, you should choose answer (C). Notice how this has been done in the example given.

Mark on **one** answer for each question. To change an answer, completely erase your old answer and then mark your new answer on the answer sheet. Mark the answer sheet carefully so that the test-scoring machine can record your test score accurately.

⚙ ANSWER SHEET ⚙

LISTENING SECTION

1 Ⓐ Ⓑ Ⓒ Ⓓ	26 Ⓐ Ⓑ Ⓒ Ⓓ	51 Ⓐ Ⓑ Ⓒ Ⓓ	76 Ⓐ Ⓑ Ⓒ Ⓓ
2 Ⓐ Ⓑ Ⓒ Ⓓ	27 Ⓐ Ⓑ Ⓒ Ⓓ	52 Ⓐ Ⓑ Ⓒ Ⓓ	77 Ⓐ Ⓑ Ⓒ Ⓓ
3 Ⓐ Ⓑ Ⓒ Ⓓ	28 Ⓐ Ⓑ Ⓒ Ⓓ	53 Ⓐ Ⓑ Ⓒ Ⓓ	78 Ⓐ Ⓑ Ⓒ Ⓓ
4 Ⓐ Ⓑ Ⓒ Ⓓ	29 Ⓐ Ⓑ Ⓒ Ⓓ	54 Ⓐ Ⓑ Ⓒ Ⓓ	79 Ⓐ Ⓑ Ⓒ Ⓓ
5 Ⓐ Ⓑ Ⓒ Ⓓ	30 Ⓐ Ⓑ Ⓒ	55 Ⓐ Ⓑ Ⓒ Ⓓ	80 Ⓐ Ⓑ Ⓒ Ⓓ
6 Ⓐ Ⓑ Ⓒ Ⓓ	31 Ⓐ Ⓑ Ⓒ	56 Ⓐ Ⓑ Ⓒ Ⓓ	81 Ⓐ Ⓑ Ⓒ Ⓓ
7 Ⓐ Ⓑ Ⓒ Ⓓ	32 Ⓐ Ⓑ Ⓒ	57 Ⓐ Ⓑ Ⓒ Ⓓ	82 Ⓐ Ⓑ Ⓒ Ⓓ
8 Ⓐ Ⓑ Ⓒ Ⓓ	33 Ⓐ Ⓑ Ⓒ	58 Ⓐ Ⓑ Ⓒ Ⓓ	83 Ⓐ Ⓑ Ⓒ Ⓓ
9 Ⓐ Ⓑ Ⓒ Ⓓ	34 Ⓐ Ⓑ Ⓒ	59 Ⓐ Ⓑ Ⓒ Ⓓ	84 Ⓐ Ⓑ Ⓒ Ⓓ
10 Ⓐ Ⓑ Ⓒ Ⓓ	35 Ⓐ Ⓑ Ⓒ	60 Ⓐ Ⓑ Ⓒ Ⓓ	85 Ⓐ Ⓑ Ⓒ Ⓓ
11 Ⓐ Ⓑ Ⓒ Ⓓ	36 Ⓐ Ⓑ Ⓒ Ⓓ	61 Ⓐ Ⓑ Ⓒ Ⓓ	86 Ⓐ Ⓑ Ⓒ Ⓓ
12 Ⓐ Ⓑ Ⓒ Ⓓ	37 Ⓐ Ⓑ Ⓒ Ⓓ	62 Ⓐ Ⓑ Ⓒ Ⓓ	87 Ⓐ Ⓑ Ⓒ Ⓓ
13 Ⓐ Ⓑ Ⓒ Ⓓ	38 Ⓐ Ⓑ Ⓒ Ⓓ	63 Ⓐ Ⓑ Ⓒ Ⓓ	88 Ⓐ Ⓑ Ⓒ Ⓓ
14 Ⓐ Ⓑ Ⓒ Ⓓ	39 Ⓐ Ⓑ Ⓒ Ⓓ	64 Ⓐ Ⓑ Ⓒ Ⓓ	89 Ⓐ Ⓑ Ⓒ Ⓓ
15 Ⓐ Ⓑ Ⓒ Ⓓ	40 Ⓐ Ⓑ Ⓒ Ⓓ	65 Ⓐ Ⓑ Ⓒ Ⓓ	90 Ⓐ Ⓑ Ⓒ Ⓓ
16 Ⓐ Ⓑ Ⓒ	41 Ⓐ Ⓑ Ⓒ Ⓓ	66 Ⓐ Ⓑ Ⓒ Ⓓ	91 Ⓐ Ⓑ Ⓒ Ⓓ
17 Ⓐ Ⓑ Ⓒ	42 Ⓐ Ⓑ Ⓒ Ⓓ	67 Ⓐ Ⓑ Ⓒ Ⓓ	92 Ⓐ Ⓑ Ⓒ Ⓓ
18 Ⓐ Ⓑ Ⓒ	43 Ⓐ Ⓑ Ⓒ Ⓓ	68 Ⓐ Ⓑ Ⓒ Ⓓ	93 Ⓐ Ⓑ Ⓒ Ⓓ
19 Ⓐ Ⓑ Ⓒ	44 Ⓐ Ⓑ Ⓒ Ⓓ	69 Ⓐ Ⓑ Ⓒ Ⓓ	94 Ⓐ Ⓑ Ⓒ Ⓓ
20 Ⓐ Ⓑ Ⓒ	45 Ⓐ Ⓑ Ⓒ Ⓓ	70 Ⓐ Ⓑ Ⓒ Ⓓ	95 Ⓐ Ⓑ Ⓒ Ⓓ
21 Ⓐ Ⓑ Ⓒ	46 Ⓐ Ⓑ Ⓒ Ⓓ	71 Ⓐ Ⓑ Ⓒ Ⓓ	96 Ⓐ Ⓑ Ⓒ Ⓓ
22 Ⓐ Ⓑ Ⓒ	47 Ⓐ Ⓑ Ⓒ Ⓓ	72 Ⓐ Ⓑ Ⓒ Ⓓ	97 Ⓐ Ⓑ Ⓒ Ⓓ
23 Ⓐ Ⓑ Ⓒ	48 Ⓐ Ⓑ Ⓒ Ⓓ	73 Ⓐ Ⓑ Ⓒ Ⓓ	98 Ⓐ Ⓑ Ⓒ Ⓓ
24 Ⓐ Ⓑ Ⓒ	49 Ⓐ Ⓑ Ⓒ Ⓓ	74 Ⓐ Ⓑ Ⓒ Ⓓ	99 Ⓐ Ⓑ Ⓒ Ⓓ
25 Ⓐ Ⓑ Ⓒ	50 Ⓐ Ⓑ Ⓒ Ⓓ	75 Ⓐ Ⓑ Ⓒ Ⓓ	100 Ⓐ Ⓑ Ⓒ Ⓓ

READING SECTION

LISTENING COMPREHENSION

This is the listening section of the test. There are three parts to this section.

PART I

Directions You will see a picture in your test book and you will hear four short statements.

Look at the picture in your test book and choose the statement that best describes what you see in the picture. Then mark your answer on your answer sheet.

Look at the sample below and listen to the four statements.

Statement (B), "The boys are reading" best describes what you see in the picture. Therefore, you should choose answer (B).

Sample Answer

Now let us begin Part I with question number one.

1.

2.

3.

4.

GO ON TO THE NEXT PAGE

5.

6.

7.

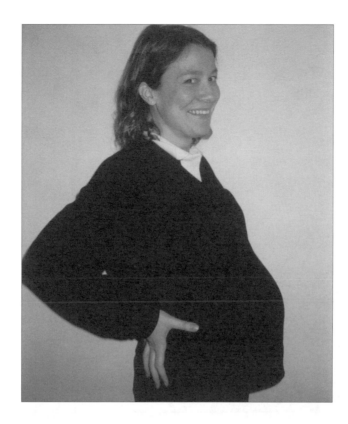

8.

GO ON TO THE NEXT PAGE

9.

10.

11.

12.

GO ON TO THE NEXT PAGE

13.

14.

15.

PART II

16. Mark your answer on your answer sheet.
17. Mark your answer on your answer sheet.
18. Mark your answer on your answer sheet.
19. Mark your answer on your answer sheet.
20. Mark your answer on your answer sheet.
21. Mark your answer on your answer sheet.
22. Mark your answer on your answer sheet.
23. Mark your answer on your answer sheet.
24. Mark your answer on your answer sheet.
25. Mark your answer on your answer sheet.
26. Mark your answer on your answer sheet.
27. Mark your answer on your answer sheet.
28. Mark your answer on your answer sheet.
29. Mark your answer on your answer sheet.
30. Mark your answer on your answer sheet.
31. Mark your answer on your answer sheet.
32. Mark your answer on your answer sheet.
33. Mark your answer on your answer sheet.
34. Mark your answer on your answer sheet.
35. Mark your answer on your answer sheet.

Directions Now, you will hear several short talks or conversations.

In your test book, you will read a question followed by four answers. Choose the best answer to each question and mark it on your answer sheet.

Now, let us begin Part III with question number 36.

36. What is their problem?

    (A) They are sick.
    (B) They need new pants.
    (C) They overate.
    (D) The horse's saddle is loose.

37. What is the problem?

    (A) Their waitress is late.
    (B) It's past ten o'clock.
    (C) They've lost their glasses.
    (D) The food is cold.

38. Who is listening to the talk?

    (A) A theater audience.
    (B) Ferry boat passengers.
    (C) Pedestrians at a crosswalk.
    (D) Race car drivers.

39. Why can't they do their homework?

    (A) They left it at school.
    (B) They don't know what it is.
    (C) There's too much of it.
    (D) They missed class.

40. Where are the washing instructions?

    (A) On the Web.
    (B) In the owner's manual.
    (C) On the label.
    (D) On the soap box.

41. What kind of music does the woman like?

    (A) Jazz.
    (B) Rock 'n' roll.
    (C) Classical.
    (D) Pop.

42. What should shoppers do?

    (A) Lock their car doors.
    (B) Go to the sale floor.
    (C) Buy a new watch.
    (D) Exit from specific doors.

43. When did the woman's parents get divorced?

    (A) When she was a baby.
    (B) Several years ago.
    (C) Last year.
    (D) Last week.

44. Where is the announcement being heard?

    (A) At a restaurant.
    (B) In a school.
    (C) On a bus.
    (D) In a mini-market.

45. Where will the sports team practice today?

    (A) On the track.
    (B) In the field.
    (C) At a club.
    (D) In the gym.

46. What time does the cafeteria open?

    (A) Late at night.
    (B) Early in the morning.
    (C) Just before lunch.
    (D) At dinner time.

47. Why doesn't the woman want to buy the shoes?

    (A) They're black.
    (B) She doesn't like the store.
    (C) They don't fit.
    (D) They're too expensive.

48. Who are they voting for?

    (A) School president.
    (B) The funniest comic.
    (C) Class colors.
    (D) Their favorite ballet.

49. Which team will the woman join?

    (A) Tennis.
    (B) Swimming.
    (C) Ping-Pong.
    (D) Baseball.

50. When do listeners need to be careful?

    (A) Stepping off the boat.
    (B) Going in the cave.
    (C) Climbing the ladder.
    (D) Sailing fast.

This is the end of the Listening Comprehension portion of the test. Turn to Part IV of the test.

YOU WILL HAVE THIRTY-FIVE MINUTES TO COMPLETE PARTS IV AND V OF THE TEST.

READING

This is the reading section of the test. There are two parts to this section.

PART IV

Directions This part of the test has incomplete sentences. There are four words or phrases, marked (A), (B), (C), and (D), under each sentence. Choose the one word or phrase that best complete the sentences. Then mark your answer on your answer sheet.

Example:

Please turn off your computer at the ------- of the day.

(A) ends
(B) ending
(C) end
(D) ended

Sample Answer
Ⓐ Ⓑ ⬤ Ⓓ

The sentence should read, "Please turn off your computer at the end of the day." Therefore, you should choose answer (C).

Now begin work on the questions.

51. She enjoys ------- in her free time.

   (A) sing
   (B) to sing
   (C) sings
   (D) singing

52. He is ------- a model airplane.

   (A) build
   (B) builder
   (C) built
   (D) building

53. We bought a ------- lemons.

   (A) few
   (B) little
   (C) some
   (D) any

54. She ------- for three months in Australia last year.

   (A) travels
   (B) traveled
   (C) is traveling
   (D) has been traveling

GO ON TO THE NEXT PAGE

55. ------- these dishes will take at least an hour.

(A) I wash
(B) The wash
(C) Washing
(D) Wash

56. All ------- of the photography club need digital cameras.

(A) mains
(B) members
(C) marks
(D) matters

57. Antonio will probably ------- the larger suitcase.

(A) pack
(B) to pack
(C) packing
(D) will pack

58. The president ------- in this city since 1996.

(A) lives
(B) is living
(C) lived
(D) has lived

59. There was a ------- at the wedding who knew how to swing.

(A) dancer
(B) deck
(C) door
(D) dollar

60. You had ------- study for the exam.

(A) go
(B) supposed to
(C) better
(D) ought

61. Maybe the show was -------.

(A) cancelled
(B) cancellation
(C) cancel
(D) canceling

62. You can't have dessert ------- you eat your dinner.

(A) but
(B) unless
(C) however
(D) whether

63. ------- will you graduate?

(A) When
(B) What
(C) As
(D) That

64. You can borrow my ------- if it gets really cold.

(A) coat
(B) coast
(C) course
(D) cooler

65. The police officer told me to stand -------.

(A) up
(B) down
(C) with
(D) for

66. He can't help us paint because he's too -------.

(A) busy
(B) busied
(C) business
(D) busily

67. These days, all cars run on unleaded
------.

(A) gasoline
(B) petroleum
(C) windows
(D) paint

68. After you collect the money, you need to count ------.

(A) it
(B) them
(C) they
(D) anything

69. The music was so ------ that it hurt my ears.

(A) lazy
(B) lonely
(C) lend
(D) loud

70. She has a two-inch scar on her ------ that will never heal.

(A) face
(B) fact
(C) facet
(D) farce

71. This lake is much ------ than the one near my house.

(A) deep
(B) deeper
(C) deeply
(D) deepness

72. Your dress is really too ------ for the event.

(A) fantasy
(B) festival
(C) fancy
(D) fashion

73. The photograph showed the mayor voting in the ------.

(A) election
(B) estimate
(C) equality
(D) eagerness

74. If you don't pay ------ during class, you're bound to fail.

(A) motion
(B) attention
(C) concentration
(D) intention

75. The children think that they can ------ a six-foot hole.

(A) due
(B) die
(C) duty
(D) dig

76. The ------ office is on Main Street.

(A) dentists
(B) dentist's
(C) dentist whose
(D) of the dentist

77. I asked ------ server for a fork.

(A) to
(B) my
(C) for
(D) we

78. The geology professor ------ here since 1988.

(A) teach
(B) taught
(C) has taught
(D) was teaching

GO ON TO THE NEXT PAGE

79. We ------- like to exchange this swimsuit.

    (A) are

    (B) could

    (C) would

    (D) ought

80. Tomorrow I'm going to ------- a haircut at 4:30.

    (A) get

    (B) be

    (C) make

    (D) act

Part V

Directions The questions in this part of the test are based on reading materials such as notices, letters, forms, and advertisements. Choose the one best answer, (A), (B), (C), or (D), to each question. Then mark your answer on your answer sheet.

Read the following example.

NOTICE

CAFETERIA CLOSED

Will reopen Monday, June 5

What will happen on June 5?

(A) The workers will take a day off.
(B) The cafeteria will open.
(C) The prices will go down.
(D) The school will close.

Sample Answer

The notice says that the cafeteria is closed and will open again on June 5. Therefore, you should choose answer (B).

Now begin work on the questions.

DO NOT DISTURB

TESTING IN PROGRESS

81. What should the reader NOT do?

(A) Make noise
(B) Interview
(C) Progress
(D) Test

82. What is happening?

(A) A progression
(B) An exam
(C) A disturbance
(D) A job fair

Questions 83—84 refer to the following sign.

Pool Entry

Fee covers one swim session only (2 hours)

Adults (19 and over)	$4.00
Teens (12-18)	$3.00
Children (4-11)	$2.00
3 and under	free

83. What do the costs cover?

(A) All-day pool access
(B) A two-hour massage
(C) Movie entry
(D) A swim period

84. Who pays the least?

(A) Senior citizens
(B) Adults
(C) School-aged children
(D) Babies

GO ON TO THE NEXT PAGE

Questions 85–86 refer to the following sign.

Welcome To Texas

Wear your seat belt!
Laws strictly enforced.

85. What is one purpose of this sign?

(A) To tell riders to use their safety belt
(B) To sell Texas-style belts
(C) To say farewell to people who are leaving
(D) To explain seat availability

86. Where would you see this sign?

(A) At the Texas border
(B) In a Texas jail
(C) In a store
(D) At a school

Questions 87–88 refer to the following sign.

All red-tag items are $20^\%$ off.

Blue-tag items are $30^\%$ off.

Open a Marteen's charge card today and save an additional 10%.

87. Where would you see this sign?

(A) An elementary school
(B) A church
(C) A sports club
(D) A store

88. What is the purpose of the sign?

(A) To explain discounts
(B) To estimate weight loss
(C) To teach math
(D) To tell sizes

Questions 89—90 refer to the following coupon.

MINDY's STELLAR CLIPS

Walk in for a
HAIRCUT TODAY
and receive a
free bottle of EverFresh Shampoo
(8 ounce size) *Retail value: $3.95*

Phone: 555-667-4409

89. What is the coupon for?

(A) Shampoo
(B) A haircut
(C) Conditioner
(D) $3.95

90. How can you get the offer?

(A) Make an appointment immediately.
(B) Buy a bottle of shampoo.
(C) Get a haircut today.
(D) Call now.

Questions 91—92 refer to the following sign.

Merry-Go-Round Rules

▮ Children under 6 must be accompanied by an adult (18 years or over).

▮ Accompanying adult rides free if standing.

▮ No changing horses after ride has started.

91. Where would you see this sign?

(A) On a Ferris wheel
(B) On a bicycle
(C) On a horse cart
(D) On a fair ride

92. What is the purpose of the sign?

(A) To tell prices
(B) To warn riders
(C) To give rules
(D) To explain how to ride

GO ON TO THE NEXT PAGE

Questions 93—94 refer to the following note.

> All burgers come with ketchup, lettuce, and tomato.
>
> Optional toppings 40 cents each: onion, pickles, cheese, peppers.

93. How many toppings come automatically?

   (A) None
   (B) Three
   (C) Four
   (D) Seven

94. Where would you see this note?

   (A) A pizzeria
   (B) A vegetarian restaurant
   (C) A fast-food restaurant
   (D) A bakery

Questions 95—96 refer to the following advice?

> **Refrigerate after opening.**
> **Contents are perishable.**

95. Where would you see this advice?

   (A) On a refrigerator
   (B) On a jar of food
   (C) On a bouquet of flowers
   (D) On a box of ice cream

96. What does the advice tell you how to do?

   (A) Store something
   (B) Open something
   (C) Serve something
   (D) Cook something

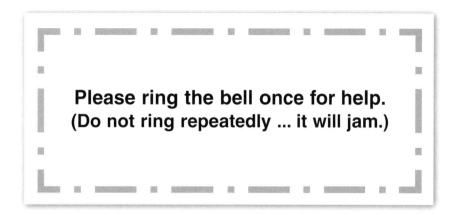

97. What will you get if you ring the bell?

(A) Assistance
(B) Trouble
(C) Repeated instructions
(D) The machine will start

98. What will happen if you ring the bell several times?

(A) You'll get help.
(B) The fire department will come.
(C) The message will repeat.
(D) It will stop ringing.

Questions 99–100 refer to the following advertisement.

2BR APARTMENT available immediate-ly.
Lrg. kitchen. 1.5 baths.
Laundry in bldg. Light, clean, new carpet/paint.
No pets/smokers. $800/mo.
Deposit first/last.
Call now 777-3059.

99. What is the advertisement for?

(A) A washer and dryer
(B) A house
(C) An apartment
(D) A car

100. Which person should not call?

(A) A dog owner
(B) A student
(C) A couple with children
(D) A painter

Stop! This is the end of the test. If you finish before time is called, you may go back to Parts IV and V and check your work.

LISTENING COMPREHENSION

This is the listening section of the test. There are three parts to this section.

PART I

Directions You will see a picture in your test book and you will hear four short statements.

Look at the picture in your test book and choose the statement that best describes what you see in the picture. Then mark your answer on your answer sheet.

Look at the sample below and listen to the four statements.

Statement (B), "The boys are reading" best describes what you see in the picture. Therefore, you should choose answer (B).

Sample Answer
 Ⓐ ● Ⓒ Ⓓ

Now let us begin Part I with question number one.

1.

2.

3.

4.

GO ON TO THE NEXT PAGE

5.

6.

7.

8.

GO ON TO THE NEXT PAGE

9.

10.

11.

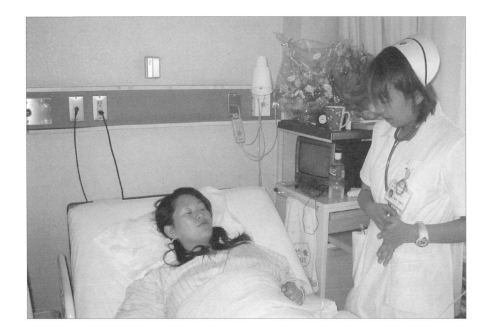

12.

GO ON TO THE NEXT PAGE ➔

13.

14.

15.

PART II

Directions Now, you will hear a question or statement followed by three responses. Choose the best response to each question or statement.

Now, listen to a sample question.

You will hear: Good morning, John. How are you?

You will also hear: (A) I am fine, thank you.
                               (B) I am in the living room.   _Sample Answer_
                               (C) My name is John.   ● Ⓑ Ⓒ

The best response to the question "How are you" is choice (A), "I am fine, thank you." Therefore, you should choose answer (A).

Now let us begin Part II with question number 16.

16. Mark your answer on your answer sheet.
17. Mark your answer on your answer sheet.
18. Mark your answer on your answer sheet.
19. Mark your answer on your answer sheet.
20. Mark your answer on your answer sheet.
21. Mark your answer on your answer sheet.
22. Mark your answer on your answer sheet.
23. Mark your answer on your answer sheet.
24. Mark your answer on your answer sheet.
25. Mark your answer on your answer sheet.
26. Mark your answer on your answer sheet.
27. Mark your answer on your answer sheet.
28. Mark your answer on your answer sheet.
29. Mark your answer on your answer sheet.
30. Mark your answer on your answer sheet.
31. Mark your answer on your answer sheet.
32. Mark your answer on your answer sheet.
33. Mark your answer on your answer sheet.
34. Mark your answer on your answer sheet.
35. Mark your answer on your answer sheet.

Directions Now, you will hear several short talks or conversations.

In your test book, you will read a question followed by four answers. Choose the best answer to each question and mark it on your answer sheet.

Now, let us begin Part III with question number 36.

36. What is happening?

(A) The man has no receipt.
(B) The man didn't pay.
(C) Aisle six is closed.
(D) The man needs to go to the cashier.

37. How did she get into the pool?

(A) She tripped.
(B) She slipped.
(C) The lifeguard made her swim.
(D) Somebody pushed her.

38. Who are Tracy and Louis Ellen?

(A) Soccer players.
(B) Hairdressers.
(C) Tennis players.
(D) Swimmers.

39. What does the woman need to do?

(A) Sew the zipper.
(B) Look inside the backpack.
(C) Enter the building.
(D) Put the book in the backpack.

40. Why do they want to celebrate?

(A) They found her wallet.
(B) They're getting married.
(C) It's the man's birthday.
(D) They passed the exam.

41. What should Ms. Klinehammer do?

(A) Wait in lane 7.
(B) Answer the telephone.
(C) Call Wade.
(D) Move forward.

42. Where are they?

(A) A movie theater.
(B) An elementary school.
(C) A train.
(D) A swimming pool.

43. What does the man want?

(A) A shirt.
(B) Salt.
(C) Pepper.
(D) Sugar.

44. What is the topic of the talk?

(A) Traffic.
(B) Weekend entertainment.
(C) A computer system.
(D) Weather.

45. Why is the flight cancelled?

(A) A storm.
(B) Fog.
(C) A strike.
(D) High coastal waters.

GO ON TO THE NEXT PAGE

46. What is the man trying on?

(A) Pants.
(B) A jacket.
(C) A jumper.
(D) Shoes.

47. Which aisle can take the next customer?

(A) 1
(B) 2
(C) 3
(D) 4

48. What did the woman do?

(A) Memorize the first part.
(B) Wash the car.
(C) Write the music.
(D) Drive in reverse.

49. Why are the man's eyes red?

(A) He's been swimming.
(B) A ball hit his face.
(C) He may be sick.
(D) Because it's cold outside.

50. When did they start to show the African stamps?

(A) The 19th century.
(B) At 3:40.
(C) A few minutes ago.
(D) At ten minutes to 8:00.

This is the end of the Listening Comprehension portion of the test. Turn to Part IV of the test.

YOU WILL HAVE THIRTY-FIVE MINUTES TO COMPLETE PARTS IV AND V OF THE TEST.

READING

This is the reading section of the test. There are two parts to this section.

PART IV

Directions This part of the test has incomplete sentences. There are four words or phrases, marked (A), (B), (C), and (D), under each sentence. Choose the one word or phrase that best complete the sentences. Then mark your answer on your answer sheet.

Example:

Please turn off your computer at the ------- of the day.

(A) ends
(B) ending
(C) end
(D) ended

Sample Answer
Ⓐ Ⓑ ● Ⓓ

The sentence should read, "Please turn off your computer at the end of the day." Therefore, you should choose answer (C).

Now begin work on the questions.

---

51. ------- Marcus 19 years old?

(A) Is
(B) Who
(C) Are
(D) He

52. ------- my glasses.

(A) This is
(B) That is
(C) The one is
(D) These are

53. Her wedding is on the ------- of May.

(A) two eight
(B) twenty-eight
(C) twenty-eighth
(D) twentieth and eighth

54. The lamp is ------- the living room.

(A) on
(B) in
(C) over
(D) under

GO ON TO THE NEXT PAGE

55. Teresa and Colleen are ------- from Ireland.

(A) they
(B) either
(C) both
(D) and

56. The hostess served ------- way too much food.

(A) he
(B) him
(C) his
(D) he's

57. Buy a loaf of ------- when you're at the store.

(A) books
(B) boxes
(C) butter
(D) bread

58. The manager ------- to send this fax before noon today.

(A) likes
(B) is liking
(C) would like
(D) liked

59. We had ------- cancel our reservations by 11:59 last night.

(A) to
(B) must
(C) supposed
(D) and

60. While we were ------- cards, we heard a strange sound.

(A) play
(B) played
(C) playing
(D) having played

61. This black wallet is much ------- expensive than the brown.

(A) too
(B) more
(C) so
(D) as

62. Are you ------- by cash or by credit card?

(A) selling
(B) paying
(C) changing
(D) trying on

63. Several students are going ------- class on Thursday.

(A) miss
(B) to miss
(C) missing
(D) will miss

64. Marty became an electrician and I did -------.

(A) become
(B) too
(C) added
(D) neither

65. That restaurant serves a lot of spicy ------- salty food.

(A) but
(B) though
(C) with
(D) and

66. Last Sunday, we ------- on Lake Wingo in my sister's boat.

(A) saw
(B) swam
(C) sailed
(D) snowed

67. The students learned how to ------- their robots remotely.

(A) care

(B) control

(C) caution

(D) communicate

68. Tony Markoni is the ------- cook in the city.

(A) better

(B) best

(C) well

(D) more

69. I always ------- my seat belt when I drive.

(A) wear

(B) wore

(C) am wearing

(D) was wearing

70. Which ------- are you flying on?

(A) air

(B) airport

(C) airborne

(D) airline

71. The actress ------- tired of signing autographs.

(A) are

(B) will

(C) was

(D) been

72. My ——–- is a member of the gymnastics club.

(A) cream

(B) course

(C) cousin

(D) cost

73. You need to ------- that shirt.

(A) butter

(B) better

(C) button

(D) bother

74. She ------- her meeting with the marketing department.

(A) cancelled

(B) carted

(C) cleaned

(D) concerned

75. The train was ------- crowded that we had to stand.

(A) too

(B) such

(C) very

(D) so

76. The dishwasher is completely -------.

(A) hungry

(B) lonely

(C) honest

(D) empty

77. Seven police cars arrived at the scene of the -------.

(A) accident

(B) attention

(C) appliance

(D) advertisement

78. My sister ordered the daily ------- from the menu.

(A) spectacle

(B) special

(C) speaker

(D) spark

GO ON TO THE NEXT PAGE

79. He always keeps his wallet ------- his back pocket.

(A) on
(B) behind
(C) beside
(D) in

80. You can either rent ------- buy these skateboards.

(A) or
(B) and
(C) nor
(D) either

Part V

Directions The questions in this part of the test are based on reading materials such as notices, letters, forms, and advertisements. Choose the one best answer, (A), (B), (C), or (D), to each question. Then mark your answer on your answer sheet.

Read the following example.

NOTICE

CAFETERIA CLOSED

Will reopen Monday, June 5

What will happen on June 5?

(A) The workers will take a day off.
(B) The cafeteria will open.
(C) The prices will go down.
(D) The school will close.

Sample Answer

The notice says that the cafeteria is closed and will open again on June 5. Therefore, you should choose answer (B).

Now begin work on the questions.

Questions 81—82 refer to the following information.

First Royal Cinemas

Presenting
Who Says?

7:15 P.M. Sunday 11/18/02
Adult $8.00
Auditorium 9
Admit One. Good this date only.

---

81. What is the title of the movie?

    (A) First Royal Cinemas.

    (B) Who Says?

    (C) Auditorium 9.

    (D) Admit One.

82. Which theater is the show in?

    (A) One

    (B) Two

    (C) Eight

    (D) Nine

Absence Codes

U = unexcused   H = holiday
E = excused   V = vacation
L = late   P = personal
I = illness   W = warning
S = suspended*   D = discipline

*Document in employee's file.

83. Which code shows that a worker is sick?

(A) L
(B) I
(C) S
(D) W

84. Which code shows that an employee is in trouble?

(A) H
(B) V
(C) P
(D) D

Questions 85–86 refer to the following questionnaire.

I want a dog for: (Check any responses that fit.)

XX Friendship   **XX** Hobby
____ Exercise   ____ To make money
XX The kids   ____ To show
____ Security, guarding   **XX** Other
____ Prestige   <u>Christmas gift for family</u>

85. What is one reason that this person wants a dog?

(A) For safety
(B) To help her health
(C) For her children
(D) She is blind.

86. What is NOT a reason that this person wants a dog?

(A) For fun
(B) As a friend
(C) To show off
(D) As a gift

GO ON TO THE NEXT PAGE

> **Night Stop Program**
> (available 9 P.M. to 5 A.M.)
> For your safety at night, you may ask to exit the bus anywhere along your route, even if it is not a regular bus stop. To do so, go to the front of the bus and ask your driver at least one block before you want to get off. Safety considerations will determine if s/he can comply with your request.

87. Who is this notice for?

(A) Drivers
(B) Riders
(C) Stop attendants
(D) Nighttime taxi passengers

88. What determines a driver's stopping at night?

(A) Safety
(B) Payment
(C) Weather
(D) If it's a regular stop

89. What should you do if you want to stop?

(A) Ring the bell.
(B) Pull the string.
(C) Shout to the driver.
(D) Approach the driver to ask.

Questions 90—91 refer to the following advertisement.

The YYCB offers fun for every family.

Active Older Adults	Open Camp
Child Watch (while you work out)	Senior Programs
Family Swim	Teen Programs
School-Age Child Care	Camping
Swim Lessons	Family Nights
Birthday Parties	Summer Enrichment
Day Camp	Youth Sports

---

90. Who would be interested in this advertisement?

(A) Active families
(B) Airline passengers
(C) Job seekers
(D) Shoppers

91. What do they NOT offer?

(A) Babysitting
(B) Parties
(C) Swimming
(D) Reading classes

GO ON TO THE NEXT PAGE

Questions 92—94 refer to the following article.

> ***Tiffany Turner***, age 12, is the grand-prize winner for the 8 to 14 age group national spelling contest. Miss Turner is a sixth-grade student at the Trenton Learning Center in Memphis, Tennessee. Miss Turner took the victory from 62 finalists by spelling "phenomenal" correctly. Her prize is an all-expenses-paid vacation for four to Hawaii. Second prize went to Jeremy Lock: a Swift 10-speed bicycle. Third prize went to Dina McGilvra: a fifty-dollar gift certificate to the Nanton Mall.

92. What event did Miss Turner win?

(A) A running race
(B) An art competition
(C) A spelling bee
(D) A math contest

93. What did she win?

(A) A trip
(B) A bicycle
(C) Money
(D) Books

94. How many children competed?

(A) 12
(B) 62
(C) 10
(D) 3

Questions 95–96 refer to the following table of contents.

Table of Contents

8 Kids and Fall Safety
Back to school means back to sports and an eye on safety.

14 All Aboard!
Take a scenic railroad trip into the past.

19 Road Lessons
Car crashes happen every day. Learn tips to be a safe pedestrian.

32 Swing is the Thing
Swing music had skirts flying at Saturday's dance.

95. Which is NOT an article in this publication?

(A) Safety for school children
(B) Car accidents
(C) A recent dance
(D) Park toys

96. Who would be interested in this magazine?

(A) Employers
(B) Families
(C) Medical doctors
(D) Sick people

Questions 97–98 refer to the following advertisement.

Excitement and energy are everywhere at the **Stand Up Artist's Coffee House**. On the stage, you can hear drumming, bells, Indian rhythms, poetry, solo singers, dancers, and original music. At the bar, you can order fine coffee and tea beverages as well as easy snacks and pastries.
Admission: $5

97. What are they advertising?

(A) A show
(B) A concert
(C) A coffee house
(D) A music CD

98. What can you eat at the coffee house?

(A) A large dinner
(B) Indian food
(C) Imported taste treats
(D) Light foods

GO ON TO THE NEXT PAGE

> ## You're Invited to a Birthday Party
> At Megan's house (10012 Blackberry Road)
> Thursday, April 17th, 5 P.M.
> Please RSVP 446-5550
> No gifts, please

99. What is this note?

(A) A postcard from a vacation
(B) A change-of-address form
(C) A party invitation
(D) An advertisement

100. What should the receiver do?

(A) Send a letter.
(B) Order now.
(C) Buy a gift.
(D) Call.

Stop! This is the end of the test. If you finish before time is called, you may go back to Parts IV and V and check your work.

Answer Key and Audio Script for Part I to Part III

Answer Key for Part IV and Part V

Answer Key and Audio Script for Practice Test 1 and 2

Test Hint 2 Practice Two

2. people

3. things or places

4. things

5. quantities and animals

6. actions

Test Hint 3 Practice One

1.
   (A) The pizza is <u>on</u> the chair.
   (B) The pizza is <u>in</u> a box.
 √ (C) The pizza is <u>under</u> the lamp.
   (D) The pizza is <u>next to</u> the window.

2.
   (A) The umbrella is <u>in</u> his bag.
 √ (B) The pedestrian is <u>in front of</u> the crowd.
   (C) A flag is flying <u>next to</u> the ferry boat.
   (D) There are benches <u>behind</u> the man.

3.
   (A) The escalators are <u>between</u> the staircases.
 √ (B) The stairs are <u>between</u> the escalators.
   (C) The people are walking <u>up</u> the stairs.
   (D) The stairs are <u>to the left of</u> the elevator.

4.
   (A) The man is <u>to the left of</u> the refrigerator.
   (B) The bottles are <u>above</u> the boxes.
   (C) The man is putting the bottle <u>on</u> the table.
 √ (D) The basket is hanging <u>on</u> the shopper's arm.

Test Hint 3 Practice Two

Prepositions	Question 1	Question 2	Question 3	Question 4
above				√
behind		√		
between			√√	
in	√	√		
in front of		√		
next to	√	√		
on	√			√√
to the left of			√	√
under	√			
up			√	

Test Hint 4 Practice

1.
 √ (A) There are <u>two</u> children.
   (B) There are <u>three</u> children.
   (C) There are <u>four</u> children.
   (D) There are <u>five</u> children.

2.
   (A) <u>One</u> girl is playing the piano.
 √ (B) <u>A couple</u> girls are playing the piano.
   (C) <u>Several</u> girls are playing the piano.
   (D) <u>A few</u> girls are playing the piano.

3.
   (A) There are <u>a couple</u> people in the park.
   (B) There are <u>a few</u> people in the park.
 √ (C) There are <u>a lot of</u> people in the park.
   (D) There are <u>thousands of</u> people in the park.

4.
 √ (A) <u>A few</u> girls are studying.
   (B) <u>Several</u> girls are studying.
   (C) <u>Lots of</u> girls are studying.
   (D) <u>Many</u> girls are studying.

Test Hint 5 Practice and Test Hint 6 Practice

1.   (A) This is a museum.
     (B) This is a laboratory.
  √ (C) This is a library.
     (D) This is a factory.

2.   (A) He's a veterinarian.
  √ (B) He's a dentist.
     (C) He's an electrician.
     (D) He's a graduating senior.

3.   (A) There's been a fire.
  √ (B) There's been a flood.
     (C) There's been a lot of fog.
     (D) There's been an invasion.

4. √ (A) The girls are in a race.
     (B) The girls are in the forest.
     (C) The girls are on a runway.
     (D) The girls are at a meeting.

Test Hint 7 Practice One and Practice Two

1.   (A) The worker is painting the walkway.
     (B) Water is pouring into the hole.
     (C) The man is riding in the truck.
  √ (D) The man is digging in the hole.

2. √ (A) The students are graduating.
     (B) The graduates are singing.
     (C) Every desk is occupied.
     (D) They are all wearing raincoats.

3.   (A) The woman is washing his hair.
  √ (B) The man is getting a haircut.
     (C) The hare is sitting quietly.
     (D) The man is riding a horse.

4. √ (A) They're building a new wall.
     (B) They're unloading wood from the truck.
     (C) They're looking at the forest.
     (D) They're both standing on ladders.

5.   (A) They're chatting on the sofa.
  √ (B) The man is pushing a button.
     (C) They're playing with a remote control car.
     (D) They are getting haircuts.

6.   (A) The man is building a fence around the driveway.
     (B) The man is carrying heavy luggage.
     (C) The man is walking into the garage.
  √ (D) The man is moving the garbage cans.

Test Hint 8 Practice One and Practice Two

1. a. T   b. T   c. F   d. F   e. T   f. F   **3.** a. F   b. T   c. F   d. T   e. F   f. T

2. a. F   b. F   c. T   d. T   e. T   f. F   **4.** a. T   b. F   c. T   d. T   e. F   f. T

Vocabulary Power!

look	build	use	take
wear	ride	erase	hang
comb	throw	play	smile
stand	press	hit	hold

Test Hint 9 Practice One and Practice Two

1. √ (A) He's a baseball player.
   (B) He's a soccer player.
   (C) He's a tennis player.
   (D) He's a basketball player.

2. (A) She's putting away her book.
   √ (B) She's turning the page.
   (C) She's reading to the child.
   (D) She's doing her art.

3. (A) He's wearing glasses.
   (B) He's mowing the grass.
   (C) He's cleaning the class.
   √ (D) He's wiping his glasses.

4. √ (A) It's an ambulance.
   (B) It's a police car.
   (C) It's a fire truck.
   (D) It's a helicopter.

Test Hint 10 Practice

1. (A) He's writing a note.
   √ (B) He's marking the wood.
   (C) He's fixing his headphones.
   (D) He's buying some wood.

2. (A) The children are seating the guests.
   (B) The children are washing the dishes.
   √ (C) The children are eating their meals.
   (D) The children are making their dinner.

3. (A) Her apron is on the hanger.
   (B) One woman is pointing to the clock.
   (C) They're painting the house.
   √ (D) They're learning to paint.

4. (A) They're trying on clothes.
   (B) They're happy to be at the party.
   √ (C) They're putting their coats on hooks.
   (D) They're putting on their jackets.

Test Hint 11 Practice

1. (A) He's billing the client.
   √ (B) He's a builder.
   (C) He's looking at the food.
   (D) He's a manager.

2. √ (A) The family is having breakfast.
   (B) They are setting the table.
   (C) Each person has a light cap.
   (D) The boat looks stable.

3. (A) One woman is pointing at the other woman.
   (B) She is going to hang her picture on the wall.
   (C) The lady is using a hairbrush.
   √ (D) The teacher is looking at one student's work.

4. √ (A) The students just arrived in the classroom.
   (B) They're looking at the goats.
   (C) They're smelling something.
   (D) They've hooked two big fish.

Test Hint 12 Practice One and Practice Two

1. √ (A) The women are airplane passengers.
   (B) The passengers are waiting for take-off.
   (C) All the seats are empty.
   (D) They're riding motorcycles.

2. (A) The woman is holding the baby.
   (B) The woman is a graduate.
   (C) The woman is in an ambulance.
   √ (D) The woman is pregnant.

3. (A) They built a snowman.
   √ (B) It's cold and snowing.
   (C) The skiers are in the house.
   (D) Fog has settled in.

4. (A) His hands are dirty.
   √ (B) He's throwing away garbage.
   (C) He's storing things in a bin.
   (D) He's throwing rocks in the lake.

Part I Practice Test

Audio Script	Explanatory Answer
1. (A) The student is peeling an apple. (B) The student is molding the clay. (C) The student is painting something. (D) The student is using the ashtray.	(A) There is a student. (B) There may be clay. √ (C) The student is painting a small pot. (D) The pot looks like an ashtray.
2. (A) All of the seats are taken. (B) Many passengers are standing. (C) They are riding in an airplane. (D) The train car isn't very crowded.	(A) There are seats. (B) Only one passenger is standing. (C) People are "riding." √ (D) The car has many open seats.
3. (A) There is a tire. (B) There are a couple of tires. (C) There are several tires. (D) There are lots of tires.	(A) There is not one tire. (B) There aren't two tires. (C) There are more than "several." √ (D) There are many tires.
4. (A) One girl is sitting in front of the other girl. (B) The girls are looking in a mirror. (C) The girls are sitting next to a plant. (D) Both girls are in a park.	(A) The girls are sitting behind each other. (B) They look similar. √ (C) They are next to the plant. (D) "Park" relates to plants and sitting.
5. (A) They are picking flowers. (B) They just got married. (C) They are wearing tuxedos. (D) They look unhappy.	(A) There are flowers. √ (B) They just got married. (C) Only the man is wearing a tuxedo. (D) "Unhappy" sounds like "happy."
6. (A) She's a dentist. (B) She's an engineer. (C) She's a musician. (D) She's a nurse.	√ (A) The woman is a dentist. (B) The equipment relates to engineering. (C) Earphones relate to music. (D) Nurses relate to medical settings.
7. (A) The fire is out of control. (B) The firemen are washing the engine. (C) The fire truck is in the street. (D) The ladders are being painted.	(A) "Fire" relates to "fire truck." (B) There is an engine. √ (C) The truck is in the street. (D) There are ladders.
8. (A) Passengers are waiting for the train. (B) There are many tracks. (C) The engine is being repaired. (D) Containers are stacked on the train car.	(A) There is a train. Passengers relate to trains. √ (B) There are lots of tracks. (C) There is an engine. (D) Containers relate to train cars. There is a train car.

Test Hint 13 Practice

1. (M)   Who caught the ball?
   (W)   (A)   My uncle built it.
       √   (B)   Jerry, in left field.
         (C)   She's in the hall.

2. (M)   What time is your haircut?
   (W)   (A)   Thanks, I like it too.
         (B)   It's a new style.
       √   (C)   3:30.

3. (M)   When can we finish our homework?
   (W)   (A)   Mostly math homework.
         (B)   She assigned it yesterday.
       √   (C)   We'll do it tonight.

4. (M)   Why does your stomach hurt?
   (W)   (A)   To the doctor, right away.
       √   (B)   I ate some bad fish.
         (C)   I weigh 60 kilos.

5. (M)   How did you lose your luggage?
   (W)   √   (A)   I left it in the taxi cab.
         (B)   Three bags.
         (C)   Let's tighten the handle.

6. (W)   Where does this train go?
   (M)   (A)   Too many passengers.
         (B)   Track 17 is closed.
       √   (C)   To Chicago.

7. (W)   Is she pregnant?
   (M)   (A)   Three kids.
       √   (B)   Yes, four months pregnant.
         (C)   No, she doesn't.

8. (W)   Which club did you join, photography or badminton?
   (M)   √   (A)   Photography.
         (B)   The net was too high.
         (C)   I can't find the room.

Test Hint 14 Practice

1. (M)   Who won the soccer match?
   (W)   (A)   On the field.
         (B)   It ended at 5:30.
       √   (C)   We did.

2. (M)   What's your favorite kind of music?
   (W)   √   (A)   Jazz.
         (B)   At the concert.
         (C)   Because it's easy to dance to.

3. (M)   When did Mika turn on the TV?
   (W)   (A)   She was bored.
         (B)   With the remote control.
       √   (C)   An hour ago.

4. (M)   Where did they leave their backpacks?
   (W)   (A)   Amy and John.
       √   (B)   On the school bus.
         (C)   Their backpacks.

5. (M)   Why are you ordering so much food?
   (W)   √   (A)   I'm really hungry.
         (B)   Two hamburgers and three large fries.
         (C)   From the server.

6. (M)   How did you pay?
   (W)   (A)   The cashier.
       √   (B)   In cash.
         (C)   Forty dollars.

7. (W)   How many words do we have to memorize?
   (M)   √   (A)   There are 100 on the list.
         (B)   In the dictionary.
         (C)   For the test.

8. (W)   What size shoes does he wear?
   (M)   (A)   Seventy dollars.
         (B)   White, with blue stripes.
       √   (C)   He wears a 44.

Test Hint 15 Practice

1. (W)   Did he catch the ball?
   (M)   (A) Baseball season.
        √ (B) Yes, he did.
          (C) With live music.

2. (W)   Can I sit here?
   (M) √ (A) Yes, you can.
          (B) Seat 42A.
          (C) In the car.

3. (W)   Was it raining when you left?
   (M)   (A) My umbrella.
          (B) I left it in my suitcase.
        √ (C) No, it wasn't.

4. (W)   May I look at your ticket?
   (M) √ (A) Yes, you may.
          (B) From the agent.
          (C) If she comes.

5. (W)   Is your wallet in your back pocket?
   (M) √ (A) No, it isn't.
          (B) For the meal.
          (C) We rode back in a wagon.

6. (W)   Did you understand the grammar?
   (M)   (A) My English teacher.
        √ (B) Yes, I did.
          (C) My grammar book.

7. (W)   Do you take credit cards?
   (M) √ (A) I'm sorry, no, we only take
              cash.
          (B) They have a credit card.
          (C) No, she isn't.

8. (W)   Are you going to fix the window?
   (M) √ (A) No, we aren't.
          (B) With a ball.
          (C) Broken glass.

Test Hints 16 and 17 Practice

1. (W)   That car was too expensive.
   (M)   (A) I got a speeding ticket.
        √ (B) Used cars are usually much
              cheaper.
          (C) The luggage is in the trunk.

2. (W)   My husband sings in the choir.
   (M)   (A) On the radio.
          (B) He does electrical wiring.
        √ (C) My wife does, too.

3. (W)   I don't feel good at all.
   (M) √ (A) Maybe you caught a cold.
          (B) Like sandpaper.
          (C) Then put it on your credit
              card.

4. (W)   My grandfather memorized that poem.
   (M)   (A) I met your grandmother, too.
        √ (B) He didn't make a single
              mistake.
          (C) I can't remember which street.

5. (W)   If I keep snacking like this, I'll surely
         gain weight.
   (M) √ (A) Snacking is a terrible habit.
          (B) The waiter brought our
              change.
          (C) You forgot to feed the snake.

6. (W)   We won the game!
   (M)   (A) Your biology professor was
              there.
          (B) She said that her stomach hurt.
        √ (C) Congratulations. I knew you
              would.

Test Hint 18 Practice One

1. (M) When will the talk start?
    (W)   (A) Yesterday.
      √ (B) Right after the lunch.
        (C) The speaker was my high
            school teacher.

2. (W) How many chairs do we need?
    (M)   (A) Sixty-five days.
      √ (B) Enough for all the parents.
        (C) That will be fine.

3. (M) Which color would you like, the gold
        or the red?
    (W)   (A) Yes, I do.
      √ (B) Whichever one is cheaper.
        (C) For the top of the package.

4. (W) Can I use your pen?
    (M)   (A) Of course we can.
        (B) No, you did not.
      √ (C) Sorry, it's broken.

5. (M) Whose brush is this?
    (W) √ (A) We all share the same brush.
        (B) I will.
        (C) You're making me blush.

6. (W) Could you please hold my umbrella?
    (M) √ (A) My hands are full.
        (B) They can't do it now.
        (C) No, I didn't know that.

7. (W) Did you get your change?
    (M)   (A) Yes, she did.
      √ (B) The waiter gave it to me.
        (C) No, we aren't.

8. (W) Why is your hair wet?
    (M) √ (A) I forgot my umbrella today.
        (B) Lots of water.
        (C) She gives a good haircut.

Test Hint 18 Practice Two

Questions	Direct Answers
1. When will the talk start?	c. At 2:00.
2. How many chairs do we need?	h. We need at least 60.
3. Which color would you like, the gold or the red?	e. Whichever one is cheaper.
4. Can I use your pen?	f. No, you can't.
5. Whose brush is this?	a. It's my brush, but everybody uses it.
6. Could you please hold my umbrella?	b. No, I can't.
7. Did you get your change?	g. Yes, I got my change.
8. Why is your hair wet?	d. It's raining outside.

Test Hint 19 Practice

1. (W) Do you want juice or milk?
    (M) √ (A) Juice, please.
        (B) Yes, thank you.
        (C) I'm thirsty.

2. (W) Can we return it or exchange it?
    (M)   (A) She returns next Friday.
        (B) She forgot to take her change.
     √ (C) Either, if you have the receipt.

3. (W)   Is it green or blue?

   (M)
- (A) Yes, it is.
- √ (B) It's green and white.
- (C) The color is.

4. (W)   Which test was hard, the math or the science?

   (M)
- (A) Tomorrow.
- √ (B) Science tests are always harder.
- (C) An "A+."

5. (W)   Are we meeting on Wednesday or Thursday?

   (M)
- √ (A) Wednesday.
- (B) In the evening.
- (C) That's the middle of the week.

6. (W)   Do you speak German or Italian?

   (M)
- √ (A) I speak both.
- (B) Berlin.
- (C) It was too hot there.

Test Hint 20 Practice

1. (M)   How much is this motorcycle?

   (W)
- (A) Four doors.
- (B) Smooth and steady.
- √ (C) Today only, it's $4,500.

2. (M)   When can we visit the hospital?

   (W)
- (A) Last week.
- √ (B) Allen's not there anymore.
- (C) At the parking lot.

3. (M)   Do you have a boyfriend?

   (W)
- (A) Yes, he is.
- √ (B) Actually, I'm married.
- (C) No, they can't.

4. (W)   What was your score on the test?

   (M)
- √ (A) I got a ninety.
- (B) Biology.
- (C) Last Tuesday.

5. (W)   Who took the train?

   (M)
- (A) The students are studying.
- (B) Katie and Mark are in training.
- √ (C) Everybody came by bus.

6. (W)   Should I still apply?

   (M)
- √ (A) We're not accepting any more applications.
- (B) You should always wipe your feet.
- (C) No, he couldn't.

7. (W)   Have you ever met my husband?

   (M)
- (A) No, he isn't.
- √ (B) I met him at the New Year's party.
- (C) Yes, they have two melons.

8. (W)   Will they remember to lock the door?

   (M)
- (A) No, I haven't.
- (B) Yes, she is planning to go.
- √ (C) I put a note on the door to remind them.

Test Hint 21 Practice

1. (W)   Is that restaurant expensive or cheap?
   (M)   (A) These shoes were pretty expensive.
           (B) I ordered chips at the restaurant.
      √ (C) We had dinner for forty dollars in total.

2. (W)   What kind of movies do you watch?
   (M)   (A) My watch is broken again.
      √ (B) I like romance and drama.
           (C) At the King Movie Theater near our house.

3. (W)   What does her face look like?
   (M) √ (A) It's small—she's very petite.
           (B) We always face the front.
           (C) It looks like rain.

4. (W)   Did you lose your ring, or did you just forget it?
   (M) √ (A) I forgot to put it on this morning.
           (B) My phone is ringing.
           (C) She lost four kilos.

5. (W)   What color are the Ping-Pong balls?
   (M)   (A) I like Ping-Pong.
      √ (B) They're orange.
           (C) This table is my favorite color.

6. (W)   Do you want to work part-time or full-time?
   (M)   (A) It's partly your fault.
           (B) I'm full.
      √ (C) I can only work about ten hours a week.

7. (W)   How do you open this box?
   (M) √ (A) Push this button, then it will open.
           (B) In the box.
           (C) The store just opened.

8. (W)   Who took this great photograph?
   (M)   (A) They took the camera, too.
           (B) We'll put the photograph in a frame.
      √ (C) My sister did, on the ferryboat.

Test Hint 22 Practice

1. (W)   Would you like honey in your tea?
   (M)   (A) That tree is too much money.
           (B) She's very funny.
      √ (C) Just a little bit.

2. (W)   How far is it to the top of the hill?
   (M)   (A) Just down the hall.
      √ (B) About 500 meters.
           (C) With a long tape.

3. (M)   When did you hurt your back?
   (W)   (A) We just heard the news.
           (B) On a hard rock.
      √ (C) Last winter, when I was skiing.

4. (M)   Why can't we go to the fair?
   (W) √ (A) We don't have time.
           (B) A fear of flying.
           (C) She kicked the ball unusually far.

5. (W)   Do you like my new dress?
   (M) √ (A) It looks very pretty.
           (B) On the desk.
           (C) I'd like to rest.

6. (W)   Who's ready for dinner?
   (M)   (A) Usually in the winter.
      √ (B) Surely the kids are hungry.
           (C) John's the winner.

7. (M)   I see a big fly in the bathtub.
   (W)   (A) We could fry the fish.
        √ (B) He's been in there for days.
           (C) The soap is in a bag in the
               cupboard.

8. (M)   Shall I e-mail it, or fax it to you?
   (W)   (A) I need all the facts, first.
           (B) She's a female.
        √ (C) I don't have a fax machine.

Test Hint 23 Practice

1. (W)   Can you work a few extra hours
         tonight?
   (M) √ (A) I can only stay until eleven
           o'clock.
        (B) She just got a new job.
        (C) We get paid on Thursdays.

2. (W)   Did you color your hair?
   (M)   (A) It's too long.
        √ (B) Yes, it was turning gray.
           (C) We just bought some paint.

3. (W)   How much is that old stamp worth?
   (M)   (A) At the post office.
        √ (B) Hundreds of dollars.
           (C) She sent the letter yesterday.

4. (M)   Where do your grandparents live?
   (W)   (A) Ninety and ninety-five years
               old.
           (B) Lots of presents for the children.
        √ (C) In a small apartment in
               Sapporo.

5. (M)   How about a snack?
   (M)   (A) For dinner.
        √ (B) I'm not hungry.
           (C) Thanks, but I already did it.

6. (W)   He isn't the professor, is he?
   (M) √ (A) He is, and he's only twenty-five.
           (B) Both tests and homework.
           (C) A very long lecture.

Part II Practice Test

Audio Script	Explanatory Answer
1. (M) Who won the first prize? (W) (A) The score was 92 to 88. (B) I always buy a ticket. (C) Joe won it.	The man asks who won. (A) 92 to 88 is a score. It doesn't answer who won. (B) "I" may answer "who." "Ticket" relates to "won." √ (C) Joe won the first prize.
2. (M) What time do you want to get your haircut? (W) (A) Short on the sides, long on top. (B) Three or three thirty. (C) Twenty dollars is the most I'll pay.	The man asks about a haircut time. (A) "Short" and "long" describe the kind of haircut. √ (B) Three or three-thirty is a time. (C) "Twenty dollars" tells the amount of a haircut.
3. (M) I hope you found your earrings. (W) (A) She wore a necklace, too. (B) They were next to the mirror. (C) Diamond, for my birthday.	The man hopes that the woman found her earrings. (A) "Necklace" relates to "earring." √ (B) The woman found her earrings next to the mirror. (C) "Diamond" and "birthday" relate to earrings.
4. (W) What hobbies do you like? (M) (A) Photography and painting. (B) It's my very favorite one. (C) Only on the weekends.	The woman asks about the man's hobbies. √ (A) The man likes photography and painting. (B) "Hobbies" may relate to "favorite." (C) "Hobbies" relate to "weekends."
5. (W) Are those his parents, or grandparents? (M) (A) His grandparents. They're really young. (B) Her parents are both from Ireland. (C) I'd like a pair, thank you.	The woman asks about some people. √ (A) The people are his young grandparents. (B) "Parents" repeats. (C) "Pair" sounds like "parents."
6. (M) Where can we go to catch butterflies? (W) (A) Butter with jam or honey. (B) You can go to bed if you're tired. (C) There are lots by the pond.	The man asks where they can find butterflies. (A) "Butter" repeats from "butterflies." (B) "Go" repeats. √ (C) There are butterflies near the pond.
7. (M) When was the wedding? (W) (A) In July. (B) A long marriage. (C) The bride wore a green dress.	The man asks the time of the wedding. √ (A) The wedding was in July. (B) "Marriage" relates to "wedding." "Long" relates to "when." (C) "Bride" relates to "wedding."

8. (W)	Why is there garbage in the entry?	There is garbage in an entryway. Why?
(M)	(A) In the garage.	(A) "Garage" sounds like "garbage."
	(B) I need to take it out.	√ (B) "Take it out" refers to the garbage.
	(C) Tea bags on the floor.	(C) Garbage in the entry could relate to "tea bags on the floor."
9. (M)	How did you find your job?	The man asks how the woman found her job.
(W)	(A) Nine to six, Monday through Friday.	(A) "Nine to six" and "Monday through Friday" relate to jobs.
	(B) I just decided to quit.	(B) "Quit" relates to jobs.
	(C) In the newspaper.	√ (C) She read about the job in the newspaper.
10. (M)	Which professor do you want?	The man asks the woman her professor preference.
(W)	(A) In my senior year.	(A) "Senior year" relates to "professor."
	(B) Professor Carter.	√ (B) She wants Professor Carter.
	(C) This will be safer.	(C) "Safer" sounds like "professor."

Test Hint 24   Practice

Audio Script

1. (D) (M) I'd like to make an appointment to see the dentist.

(W) Are you having any specific trouble?

(M) No, it's just a regular check-up and teeth cleaning.

2. (C) (M) How much is it to mail this letter to France?

(W) First class mail . . . $2.15.

(M) Fine. Here's one, two, three dollars.

3. (B) (W) All passengers bound for Tokyo, your train is now boarding on track 27. The Tokyo express is now boarding on track 27. Thank you.

4. (B) (M) When does the sale start?

(W) It starts next week on Tuesday.

(M) Tuesday the third? Great. I'll come back then.

5. (C) (M) My flight was canceled and I missed my meeting in New York.

(W) Why was the flight cancelled?

(M) There was a storm in New York and lots of snow on the runway.

6. (C) (M) And it's . . . two points for the Greenbacks! The score is now 66 to 72, so this game is not over yet. Now, Logan, number 52, has the ball, he's taking it down center court, and he shoots . . . no, it's off the rim. But here comes Kelly, and he tips it in . . . BASKET!

Test Hint 25 Practice

Audio Script

1. (C) (M) I'd like to try on this watch.

(W) Sure. I'll unlock the case here . . .

(M) I need a waterproof watch, to swim in.

2. (D) (M) Is that your uniform?

(W) No, it's your son's uniform. It was at our house.

(M) Wow, my son has been looking for it all week.

3. (D) (M) What year is your daughter in at school?

(W) She's in her first quarter at the university.

(M) Ah . . . a college freshman. That's a fun time.

4. (C) (M) Why don't you try on those boots?

(W) I don't think they're in style.

(M) Yeah . . . those were in fashion about three years ago.

5. (B) (M) Who is that playing the guitar?
   (W) That's my daughter, practicing for her lesson.
   (M) She sounds like a professional.

6. (A) (M) We need to make an appointment at the photographers.
   (W) I'll make it on the Web.
   (M) Great. Then I don't need to call.

Test Hint 26 Practice

Audio Script

1. (B) (M) <u>Your homework</u> for this weekend starts on page 72 of the <u>textbook</u>. Do exercise 2, 3, 4, and 6. That's page 72, exercises 2, 3, 4, and 6. <u>I'll see you on Monday</u>.

2. (D) (M) Attention, ladies and gentlemen. A woman's wedding ring has been turned in <u>to the lost and found</u>. A woman's wedding band was just found in the ladies restroom and it has been <u>turned in</u> to the <u>lost and found</u>. Please come to <u>customer service</u> to <u>claim it</u>. Thank you.

3. (C) (M) <u>Watch your step</u> as you <u>get off the bus</u>. <u>Be careful</u>, these <u>stairs are mighty steep</u>. Please <u>watch your step</u>, ma'am.

4. (C) (W) Have you <u>paid your tuition</u> yet?
   (M) I went to pay yesterday, but the line was too long.
   (W) Everything is slow on the <u>first day of the quarter</u>.

5. (A) (W) <u>Theater patrons</u>. There are <u>five minutes until curtain</u>. Please return to your seats. <u>Intermission is now ending</u>. Please <u>return to the theater</u>.

6. (C) (W) There is <u>no smoking</u> inside the terminal building except in <u>designated smoking areas</u>. <u>Designated smoking areas</u> are located on the main level and the third floor. The airport authority thanks you for <u>not smoking inside the terminal</u>, except in <u>designated smoking areas</u>.

Test Hint 27 Practice

Audio Script

1. (B) (M) Excuse me, would you please sit down? I can't see.
   (W) I can't see either. The man in front of me is standing up.
   (M) Nobody can see, because everybody is standing up.

2. (B) (M) I'm looking for their newest CD ...
   (W) Lemon Lime hasn't been released yet.
   (M) Music News said that it was supposed to be in stores today.

3. (C)   (M)   Did you finish your homework?

(W)   Yes, but my dog ate it.

(M)   Your homework is due today by 3:30.

4. (A)   (M)   Have you had dinner?

(W)   No, and I missed lunch, too.

(M)   Why don't we go out for dinner tonight.

5. (C)   (W)   Can I borrow your umbrella?

(M)   If you bring it back by 5:00.

(W)   Sure. I'm just running to the post office.

6. (B)   (W)   I'll pick you up after work.

(M)   Can you get me in front of the library?

(W)   Sure. The library, then, four o'clock.

Test Hint 28 Practice

Audio Script

1. (A)   (M)   I'd like to make an appointment to discuss my classes for next semester.

(W)   The professor is booked this week. How about next week?

(M)   It needs to be this week, because I need to register by Friday.

2. (A)   (W)   Sunshine Airlines thanks you for choosing our carrier. As a reminder, check-in begins three hours before the scheduled departure time. You must be at your gate 30 minutes prior to departure time. Boarding begins 20 minutes prior to departure. Thank you.

3. (B)   (M)   My wife and daughter work out together.

(W)   What do they do for a workout?

(M)   They play tennis or ride their bicycles.

4. (C)   (M)   Our team uniforms have arrived, and you can pick yours up in my office after practice. Uniforms are in my office, ready after practice. You'll want to double-check the size and the spelling of your name before we wear them, so we can catch any errors.

Test Hint 29 Practice

Audio Script

1. (C)   (W)   Is this red hat still in style?

(M)   It looks good to me, and it matches your belt.

(W)   Hat styles don't change much, do they?

2. (A)   (W)   You are much too late to join this tour.

(M)   Our car was stuck in the snow.

(W)   You are too late, regardless of your reasons.

3. (C)   (W)   We'd like dinner reservations for seven o'clock.

         (M)   We're booked at seven. How about 6:30?

         (W)   If we can't come at seven, we'll go somewhere else.

4. (D)   (W)   Can you help me clean the house on Saturday morning?

         (M)   It doesn't look dirty to me.

         (W)   That's because I clean it every Saturday.

5. (C)   (W)   How do you start the timer?

         (M)   Push the button.

         (W)   This button? I already pushed it.

6. (B)   (W)   Where is the gym?

         (M)   It's on the first floor, at the north end of the building.

         (W)   Oh, I'll have to go downstairs.

7. (A)   (W)   What's wrong with your uniform?

         (M)   When I washed it, the colors ran.

         (W)   The white part looks pink now.

8. (B)   (W)   We're taking our grandchildren to Disneyland for vacation.

         (M)   They'll love it. There's so much to do there.

         (W)   I know: rides, music, stores, Disney characters, games . . .

Test Hint 30 Practice Two

3.   party, four, table, hostess, now seating, Hatsfield party of four

4.   bags, the bag you claim, matching the claim check, tag, luggage

5.   fifteen–love, serving, net ball, net, second serve, returns, comes to net, rally, deep left, alley, return, it's out, thirty–love

6.   show, opened, visitors, art, famous, Impressionism, art is timeless, Picasso

7.   call waiting, line three, caller, line three

8.   shoppers, six items, changing rooms, try on, clerk, store, changing room

Test Hint 31 Practice

2.	museum	**9.**	bus
3.	TV	**10.**	sports event
4.	school	**11.**	airport
5.	restaurant	**12.**	beach/pool
6.	office	**13.**	store
7.	post office	**14.**	theater
8.	radio		

Test Hint 32 Practice

1. (B)	(W)	I'm new. I work in the cosmetics department.	
	(M)	Oh, I work in the children's department. My name is Robert.	
	(W)	I'm Becky. It's nice to meet you.	
2. (A)	(M)	Do you want to play badminton?	
	(W)	That's a good idea. Then we can swim.	
	(M)	Let's go to the gym. The basketball courts are set up for badminton on Tuesdays.	
3. (B)	(M)	Have you registered for classes yet?	
	(W)	I registered on-line last night.	
	(M)	I still need to pay my tuition.	
4. (D)	(W)	Shoppers: Up to six items may be taken into the fitting rooms. If you would like to try on more than six items, please leave them with the clerk at the fitting room entry. You are allowed only six items in the fitting rooms at one time.	
5. (B)	(M)	Has the bus arrived yet?	
	(W)	No. It's going to be thirty minutes late.	
	(M)	If we have a half an hour, why don't we go get a coffee?	
6. (C)	(M)	How much tip should we leave?	
	(W)	Well, fifteen percent is standard. But he was a great waiter.	
	(M)	Let's leave twenty percent, then. Here's a five-dollar bill.	
7. (C)	(M)	Coffee, soda! We have coffee for sale, ladies and gentleman! Take it now. Fresh, hot coffee. Ice cold soda. Juice. All kinds of beverages.	
8. (D)	(M)	You need to practice every day to memorize this piece.	
	(W)	I'm not good at memorizing music.	
	(M)	You need to try. All of my students are learning their songs by heart.	

Test Hint 33 Practice One and Practice Two

	Audio Script	Practice One	Practice Two
1. (W)	I like living in the city.	**1.** Where does the woman live?	**1.** Where does the man live?
(M)	Really? I thought you'd miss us in the countryside. I still love it there.	√ (A) In a city.	(A) In a city.
(W)	I do miss it. But now I can go out any time: movies, shows, restaurants. You name it.	(B) In the countryside.	√ (B) In the countryside.
		(C) On a farm.	(C) On a farm.
		(D) At a university.	(D) At a university.

2.	(W)	I'll call and make the dinner reservations.	**2.**	What will the woman do?	**2.**	What will the man do?

2.
(W) I'll call and make the dinner reservations.
(M) Great. I'll go pick up the car.
(W) After they're made, I'll meet you out front.

2. What will the woman do?
√ (A) She'll make restaurant reservations.
(B) She'll pick up the car.
(C) She'll eat meat.
(D) She'll call her husband.

2. What will the man do?
(A) He'll make restaurant reservations.
√ (B) He'll pick up the car.
(C) He'll eat meat.
(D) He'll call his wife.

3.
(W) I'm tired of studying. This is too much homework!
(M) I'm tired of waiting. When will you be finished?
(W) You've been really patient. Let me change my clothes and we can go.

3. What has the man been doing?
(A) Changing his clothes.
(B) Doing his homework.
√ (C) Waiting.
(D) Cleaning.

3. What has the woman been doing?
(A) Changing her clothes.
√ (B) Doing her homework.
(C) Waiting.
(D) Cleaning.

4.
(W) This chicken isn't cooked. I'm sending it back.
(M) That's strange. Mine is cold.
(W) Mine is raw and yours is cold! Let's send them both back.

4. Why is the woman returning her chicken?
(A) It's cold.
(B) It's strange.
√ (C) It isn't cooked.
(D) It's too salty.

4. Why is the man returning his chicken?
√ (A) It's cold.
(B) It's strange.
(C) It isn't cooked.
(D) It's too salty.

5.
(W) I gave my tickets to my secretary.
(M) I gave my tickets to my older son, Erik.
(W) My secretary knows Erik—she met him at the family picnic.

5. Who did the man give his tickets to?
(A) His secretary.
(B) His brother.
(C) The woman.
√ (D) His older son.

5. Who did the woman give her tickets to?
√ (A) Her secretary.
(B) Her brother.
(C) The man.
(D) Her older son.

6.
(W) I have a customer holding on line one.
(M) And I have to run to a meeting.
(W) We'll have to talk about this problem later.

6. What does the man need to do now?
(A) Talk to a customer.
√ (B) Go to a meeting.
(C) Talk to the woman.
(D) Solve a problem.

6. What does the woman need to do now?
√ (A) Talk to a customer.
(B) Go to a meeting.
(C) Talk to the man.
(D) Solve a problem.

Part III Practice Test

Audio Script	Explanatory Answer
1. (W) What time do we need to be at the airport? (M) We should check in at least an hour in advance. (W) Our flight's at three, so we should be there by two o'clock.	The man and woman have a flight at three o'clock. They need to arrive at the airport by two o'clock. (A) "One" means "an." √ (B) "Two" repeats. They need to arrive by 2:00. (C) "Three" repeats. It is their flight time. (D) "Four o'clock" is one hour after their flight.
2. (W) You gave me the wrong change. (M) That's seven dollars and thirty-two cents. (W) I know, but I gave you a twenty.	The woman is a customer. She bought something. The man is a cashier. He gave the woman change. The woman says that the change is wrong. She says that she paid with a twenty-dollar bill. (A) "Pay" relates to change and money. (B) "Return" relates to "gave you." (C) "Money" relates to $7.32. √ (D) The man gave the wrong change.
3. (W) Yolanda won a new car at the baseball game. (M) You're kidding. I saw her in the red sports car. (W) That's it! Her ball game ticket had a winning number on it.	Yolanda won a new car. She won the car at a baseball game. She won because she had a winning ticket number. (A) "Ticket" and "baseball game" repeat. (B) Vacations are a common prize. (C) "Telephone" relates to "number." √ (D) "Automobile" means "car."
4. (M) What's your favorite kind of ice cream? (W) I like blackberry. (M) It's especially good if they put real blackberries in it.	They like blackberry ice cream. (A), (B), and (D) These are all likable ingredients in ice cream. √ (C) The man likes real blackberries in his ice cream.

5. Attention shoppers: The women's department half-yearly sale starts tomorrow. Don't miss great bargains in every women's wear department. Shoes and boots are up to 70% off. Casual wear and separates are never a better price. You'll find lingerie, accessories, even makeup and personal care items, all at low, low prices. Claiborne's opens tomorrow at 8 A.M. Don't be late!

The announcement is for shoppers in a department store. A new sale starts tomorrow. Many items will be on sale.

√ (A) The announcement is about a sale.
   (B) The store's opening time is named: "8:00."
   (C) "Department" repeats.
   (D) "Return" relates to the goal of the announcement. The store wants shoppers to return tomorrow.

---

6. (M) Excuse me. Did you lose an earring?
   (W) Oh my gosh, yes. Thank you. Where did you find it?
   (M) It was right under your chair.

The man found the woman's earring. It was under her chair.

√ (A) He gave her the earring.
   (B) "Jewelry" relates to earrings.
   (C) "Chair" repeats.
   (D) "Hearing" sounds like "earring."

---

7. (M) We had to memorize every president's name for the test.
   (W) I don't think I could name even ten presidents.
   (M) Only two students got 100%.

The speakers are students.
They are talking about a test. For the test, they learned the names of all of the presidents.

√ (A) The test was about the presidents.
   (B) "100%" relates to mathematics.
   (C) Spelling relates to school.
   (D) "Russian" is not mentioned.

---

8. The Lacey Aquatics Center would like to remind you that there is no running on the decks. No roughhousing, and no diving into the pool. Food and beverages are not allowed in the pool area. Remember: Safe swimmers are happy swimmers.

The announcement is at a swimming pool. Swimmers must not run. They mustn't play rough. They mustn't dive. They may not eat or drink near the pool.

   (A) "Restaurant" relates to "food and beverages."
   (B) Some of these rules may apply to a school.
   (C) "Dock" sounds like "deck."
√ (D) "Pool" relates to "aquatics center."

Test Hint 34 page 66

1. (C)

The students were early <u>and</u> the teacher was, too. "And" is a coordinate conjunction. The students were early. The teacher was early.

2. (B)

My glasses <u>are</u> broken. "Glasses" is a plural noun.

3. (A)

I start work <u>at</u> 7:30 on Tuesdays. "At" is often used with time.

4. (B)

My snack was <u>bigger</u> than my lunch. Two things are being compared: a snack and a lunch. The snack was bigger.

5. (B)

Yesterday, we <u>helped</u> my friend move into his new apartment. The verb is in the simple past. The helping happened yesterday.

6. (C)

We are planning <u>to build</u> a birdhouse for that tree. The verb "plan" is followed by an infinitive.

7. (C)

The painter isn't painting this area <u>anymore</u>. The painter has already painted the area. She is no longer painting that area.

8. (D)

Last weekend, we went <u>sailing</u> on Lake Michigan. "Go sailing" is a set expression. "Go" is followed by the "-ing" form of many set words.

Count Nouns pages 70-71

1. (B)

My boss gave me two <u>books</u> to read during the break. "Two" indicates that a plural noun will follow. "Books" is a plural noun.

2. (C)

There are two <u>faxes</u> on your desk. "Faxes" is a regular plural count noun.

3. (B)

The dentist had to pull her four front <u>teeth</u>. "Teeth" is the plural of "tooth."

4. (C)

These CDs <u>are</u> on sale today. The plural "CDs" requires a plural verb.

5. (D)

Nine of the students <u>were</u> late to class. "Nine of the students" is plural. It requires a plural verb.

Determiners before Count Nouns
pages 71-73

1. (C)

My new sweater has <u>a</u> large green button at the top. "A" means one. "button" is a singular count noun.

2. (B)

Did you see <u>the</u> horse that fell in the river? "The" shows that the horse is specified. This horse is the horse that fell in the river. "Horse" is a count noun.

3. (C)

Eriko missed <u>six</u> questions on the math test. "Questions" is a plural count noun. "Six" is also plural.

4. (D)

Martin made <u>several</u> field goals during the second half. "Field goals" is a plural count noun. It requires a plural determiner.

5. (D)

<u>Both</u> contact lenses fell on the floor. "Contact lenses" is a plural count noun.

6. (D)

We didn't buy <u>any</u> erasers because they were sold out. "Any" is common in negative sentences.

7. (C)

Are there <u>any</u> cookies in the kitchen? "Any" is common in questions.

Non-Count Nouns pages 73-75

1. (A)

The taxi driver had to stop to put <u>gas in</u> his cab. "Gas" is a non-count noun. (B), (C), and (D) are also non-count nouns. However, their meanings don't make sense in this sentence.

2. (B)

The tea <u>is</u> boiling on the stove. Non-count nouns always take a singular verb.

3. (D)

She packed <u>some</u> jewelry in her suitcase. "Jewelry" is a non-count noun. The sentence is affirmative. Use "some."

4. (C)

There <u>was</u> snow on the ground and we could hardly walk. "Snow" is a non-count noun. Non-count nouns always take a singular verb.

5. (A)

How <u>much</u> money is in the piggy bank? "Money" is a non-count noun.

6. (C)

We ate <u>a lot of</u> rice at lunchtime. "Rice" is a non-count noun. The sentence is affirmative. Choices (A) and (B) occur before count nouns. (D) "Any" is usually used in negative sentences or questions.

7. (B)

There wasn't <u>any</u> lightning at the airport at 2 P.M. "Any" is common in negative statements.

8. (B)

<u>There is no</u> information about the election. "Information" is a non-count noun. The sentence is affirmative. Look at this sentence with the same idea, different grammar: There isn't any information about the election.

Gerunds page 76

1. (C)

<u>Living</u> in the dormitories saves students time and money. The gerund is the subject of the sentence.

2. (C)

He quit <u>working</u> so that he could focus on his education. The gerund is the object of the verb "quit."

3. (D)

They paid for the new sign by <u>collecting</u> money from all the club members. The gerund is the object of the preposition "by."

Vocabulary Power!

a. question
b. education
c. collection

Infinitives page 77

1. (B)

<u>To grade</u> all these papers by 5:00 will be almost impossible. The infinitive is the subject of the sentence.

2. (B)

The younger children seem <u>to miss</u> school more often than the older students. The infinitive is the object of the verb "seem."

3. (C)

We're going to stay in Barcelona <u>to visit</u> my sister-in-law. The infinitive shows the purpose of the visit. Look at this sentence: We're going to stay in Barcelona in order to visit my sister-in-law.

Subject Pronouns page 78

1. (A)

<u>They</u> waited in line for over an hour. "They" is the subject of the sentence.

2. (D)

<u>She</u> listens to music when she takes a shower. "She" is the subject of the clause.

Object Pronouns pages 78-79

1. (C)

John gave <u>us</u> the letter. "Us" is an indirect object. "The letter" is the direct object.

2. (B)

Please come to <u>me</u> if you have any problems. "Me" is the object of the preposition "to."

3. (A)

We took the dogs for a walk and fed <u>them</u>. "Them" is the object of the sentence.

4. (B)

We talked to Mark at the party, but neither of us liked <u>him</u> very much. "Him" is a direct object.

5. (D)

The professor <u>told it to the students</u>. "It" is the direct object. "It" is a pronoun. It comes before the indirect object, "to the students."

6. (D)

My grandmother used to sing <u>it to me</u> when I was younger. "It" is the direct object. "It" is a pronoun. It comes before the indirect object, "to me."

Possessive Pronouns page 79

1. (D)

Your apartment is bigger than <u>mine</u>. "Mine" means "my apartment."

2. (C)

This is <u>her</u> basketball, but the soccer ball is ours. The basketball is hers.

Reflexive Pronouns page 80

1. (B)

Marcus cut <u>himself</u> while he was grating the carrot. Marcus is both the receiver and the doer of the action.

2. (A)

I dumped my boyfriend because he talked only about <u>himself</u>. The reflexive pronoun is the object of the preposition "about."

3. (D)

Jessica prefers to go jogging by <u>herself</u> because she can set her own pace. "By herself" means "alone."

4. (B)

My husband wants to paint the house <u>by</u> himself. "By himself" means "without help."

Ordinal numbers page 81

1. (B)

This semester begins on September <u>seventh</u>. Dates are usually given with an ordinal number.

2. (B)

My granddaughter is in the <u>fifth</u> grade. The ordinal shows the girls position in school.

Comparatives page 82

1. (C)

Our uniforms are <u>warmer</u> than theirs. Two things are being compared. Our uniforms are warmer than their uniforms.

2. (D)

Her employer is <u>more relaxed</u> than her boss. Two people are being compared. Someone's employer is more relaxed than her boss.

3. (B)

There were more <u>more graduates</u> this year than last year. The number of graduates is being compared. This year, there were more graduates.

4. (C)

Your daughter works <u>more slowly</u> than other children in the class. "Slowly" is an adverb. One girl's work speed is being compared to her classmates' work speed.

5. (D)

We sold <u>fewer</u> bicycles this year than last year. "Bicycles" is a count noun, so the comparative word "fewer" is used.

Superlatives pages 83-84

1. (C)

The apple is small, the lemon is smaller, and the apricot is the <u>smallest</u>. Three things are being compared.

2. (C)

This is the <u>sweetest</u> coffee I've ever had. The speaker is comparing this coffee to every other coffee in his life.

3. (A)

Driving an automobile is one of the <u>most</u> dangerous things we do in life. Driving is being compared to all of the other activities in our lives.

4. (A)

That was the <u>most</u> candy I've ever seen in my life. The superlative here compares the amount of candy.

5. (D)

Last night, I saw the <u>best</u> movie that I've ever seen. "Best" is the superlative form of "good."

6. (D)

Six hundred miles is the <u>farthest</u> that I've driven in one day. "Farthest" is the superlative form of "far."

Equivalents (as . . . as) page 84

1. (C)

His Japanese is <u>as</u> good as a native speaker's. The man speaks Japanese as well as a Japanese person speaks Japanese.

2. (B)

Sleeping is <u>as</u> natural as eating. Two things are being compared. Their naturalness is the same.

Vocabulary Power!

a. native
b. natural

3. (D)

My mother's <u>nationality</u> is Canadian because she was born in Quebec. Your nationality shows your country. One's passport shows one's nationality.

4. (A)

We like to go hiking because we enjoy nature. "Nature" means "outdoors."

Possessive Adjectives and Nouns

pages 85-86

1. (A)

My car is parked on the street. "My" shows that I own the car.

2. (D)

My husband drove over his bicycle in the driveway by accident. The husband owned the bicycle that he drove over.

3. (C)

Our seats are in aisle 17, row 4. The seats are ours.

4. (D)

By accident, the badminton player's racket was left in the car. The player owned the racket.

5. (D)

All men's haircuts are 10% off, even if you pay by credit card. The haircuts are for men.

Vocabulary Power!

a. by accident
b. by far
c. by credit card

Participles as Adjectives pages 86-87

1. (D)

My sister is going to get married in July. "Married" is a past participle. "Get married" is a set expression.

2. (A)

My ex-boyfriend has a broken heart. His heart broke. It is now broken. "Broken" is a past participle.

3. (D)

I am used to riding this broken bicycle, and it's not for sale. "Used to" is a set expression.

4. (A)

The students are done with the assignment. "Done with" is a set expression.

Prepositions of Location pages 88-89

1. (A)

The truck driver left his license at the police station. Only "at" makes sense here. "In" is also a possibility: The truck driver left his license in the police station.

2. (D)

The children played next to the lake. "Next to the lake" is a prepositional phrase.

Vocabulary Power!

Prepositions

about *L*	below *L*	next to *L*
above *L*	beside *L*	of
according to	by *L*	through *L*
across *L*	except	toward *L*
around *L*	for	up *L*
at *L*	from *L*	with *L*

3. (A)

She rents an apartment on the edge of town. Only "on" makes sense. It is a preposition of location. The other choices, (B), (C), and (D) are not.

4. (C)

After the first quarter, tuition always goes up. Only "after" makes sense.

5. (D)

The criminal had used fake ID, <u>according to</u> the newspaper. Only (D) makes sense.

Prepositions with Indirect Objects
pages 89-90

1. (B)

They gave a T-shirt <u>to everyone</u> at the concert. "Everyone" is the indirect object. "T-shirt" is the direct object. The indirect object comes after the direct object. It needs a preposition.

2. (B)

Mrs. Cameron taught the song <u>to the students</u>. "Students" is the indirect object. "Song" is the direct object. The indirect object comes after the direct object. It needs a preposition.

3. (A)

The store gave all <u>workers</u> a 4% raise. "Workers" is the indirect object. "A 4% raise" is the direct object. The indirect object comes before the direct object. No preposition is needed.

4. (A)

The new manager sent <u>all employees</u> a letter. "Employees" is the indirect object. "A letter" is the direct object. The indirect object comes before the direct object. No preposition is needed.

5. (B)

We made a birdhouse <u>for</u> my brother. The verb "make" usually take an indirect object with the preposition "for." The indirect object (my brother) comes after the direct object (birdhouse).

6. (A)

We made <u>my brother</u> a birdhouse. "My brother" is the indirect object. "A birdhouse" is the direct object. The indirect object comes before the direct object. No preposition is needed.

Prepositions in Two-Word Verbs
page 90

1. (B)

We looked <u>up</u> the word in the dictionary. "Look up" is a two-word verb. It means "search for information." She looked up his number in the phone book.

Coordinating and Correlative Conjunctions pages 91-92

1. (B)

Carl read the report, <u>and</u> his boss read it too. "And" is a coordinate conjunction. It connects two sentences. Carl read the report. His boss read it.

2. (B)

They will graduate not in June, <u>but</u> in December. "But" connects two prepositional phrases: "in June" and "in December."

3. (C)

Most students would support <u>either</u> a ball field or a tennis court. "Either . . . or" is a correlative conjunction. Students support one or the other.

4. (D)

Our company will <u>neither</u> export nor import shoes. "Neither . . . nor" is a correlative conjunction.

5. (D)

<u>Both</u> the airport and the seaport were closed because of fog. "Both . . . and" is a correlative conjunction.

Vocabulary Power!

a. report
b. support
c. export
d. import

e.   airport

f.   seaport

6. (D)

The ship will arrive in the <u>port</u> at 4 P.M. Only (D) makes sense.

7. (D)

Tea is <u>imported</u> from China, but it's quite expensive here. Only "imported" completes this sentence correctly.

Verb "to have" page 93

1. (B)

I don't <u>have</u> my schedule with me. The negative is formed with an auxiliary (don't) and the base form of the verb.

2. (A)

She <u>has</u> enough money for the bus and for lunch. "She" requires the third person singular form of the verb.

3. (D)

<u>Do you have</u> luggage for your trip? In yes-no questions, the subject comes between the helping verb and main verb.

4. (C)

The electronics department <u>had</u> many customers yesterday. The past tense of "have" is "had."

Verb "to be" pages 94-96

1. (A)

I <u>am</u> on the volleyball team because I'm so tall. The first person singular of "be" is "am."

2. (B)

What <u>is</u> your excuse for being late? The third person singular of "be" is "is."

3. (C)

Police <u>are</u> looking into the cause of the accident. "Police" takes the third person plural verb.

4. (C)

<u>You're</u> going to wash the dishes, aren't you? "You're" is a contraction of "you + are."

5. (B)

She <u>was</u> so sick yesterday that she stayed home from school. "Was" is the past form of "be."

6. (A)

<u>Are the girls</u> ready to leave for their dance class? In a question, "be" comes before the subject. It doesn't take an auxiliary.

Vocabulary Power

a.   because

b.   excuse

c.   cause

7. (C)

The car stopped running <u>because</u> we were out of gas. "Because" introduces the reason for their lateness.

8. (B)

<u>Excuse</u> me, is the manager available? Only "excuse" makes sense in this sentence.

Simple Present pages 96-97

1. (B)

Kayoko is in trouble because she <u>misses</u> class every Thursday. The simple present shows usual activities.

2. (D)

They <u>own</u> two houses in Korea. The simple present shows general facts.

3. (C)

I <u>don't work</u> in the computer science department. The negative is formed with an auxiliary (don't) and the base form of the verb.

4. (D)

<u>Do</u> you remember if the party is in the afternoon or in the evening? In yes-no questions, the subject comes between the helping verb (do) and the main verb.

5. (D)

The fire <u>in</u> the men's department cost the store millions. "In" is often used to show that something is in a location. "In a department" is an expression.

6. (D)

At least they don't yell <u>in</u> front of their children. "In front of" means "in the presence of."

7. (*Answers will vary.*)

My grandson always ------- when he runs downhill.

Present Progressive page 98

1. (C)

The art teacher <u>is grading</u> students' photographs now. The present progressive shows that something is happening now.

2. (A)

The police officer <u>looks</u> at a driver's ID whenever he stops a car. The simple present shows habitual action.

3. (D)

Are you <u>playing</u> on the soccer team this spring? The present progressive shows future time.

4. (A)

He's <u>applying</u> for his student visa next week. The present progressive shows future time.

Simple Past pages 99-100

1. (C)

Hiroshi <u>called</u> his cousin this morning on his cell phone. The simple past shows that something began and ended in the past.

2. (D)

The airport <u>will open</u> next week on Friday. "Next week on Friday" refers to the future.

3. (B)

He <u>finished</u> the test on time. The simple past shows that something began and ended in the past.

4. (C)

We <u>heard</u> about the accident on the radio. The simple past shows that something began and ended in the past.

Vocabulary Power

a. on his cell phone

b. on Friday

c. on time

d. on the radio

f. on vacation

5. (A)

How many postcards did you write while you were <u>on</u> vacation? "On vacation" is a set expression.

"Used To" page 100

6. (A)

Our company used to <u>fix</u> water pipes, but now we only sell new ones. "Used to" is followed by a verb in the base form.

Past Progressive pages 101-102

1. (D)
That employee wasn't <u>working</u> on this computer at 4:00. The past progressive describes a past action that was in progress at a specific time.

2. (B)
She <u>was</u> getting off the bus when the man approached her. Form the past progressive with a past form of "be" + "-ing verb."

3. (C)
While she <u>was looking up</u> the new word, she found the other word that we didn't know. The past progressive can describe two past actions. One action is simple and short in length. The other action is longer. The past progressive is used to describe the long action.

4. (D)
Was it pouring rain when you <u>picked up</u> your husband from work? The past progressive can describe two past actions. One action is simple and short in length. The other action is longer. The simple past is used to describe the shorter action.

Vocabulary Power!

a. put away
b. get off
c. fill in
d. wake up
e. figure out
f. look up
g. pick up

Two-Word Verbs

fill in	*write*
look up	*search for*
figure out	*answer*
pick up	*take*

get back (from)	*return*
put away	*organize*
get off	*disembark*
put on	*dress*
get in	*enter*
take off	*remove*
get on	*board*
throw away	*put in the garbage*
get out	*go*
try on	*wear a short time*
give up	*quit*
turn off	*stop*
grow up	*get older*
turn on	*start*
hand in	*give*
wake up	*awake*

Note: Answers may vary.

5. (A)
You should always <u>turn off</u> the light before you leave the house. Only "turn off" makes sense.

6. (D)
He tried <u>on</u> his tuxedo, but it was much too tight. "Try on" means "wear clothes for a short time to see if you like them."

7. (B)
Our records show that he <u>paid</u> for his glasses with a credit card. The simple past indicates an activity that started and ended in the past.

Future with "will" pages 101-103

1. (A)
We will <u>be</u> careful when we cross the street. To show future time, "will" is followed by the simple form of the verb.

2. (B)
The fog <u>will</u> lift by mid-afternoon. To show future time, "will" is followed by the simple form of the verb.

3. (D)

You <u>won't</u> be able to graduate this semester if you don't take the test. "Won't" is the contracted form of "will not."

Vocabulary Power!

a. soon
b. by mid-afternoon
c. this semester

Expressions of the Future page 103

Answers will vary.
ASAP (as soon as possible) *2*
soon *4*
by Thursday *10*
ten years from now *12*
immediately (right away) *1*
the day after tomorrow *9*
in a minute *3*
this afternoon *5*
later on *6*
tomorrow evening *8*
next month *11*
tonight *7*

Future with "be going to" page 104

1. (B)

I <u>am going</u> to take my visor to the baseball game tonight. "Be going to" shows future time. "Tonight" indicates the future.

2. (A)

The students <u>got</u> their student ID's last Tuesday. "Last Tuesday" refers to the past. "Got" is the past form of "get."

3. (B)

Are the tourists going <u>to need</u> a visa to enter Morocco? The future with "be going to" is made of "be going" + infinitive.

Vocabulary Power!

a. visit
b. visor
c. visa

Helping Verbs (Auxiliary Verbs)
pages 104-106

1. (C)

You <u>mustn't</u> smoke in the lobby because it's against the law. Only the verb "mustn't" adds a logical meaning to this sentence.

2. (A)

Can they <u>play</u> badminton on Wednesday? When a verb follows a helping verb, it is in its base form.

3. (C)

If her purse was stolen, she <u>has got to</u> call the police. "Has got" means "must." It is followed by the infinitive.

4. (B)

<u>Would</u> you please wait for me in the lobby? Only "would" makes sense in this sentence.

5. (C)

You <u>have to</u> dry your hair before we take the photograph. Only "have to" makes sense in this sentence.

6. (C)

We <u>would rather</u> meet you for coffee than for lunch. "Would rather" shows the speaker's preference.

Passive pages 106-107

1. (D)

The employee was <u>given</u> a raise. Somebody gave the employee a raise.

2. (A)

Was the history class taught <u>by</u> the mathematics professor? The subject of an active sentence may become a "by phrase."

3. (C)

My photo has already been <u>taken</u>. Somebody took my photo.

Present Perfect pages 107-108

1. (D)

These employees <u>have lived</u> in this dormitory since May. "Since" is the key to the present perfect in this sentence.

2. (C)

She <u>has</u> seen that movie seven times. The present perfect is made of the present tense of "have" + the past participle.

3. (B)

My secretary has already <u>gone</u> to an office supply store to look for those covers. The present perfect is made of the present tense of "have" + the past participle.

Verb Tense Review of Seven Basic Tenses page 108

1. (C)

At 3:00 tomorrow, Beth <u>will get</u> a haircut. "3:00 tomorrow" keys the future tense.

2. (C)

She can't join us for coffee because she <u>is getting</u> a haircut right now. "Now" keys the present progressive tense.

3. (B)

Actually, she <u>got</u> her hair cut twice yesterday! The action started and ended in the past.

4. (D)

When she <u>was getting</u> her first haircut, there was an earthquake. There were two actions in the past. She was getting her haircut. The haircut was interrupted by the earthquake.

Adverbs of Frequency pages 109-110

1. (A)

She worries about her weight so she <u>often</u> exercises. Grammatically, all of the answer choices work. However, only "often" makes sense in this sentence.

2. (D)

They both hate to cook so they <u>always</u> eat out. Grammatically, all of the answer choices work. However, only "always" makes sense in this sentence.

3. (D)

<u>We can rarely eat eggs</u> because of the cholesterol. Place the adverb (rarely) after the first helping verb.

4. (A)

The sale clothes <u>are never in the front</u> of the store. Place the adverb after "be" if it is the main verb.

IX. Part IV Practice Test pages 111-112

1. (C)

My brother has a pet snake, but my father is <u>scared</u> of it. The snake scares the father. The snake is scary. The father is scared.

2. (A)

These <u>cherries</u> were picked from the tree by my grandparents. Cherries grow on trees. Only "cherries" makes sense.

3. (C)

She wrapped her jewelry in tissue and put <u>it</u> in her purse. "Jewelry" is a non-count noun.

4. (C)

All of the sports <u>equipment</u> is stored in the gym. Only "equipment" makes sense.

5. (B)

The tour guide <u>and</u> several passengers slipped on the ice. The tour guide slipped. The passengers slipped.

6. (B)

They didn't bake any cookies because everyone were <u>full</u>. They were not hungry, so they didn't make cookies.

7. (C)

The tickets in her wallet <u>are</u> for the play tonight. The plural subject is "tickets." It must agree with the verb. Do not be confused by the prepositional phrase "in her wallet."

8. (B)

Visibility was low because of the <u>fog</u>. Only "fog" makes sense.

9. (D)

In their home, they speak <u>in</u> German. "In" + language is a set form.

10. (C)

I can't help you right now because I <u>am cooking</u> this pudding. "Right now" keys the present progressive.

11. (A)

Did you <u>hear</u> the announcement about the sale? This is a yes-no question. The subject comes between the helping verb and the main verb. The main verb is in its base form.

12. (A)

<u>When did they issue</u> the new company ID cards? This is a question with an information word. The question word comes before the helping verb.

13. (C)

My grandson <u>is going to</u> ride his scooter. "Be going" + infinitive shows future time.

14. (A)

Makiko <u>has</u> already talked to her math teacher about the book. "Already" keys the present perfect.

15. (D)

Professors must turn in their grades promptly after the end of the <u>quarter</u>. Only "quarter" makes sense here.

Test Hint 50 Practice

1. (B)
If you arrive late, you will miss the test. The ticket says, "No one will be allowed in after the test starts." (A) "Scores" relate to tests. (C) Waiting to break may seem like a reasonable possibility. (D) "Register" and "test" repeat.

2. (D)
Payment is not mentioned. (A), (B), and (C) These items are named in the last paragraph.

3. (C)
Most of their customers are young adults, 20-30 years old. (A), (B), and (D) These groups are customers, but they are a small percentage of customers.

4. (B)
The chart is for 11 months of sales: January 1 through November 30. (A) "10" is a percentage in the chart. (C) Many sales charts cover one year, or 12 months.

5. (A)
Angel Mountain has started to allow snowboarding. (B) "Skiing" is mentioned many times. (C) "History" is repeated. (D) "Airplane rides" relate to the view from the gonodola in the first paragraph.

6. (B)
Dylan White says that the skiers aren't open to change. In other words, they are close-minded. (C) "Wild and young" repeats. However, it refers to the snowboarders, not to the skiers.

7. (A)
You can see snowboard tracks in the snow. In order to answer this question, you must read both the first and the second paragraphs in the article. (B) "Angel" repeats. (C) The snowboard tracks are shaped like snakes. (D) This may seem like a logical answer.

Test Hint 51 Practice

1. (B)
The gym's surface will be redone. (A) A sports event is a logical reason to close a gym. (C) "April" repeats, and April dates are given. (D) "Service" might look like "surface."

2. (C)
The gym reopens on April 8. (A) "April" repeats. (B) "April 7" is the last day that the gym is closed. (D) "April 18" looks like "April 8."

3. (A)
"All of your money" means "full refund." (B) and (C) These are common options in stores, but they are not part of this policy. (D) "Original receipt" repeats.

4. (D)
"Cash register receipt" means "original receipt." (A) and (C) These options are commonly shown if you return something. (B) "Policy" repeats. The policy is probably posted in the store or on the receipt. The customer doesn't have to show it.

5. (A)
The city got a high score for its recycling program. (B) "Solid waste" repeats. (C) "Customers" repeats. (D) "Recycling" repeats.

6. (C)
"October" is in the fall. (A) "1991" repeats. (B) "Five" repeats.

Vocabulary Power!

a. resurface
b. return
c. refund
d. reopen
e. recycle

Test Hint 52 Practice One

Type of Reading for Questions 1 and 2

rules

1. Ⓐ Ⓑ Ⓒ Ⓓ

Type of Reading for Questions 3 and 4

subscription

3. Ⓐ Ⓑ Ⓒ Ⓓ

Type of Reading for Questions 5 and 6

schedule

5. Ⓐ Ⓑ Ⓒ Ⓓ

Type of Reading for Questions 7 and 8

sign

7. Ⓐ Ⓑ Ⓒ Ⓓ

(Answers will vary. All are reasonable choices.)

Test Hint 52 Practice Two

1. (B)

The sign explains the rules for the pool. (A) Many pools have a sign with prices. (C) and (D) These options relate to swimming, but they are not mentioned here.

2. (A)

This sign is at a pool. (B), (C), and (D) These are logical places to find a sign.

3. (B)

The form is for newspaper subscribers. (A) "Clocks" relates to "Times."

4. (B)

Mariana Perka wants to subscribe to the newspaper. She is a reader. (A) "Writers" relate to newspapers. (C) Mariana might mail this form.

5. (A)

The purpose of the schedule is to give bus times. (B) "Wheelchair access" is repeated. (C) The street numbers could relate to a city map. (D) "Times" relate to the times in the schedule.

6. (C)

A bus rider would use this schedule.

7. (B)

The purpose of the sign is to warn drivers. The road is slippery when it is wet. (A) and (C) These are good options, because a road sign may close a road or post a speed limit. (D) This choice is not logical, because road signs don't give directions.

8. (A)

A driver should drive slower if the road is wet. "Drive slower" means "reduce speed." (C) "Change lanes" is repeated. (D) "Lane" is repeated.

Test Hint 53 Practice

1. (C)

A sale is being advertised. See these words in different fonts or bigger sizes: sale, sale event, big discounts, nonstop discounts, sale of the year. (A) and (D) The sale is at a store. (B) "Fashion" repeats.

2. (D)

The sale is an all-day sale. See these words in different fonts or bigger sizes: 24-hour sale, all-day, from 12:01 A.M. to 11:59 P.M.

3. (B)

The ticket is for a play. See the capital words in different fonts: Performata Theater. (A) "Take-Off" relates to "flight." (C) Buses relate to tickets. (D) Lectures also may require tickets.

4. (A)

The ticket can't be returned for cash. See the capital-letter note at the bottom that repeats: NO REFUNDS.

5. (A)

You would see this sign at a government office. See the first sentence: Welcome to the Department of Animal Control. (B) A restaurant may relate to taking a number and a seat. (C) Animals relate to pets. (D) Zoos relate to pets.

6. (B)

The purpose of the directions is to shorten the wait. See the first sentence before the bullets: To minimize your wait.

Test Hint 54 Practice One

1. (A)

The purpose of the form is to gather health information. See the title: Health History. (B) Many illnesses are named in the form. (C) and (D) "Patient" relates to health forms.

2. (D)

The patient has a history of heart disease and headaches. (A), (B), and (C) These options are mentioned in the form, but none is checked.

3. (A)

The warning tells you how to open something. (B) Anybody can use this item. (C) The warning doesn't name the contents. It says that the contents are under pressure. The contents might be a carbonated beverage. (D) Storage isn't discussed.

4. (B)

You might see this warning on a carbonated drink, such as soda pop or champagne. (A), (C), and (D) None of these items is packed under pressure.

5. (B)

Mr. Soriano got the letter because he traveled 60,000 miles. (A) "Upgrade" and "voucher" repeat. (C) Travel with family or friends is mentioned. (D) The letter is about an airline's program.

6. (D)

With one bonus upgrade, a person can move to business class. With two, a person can go to first class. (A) "Treat" relates to "free." (B) You may bring a traveling companion, but not for free. (C) Discounted tickets are a logical gift from an airline.

7. (A)

Mr. Soriano or anyone he travels with can use the voucher. See this sentence: You can also use this voucher to treat any friend, family member, or acquaintance traveling in your company. Note that "in your company" means "together with you." It does not mean "in your corporation." You can guess this by the list of people already named: any friend, family member, or acquaintance. (B), (C), and (D) These people are all mentioned.

Practice Two

Answers will vary.

Test Hint 55 Practice

1. (D)

The purpose of these instructions is to explain how to open a door.

2. (C)

You should turn the handle after the light comes on. Instructions are usually given in order.

3. (C)

Ms. Taylor is a photographer and journalist, or a "photojournalist."

4. (A)

She is "based in New York."

5. (A)

The invitation is to "a public lecture."

6. (C)

The event is in Lawrence Hall.

Test Hint 56 Practice

1. (C)

Mustafa Kemal Ataturk was the father of Turkey. "Father" means "founder."

2. (B)

Ataturk "created the Republic of Turkey." It was an independent nation.

3. (B)

After 1923, Turkey was an independent democracy.

4. (A)

A "job hunter" is a "job applicant." This form is for a person that is looking for a job.

5. (C)

The sophomore year in college is the second year in college.

6. (D)

"CPR" stands for cardiopulmonary resuscitation.

Test Hint 57

1. (D)

Harold Gerrard is a pilot. A captain in an airline is a pilot. (A) "Employer" relates to "employee." (B) "Passenger" relates to airlines.

2. (B)

He works for Blue Heights Airline. The airline is his "employer." (A) His name repeats. (C) "Captain" repeats. (D) "A-1" repeats.

3. (B)

California grade-schoolers can name the most cities. (A), (C), and (D) These groups of students are all named.

4. (B)

Klingham learned the state names for a test. (A), (C), and (D) These options may be reasons to learn a state name. However, none is mentioned.

5. (D)

Martin Anderson has a bad memory in general. (A) Busyness is a common reason to forget things. (B) His mother is mentioned. (C) "Reading" relates to studying.

Vocabulary Power!

a. capital
b. captain

a. remember
b. memorize
c. memory

Test Hint 58

1. (B)

The topic of the article is an election.

2. (A)

Yesterday there was a vote.

3. (D)

A public relations worker reported that the numbers were very close.

Part V Practice Test

1. (B)

You would see this sign on a truck. The sign is about the truck. (A) "Track" sounds like "truck." (C) Cranes often have cautions. (D) Wheelchairs may require caution. Wheelchairs may stop or back frequently.

2. (D)

"Often" means "frequently."

3. (C)

The Department of Licensing deals with licenses. "Licenses" are mentioned many times in the listing. (A) "Registration" repeats. (B) A National Tax Agency may relate to a government Web site. (D) "Housing" may also have a governmental Web site.

4. (B)

A person who moves would have a new address. See the third point in the list. (A) and (C) These are likely reasons to visit a government Web site. (D) "High school" relates to "teen."

5. (B)

In Japan, maitake mushrooms are used to treat high blood pressure. (A) "Cholesterol" repeats. (C) Liver disorders are not mentioned. (D) "Blood" repeats.

6. (D)

The health community is "just starting to understand" the health value of mushrooms. (A) "Health" repeats. (C) "Benefits" repeats.

7. (A)

The advertisement describes an apartment that is for rent. (B) "Rent" and "apartment" repeat. (C) and (D) "Apartment" repeats.

8. (D)

"Walk to shopping" means that the apartment is near shops. (A) "Washer" repeats. (B) The washer and dryer are in the building. They are not in the apartment. (C) "Damage" repeats.

9. (B)

This is a ballot. Students will vote for their school's government. (A) "Student body" repeats. (C) Candidates are named. Their positions are not. (D) "Student body government" repeats.

10. (C)

Four students will be elected: president, vice-president, secretary, and treasurer. (A) "One" is the number of candidates you can vote for for each office. (B) "Two" is the number of candidates for each office. (D) "Eight" is the total number of candidates.

Quick Answer Key (See Explanatory Answers on Following Pages)

Part I

1. C	4. A	7. A	10. A	13. C
2. C	5. A	8. C	11. D	14. D
3. C	6. D	9. C	12. B	15. C

Part II

16. B	20. A	24. B	28. B	32. C
17. C	21. C	25. A	29. B	33. B
18. A	22. A	26. B	30. A	34. A
19. B	23. A	27. C	31. B	35. B

Part III

36. C	39. C	42. D	45. D	48. B
37. A	40. C	43. C	46. C	49. A
38. B	41. A	44. C	47. D	50. B

Part IV

51. D	57. A	63. A	69. D	75. D
52. D	58. D	64. A	70. A	76. B
53. A	59. A	65. A	71. B	77. B
54. B	60. C	66. A	72. C	78. C
55. C	61. A	67. A	73. A	79. C
56. B	62. B	68. A	74. B	80. A

Part V

81. A	85. A	89. A	93. B	97. A
82. B	86. A	90. C	94. C	98. D
83. D	87. D	91. D	95. B	99. C
84. D	88. A	92. C	96. A	100. A

Score _____ / 100

Audio Script	Explanatory
1. (A) They are looking at the calendar. (B) They're working on the computer. (C) The teacher is writing something. (D) The students are at the chalkboard.	(A) There is a calendar on the wall. (B) There is a computer behind them. √ (C) We can guess that the older woman is a teacher. She is writing. (D) "Chalkboard" is related to school.
2. (A) There are beautiful flutes. (B) The bananas are hanging in a tree. (C) The room is full of fruit. (D) The food is in a cabinet.	(A) "Flutes" sounds like "fruits." (B) There are bananas, but not a tree. √ (C) There is a lot of fruit. (D) "Food" sounds like "fruit."
3. (A) The man is painting the scenery. (B) The man is conducting a meeting. (C) The man is pointing at something. (D) The man is handing out information.	(A) "Painting" sounds like "pointing." There is scenery. (B) His business suit may relate to a meeting. Pointing also relates to meetings. √ (C) He is pointing. (D) "Handing out" relates to "hand."
4. (A) The man is pouring the water. (B) The man is drinking the water. (C) The man is cleaning up the water. (D) The man is splashing the water.	√ (A) He is pouring water. (B) There is "water." (C) There is "water." (D) He is pouring carefully so it doesn't splash.
5. (A) There are flags near the lighthouse. (B) The gate is wide open. (C) Tourists look from the balcony. (D) Workers will paint the building.	√ (A) There are flags. (B) "Gate" relates to the fence. (C) The lighthouse has a balcony. (D) The building needs to be painted.
6. (A) The man is pounding a nail. (B) The man is pouring some cream. (C) The man is putting on a jacket. (D) The man is painting the window frame.	(A) "Pounding a nail" relates to work. (B) "Pour" sounds like "paint." (C) "Put" sounds like "paint." "Jacket" relates to a "coat" of paint. √ (D) He is painting.
7. (A) The woman is pregnant. (B) The woman is embarrassed. (C) The woman is a passenger. (D) The woman is a patient.	√ (A) She is pregnant. (B) She doesn't look embarrassed. (C) She isn't a passenger. (D) "Patient" relates to being pregnant.
8. (A) There are several boats on the river. (B) The lake is calm. (C) The river comes from the mountains. (D) There are waves on the ocean.	(A) There is a river. (B) "Lake" relates to "river." √ (C) The river comes from the mountains. (D) "Ocean" relates to "river."
9. (A) The worker is parking his car. (B) The worker is sleeping in the street. (C) The worker is sweeping the street. (D) The worker is pushing the garbage can.	(A) There is a "parking" area. (B) "Sleeping" sounds like "sweeping." √ (C) He is sweeping the street. (D) There is a garbage can.

10. (A) The graduates are singing. (B) The singers are clapping. (C) The students are starting college. (D) They are wearing bathrobes.	√ (A) They are singing. (B) They are singing. (C) "Students" and "college" relate to graduation. (D) "Bathrobes" relate to "gowns."
11. (A) The books are on the table. (B) They're eating their lunch. (C) One woman is putting sugar in her tea. (D) One woman is serving drinks.	(A) There are "books" and a "table." (B) "Tea" relates to "lunch." (C) "Sugar" relates to "tea." There is "tea." √ (D) She is serving tea.
12. (A) The dogs are resting. (B) The dogs are racing. (C) The dogs are riding the sled. (D) The dogs are rowing.	(A) "Rest" sounds like "race." √ (B) They are racing. (C) There is a "sled," and a man is "riding" it. (D) "Row" sounds like "ride."
13. (A) The man is smoking a pipe. (B) The man is painting the porch. (C) The man is blowing bubbles. (D) The man is chewing bubblegum.	(A) "Smoke" and "blow" both relate to the mouth. His stick may look like a pipe. (B) There is a porch. √ (C) He is blowing bubbles. (D) "Chew" and "blow" both relate to the mouth. "Bubble" repeats.
14. (A) The children are bored. (B) The children are sick. (C) The children are sad. (D) The children are happy.	(A) "Bored" means "not interested." (B) The children look healthy. (C) The children are smiling. √ (D) They are smiling and happy.
15. (A) She's a registered nurse. (B) She's a waitress. (C) She's a cashier. (D) She's a banker.	(A) "Registered" sounds like "register." There is a cash register. (B) A waitress may wear a scarf and apron. √ (C) She is a cashier. (D) "Banker" relates to money.
16. (W) Did you hear the ambulance go by? (M) (A) She is sick. (B) It was loud. (C) No, I won't.	The woman asks about the ambulance. (A) "Sick" relates to ambulances. √ (B) The ambulance made lots of noise. (C) "Won't" doesn't match the question.
17. (M) Where is Mark's bicycle? (W) (A) The cafeteria is open. (B) A flat tire. (C) In the garage.	The man asks about a bicycle. (A) A bicycle might be in a cafeteria. (B) "A flat tire" relates to bicycles. √ (C) It is in the garage.
18. (W) Your chemistry professor didn't really say that, did she? (M) (A) Yes, she did. (B) It's her profession. (C) At 212 degrees Fahrenheit.	"Did your chemistry professor say that?" √ (A) Yes, the professor said it. (B) "Profession" sounds like "professor." (C) "212 degrees F" relates to chemistry.
19. (M) Don't you want to travel overseas? (W) (A) Dark blue with big waves. (B) International flights tire me out. (C) I don't want to look over at her now.	"Do you want to travel overseas?" (A) "Blue" and "waves" describe seas. √ (B) "International" means "overseas." The flight tires her, so she doesn't want to. (C) "Over" repeats.

20. (W) Why don't you meet me at the theater?
(M) (A) Sure, I'll see you there.
(B) The actor is famous.
(C) I'd like to introduce you.

The woman suggests meeting at the theater.
√ (A) The man will see her at the theater.
(B) "Actor" relates to "theater."
(C) "Introduce" relates to "meet."

21. (W) How many months pregnant is she?
(M) (A) One month ago.
(B) She had twins.
(C) Six, I think.

The woman asks about her pregnancy.
(A) "Month" repeats.
(B) "Twins" relates to pregnant.
√ (C) She is six months pregnant.

22. (W) Is he a talented painter, or is he just learning?
(M) (A) This is the third house he's painted.
(B) At the museum.
(C) He's a senior in high school.

She asks about the painter's experience.
√ (A) He has little experience. He has only painted 2 other houses.
(B) "Museum" relates to painters.
(C) "Learning" relates to high school.

23. (W) Have you ever read this biography?
(M) (A) No, I haven't.
(B) Both books are on sale.
(C) She wrote it independently.

The woman asks if the man has read the book.
√ (A) The man hasn't read it.
(B) "Books" relates to "biography."
(C) "Independently" may relate to biographies.

24. (W) That announcement was confusing.
(M) (A) She had a head injury.
(B) I didn't understand it either.
(C) The principal, I think.

The announcement was unclear.
(A) A "head injury" relates to confusion.
√ (B) The man agrees: it wasn't clear.
(C) A principal makes announcements.

25. (W) Did you see zebras or bears?
(M) (A) We saw zebras.
(B) I went to the zoo.
(C) It hurt my bare hands.

The woman asks about zoo animals.
√ (A) He saw zebras.
(B) "Zoo" relates to animals.
(C) "Bare" is a homonym with "bear."

26. (M) Why did you exchange the sweater?
(W) (A) She chased me from the store.
(B) It was too small.
(C) My money back.

The woman returned her sweater and got a different sweater. Why?
(A) "Chase" sounds like "exchange," and "store" relates to exchanges.
√ (B) The sweater was too small.
(C) "Money back" relates to exchanges.

27. (M) How long did he study flower arranging?
(W) (A) Japanese and Western style.
(B) The flowers are pink and white.
(C) For seven years.

The man asks about someone's study of flower arranging.
(A) Japanese and Western are two styles of flower arranging.
(B) "Flower" repeats.
√ (C) He studied for seven years.

28. (W) The court found him guilty.
(M) (A) I thought he was lost.
(B) The newspapers sure showed him that way.
(C) He drank all of the goat's milk.

A judge thinks that the man did a bad thing.
(A) "Lose" relates to a court case.
√ (B) The newspapers presented the man as guilty.
(C) "Goat" may sound like "court."

29. (W)	What's your favorite sport?		The woman asks the man's sport preference.
(M)	(A) At the beach.		(A) The beach is where he plays.
	(B) Volleyball.	√	(B) "Volleyball" is his favorite.
	(C) Yes, I can.		(C) The question is not a "yes-no."

30. (M) Have you checked your calendar to see about next Friday?

The man wants to know if the woman is free on Friday.

(W) (A) Yes, and I'm free.
   (B) Next Friday is the nineteenth.
   (C) My calendar fell off the wall.

√ (A) Her calendar shows that she's free.
   (B) "Friday" repeats.
   (C) "Calendar" repeats.

31. (M) Who do we know who's driving to the concert?

They may be looking for a ride to the concert.

(W) (A) They don't like rock 'n' roll.
   (B) My sister's friend is driving.
   (C) I know how to drive.

   (A) "Rock 'n' roll" relates to concerts.
√ (B) The sister's friend is driving.
   (C) "Drive" and "know" repeat.

32. (W) Why did the cream spoil?

The milk is bad. They wonder why.

(M) (A) Because he can't answer it.
   (B) It spilled on the floor.
   (C) It wasn't refrigerated.

   (A) "Because" often answers a "why-" question.
   (B) "Spill" relates to cream.
√ (C) It wasn't kept cold.

33. (W) Where is the water fountain?

The woman probably wants to drink water.

(M) (A) Juice, please.
   (B) Down the hallway.
   (C) A fountain pen.

   (A) "Juice" relates to water.
√ (B) The fountain is in the hall.
   (C) "Fountain" repeats.

34. (M) How long have they lived in their house?

The man asks about their residence.

(W) (A) A few months.
   (B) Just down the street.
   (C) About fifteen meters.

√ (A) Two or three months.
   (B) This answers "Where is their house?".
   (C) This answers "How far away is their house?"meter

35. (M) Is it Miss, or Mrs.?

He asks about her name.

(W) (A) I missed it.
   (B) Mrs.
   (C) Yes, it is.

   (A) "Missed" sounds like "miss."
√ (B) She is married.
   (C) The question can't be answered "yes."

36. (W) That buffet was delicious, but I ate way too much.

They are at a restaurant with a buffet. They both ate too much food. The man's pants feel tight. The woman wishes that she didn't eat dessert.

(M) Me too. I may have to loosen my belt.

(W) I shouldn't have eaten dessert.

   (A) Sick people often complain.
   (B) "Pants" relates to belts.
√ (C) They ate a lot.
   (D) "Loose" repeats.

37. (M) Where is our waitress?

They are in a restaurant. They are waiting for their waitress. She is coming.

(W) We've been waiting for at least 10 minutes.

(M) Here she comes now.

√ (A) The waitress is late.
   (B) "Ten" repeats.
   (C) "Lost" relates to "where?" "Glasses" relates to restaurants.
   (D) "Food" relates to restaurants. "Cold" relates to waiting.

38. We are arriving at Bilman Island. All passengers must disembark the vessel. Walk-on passengers please proceed to the upper deck. Drive-on passengers, please return to your vehicles.

Passengers are on a ferry boat. They hear this announcement. The ferry is arriving at the island. Foot passengers must get off of the ferry. The exit is on the upper deck. Car passengers must go to their cars.
- (A) "Theater" relates to "walk-on."
- √ (B) Boat passengers.
- (C) "Pedestrians" relates to "walk-on passengers."
- (D) "Drivers" relates to "drive-on passengers."

39. (M) I can't memorize all these words.
(W) Me neither. There are over fifty words.
(M) She always gives too much homework.

They are trying to learn words. It is their homework. There are too many words. They can't learn them all.
- (A) "School" relates to homework.
- (B) "Know" relates to memorize.
- √ (C) "Too much" repeats.
- (D) "Miss class" relates to homework.

40. (W) Where are the washing instructions for this shirt?
(M) They're on the label. It should be in the collar here.
(W) Oh I see them, they're sewn in this side seam.

The woman wants to know how to wash the shirt. The washing directions are on the label. The label is in the side of the shirt.
- (A) and (B) "The Web" and "an owner's manual" are common places to find instructions.
- √ (C) They are on the label.
- (D) "Soap" relates to washing.

41. (W) Thanks for the CD. I really like jazz.
(M) Do you know the group?
(W) I do. I heard them perform at Jazzfest 2000.

The man gave the woman a jazz CD. She says thank you. She heard the jazz band in concert.
- √ (A) The woman likes jazz.
- (B), (C), and (D) These types of music relate to CDs, groups, and performances.

42. Shoppers! The time is now 9:00. The store is closing. Please exit from the north doors. All other exits will be locked. Again, please exit from the north doors-direct access to the parking garage.

Shoppers are in a store. They hear an announcement. The store is closing. Shoppers must leave from the north doors. Other doors are locked.
- (A) "Lock" and "doors" repeat.
- (B) In stores, announcements about "sales" are common.
- (C) "Watch" relates to 9:00.
- √ (D) Shoppers must leave from the north doors.

43. (M) Is that your mom?
(W) No, it's my new stepmom.
(M) Oh, I forgot. Your parents got divorced last year, didn't they.

They are discussing a woman. She is the speaker's step-mom. Her parents are divorced. Her father remarried.
- (A) "Baby" relates to mom.
- (B) "Year" repeats.
- √ (C) They divorced last year.
- (D) "Last" repeats.

44. Our next stop is Tuskaloola. There's a small restaurant, a mini market, and, of course, restrooms. This is our last stop for about a hundred miles or so, so take advantage of it.

The announcement is on a bus. The bus will stop. At the stop, there is a restaurant, market, and bathrooms. The bus will not stop again for a long time.

    (A) "Restaurant" repeats.
    (B) There are many announcements in schools.
√ (C) They are on a bus.
    (D) "Mini-market" repeats.

---

45. The track team will meet in the gym today. Attention track team members: Your practice will be in the gymnasium this afternoon due to the bad weather.

This announcement is in a school. The weather is bad. So, the track team will meet in the gym.

    (A) "Track" repeats.
    (B) A "field" is a logical place for a track meet.
    (C) A "club" is a logical place for a track team to meet.
√ (D) They will meet in the gym. "Gym" is short for "gymnasium."

---

46. (W) What time does the cafeteria open?
    (M) Just before lunch, around 11, I think.
    (W) Too bad. I missed my morning coffee and I was up late last night.

The woman wants to go to the cafeteria. She wants coffee. She is tired. The cafeteria opens at about 11:00.

    (A) "Late" and "night" repeat.
    (B) "Early" relates to "morning coffee."
√ (C) 11:00 is just before lunch.
    (D) "Dinner" relates to cafeterias.

---

47. (W) These shoes are $140!
    (M) That's twice as much as the other black ones.
    (W) Let's go back to the less expensive store.

The woman is surprised by the price of the shoes. They are expensive. They are two times more expensive than the other shoes.

    (A) "Black" repeats.
    (B) "Store" repeats.
    (C) Fit is a common reason not to buy something.
√ (D) The shoes are too expensive.

---

48. It's time to vote for your favorite comedian, and you can only vote for one. To remind you, we first heard Stella on her mother's new car. Then we heard Jason on the price of sports shoes. And last was Mary Jean, who told us about her unexpected hair color. These are three great young comics, but you have to choose the best one! Please take out your ballots.

The audience heard three comedians. One talked about her mom's car. One talked about sports shoes. One talked about hair color. They were all very funny. The audience must vote for the funniest comedian.

    (A) "School president" is somebody we vote for.
√ (B) They are voting for the funniest comic.
    (C) "Class colors" are often voted on.
    (D) "Favorite" repeats, and "ballet" may sound like "ballot."

---

49. (W) Which team are you going to join?
    (M) I like Ping-Pong, and they only meet once a week.
    (W) I think I'll do tennis, because I get better exercise.

They are discussing sports teams. The man likes Ping-Pong. The woman likes tennis.

√ (A) She will join the tennis team.
    (B) Swimming isn't named.
    (C) "Ping-Pong" is the team the man will join.
    (D) "Baseball" isn't named.

50. Remember, watch your head as you enter the cave. The ceiling is very low, and we have accidents all of the time. Watch your head as you enter the cave.

People are going into a cave. The ceiling is low. They may hit their heads. They should be careful.
   (A) You should be careful when you step off a boat.
√ (B) They are entering a cave.
   (C) You could hit your head while climbing a ladder.
   (D) You should be careful when you sail fast.

51. (D)
She enjoys <u>singing</u> in her free time. "Enjoys" is followed by the *-ing* form.

52. (D)
He is <u>building</u> a model airplane. This is the present continuous.

53. (A)
We bought a <u>few</u> lemons. "Lemons" is a count noun. Look at the grammar of these similar sentences: *We bought little lemons. We bought a little lemon. We bought some lemons. We didn't buy any lemons.*

54. (B)
She <u>traveled</u> for three months in Australia last year. This is the simple past tense. The activity happened in the past. It happened at a set time. It is now finished.

55. (C)
<u>Washing</u> these dishes will take at least an hour. "Washing" is a gerund. A gerund may be the subject of a sentence.

56. (B)
All <u>members</u> of the photography club need digital cameras. Only "members" makes sense in this sentence.

57. (A)
Antonio will probably <u>pack</u> the larger suitcase. This is the simple future tense. *He will pack the suitcase.*

58. (D)
The president <u>has lived</u> in this city since 1996. This is the present perfect. The activity began in the past. It continues into the present.

59. (A)
There was a <u>dancer</u> at the wedding who knew how to swing. "Swing" is a type of dance. A person can swing.

60. (C)
You had <u>better</u> study for the exam. "Had better" is a set expression that means "should." Think about these similar sentences, which are also correct: *You are supposed to study for the exam. You ought to study for the exam.*

61. (A)
Maybe the show was <u>cancelled</u>. "Cancelled" is a participle. This sentence is passive.

62. (B)
You can't have dessert <u>unless</u> you eat your dinner. "Unless" shows the condition. If you eat your dinner, you can have dessert.

63. (A)
<u>When</u> will you graduate? "When" asks about time. Think about this correct sentence, too: *What day will you graduate?*

64. (A)
You can borrow my <u>coat</u> if it gets really cold. Only a coat would help somebody in the cold.

65. (A)

The police officer told me to stand <u>up</u>. "Stand up" is a two-word verb. It means "stand."

66. (A)

He can't help us paint because he's too <u>busy</u>. "Busy" is an adjective. It describes the man.

67. (A)

These days, all cars run on unleaded <u>gasoline</u>. This tests your vocabulary knowledge.

68. (A)

After you collect the money, you need to count <u>it</u>. "Money" is a non-count noun. This may seem strange, especially in this sentence. A non-count noun is singular.

69. (D)

The music was so <u>loud</u> that it hurt my ears. This tests your vocabulary knowledge.

70. (A)

She has a two-inch scar on her <u>face</u> that will never heal. A "scar" is a mark from a cut. This questions tests your vocabulary knowledge.

71. (B)

This lake is much <u>deeper</u> than the one near my house. This is a simple comparison. One lake is deeper than the other.

72. (C)

Your dress is really too <u>fancy</u> for the event. "Fancy" means dressy. This is a vocabulary question.

73. (A)

The photograph showed the mayor voting in the <u>election</u>. This is a vocabulary question. All of the options are advanced words, so it is a difficult question.

74. (B)

If you don't pay <u>attention</u> during class, you're bound to fail. This is a vocabulary question. All of the options are advanced words, so it is a difficult question.

75. (D)

The children think that they can <u>dig</u> a six-foot hole. This is a vocabulary question.

76. (B)

The <u>dentist's</u> office is on Main Street. "Dentist's" is a possessive noun.

77. (B)

I asked <u>my</u> server for a fork. "Ask" is not followed by the preposition "to."

78. (C)

The geology professor <u>has taught</u> here since 1988. This is the present perfect. The activity began in the past. It continues in the present.

79. (C)

We <u>would</u> like to exchange this swimsuit. "Would like" means "want."

80. (A)

Tomorrow I'm going to <u>get</u> a haircut at 4:30. "Get a haircut" is a set expression.

81. (A)

"Disturb" means "make noise." This sign would be on the door of a school classroom. In the classroom, students are taking a test. (B) "Interview" is not mentioned. (C) "Progress" repeats. (D) "Test" repeats.

82. (B)

"Exam" means "test." (A) "Progress" repeats. (C) "Disturb" repeats. (D) "Job fair" is not mentioned.

83. (D)

"Swim period" means "swim session." (A) "Pool" repeats. The cost doesn't pay for the whole day. (B) "Two-hour" repeats. (C) These prices might be typical movie prices.

84. (D)

Babies are free, so they pay the least. (A) and (B) Senior citizens and adults pay the adult price of $4. (C) School children pay $2 or $3.

85. (A)

The sign says "Wear your seat belt!" "Seat belt" means "safety belt." This is a road sign. (B) "Texas" repeats and "belts" repeats. (C) "Farewell" means goodbye. (D) "Seat" repeats.

86. (A)

The sign says "Welcome to Texas." So, it must be at the border. (B) "Texas" repeats, and "jail" relates to "laws." (C) and (D) are not mentioned.

87. (D)

The sign talks about discount prices. So, it must be in a store. (A), (B), and (C) These places often have signs, but not about discount prices and charge cards.

88. (A)

The sign explains discounts. (B) Weights may be given as percentages. (C) Percentages relate to math. (D) Numbers and shopping relate to sizes.

89. (A)

The coupon is for a bottle of shampoo. If you get a haircut, you get free shampoo. (B) "Haircut" repeats. (C) Conditioner relates to haircuts. (D) $3.95 is the value of the shampoo.

90. (C)

If you get a haircut today, then you get free shampoo. "Shampoo" is the offer. (A) "Appointments" relate to haircuts. (B) "Shampoo" repeats, but you don't have to buy any. (D) "Call" relates to the phone number.

91. (D)

A merry-go-round is a "fair ride." (A) A Ferris wheel would have similar rules. (B) "Bicycles" relate to "rides." (C) "Horse" repeats.

92. (C)

The first line of the sign says "Rules." This sign gives rules. (A) "Prices" relates to "free." (B) This is not a warning. However, a ride may post warnings. (D) "Ride" repeats.

93. (B)

"Automatically" means "without doing anything." All burgers come with three toppings: ketchup, lettuce, and tomato. You don't have to ask. You don't have to pay extra. (A) "None" is not mentioned. (C) Four toppings are available if you order them: onion, pickles, cheese, peppers. (D) The total number of possible toppings is seven.

94. (C)

This sign is about "burgers." Fast-food restaurants sell burgers. (A) A pizzeria doesn't normally sell burgers. However, a pizzeria uses toppings. (B) "Vegetarian" means "no meat." This is a burger restaurant. (D) "Bakery" is not mentioned.

95. (B)

A "jar" has "contents." A jar goes in the refrigerator. Food is perishable (it can go bad). So, this advice must be on a jar of food. (A) "Refrigerator" repeats. (C) A bouquet doesn't have contents. (D) Ice cream doesn't go in the refrigerator. Note: You do not need to understand the word "perish" in order to answer this question.

96. (A)

"Store" means "keep." This jar needs to be kept in the refrigerator. (B) Jars open, but this advice doesn't tell you how to open a jar. (C) "Serve" relates to food. (D) "Cook" relates to refrigeration and perishing. Note: You do not need to understand the word "perish" in order to answer this question.

97. (A)

"Assistance" means "help." (B) "Trouble" isn't mentioned. (C) "Repeat" repeats. (D) A starting machine may relate to a jam.

98. (D)

"Ring the bell several times" means "ring repeatedly." "Stop ringing" means "jam." (A) "Help" means "assistance." (B) Ringing some bells may call the fire department. (C) "Repeat" repeats.

99. (C)

A two-bedroom apartment is for rent. (A) A washer and dryer may be found in an apartment. (B) Houses relate to apartments and rent. (D) A car is not mentioned.

100. (A)

The advertisement says "no pets." A person with a dog has a pet. (B) Students are not mentioned. (C) Some apartments may not want children. (D) "Paint" repeats.

○ ANSWER SHEET ○

LISTENING SECTION

1 Ⓐ Ⓑ Ⓒ Ⓓ   26 Ⓐ Ⓑ Ⓒ Ⓓ
2 Ⓐ Ⓑ Ⓒ Ⓓ   27 Ⓐ Ⓑ Ⓒ Ⓓ
3 Ⓐ Ⓑ Ⓒ Ⓓ   28 Ⓐ Ⓑ Ⓒ Ⓓ
4 Ⓐ Ⓑ Ⓒ Ⓓ   29 Ⓐ Ⓑ Ⓒ Ⓓ
5 Ⓐ Ⓑ Ⓒ Ⓓ   30 Ⓐ Ⓑ Ⓒ
6 Ⓐ Ⓑ Ⓒ Ⓓ   31 Ⓐ Ⓑ Ⓒ
7 Ⓐ Ⓑ Ⓒ Ⓓ   32 Ⓐ Ⓑ Ⓒ
8 Ⓐ Ⓑ Ⓒ Ⓓ   33 Ⓐ Ⓑ Ⓒ
9 Ⓐ Ⓑ Ⓒ Ⓓ   34 Ⓐ Ⓑ Ⓒ
10 Ⓐ Ⓑ Ⓒ Ⓓ   35 Ⓐ Ⓑ Ⓒ
11 Ⓐ Ⓑ Ⓒ Ⓓ   36 Ⓐ Ⓑ Ⓒ Ⓓ
12 Ⓐ Ⓑ Ⓒ Ⓓ   37 Ⓐ Ⓑ Ⓒ Ⓓ
13 Ⓐ Ⓑ Ⓒ Ⓓ   38 Ⓐ Ⓑ Ⓒ Ⓓ
14 Ⓐ Ⓑ Ⓒ Ⓓ   39 Ⓐ Ⓑ Ⓒ Ⓓ
15 Ⓐ Ⓑ Ⓒ Ⓓ   40 Ⓐ Ⓑ Ⓒ Ⓓ
16 Ⓐ Ⓑ Ⓒ   41 Ⓐ Ⓑ Ⓒ Ⓓ
17 Ⓐ Ⓑ Ⓒ   42 Ⓐ Ⓑ Ⓒ Ⓓ
18 Ⓐ Ⓑ Ⓒ   43 Ⓐ Ⓑ Ⓒ Ⓓ
19 Ⓐ Ⓑ Ⓒ   44 Ⓐ Ⓑ Ⓒ Ⓓ
20 Ⓐ Ⓑ Ⓒ   45 Ⓐ Ⓑ Ⓒ Ⓓ
21 Ⓐ Ⓑ Ⓒ   46 Ⓐ Ⓑ Ⓒ Ⓓ
22 Ⓐ Ⓑ Ⓒ   47 Ⓐ Ⓑ Ⓒ Ⓓ
23 Ⓐ Ⓑ Ⓒ   48 Ⓐ Ⓑ Ⓒ Ⓓ
24 Ⓐ Ⓑ Ⓒ   49 Ⓐ Ⓑ Ⓒ Ⓓ
25 Ⓐ Ⓑ Ⓒ   50 Ⓐ Ⓑ Ⓒ Ⓓ

READING SECTION

51 Ⓐ Ⓑ Ⓒ Ⓓ   76 Ⓐ Ⓑ Ⓒ Ⓓ
52 Ⓐ Ⓑ Ⓒ Ⓓ   77 Ⓐ Ⓑ Ⓒ Ⓓ
53 Ⓐ Ⓑ Ⓒ Ⓓ   78 Ⓐ Ⓑ Ⓒ Ⓓ
54 Ⓐ Ⓑ Ⓒ Ⓓ   79 Ⓐ Ⓑ Ⓒ Ⓓ
55 Ⓐ Ⓑ Ⓒ Ⓓ   80 Ⓐ Ⓑ Ⓒ Ⓓ
56 Ⓐ Ⓑ Ⓒ Ⓓ   81 Ⓐ Ⓑ Ⓒ Ⓓ
57 Ⓐ Ⓑ Ⓒ Ⓓ   82 Ⓐ Ⓑ Ⓒ Ⓓ
58 Ⓐ Ⓑ Ⓒ Ⓓ   83 Ⓐ Ⓑ Ⓒ Ⓓ
59 Ⓐ Ⓑ Ⓒ Ⓓ   84 Ⓐ Ⓑ Ⓒ Ⓓ
60 Ⓐ Ⓑ Ⓒ Ⓓ   85 Ⓐ Ⓑ Ⓒ Ⓓ
61 Ⓐ Ⓑ Ⓒ Ⓓ   86 Ⓐ Ⓑ Ⓒ Ⓓ
62 Ⓐ Ⓑ Ⓒ Ⓓ   87 Ⓐ Ⓑ Ⓒ Ⓓ
63 Ⓐ Ⓑ Ⓒ Ⓓ   88 Ⓐ Ⓑ Ⓒ Ⓓ
64 Ⓐ Ⓑ Ⓒ Ⓓ   89 Ⓐ Ⓑ Ⓒ Ⓓ
65 Ⓐ Ⓑ Ⓒ Ⓓ   90 Ⓐ Ⓑ Ⓒ Ⓓ
66 Ⓐ Ⓑ Ⓒ Ⓓ   91 Ⓐ Ⓑ Ⓒ Ⓓ
67 Ⓐ Ⓑ Ⓒ Ⓓ   92 Ⓐ Ⓑ Ⓒ Ⓓ
68 Ⓐ Ⓑ Ⓒ Ⓓ   93 Ⓐ Ⓑ Ⓒ Ⓓ
69 Ⓐ Ⓑ Ⓒ Ⓓ   94 Ⓐ Ⓑ Ⓒ Ⓓ
70 Ⓐ Ⓑ Ⓒ Ⓓ   95 Ⓐ Ⓑ Ⓒ Ⓓ
71 Ⓐ Ⓑ Ⓒ Ⓓ   96 Ⓐ Ⓑ Ⓒ Ⓓ
72 Ⓐ Ⓑ Ⓒ Ⓓ   97 Ⓐ Ⓑ Ⓒ Ⓓ
73 Ⓐ Ⓑ Ⓒ Ⓓ   98 Ⓐ Ⓑ Ⓒ Ⓓ
74 Ⓐ Ⓑ Ⓒ Ⓓ   99 Ⓐ Ⓑ Ⓒ Ⓓ
75 Ⓐ Ⓑ Ⓒ Ⓓ   100 Ⓐ Ⓑ Ⓒ Ⓓ

Quick Answer Key (See Explanatory Answers on Following Pages)

Part I

1. D	4. A	7. B	10. D	13. D
2. C	5. D	8. A	11. B	14. A
3. B	6. B	9. C	12. A	15. D

Part II

16. A	20. A	24. B	28. A	32. C
17. C	21. B	25. B	29. B	33. A
18. A	22. C	26. C	30. A	34. A
19. B	23. A	27. B	31. B	35. A

Part III

36. D	39. B	42. C	45. B	48. A
37. D	40. D	43. B	46. B	49. C
38. C	41. B	44. D	47. D	50. C

Part IV

51. A	57. D	63. B	69. A	75. D
52. D	58. C	64. B	70. D	76. D
53. C	59. A	65. D	71. C	77. A
54. B	60. C	66. C	72. C	78. B
55. C	61. B	67. B	73. C	79. D
56. B	62. B	68. B	74. A	80. A

Part V

81. B	85. C	89. D	93. A	97. C
82. D	86. C	90. A	94. B	98. D
83. B	87. B	91. D	95. D	99. C
84. D	88. A	92. C	96. B	100. D

Score _____ / 100

Audio Script	Explanatory
1. (A) The men are looking at the painting. (B) The men are looking at the artist. (C) The men are looking at the structure. (D) The men are looking at the statue.	(A) "Painting" relates to sculpture. (B) A sculpture is art. (C) "Structure" sounds like "sculpture." √ (D) It is a statue.
2. (A) Both girls put their hair in curlers. (B) They are studying in the library. (C) One girl is putting up the other girl's hair. (D) They are looking at pieces of jewelry.	(A) There is hair. (B) They are in a library. √ (C) One girl is doing the other's hair. (D) There is jewelry.
3. (A) He is taking a bath. (B) He is swimming. (C) He is cleaning the pool. (D) He is flying over water.	(A) "Bath" relates to water. √ (B) He is swimming. (C) There is a pool. (D) He's doing the "butterfly stroke." There is water.
4. (A) They're checking the price. (B) They're paying for the shirt. (C) They're trying on the shirt. (D) They're hanging it up.	√ (A) They are looking at the price tag. (B) There is a shirt. (C) There is a shirt. (D) There is a hanger.
5. (A) The door is locked. (B) There's a key in the lock. (C) There's a rock on the gate. (D) The lock is hanging from a chain.	(A) There is a lock. (B) There is a lock. (C) "Rock" sounds like "lock." There is a gate. √ (D) The lock is on the chain.
6. (A) He's getting his teeth cleaned. (B) He's getting his hair cut. (C) He's getting his hair dyed. (D) He's getting his head measured.	(A) Teeth cleaning is a personal service. √ (B) He's getting a haircut. (C) There is hair. (D) She is focusing on his head.
7. (A) The girl is serving the ball. (B) The girl is hitting the ball. (C) The girl is playing at net. (D) The girl is chasing the ball.	(A) "Serve" relates to tennis. There is a ball. √ (B) She is hitting the ball. (C) "Net" relates to tennis. (D) There is a ball.
8. (A) The boy is playing with his toys. (B) The train is crowded. (C) The door is broken. (D) The child is having fun with his friends.	√ (A) He is playing with a train set. (B) There is a train. (C) The door, in the back of the picture, is torn. It isn't broken. (D) There is a child having fun. However, he is alone.
9. (A) The man is reading a book. (B) The man is examining his airline ticket. (C) The man is looking at his passport. (D) The man is filling out a form.	(A) The man is reading something. (B) He is probably in an airport. √ (C) He is looking at his passport. (D) "Form" relates to passports.

10. (A) The students are listening to a lecture.
(B) They are sharing a calculator.
(C) The professor has written all over the board.
(D) They are studying together.

(A) There are students.
(B) There are many calculators.
(C) "Professor" relates to students and studying.
√ (D) They are studying.

11. (A) They are a doctor and a nurse.
(B) They are a nurse and a patient.
(C) They are an engineer and a child.
(D) They are a technician and a student.

(A) "Doctor" relates to nurse. There is a nurse.
√ (B) One woman is a nurse. The sick woman is the patient.
(C) The electrical equipment may relate to "engineer."
(D) The electrical equipment may relate to "technician."

12. (A) The musicians are playing at the beach.
(B) The concert is sold out.
(C) The guitar players are in a performance hall.
(D) The audience is clapping.

√ (A) The are playing guitars in the sand.
(B) "Concert" relates to music.
(C) There are guitars and players.
(D) There is an audience.

13. (A) He's signing the documents.
(B) He's looking in the phone book.
(C) He's calculating the bill.
(D) He's looking at the menu.

(A) The menu may look like documents.
(B) The menu may look like a phone book.
(C) "Bills" relate to restaurants.
√ (D) He's looking at a menu.

14. (A) The women are looking at a document.
(B) The women are wearing glasses.
(C) The women are looking in the mirror.
(D) The women are typing on the keyboard.

√ (A) They are looking at a document.
(B) There are glasses in the picture. Only one woman has glasses.
(C) The women are looking at something.
(D) There is a keyboard.

15. (A) The passengers are getting off of the bus.
(B) The passengers are waiting for the bus.
(C) The passengers are waving to the bus.
(D) The passengers are getting on the bus.

(A) "Get off" relates to buses.
(B) They are finished waiting. The bus has arrived.
(C) There is a bus.
√ (D) They are getting on the bus.

16. (W) Did you get your hair cut?

(M) (A) Yes, I did.

(B) I need a bandage.

(C) My favorite shampoo.

The woman asks about a hair cut.

√ (A) The man says that he got his hair cut.

(B) "I" is often a good answer to a question with "you."

(C) "My" is often a good answer to a question with "you." "Shampoo" relates to "hair cut."

---

17. (M) Which would you like, potatoes or fries?

(W) (A) Salad.

(B) I would.

(C) French fries.

The man offers either potatoes or French fries.

(A) "Salad" isn't offered.

(B) "Would" repeats.

√ (C) "French fries" are "fries."

---

18. (W) Why don't we play tennis this weekend?

(M) (A) Great. I like tennis.

(B) She's playing on Saturday.

(C) Two or three balls.

The woman wants to play tennis.

√ (A) The man likes tennis. He wants to play.

(B) "Play" repeats.

(C) "Balls" relate to tennis.

---

19. (M) You haven't tried it on, have you?

(W) (A) I have three.

(B) I have, and it doesn't fit.

(C) Fifty percent off.

The man asks if the woman tried something on. It is probably clothes.

(A) "I" is often a good answer to a question with "you." "Have" repeats.

√ (B) The woman has tried it on. It doesn't fit her.

(C) "Fifty percent" could be a discount. It relates to shopping and "trying on" clothes.

---

20. (W) Don't you want dessert?

(M) (A) I'm full.

(B) No, I haven't.

(C) In the desert.

The woman offers dessert.

√ (A) The man is full. So, he doesn't want dessert.

(B) "I" is often a good answer to a question with "you." "No" is often a good response to "Do you?"

(C) "Desert" sounds like "dessert."

---

21. (M) Where does she live now?

(W) (A) For two years.

(B) In an apartment.

(C) She works at the airport.

The man asks where she lives.

(A) This answer is for a different question: "How long has she lived there?"

√ (B) She lives in an apartment.

(C) This answer is for a different question: "Where does she work now?"

---

22. (M) How did you make the reservations?

(W) (A) To Hawaii.

(B) You did.

(C) On the Web.

The man asks how she made reservations.

(A) "To Hawaii" relates to making reservations.

(B) "You" and "did" repeat.

√ (C) She made her reservations online.

---

23. (W) Your jacket has a stain on the back.

(M) (A) I know. I'm going to return it.

(B) I always pay by credit card.

(C) I didn't think it was that cold today.

There is a mark on the back of the man's jacket.

√ (A) The man knows about the mark. He plans to return the jacket.

(B) Paying with a credit card may relate to a jacket.

(C) "Cold" relates to "jacket."

24. (W) When is check-in?
 (A) A personal check.
 (B) Two hours before the flight.
 (C) On the plane.

The woman asks about check-in time. They are probably in an airport.
 (A) "Check" repeats.
 √ (B) Check-in is two hours before the flight.
 (C) "Plane" relates to "check-in."

25. (W) Where is the fax machine?
 (M) (A) She lives in Osaka.
 (B) On the third floor.
 (C) The papers.

The woman asks where the fax machine is.
 (A) "In Osaka" answers "where."
 √ (B) The machine is on the third floor.
 (C) "Papers" relate to "fax machine."

26. (W) Who manages the parking lot?
 (M) (A) He asked my teacher.
 (B) Very much.
 (C) The building manager does.

The woman asks about the parking area.
 (A) "He" is a good answer to "who."
 (B) "Very much" answers questions with "how" or "how much."
 √ (C) The manager runs the parking lot.

27. (W) Which quarter are you taking biology?
 (M) (A) Half.
 (B) Winter.
 (C) My mathematics professor.

The woman asks about the man's plans to take biology.
 (A) "Half" relates to "quarter."
 √ (B) The man will study biology in the winter quarter.
 (C) "Mathematics professor" relates to a biology class.

28. (W) Roderick scored the most points in all three of the last games.
 (M) (A) He's so tall, he always scores high.
 (B) Twenty-two or twenty-three, I think.
 (C) She's paying for them, in aisle nine.

This is a statement. It is about an athlete named Roderick. He scored many points. This is not a question.
 √ (A) The man gives a reason for the points. The athlete is tall.
 (B) "Twenty-two" tells how many points he scored.
 (C) "Paying" and "aisle nine" relate to tickets for a sports event.

29. (W) Why do they close the school when it rains?
 (M) (A) It's sunny today.
 (B) The river often floods.
 (C) At 8 A.M.

The school closes when it rains. The woman wants to know why.
 (A) "Sunny" relates to rain.
 √ (B) When it rains, the river floods.
 (C) "8 A.M." is a time that school starts.

30. (W) You haven't wrapped the gift yet, have you?
 (M) (A) I did it this morning.
 (B) Stickers and a fancy notebook.
 (C) For her birthday party.

Has the man wrapped the gift?
 √ (A) He wrapped the gift this morning.
 (B) This answer tells about the gift.
 (C) This answer tells the purpose of the gift.

31. (M) Is electricity included in the rent?
 (W) (A) The electric bill is high.
 (B) It is.
 (C) You could buy a heater.

The man asks about electricity payment.
 (A) "Electric" repeats.
 √ (B) The electricity (it) is included.
 (C) "Heater" relates to electricity.

32. (M) Are you paying in cash or with a credit card?

(W) (A) I'd prefer to play cards.

(B) Tax is too steep.

(C) Cash.

The man asks how she is paying.

(A) "Play" sounds like "pay."

(B) "Tax" relates to paying.

√ (C) She is paying with cash.

---

33. (W) Would you like to see my doll collection?

(M) (A) Thanks, I'd enjoy that.

(B) I collect stamps, too.

(C) I'd like a tall one.

The woman offers to show her dolls.

√ (A) Yes, he wants to see the dolls.

(B) "Collect" repeats, and "stamps" relates to collecting.

(C) "I'd like" is a common answer to "Would you like?" "Tall" sounds like "doll."

---

34. (W) Who is your history instructor?

(M) (A) Professor Swanson.

(B) I got an A+.

(C) Too much homework.

The woman asks about the man's history teacher.

√ (A) The teacher is "Professor Swanson." "Professor" means "instructor."

(B) "A+" is a grade for a history class.

(C) "Homework" relates to history classes.

---

35. (W) Is she the coach?

(M) (A) Yes, I met her yesterday.

(B) The team is too small.

(C) We won the first game.

One woman asks about another woman.

√ (A) Yes, she is the coach. The man met her yesterday.

(B) "Team" relates to "coach."

(C) "Won the game" relates to "coach."

---

36. (W) May I see your receipt, sir?

(M) Here it is. I just paid at aisle six.

(W) Okay. You'll need to take this to the cashier to get the security tag removed.

The speakers are in a store. The man is a shopper. The woman is a store worker. The man is leaving the store. He made an alarm sound. The store worker asks to see the man's receipt. He has his receipt. He paid. Now he needs to go back to the cashier. The cashier can take the security tag off of his merchandise. Then, the alarm will not sound.

(A) "Receipt" repeats.

(B) "Pay" repeats.

(C) "Aisle six" repeats.

√ (D) The man must return to the cashier.

---

37. (W) Somebody pushed her into the pool.

(M) Did they push her on purpose?

(W) No, it was just an accident. The lifeguard had to pull her out.

A woman and man are talking about an accident. A girl was at a swimming pool. Somebody pushed her into the water. It was an accident. The lifeguard pulled the girl out of the pool.

(A) and (B) Tripping and slipping are common ways to fall into a pool.

(C) "Lifeguard" repeats.

√ (D) Somebody pushed the girl into the pool.

---

38. Fifteen-love, Louise Ellen serving. From where I'm sitting, that looks like a net ball. Net. This is her second serve. Tracy returns it. And Louise Ellen comes to net. What a rally this is. It's deep left, and she pushes Tracy all the way into the alley. Return . . . and it's out. Thirty-love.

A sports announcer is talking about a tennis game. The score is 15 to zero. Louise Ellen is serving the ball. Her first serve hits the net. Her second serve is good. Tracy hits the ball back. Louise comes to the net. It's a good rally ("What a rally this is"). Louise hits the ball far back to the left. Tracy has to go into the alley. She hits the ball out. Now the score is 30 to zero.

(A) Soccer players are athletes, like the women.

(B) "Hairdresser" relates to "net" and two women.

√ (C) They are tennis players.

(D) "Swimmers" relates to sports and "deep."

39. (W) Can you please open your backpack?

(M) I can't, the zipper is stuck.

(W) We need to search all bags before you can enter the building.

The woman is a security worker for a building. The man wants to enter the building. The woman asks the man to open his backpack. He can't open it because the zipper is broken. The woman needs to look in his bag. She looks in all bags before a person goes into the building.

(A) "Zipper" repeats, and a broken zipper may need to be sewn.

√ (B) "Look inside" means "search."

(C) "Enter the building" repeats.

(D) "Book" relates to backpack, and "backpack" repeats.

---

40. (W) I passed the test!

(M) Congratulations. So did I.

(W) Let's go celebrate.

The man and woman just took a test. The woman passed. The man passed too. They want to party.

(A), (B), and (C) These are three good reasons to party.

√ (D) "Exam" means "test."

---

41. Ms. Klinehammer, you have a call waiting on line 7. Ms. Klinehammer, caller holding, line seven.

A secretary is making an announcement in an office. The announcement is for Ms. Klinehammer. There is a telephone call for Mrs. Klinehammer. The caller is waiting on line seven.

(A) "Wait" repeats. "Lane 7" sounds like "line 7."

√ (B) She needs to answer the telephone.

(C) "Call" repeats. "Wade" sounds like "wait."

(D) "Move forward" relates to lines.

---

42. (M) Tickets! May I see your tickets please.

(W) Here's my ticket. My son is only three.

(M) Under three, ride free.

The woman is riding a train or bus. The man needs to see everybody's tickets. The woman shows her ticket to the man. The woman's son doesn't have a ticket. He is only three years old. Riders who are under three years old don't pay.

(A) "Movie theater" relates to "ticket."

(B) "Elementary school" relates to a young son.

√ (C) They are on a train.

(D) "Swimming pool" relates to tickets.

---

43. (M) Can you pass the salt?

(W) The shaker is empty.

(M) Don't we have any more?

The man and the woman are eating at a table. The man wants the salt. There is no salt in the salt shaker. The man wonders if there is more.

(A) "Shirt" sounds like "salt."

√ (B) He wants salt.

(C) "Pepper" relates to salt.

(D) "Sugar" is often passed at a table.

---

44. This is WKBZ at 1550 on your A.M. dial with a weather update. Storm warnings are in effect throughout the evening and into the weekend. Expect westerly winds up to 40 miles per hour with gusts up to 60 miles per hour. We've already had reports of lightning along the coast, and that system is just going to keep on coming.

The announcement is on the radio. It is about the weather. There may be a storm tonight or this weekend. There may be strong winds. There is already lightning near the ocean. The bad weather is moving inland.

(A) "Traffic" is a typical topic of radio announcements.

(B) "Weekend" repeats.

(C) "System" repeats.

√ (D) The announcement is about weather.

45. (M) Your flight has been canceled due to fog in Vancouver.
(W) Oh, no. Are there any flights into Seattle?
(M) The whole west coast is fogged in.

The speakers are at an airport. The man works for an airline. The woman is a passenger. The man says that the woman's plane will not go to Vancouver. There is fog in Vancouver. The woman asks about planes to Seattle. There are no planes to Seattle. There is fog all over the west coast.

(A) A storm is a common reason to cancel a flight.
√ (B) Fog is canceling the flights.
(C) A strike is a common reason to cancel a flight.
(D) "Coast" repeats.

46. (M) The sleeves are too short.
(W) That jacket is out of style, anyway.
(M) I guess I can't wear this.

The man and woman are talking about a jacket. The sleeves are short. It is out of style. The man shouldn't wear it.

(A) "Pants" do not have sleeves.
√ (B) He is trying on a jacket.
(C) The speakers do not talk about a jumper.
(D) "Shoes" do not have sleeves.

47. I can take the next customer in Aisle 4. Cash only. Next cash customer in aisle 4, please.

A cashier in a store is making an announcement. She is free. She can help a customer. The next customer should go to her cash register. She is in aisle 4. She can only accept cash.

(A) "One" relates to "next."
(B) "Two" relates to "next."
(C) "Three" isn't mentioned.
√ (D) Aisle 4 is open.

48. (M) Did you memorize the music?
(W) I memorized everything except the last verse.
(M) We can practice in the car.

The man and woman are talking about music. They are probably going to a concert. The woman memorized most of a song. However, she didn't memorize the last part. She can practice it in the car.

√ (A) She memorized the first part of the song.
(B) "Car" repeats.
(C) "Music" repeats.
(D) "Drive" relates to car. "Reverse" sounds like "verse."

49. (M) I think I caught a cold last week.
(W) Your eyes look kind of red.
(M) They are, red and itchy. It's flu season, I guess.

The man is sick. He got sick last week. His eyes look red.

(A) Swimming makes your eyes red.
(B) A ball could make your eyes red.
√ (C) "Sick" means "cold" and "flu."
(D) "Cold" repeats.

50. Stamp Collectors, listen up! The Association of African Stamp Collectors has just opened its new exhibit. With stamps from Zaire, the Ivory Coast, South Africa, Morocco-some rare stamps dating to the 19th century. The African Stamp Collectors' table is Number 34. Booth Number 34, near the cafeteria entrance. African Stamps has just opened its display.

This announcement is at a show of collections. The announcement is about an African stamp show. The African stamp exhibit is new. The African stamps are from many African countries. The African stamps are rare and old. The African stamp show is at table number 34. This table just opened.

(A) "Nineteenth century" repeats.
(B) "3:40" sounds like "34."
√ (C) The display "just" opened.
(D) "Ten minutes to eight" may sound like "opened its display."

51. (A)

<u>Is</u> Marcus 19 years old? "Marcus" is a singular, third person. "Is" is a third person singular verb.

52. (D)

<u>These are</u> my glasses. "Glasses" is plural. It requires a plural pronoun and verb, "glasses," "are."

53. (C)

Her wedding is on the <u>twenty-eighth</u> of May. Dates are given as ordinal numbers. A wedding can be on only one day.

54. (B)

The lamp is <u>in</u> the living room. A lamp can be <u>in a living room</u>. It can hang <u>from the ceiling</u>. It can be <u>on a table</u>. A lamp can't be "on, over, under" a living room.

55. (C)

Teresa and Colleen are <u>both</u> from Ireland. Two girls are from Ireland.

56. (B)

The hostess served <u>him</u> way too much food. "Him" is an indirect object. If this sentence is difficult for you, make it easier: The hostess served <u>him</u> food. ("Food" is the direct object.) See page 109.

57. (D)

Buy a loaf of <u>bread</u> when you're at the store. "Loaf" is commonly used to count packages of bread.

58. (C)

The manager <u>would like</u> to send this fax before noon today. "Would like" shows preference. It means "want." The manager wants to send his fax before noon today. The other options do not match the time and meaning of this sentence.

59. (A)

We had <u>to</u> cancel our reservations by 11:59 last night. "Have to" is a modal auxiliary. It means "must."

60. (C)

While we were <u>playing</u> cards, we heard a strange sound. Two past actions are happening at the same time. People were playing cards. A sound interrupted their game. "Were playing" must be past progressive. "Heard" must be simple past.

61. (B)

This black wallet is much <u>more</u> expensive than the brown. Two wallets are being compared. "More" is used in comparisons between two things.

62. (B)

Are you <u>paying</u> by cash or by credit card? All of the answer options relate to shopping. Only "paying" can be done with cash or a credit card.

63. (B)

Several students are going <u>to miss</u> class on Thursday. This sentence uses the present progressive + infinitive to show future time.

64. (B)

Marty became an electrician and I did <u>too</u>. Two people did the same thing. Marty did it. I did it too. (D) "Neither" is for negative sentences: Marty didn't become an electrician, and neither did I.

65. (D)

That restaurant serves a lot of spicy <u>and</u> salty food. The food has two features: It is both spicy and salty. (A) and (B) show a contrast, but "spicy" and "salty" do not contrast.

66. (C)

Last Sunday, we <u>sailed</u> on Lake Wingo in my sister's boat. You can sail in a boat. You cannot swim on a lake. (Rather, you swim in a lake.)

67. (B)

The students learned how to <u>control</u> their robots remotely. Only "control" completes this sentence.

68. (B)

Tony Markoni is the <u>best</u> cook in the city. Tony is being compared to all of the other cooks in the city. There are many cooks. You need the superlative form, best.

69. (A)

I always <u>wear</u> my seat belt when I drive. The simple present shows that this is a habitual, repeated action.

70. (D)

Which <u>airline</u> are you flying on? You fly on an airline, or with an airline. (A) "Which air" makes no sense. (B) You can't fly on an airport. However, you could say: "Which airport are you flying into?"

71. (C)

The actress <u>was</u> tired of signing autographs. "Actress" takes the third person singular verb. (B) If you want to talk about the future, you need to say: The actress will be tired of signing autographs.

72. (C)

My <u>cousin</u> is a member of the gymnastics club. Your cousins are the children of your parent's brother or sisters.

73. (C)

You need to <u>button</u> that shirt. "Button" means to close something with buttons.

74. (A)

She <u>cancelled</u> her meeting with the marketing department. A meeting was planned. The woman changed the plan. Now, there is no meeting.

75. (D)

The train was <u>so</u> crowded that we had to stand. "So" introduces a negative consequence, "that we had to stand."

76. (D)

The dishwasher is completely <u>empty</u>. There are no dishes in the dishwasher.

77. (A)

Seven police cars arrived at the scene of the <u>accident</u>. Police cars come to accident scenes to help people.

78. (B)

My sister ordered the daily <u>special</u> from the menu. Many restaurants have a special meal. It is usually a bargain.

79. (D)

He always keeps his wallet <u>in</u> his back pocket. Many people keep their wallets in their back pocket.

80. (A)

You can either rent <u>or</u> buy these skateboards. A person has two choices: either rent or buy. "Either . . . or" is a set expression.

81. (B)

The title of the movie is "Who Says?" (A) First Royal Cinemas is the name of the theater. (C) Auditorium 9 is the hall where the movie shows. (D) "Admit one" repeats from the ticket.

82. (D)

The show is in auditorium 9. "Auditorium" means "theater." (A) "One" means "first." (B) "Two" repeats the year, "02." (C) "Eight" is the price of the ticket.

83. (B)

"Illness" means "sick." (A) "Late" means "after the set time." (C) "Suspended" means the person is not working for a short time. (D) "Warning" means "information about a danger."

84. (D)

"Discipline" means punishment. (A) "Holiday" means a day off. (B) "Vacation" means a long holiday. (C) "Personal" means that the reason is private.

85. (C)

"Kids" means "children." (A) "Safety" means "security," but it is not checked. (B) "Health" refers to "exercise," but it is not checked. (D) "Blind" means "can't see." It is not an option.

86. (C)

"Show off" refers to "prestige." (A) We do hobbies for fun. (B) "Friendship" is a reason hat she wants a dog. (D) The dog is a Christmas gift.

87. (B)

The notice tells bus riders about nighttime bus stops. (A) Drivers would get this information from a driver's handbook. This notice talks about "you." You exit the bus and talk to the driver. "You" can't be the driver. (C) "Stop" is repeated in the title of the notice. (D) "Night" is repeated. "Taxi" riders may also be concerned with stops.

88. (A)

Read the last sentence in the notice: "Safety considerations will determine (decide)" if the driver can stop. (B) "Payment" relates to buses. (C) Weather could be a factor, but it is not mentioned. (D) "Regular stop" is repeated.

89. (D)

"Approach the driver" means "go to the front end of the bus and ask your driver." (A) and (B) Ringing a bell or pulling a cord are common ways to stop a bus. (C) Shouting is not mentioned.

90. (A)

This advertisement lists many family activities. So, active families would be interested in it. (B), (C), and (D) are common targets for advertisements. However, they are not mentioned here.

91. (D)

Reading classes are not mentioned. (A) "Babysitting" means "child care." (B) "Birthday parties" are offered. (C) "Swim lessons" are offered.

92. (C)

A "spelling bee" is a spelling contest. (A) "Race" means "contest." (B) "Competition" means "contest." (D) "Contest" is repeated.

93. (A)

"Trip" means "vacation." First prize is a vacation to Hawaii. (B) A bicycle is second prize. (C) "Money" relates to a "fifty-dollar gift certificate." (D) Books are not mentioned.

94. (B)

There were 62 finalists. (A) 12 is Tiffany's age. (C) 10 is the number of speeds on the bicycle prize. (D) 3 is the number of winners.

95. (D)

Park toys relate to children, but they are not mentioned. (A) The first article is about "Kids and Fall Safety." (B) "Road Lessons" is about car crashes. "Crash" means "accident." (C) The last article is about a swing dance.

96. (B)

The topics of the articles relate to families: children's safety, travel, dancing. (A), (C), and (D) would not be interested in these general topics.

97. (C)

The advertisement talks about a coffee house. It names many good features of the coffee house. (A) and (B) are features of the coffee house. (D) Music CDs relate to music.

98. (D)

"Light foods" means "easy snacks and pastries." (A) Dinner is not mentioned. (B) "Indian" repeats. (C) "Imported" may relate to Indian, coffee, or tea.

99. (C)

This note is an invitation to a birthday party. See the first line. (A) It is not a postcard. (B) The note gives an address, but it does not inform people about a change of address. (D) It is not an advertisement.

100. (D)

"RSVP" + phone number means "call to say if you can come." (A) A letter is not needed. (B) There is nothing to be ordered. (C) The card says, "No gifts, please." So, the receiver should not buy a gift.

The Houseplant Whisperer

Practical Guide to Caring for & Maintaining Thriving Houseplants Year-Round

Improve air quality, promote relaxation &
create a beautiful living space

MICHELLE ROSA

Humanity Publications

This here is for my Milk and Honey Babies

Apriya and Aniyah Artis

Love, Mami xoxo

The seed that fell on good soil represents those who truly hear and understand God's word and produce a harvest of thirty, sixty, or even a hundred times as much as had been planted.

— **Matthew 13:32 (NLT)**

FOREWORD

"Plants are like people - they thrive with love, attention, and a little bit of patience."

— Anonymous.

Meet our protagonist, Michelle, a young woman in her 30s passionate about houseplants. Michelle's love for plants started when she was a little girl, and she used to help her grandmother in her beautiful garden. However, it wasn't until later in life that she discovered her love for indoor house planting.

She loved being surrounded by nature in her home and was determined to make her succulent collection thrive. Michelle's dedication and hard work have paid off over the years, resulting in a thriving group of stunning succulent plants. Her home is now a serene haven filled with lush greenery, and her plants have become her companions, bringing her joy and tranquility.

She spent years learning and gaining experience in indoor house planting, and her positive attitude and hard work paid off. Her succulent plants grew tall and healthy, with leaves as green as emeralds and flowers as bright as the sun.

One day, as she was admiring her stunning succulent collection, a friend came over and marveled at the beauty of her plants. "How do you keep them alive and healthy?" her friend asked in amazement.

That's when it hit her - she wanted to share her critical tips with other nature lovers who wanted to grow their indoor houseplant collection. She wants to help people understand how to make indoor house planting easier and show them that it is possible to have a captivating succulent collection everyone admires.

And so, she created this book - She knows 95% of people agree that there is an information overload problem today. And it's precisely why when she started this book, it focused on fewer tips and more storytelling, case studies, and her personal experience helping others grow and care for their succulent plants. Her goal is to help you create a stunning indoor garden that will amaze your friends and family.

Therefore, I'm excited for you, the reader. Let's start on your journey to becoming a houseplant parent extraordinaire! Prepare yourself to explore the universe of indoor house planting and learn how to keep your succulent plants alive and thriving.

-Marianne B, Female, North America
New Houseplant Hobbyist

TABLE OF CONTENTS

Foreword v

Introduction xiii

Chapter 1 Deciding On Your First Houseplant 1

Subjective Reasons to Have Plants..3

How to Choose Houseplants 11

Location of Plant...20

Purpose of the Plant 20

Light Intensity 20

Humidity 20

Temperature...20

Chapter 2 Water – The Essence of Life 22

Cacti...23

Tropical Plants 23

Furry Leaved Plants 23

Aerial Rooted Plants 24

Bromeliads..24

Overwatering Vs Underwatering 24

5 Golden Rules for Watering 27

Watering Chart for Main Indoor Houseplants 28

Chapter 3 Growing Medium - The Power of Earth 31

What Makes an Excellent Growth Medium? 32

Types of Growth Mediums 33

Checklist of Which Potting Medium is Best Suited to the Houseplants 41

Chapter 4 Temperature and Humidity – The Power of Fire and Wind 45

Common Issues with Temperatures of the Houseplants 46

Tips to Keep the Temperature Neutral for Houseplants 48

Do Cold Tolerant Indoor Plants Exist? 48

Why Does Some Plant Prefer Higher Humidity? 51

Plants that Increase or Decrease Humidity in Homes 52

Checklist of Relative Humidity Levels of Houseplants 55

GoodWill 58

Chapter 5 Pest Control & Diseases 60

Most Common Indoor Plant Pests 61

Types of Pesticides 64

Common Houseplant Disease 66

Chapter 6 Plant Nutrition - Give Us this Day, Our Daily Bread 69

Primary Plant Nutrients 70

Secondary Plant Nutrients 71

Micronutrients 72

Essential Nutrition Guide for Flowering & Non-flowering Houseplants 73

Types of Fertilizers 75

Chapter 7 Light Control & Seasonal Changes 77

Lightening Conditions for Different Houseplants 79

Diagnosing Problems in Struggling Plants..83

Less Light..84

Top High Light, Medium Light, and Low Light Plant Picks 85

Care Routine for Plants in the "Quiet Season" 90

Chapter 8 Houseplant Propagation..93

    Types of Houseplant Propagation 94

    Air Layering 95

    Division 96

    Plantlets and Offsets 96

    Sowing Seeds...96

    10 Easy Steps to Home/indoor Propagation...................................97

Chapter 9 Understanding Which Plant is Right for You 98

    Care and Maintenance 99

    Light 99

    Space...102

    Positioning..103

    How is the View?..103

    Temperature and Humidity..104

    Pictorial Representation of Main Houseplant Types 105

    Maintenance Chart for Main Indoor Houseplants 121

Conclusion..125

Final Thoughts 128

Acknowledgments 130

References...131

To express gratitude for your purchase, I would like to extend an exclusive offer to readers of Transform Your Home into a Lush Oasis with this SPECIAL *Bonus Gift*

Planting Terrarium

Scan the QR Code Now and Flourish your Indoor Jungle!

Come join us and get free access to
all my books, both now and in the future!
Lots of people are already enjoying this exclusive offer, and
you can too.

Sign up today!

Bring the Beauty of Nature inside -

Are you excited to discover more about houseplants and cultivate healthy habits to take care of them? Then, you may find the Houseplant Hobbyist & Enthusiasts community on Facebook, very useful.

This is a wonderful community of individuals who share their love for plants and are passionate about nurturing them. Here, you can find easy-to-follow advice for looking after your houseplants, connect with other plant enthusiasts, and ask for help with any difficulties you may face.

By becoming a part of this community, you can boost your knowledge and skills to become an expert in houseplant care!

Scan the QR Code and Join Today!

INTRODUCTION

"My green thumb came only as a result of the mistakes I made while learning to see things from the plant's point of view."

— H. Fred Dale

Humans have been fans of gardening and houseplants for decades. It has been a source of joy and bread and butter for them. Millennials and Gen Zs constantly take up this hobby, even with the changing world.

You might be wondering how this activity is still prevalent in the present age. The answer lies in your existence.

Have you ever felt the sudden urge to trek across town to the gardens? Or a penchant for packing your belongings for an enticing destination?

If so, this behavior is because of your inherent tendency to link with other forms of nature, called Biophilia. It refers to your human instinct to show affection to anything perceived to be alive.

Living in an environment that helps you connect with nature has several psychological benefits. It's more than a mere appeal to grow houseplants. Being closer to nature relaxes your nerves.

While staying in a constructive environment for an extended period can wear you down emotionally, staying closer to nature can play a massive role in helping to ease your stress. So, next time, you don't need to feel guilty about your urge to have a living green wall in your office.

Even more, giant corporations are experiencing the healing power of Biophilic environments. As a result, the design of businesses, landscapes, airports, and other places is changing.

Besides the corporate world, we see a growing trend in sales of Houseplants, Succulents, and Tropical Plants in gardens. Millennials lead as the top group investing in this activity.

There are several reasons why this gloomy industry is popular among this generation. The most common ones are the competitive job market and skyrocketing tuition prices. As a result, they are delaying marriages, home purchases, and having children.

With uncertain economic and financial conditions, Generation Z prefers to be a plant parent! They are cheap and have several benefits, and ensure a flexible life.

It fulfills their need to nurture something. Even though houseplants need a lot of care and attention, they require little maintenance and can scratch your itch.

Another reason is millennials prioritize wellness and health much more than previous generations, making plants a natural draw. People generally consider plants to be the healthiest species to live with. They improve your mood, aid in water purification, reduce stress and decorate your home.

This trend has also affected employers who know how vital a healthy work environment is to millennials. They are striving to incorporate living green spaces and living walls.

Do you know? In Brooklyn, New York, the Etsy headquarters has more than 11,000 plants in their 200,000-square-foot facility.

The most crucial benefit of house planting is the community it builds. Several online and in-person activities have emerged, such as plant shows, clubs, and swaps. People can now interact better due to this shared interest.

While such trends are notorious for fading and flourishing cycles, indoor gardening is here to stay. This hobby has numerous psychological and physical advantages.

We often live in cramped places without windows or air vents, including offices, tiny homes, and other locations. Having plants in such spaces can induce feelings of escape. These plants lead to feelings of being away from physical and social demands. You are likely to experience fewer symptoms of depression and anxiety.

You might have heard a lot about how plants reduce stress. The scientific reasoning behind this fact is the changes made in your body. Plant interaction suppresses the body signals in you that indicate distress. Spend a few minutes transplanting and repotting an indoor plant. You'll witness the results yourself.

Additionally, who feels energized after a hectic workday? Well, don't worry! Plants have the power to recharge you. Keeping your mind on challenging tasks, like your job, can lead to bad feelings and mental fatigue. Looking at your indoor garden will redirect your attention, spark your interest, and restore your drained psychological and physical energy. This concept is also known as the "attention restoration theory."

Aside from mental fitness, plants can also improve physical health. Researchers found that post-operative patients with plants in their rooms recovered comparatively faster. Not only that, they required fewer pain medications and hospital stays. So, don't be shy about taking a flower bouquet to your loved one in the hospital next time.

Furthermore, plants may boost your productivity if you often feel demotivated. They help you clear your mind and decrease stress. As a result, you work to the best of your abilities.

Not only that, but this hobby can also reduce your blood pressure and headaches. They create this effect by suppressing your sympathetic nervous system, which is responsible for blood pressure, increased heart rate, pupil size, and breathing rate.

With so many great benefits, it's easy to see why indoor planting could be a fun hobby. You might wonder if I only need a pot, soil, and water. Yet, there is more to the story.

"I wish I knew these things before starting my houseplant parent journey!"

These were the words of 29-year-old Marianne, an enthusiastic plant keeper. Her sudden urge to nurture plants came from her first trip to Hawaii. After returning from her journey, she wanted everything around her to be tropical and Hawaii-inspired. A couple of months after that, she started collecting plants. It motivated her to grow some succulents and planters by herself. Yet, sadly, she faced a couple of problems that she couldn't resolve by herself. Such as:

☐ Lack of basic knowledge about the essential elements of plants that can ensure their survivability

☐ Hoarding any plant that came into her sight without learning anything about choosing beginner-friendly types

☐ Spending a lot of money so far but zero results

She got a copy of this book only three months ago. Here is what she has to say:

Marianne B, Female, 29 years old (North America):

I was constantly struggling to keep my indoor plants survive. They used to turn yellow and soon the leaves start to curl and eventually fall down. After reading this book, I came to know about my shortcomings. Now, finally! I can say I'm a proud plant parent, thanks a lot!

Fortunately, this book includes all the information that can save you from all such obstacles and hassles. With its help, you can make your houseplants happy and healthy.

The author of this book is a young professional woman in her 30s who is a passionate houseplant parent. She created this book after years of learning and experience in indoor house planting. Her positive attitude and hard work taught her how to grow, care for, and keep succulent plants alive.

She now plans to share her essential tips with other nature lovers. She aims to help people understand how they can make indoor house planting easier. Through this book, she intends to demonstrate that your dream of having a captivating succulent collection everyone admires is achievable.

The hobby takes both time and effort. So, only give this book a go if you're someone who wants to:

✔ ☐ Enjoy your life with your plants

✔ ☐ Learn about the needs of different plants

✔ ☐ Want to know beginner plant types and their growing hacks

✔ ☐ Repotting, transplanting, and propagation

Then, you're here for a treat! After going through this book, you'll achieve your desired green thumb. You'll be sipping tea with guests while they wonder how you made it all possible in no time! Are you in?

CHAPTER 1

DECIDING ON YOUR FIRST HOUSEPLANT

"Nature holds the key to our aesthetic, intellectual, cognitive, and even spiritual satisfaction."

— E. O. Wilson

The attachment you feel towards plants is not only because it's trendy. Cultivating plants, trees, and succulents is a trend passed down through generations. We can trace it back to the times of ancient Rome and Greece.

You may ask why millennials are intensely interested in this ancient concept. Well, there can be multiple reasons why people are jumping on this trend. Primarily most important, a plant fills a *"need."* It might soothe nerves, soften the stark lines of your living space, or help you escape from your screens.

Plant Parenthood is a popular term used by individuals who call their plants "babies." for Generation Z, it's a way to satisfy their natural need to care for something. Several such young people cultivating indoor plants call themselves plant parents.

Young adults are taking longer to tie the knot compared to previous generations. They are still interested in long-term commitments. They are simply delaying marriage and shouldering heavy responsibilities, including raising children.

The reasons are economic instability, a change in gender dynamics, and more women in colleges and workplaces. The uncertainty pressures them to get their lives sorted out before marriage.

In the meantime, they are looking for options to fulfill their need to nurture. It's a good choice for them because it won't significantly affect their budgets, lives, or homes. Here is where houseplants come into play.

In addition, taking care of plants also has several psychological effects. It brings out your innate tendency to love other living things. We start to think about their requirements to survive and thrive.

We create an emotional bond with our planters. This natural connection with nature forces you to take care of them. So, if you ever wonder why you're so disappointed with drooping leaves, now you've got your answer!

Furthermore, plants are known to be aesthetically pleasing. The shape and colors of plants tend to relieve your stress, help you brainstorm better ideas, and cope with your surroundings. According to a survey, about 52 percent of millennials have stated that anxiety has kept them up at night. It may also cause this age group's enthusiasm for plant parenting.

Moreover, we all need a sense of pride and accomplishment to stay motivated. Taking care of plants will give you joy and boost your self-esteem. Watching your little planters grow and sustain themselves can be weirdly rewarding for any plant parent.

The shared generation is constantly in a dilemma. Millennials and Gen Z are known to compare their lives to those of others in the social media age. As a result, they feel that they have failed in life.

By caring for plants, Generation Z feels they are doing something great. It would be reasonable to say that millennials will undoubtedly have plant babies. The circumstances make them and this hobby a match made in heaven.

Why You Should Choose Houseplants

Modern mechanical life and concrete buildings have disrupted our connection with the natural environment. Aside from their psychological impact, indoor plants are aesthetically pleasing. Something as simple as a little plant pot on a green wall can improve your overall mood immensely.

Subjective Reasons to Have Plants

There are endless benefits to investing in this joyful hobby. Here is a list of ways greenery can impact your surroundings.

Beautification

Enhancing your apartment, office, or outdoor space is a critical physical attribute. Imagine the swaying of a palm frond through your window. This scene will provide a cooling effect on your eyes.

Additionally, these plants give an architectural touch to your place. They have the power to add freshness and softness to any boring frame! Many designers and home decor enthusiasts use them for decorating shelves.

Apart from that, you can also use them to fill spaces that seem rigid. A good plant for this purpose can be a succulent. They demand very little attention while having an architectonic touch.

Moreover, plants are also known to beautify the straight lines and angles in a home. A Kentia Plant will be a fantastic solution if you search for anything comparable. Invest in beginner-level planters like Spider Plants, Ferns, and Potted Pelargoniums to give your home a tropical atmosphere. It will allow you to have a low-maintenance indoor jungle that is also very attractive.

Decor

Does the indoor jungle look too much to you? If so, carefully positioning a few pieces can even elevate a space. A more extensive statement plant will create a single focal point in your area.

You can use these versatile plants as accessories and elements of interior design. Using them smartly will transform the plain white walls of your house into a place that reflects your personality.

Try placing a Fig Tree in your high-ceiling dining room. You'll be surprised how many people are inspired by this lovely decor piece. If you're interested in a similar idea, Elephant's Ear, Pygmy Date Palm, and Citrus can be great options.

Simplicity

As "less is more" trends, many seek ideas to revamp their space. Yet, introducing greenery intermingled with this minimalist approach can be a bit challenging. Thankfully, getting that minimalist aesthetic doesn't need spending hundreds of dollars.

Regardless, there are several ways you can make that happen. First and foremost, strike a balance in your environment. Evaluate the shape of your room and let it dictate flower or plant shapes.

Let's say you have long, rectangular-shaped furniture. Orchids could be a fantastic match. A good strategy is to use the same type of plant but in different sizes. It will effortlessly make your place look more impressive.

Moreover, plants can also be a perfect choice to fill a space. Instead of bulky furniture, get a Fiddle Fig Tree or a sizeable potted plant like the Dracaena. These unique indoor choices will naturally become part of your setup.

All you need is to find a suitable corner. It can be at the end of the corridor, beside a sofa, or in the foyer. Just make sure that the place has a good amount of sunlight.

Another way indoor plants can help you with minimalistic decor is through Terrarium. You can add glass terrariums anywhere without disrupting your space's flow. Along with being dainty, they are super easy to maintain. Either lay them flat on any surface or hang them with your ceiling.

Restores Balance

Did you know? The color green can create balance and harmony around you. We continually struggle to have a peaceful time in the current fast-paced environment. You might have found yourself tense even when lying on your bed.

In that case, having indoor plants can be a great move. You can place some tiny planters near your bed as well. Seeing them will assist you in indulging in a peaceful sleep. Besides that, you'll be able to embrace a Biophilic design naturally.

For decades, plants have been used in Chinese traditions (Feng Shui) for harmonizing homes. Some fantastic options include Lucky Bamboo, Orchids, Money Plants, Parlor Palms, Peace Lily, and Boston Fern. The great thing is all of them are low-maintenance and kept alive with minimal effort.

Promotes Optimism

It is well-known that plants help you build a positive outlook toward life. Your surrounding can have a massive impact on your mindset and overall health. For instance, staying in a cluttered or unclean space will make you sick. So, you gradually lose energy and become prone to several problems.

A study suggests multiple benefits of keeping indoor plants, such as increased optimism and calmness and reduced depression, stress, and anxiety. You become more productive, active, and refreshed. Similarly, staying surrounded by fresh plants and greenery can uplift your mood.

Not only does it boost your mood and well-being, but it also enhances your sense of control and stability. Even a decrease in blood pressure and headaches is possible by having some plants by your side. Relevant research suggests that individuals in a plant-filled room experienced a four-point drop in blood pressure readings.

Objective Reasons to Have Plants

Other than visual attraction and psychological benefits, indoor plants have several perks. For instance, improvement in overall health and your environment. Here are several ways how plants contribute to your fitness.

Indoor Air Quality

The air you breathe in is full of toxins and harmful chemicals. These pollutants can cause chronic diseases and respiratory illnesses, such as asthma. In addition, ozone layer depletion has exposed us to several health problems, such as skin diseases, cataracts, cancer, and an impaired immune system.

Your small step of cultivating plants can save you and your loved ones from these life-threatening experiences. How so? Indoor planters and succulents absorb impurities and gases that are harmful to humans. According to NASA research, these plants can eliminate 87 percent of air pollutants in 24 hours.

Even though some plants can perform this activity better, all of them can contribute to the environment. The microorganism in these plants' soil also contributes to this cause.

The microbes eat the air contaminants such as organic matter and oil (waste food). They convert these products into water and carbon dioxide. In this process, naturally occurring bacteria and fungi degrade hazardous substances.

Some popular houseplants that improve air quality include Peace Lily, English Ivy, Snake Plant, Chrysanthemum, Devil's Ivy, Dracaena, and Bamboo Palm. No green thumb yet? No worries! These plant types are easy to maintain, even if you have just started as a beginner.

Therapy

Indoor plants are known to hold prestigious therapeutic value. Research suggests that interacting with a green atmosphere can help people with mental illnesses. Taking responsibility for plants promotes self-efficacy and confidence in you. As a result, it improves your mental health.

Horticultural therapy is known to have several benefits. It can be your refugee from your tough, practical life. While for several people, it is a source of joy. Additionally, you tend to feel more relaxed by planting and maintaining plants.

Regardless of the size of your home, consider adding some plants. Over time, you'll see an uplift in your mood and health. In addition, plants can help combat feelings of loneliness. Nurturing a small plant can provide a meaningful and rewarding purpose, especially when you see it grow and thrive before your eyes.

Humidity Control

Are you tired of hot weather and excessive humidity? Don't worry! Adding indoor plants to your house is an excellent way to combat humidity. Your plant partner is here to help you out.

Plants are known to be natural dehumidifiers. They tend to absorb water from the surroundings through leaves. While doing so, they release moisture back through transpiration. This process aids in regulating humidity levels while creating fresh air in space.

The humidity-absorbing houseplants are an excellent choice if you cannot water them daily. They are tough enough to survive, even if you neglect them on your busiest days. Some low-maintenance relevant plants include Peperomia, Golden Pothos (Epipremnum Aureum), Aloe Vera, Spider Plant, and Lilac.

Allergen relief

Modern houses are more energy efficient and can save you a lot of money. However, the bad news is that these houses are airtight compared to the old ones. Your place traps indoor pollutants for an extended period. As a result, people prone to allergies are more exposed to watery eyes and sneezing.

The good news is that certain plants can help you with this problem. They flush away toxins and improve air quality. Houseplants for allergy relief usually come with larger leaves. Their physical appearance also makes them an attractive statement in your place.

Some low-allergy planters can even remove dangerous chemicals, such as Formaldehyde, from your environment. Moreover, these plants flourish even with little care. Consequently, you need not be concerned about their survival.

Although, this does not mean you can completely neglect your plant baby. Nevertheless, all plants can worsen allergies if not treated correctly. Only water the soil of these plants when they become dry to the touch. Excessive water can result in the growth of molds.

Furthermore, keep cleaning the plant leaves with a damp cloth occasionally. Dusty leaves can only elevate the problem.

Still, determining which plants will thrive in a small area? NASA researched Mars and Lunar bases to determine the best plants that fit this job. The following are some of the top suggestions:

- Golden Pothos and Philodendron (controls Formaldehyde)

- Mums and Peace Lilies (for removing PCE from the air)

- Gerbera Daisies (for controlling benzene)

- Lady Palm and Bamboo Palm (to clean air gently)

Try cultivating any of them as per your concern.

Culinary Purposes

Another incredible benefit of having indoor houseplants is eating healthy organic food. You can cultivate carrots, peppers, cilantro, basil, apples, blueberries, and onions on your window sill.

Additionally, this pastime will assist in purifying the air you breathe of contaminants. You'll be surprised that changing years does not affect indoor cultivated items. Thus, you'll be able to eat them anytime around the year. Besides that, you get to live an eco-friendly lifestyle cost-effectively.

Moreover, growing your food comes with several other perks. You get to decide which type of pesticides or chemicals will come in contact with your veggies and fruits. Additionally, you can also control the time of their harvesting.

The veggies you grow in your personal spaces are more nutritious than the store-bought ones. If you had lousy luck with growing such items previously, don't worry! Try working with less variety and quantity of plants. Start small.

Some easy-to-grow edibles include bell peppers, blackberries and raspberries, cabbage cucumbers, garlic, and strawberries. You can choose some of these options and gradually add to them.

Interior Design Functionality

Do you like to decorate your home? Do you regularly make statement-making purchases? Adding indoor houseplants to your home would be an excellent addition. Your home's atmosphere will change thanks to these functional objects. They'll not only brighten up the empty room but also your soul.

However, make sure you don't clutter your space with them. Keep in mind that the size of your house and the pot matters. Having large-size planters in a confined apartment will make the area unappealing.

That said, some plants look more attractive in interior design than others. Some of the popular choices include the Sweetheart Plant, Fiddle Leaf, Fig Tree, Monstera, Palm, and Air Plants (Tillandsias). All of them are low-maintenance, fast-growing, and a treat to the eyes.

- **Reduce Stress Levels**

Life underwent dramatic changes following the unfortunate events of COVID-19. People had to stay home, leading to a lack of social interaction and a disconnection from nature.

All of this severally impacted the mental fitness of people. Sadly, they are still in its effect even after lifting the lockdown. Along with these psychological issues, people have come back to regular jobs. Many of them aren't able to cope with daily stress anymore.

Researchers all around the world started to look for options that can improve their emotional health. A relevant study revealed how plant-related tasks can impact your mental fitness. It showed that the subjects felt soothed, comfortable, and natural while interacting with plants.

Therefore, having indoor plants can prove to be life-changing for you. They will boost your productivity and reduce feelings of anxiety and depression with better concentration and memory.

Many plants are easy to care for and last for a long time. Some examples are Snake Plants, Jade Plants, English Ivy, Boston Fern, Bamboo Palm, Lavender, and Flamingo Lily.

After learning about their extraordinary qualities, you must be eager to have your plant babies. Yet, the question arises of how you will choose the best fit for you. If you're wondering the same, keep reading.

How to Choose Houseplants

Searching for low-maintenance planters and succulents for your home can be challenging, especially if you're a beginner. However, we'll discuss some unique types of houseplants below to guide you.

Flowering Houseplants

These plants add scent, enjoyment, and vibrance with a pop of color. Try one of these flowering houseplants that require minimal attention.

Begonias

Begonias can thrive easily in favorable conditions. They can be an excellent investment as a houseplant. However, make sure that you have kept them in a sunny location. Keeping them in a closed window space can harm them.

They need high to medium heat and are available in various colors. Make sure you water them regularly.

Streptocarpus

Do you love brightly colored flowers? If yes, this flowering plant could be a perfect pick. It flourishes in bright spots, but avoid placing it in direct sunlight. These plants grow quickly and are easy to take care of.

You'll need a potash-rich liquid fertilizer for a steady supply of flowers and pick off spent stalks. For watering, you must ensure that it feels dry to the touch. Overwatering can cause harm to its root system.

As streptocarpus has a shallow root system, a 15 cm or smaller pot would be enough.

Cacti and Succulents

Cacti are a popular choice as indoor houseplants for people who have busy schedules. They can tolerate drought. They have water stored in their leaves or fleshy stems. Even though they grow slowly, they can thrive under usual household conditions, such as low humidity and high temperature.

Some popular choices belonging to this family include

Dragonfruit

This tall cactus plant can serve as a houseplant. It typically bears large flowers between 6 and 12 inches in size and has hairy spines. Over time, these large flowers transform into fruits. While it usually favors direct sunlight, it can also adapt to partial shade.

Overwatering can kill Dragonfruit. So, keep your new plant buddy in moderate to low moisture levels.

Dancing Bones Cactus

Several people keep this short cactus plant as a houseplant. It has thin pencil-like small leaves with tiny flowers (having a size of roughly 1 inch). Like dragon fruit, it thrives ideally in moderate to low moisture levels. Overwatering can harm its roots, and your little partner can die.

This cactus plant type prefers staying in the shade. As far as growth is concerned, it can reach a height of 12 inches and a width of 18 inches.

Golden Barrel Cactus

This small cactus appears to be like a tiny sharp ball. It has long spines that cover the complete plant. It also produces small yellow flowers (2 to 3 inches). It can endure rough conditions like drought and poor soil.

Just like other cacti, this plant is not a fan of water. Overwatering can rot its root causing the plant to die. Thus, make sure this plant remains in moderate to dry moisture conditions.

Air Plants Tillandsia Spp.

You've probably seen those trendy hanging plants in garden apps. People call them Air Plants, and they're famous for indoor gardening. They get this unique name because they have a remarkable ability to pull moisture from the air. Most plant types don't need soil or a pot to grow.

You can try any of the well-liked options in this category that are listed below.

Maxima' Sky Plant (Tillandsia Ionantha 'Maxima' or 'Huamelula')

This beautiful Air Plant is here to make an appearance! It has coral-red leaves and produces brilliant purple-colored flowers. It can grow multiple flowers at once. This indoor houseplant requires full sun or partial shade to rise. Besides that, it grows in fluorescent light as well.

This plant has a height of 5 to 6 inches with a width of 3 to 4 inches. Thus, its size is more significant than other indoor houseplants.

Sky Plant (Tillandsia Ionantha)

This mesmerizing plant has layers of shiny green leaves. As they grow longer, they extend into shades of pink and red. This plant type is trendy all over the world. The reason is that this tough guy is extremely hard to kill.

It has a height of 6 to 12 inches. At the same time, it thrives both in bright and indirect sunlight.

Trailing and Climbing Houseplants

Have you seen those plants hanging from indoor baskets, pots, and ceilings? The branches you see are called trailing stems. Investing in this plant type would be great if you're into home decor.

Climbing houseplants can be 'trained' as per your requirements. You can make it climb on or trail over specific features of a home. It can complement various textures, furnishing, colors, and even finishes.

The two of the most in-demand houseplants include

Devil's Eye (Golden Pathos)

This trailing plant will be a great fit if you're looking for an easy-to-care option. Golden Pathos are low-maintenance and highly adaptive plants. They can withstand various environmental conditions and mediums. No soil pot? No problem! This climbing plant can thrive in a bowl filled with water.

Pathos is not a fan of direct sunlight. However, these plants respond well to indirect, bright, and low light. Only water them when they feel dry to the touch. As an estimate, watering them once a week would be enough.

String of Pearls

This adorable succulent is a houseplant that usually grows over long vines. It appears to be like tiny pearls attached to a string. These pearls are soil to touch and are round. These physical traits make them perfect for positioning in a cascade or hanging baskets. In rare cases, the strings of pearls flower into fainted white blooms.

This plant enjoys direct sunlight. Around 6 to 8 hrs of the sun is required to keep them thriving.

Indoor Palms

Indoor palms are here to give your house and conservatory an exotic and tropical vibe. They are the most cultivated plants around the globe. Whether in a modest apartment or a prominent location, this would be a great addition to your collection.

Palm Trees are known for their air-purifying abilities. They remove pollutants like carbon monoxide and dangerous Volatile Organic Compounds (VOCs) from the air. Besides beautification, having this plant has several benefits.

Moreover, these plants assist in balancing negative energy. They bring out fresh vibes and boost positivity in the environment. Some popular indoor palms include

Parlor Palm (Chamaedorea Elegans)

This beautiful plant is compact and has attractive arching leaves. They are low-maintenance and require little care. Parlor Palm thrives in medium to intense indirect bright light. On average, this plant can grow up to 10 to 12ft.

Overwatering is a straight no for these plants. Water once a week or once every two weeks. Make sure that the soil is dry and has no moisture.

Areca Palm (Dypsis Lutescens)

Here is another fantastic option for busy plant parents. This plant type can survive various environmental circumstances. It enjoys indirect bright light. However, it can withstand low light conditions. However, direct sunlight can scorch its leaves.

When the soil has dried out, only water it. Overwatering can rot its root system, causing it to die.

Narrow-Leaf / Broad-Leaf Foliage Houseplants

Are you fond of plants having attractive leaves? If so, Foliage houseplants would be an excellent option for you. They come in various sizes. Thus, you can get it as a statement piece or a smaller one to fill up any corner.

Additionally, these plants add an exotic look to your house. You can place it near your bookshelf or hide those old DVDs. Instantly, you will feel that your place looks nicely tied together.

Some types of Foliage houseplants include

Iron-Cross Begonia

People recognize this plant for its eye-catching two-tone leaves. Its name, iron-cross, comes from the brown markings on its leaves that look a lot like the iron cross seen on shields during the Crusades.

This indoor plant doesn't mind staying in the pot. It lacks humidity if the plant's leafy edges become brown and crispy. However, make sure you water it before the soil completely dries out. If the leaves start turning yellow and brown, reduce the water you give them.

Flamingo Flower (Anthurium)

The indoor plant will be a great option if you're looking for a smaller version! It will easily fit on your shelf, side table, or window sill. These show-stopping blooms can beautify your home throughout the year. It usually grows up to 12 to 18 inches.

Furthermore, this plant thrives with little to no care. Ensure you grow it in acidic soil in humid conditions (60 °F to 90 °F) and water it whenever the soil feels dry to the touch.

Ferns

Ferns are the most popular type among gardeners and other plant lovers. They come in a fantastic range for you to choose from. Some of them are fond of direct light, while others prefer shade. Make sure you choose the right spot accordingly for your baby Fern.

If you're interested in getting ferns as a houseplant, Phlebodium Blue Star - Blue Star Fern or Asparagus Setaceus - Lace Fern would be great options. These plants are low-maintenance in nature. All you need to do is to remove any dead or damaged fronds.

Phlebodium Blue Star - Blue Star Fern

This indoor houseplant can thrive under a range of different lighting. It will give your house a fresh and exotic appearance. Also, this fern type is known to detoxify harmful toxins in the air.

You'll need to water them weekly while keeping their soil wet. However, avoid watering to the point that the soil feels overly wet.

Asparagus Setaceus - Lace Fern

This decorative plant thrives in hot climates. The leaves of this plant resemble tiny leaf-like cladodes. These are super easy to grow and require a lot of water.

You should place Fern Lace in soil that retains water well. It loves direct sunlight, so keep it near a window.

Bromeliads

Do you love the tropics and sun-soaked climates? If so, Bromeliads could be for you. This plant is famous for its thick leaves that bloom into a natural rosette. It's a low-maintenance plant that adds an appealing texture to your home.

At the end point of its life, it may produce a flower or an inflorescence. This plant's leaf color, shape, and size also come in a wide variety.

Aechmea (Aechmea spp.)

This type of Bromeliad is the most resilient and long-lasting plant. Aechmea is also the reason behind its popularity among indoor houseplants. These large-sized plants have striking color flowers and plants.

These plants enjoy bright and indirect light. Keep them in a shade if you have kept them in the outer area of your house.

Guzmania (Guzmania spp.)

These spell-bounding indoor plants are available in various striking colors, such as white, purple, orange, red, and even yellow. These insignificant flowers will transform your living room.

You may use them as a tabletop plant for a pop of color. They respond well to bright but indirect light. Make sure you keep them away from direct sunlight.

Knowing about the prominent types of houseplants is essential before buying one. Besides that, you should consider some practical considerations. Such as

Location of Plant

With so much variety, there are high chances of picking the wrong plant for the wrong place. Therefore, look for a houseplant that fits into your preferred location. Otherwise, your plant baby might not be able to survive for long.

Purpose of the Plant

Are you cultivating a plant to get some health benefits? Is it because they feel you relaxed? Or to fulfill your need to nurture something? Keep that reason in mind before you select a plant. That way, you can invest in a piece that meets your requirements.

Light Intensity

Some plants respond well to direct light. In contrast, others prefer indirect light with varying brightness. You need to ensure that the plant location provides appropriate sun exposure. In another case, that plant can rot and eventually die.

Humidity

The humidity of a place is a crucial element for the thriving of a plant. Bathrooms and kitchens usually have low humidity levels. In comparison, a living room might have high humidity levels.

The plant you select should match the humidity level of the chosen location. For instance, Orchids do not prefer drier environments. At the same time, other plants might thrive in such an atmosphere.

Temperature

A room that gets too hot from the sun can damage the leaves of a plant. On the other hand, some plants might suffer in cold drafts (from freezing nights). The trick is to measure the room's temperature, not just rely on the thermostat's reading. Only introduce a plant to your space that can handle the specific temperature conditions.

Keeping track of all these crucial elements will save you from seeing your plant baby decline, unlike some plant enthusiasts that had to learn it the hard way.

Some people my age have kids, and here I'm googling "Indoor houseplants that are impossible to get killed."

A fellow millennial tweeted this, John Paul Brammer, from Brooklyn. He is an author, illustrator, content creator, and struggling plant parent! John used to take himself as a plant killer. Every plant he tried to keep alive ended up killing it.

After many trials, he finally managed to keep half of those plants alive. Do you want to know how he gained success? It was by learning the essential care requirements of the plant. If you need to learn about them, jump to the next chapter.

CHAPTER 2

WATER – THE ESSENCE OF LIFE

"My fake plants died because I did not pretend to water them"

— **Mitch Hedberg**

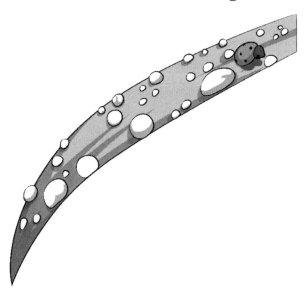

How often should I water my houseplants? How much water do they need? These are the most common queries of many plant parents at a beginner level. Don't worry if you are wondering the same things.

The frequency of water depends upon several factors, such as the type of plant, light intensity, the amount of water used, and other environmental factors. The most straightforward answer is "whenever they would need it." Unfortunately, solutions like "every other week, once a week, or a couple days won't help you.

As a rule of thumb, plants need more water in the spring and winter. At the same time, they can be left a bit dry in Autumn. When you're watering them, you can also consider their origin. For instance, if your houseplant is from a desert, it would do great with less water. If it's from the rainforest, it evolved to thrive in a humid atmosphere.

Regardless, here is a quick overview of watering some of the most popular plants.

Cacti

The majority of the plants from this family prosper in the summers. In this growing season, they benefit a lot from regular watering. The dormant phase (usually winter) follows this growth period. A great move would be mixing the horticultural grit into the potting mix. It will ensure excellent drainage. Using a top dressing of grit will reduce water splashes on plants during watering.

Tropical Plants

Many topical plants don't mind getting their compost and foliage wet. Thus, you don't need to be extra careful while watering them. A great example of such a plant would be the Boston Fern. This plant thrives in tropical zones and comes from a humid habitat. Thus, it won't matter if you get water on the foliage. However, ensure you don't leave the compost dry, only making the leaves wet.

Furry Leaved Plants

These plants with soft furry foliage don't prefer getting their stem and leaves too wet. For instance, African Violets (Streptocarpus) grow under the canopy of giant trees and plants. Even if the atmosphere is very humid, they receive little direct rainfall. You'll need to make them sit in a water tray (for approximately 20 minutes) with their pots to water them.

Aerial Rooted Plants

Plants with aerial roots are suitable for propagation, air absorption, stability, and nourishment. Swiss cheese plants (Monstera) and orchids both have aerial roots. Such plants belong to humid environments. They prefer to have their roots and leaves misted regularly.

Bromeliads

Most Bromeliads accumulate water in reservoirs or central tanks in the wilderness. Its leaves and roots retain only a tiny fraction of moisture through natural rainfall.

Even though the roots of Bromeliads like being the most, they don't enjoy being soggy. Your little pet is likely to suffer more from over-watering than under-watering.

Overwatering Vs Underwatering

Just like Bromeliads, a lot of houseplants are not a fan of excessive water. **Overwatering** can cause the death of your plant partner. The fungi bred in soggy soil can choke the insides of the root system. The signs, such as yellow, drooping leaves, are similar to underwatering.

The reason behind this similarity is the collapse of the plant's vascular system in both cases. That might trick you into thinking that your baby needs more water. Thus, you are sending them off to a death sentence.

On the other hand, an underwater plant is also not in a happy mood. In **underwatering**, the water pulled from the roots cannot keep up with the amount lost during transpiration. As a result, the microscopic leaf pores (stomata) close down to minimize loss. It means carbon dioxide cannot enter, and photosynthesis has stopped.

Severe dehydration and the baking sun kill off anything above the ground. When the rain returns, the whole plant grows back from the living root. Your plant won't endure long at that stage because it will start to rely on its energy stores. Yet, the plant still has a chance to survive. You can consider an excellent example of grass.

In underwatering, the root saves the plant, while the root causes the plant to die in overwatering. Nevertheless, educating yourself about combating overwatering can save your back.

Signs of Overwatering

There are several symptoms your plant will show when it's overwatering. The most common ones are

- Slimy and grey roots.

- Old and new leaves are falling off at the same time.

- Foul odor or root rot.

- Leaf tips are brown.

- Leaves are wilting, yellow, and brown.

- Flowers, stems, and leaves get moldy.

What to Do if You Accidentally Overwater

Water is a crucial element for your baby's growth. Yet, adding an excessive amount of it can be immensely harmful. To avoid:

- Use a pot with drainage holes. It will reduce the risk of over-watering. The total size of your pot should resemble a standard pop bottle cap.

- Water your plants in the early morning. It will allow your plant baby to absorb as much moisture as possible. At that time, the temperature would be cool and moist.

- Avoid making your plant sit in water for an extended time. It will cause root rotting and kill your houseplant. If you need to make it sit in the dish, change the water after a couple of weeks. That will ensure proper drainage with no risk of overwatering.

Tips for Avoiding Overwatering

Make these minor adjustments to avoid overwatering:

- Always water plants with a water bottle from a distance. In this manner, the liquid won't pull the soil up.

- Avoid watering your houseplants in extreme temperatures (Never above 85 degrees F and rarely below 45 degrees F)

- Ensure proper drainage holes in the pot to prevent your plant from staying in water for extended periods.

- Directly adding chemicals like fertilizers after cleaning the plant's container can irritate sensitive plants. Therefore, keep the plant in lukewarm water for 15 minutes. It will absorb some moisture before adding any other product to it.

- Just like water, adding too much fertilizer is of no good. Your plant will eventually burst because of too many nutrients and water ingestion.

Plant Types that Don't Like Overwatering

The majority of succulents are fond of dry soil. They don't enjoy frequent watering sessions and are well-adaptive to indoor growing conditions.

Learning about the exact watering needs of your pet plant can be difficult at first. However, some tips will benefit almost any plant type. Some of them are listed below.

5 Golden Rules for Watering

Upgrade your plant care game by following these simple yet effective tips:

1. Keep your plant's moisture level maintained. Even though they prefer moisture, slight drying would promote growth in your planters and succulents.

2. Make sure that you are properly watering your plant as per its need. You can water most of the houseplants infrequently. Yet, it should be enough for them to combat with next day's heat.

3. Do not leave your plant's leaf wet for a long time. Wet leaves left overnight can cause mold diseases. In the daytime, they develop slight sun marks.

4. The soil needs to be moist to promote plant growth. The water you sprayed must reach the roots. Inadequate watering causes the water only to cover the upper soil.

5. Some plants fuss about the water they receive. As a rule of thumb, plants prefer lukewarm instead of cold water. Besides that, use filtered water if you live in a place where only hard water is accessible.

To make things easier, we have added a watering table for the most common plant types (as given in Chapter 1).

Watering Chart for Main Indoor Houseplants

Categories	Type of Water	Frequency of Water
• **Flowering Houseplants** Such as Orchids, Begonias, Peace Lily, Christmas Cactus, Begonia, African Violet, and many more	Tap water would do the job However, using a filtration system for that water before its usage is preferred	• Water and mist regularly • Keep humidity maintained • Drain well
• **Cacti and Succulent** Such as Snake Plant, Cactus, Jade Plant, Adenium (Desert Rose), Lithops, and many others	Rainwater or distilled water	• Keep moist during the flowering season • Let the plant dry between waterings • Water only once per month during winters (slow-growth period) • Check moisture condition by sticking index finger in the soil every two weeks • Avoid overwatering
• **Air Plants** Such as Stricta, Brachycaulos, Caput Medusae, Aeranthos, Capitata, Streptophylla, and many more	Pond water, creek water or rainwater. Alternatively, bottle spring water or tap water that is kept in an open container overnight	• Use a mister to spray the leaves two or three times a week • Alternatively, dunk the plant in a water container for 15 seconds. Follow up by removing excessive water. • (Make sure it dries out before night and the

		temperature declines)
• **Trailing and Climbing Houseplants** Such as Golden Pothos, Heart-Leaf Philodendron, Satin Pothos, Orchid Cactus, Ed Herringbone Plant, and many others	Bottle, rain, or tap water.	• Set up in a well-draining planter • Water weekly, make sure the soil is dry to touch before watering
• **Narrow-leaf / Broad-leaf Foliage Houseplants** Such as Cast Iron Plants, Aglaonema, Dumb Cane, Kentia Palm, Lucky Bamboo, Swiss Cheese, Panda Plant, Zebra Plant, Neon Pothos, and many others	Rainwater or tap water (kept overnight)	• Regular watering roughly after every 5-10 days • Keep soil evenly moist • Ensure water is drained well
• **Ferns** Such as Osmunda Regalis, Asplenium Scolopendrium, Imbricatum, Blechnum Spicant, Dicksonia Antarctica, Matteuccia Struthiopteris, and many more	Don't use tap water directly as it contains chlorine Let the water sit in an open container to get rid of toxic chemicals	• Water your Ferns when the surface of the compost gets dried • Don't follow a routine, check whether the pot needs water • Water less if your plant is in a cool room and vice versa • Use water when it comes to room temperature
• **Bromeliads**	Distilled water or	• Water roughly every

Such as Guzmanian, Neoregelia, Vriesea, Champaca, Billbergia, Aechmea, Cryptanthus Tillandsia, and Dyckia	rainwater	two weeks • Lightly spray them even daily with a spray bottle • For a thorough watering session, wait until the 2 inch of the soil feels dry

Water plays a crucial role in plant growth. In addition to that, its absorption also indicates the soil quality and the appropriate type of soil required. Check out the next chapter to learn more about it.

CHAPTER 3

GROWING MEDIUM - THE POWER OF EARTH

"Although the surface of our planet is two-thirds water, we call it the Earth. We say we are earthlings, not waterlings. Our blood is closer to seawater than our bones to soil, but that's no matter. The sea is the cradle we all rocked out of, but it's to dust that we go. From the time that water invented us, we began to seek out dirt. The further we separate ourselves from the dirt, the further we separate ourselves from ourselves. Alienation is a disease of the unsoiled."

— Tom Robbins

All plant parents use some add-on to keep their houseplants healthy and happy. Hence, you must have the best criteria to see what makes a growing medium the best choice.

These composts are a mixture of multiple components serving different purposes. The media supports the houseplant. While fertilizers enforce nutrition, they play a vital role in plant growth and development. Besides, the pore spaces in air and water move through the plant roots.

Mediums work as enhancers of plant growth and life. There are different types, like ones with peat and ones without it. Peat is from old, broken-down plant stuff. You might be thinking, why do we need to learn about this?

Houseplants come in a wide range, requiring several potting and watering routines. Some may need moist soil-type media for a super bloom, and others may thrive with drier type. A few plants need a lot of nutrients, and many don't. Hence, you must have the best criteria in your mind to see what makes a growing medium the best choice.

What Makes an Excellent Growth Medium?

If you exclude the external factors and focus on the plant root health, then you may choose a growing medium with the following traits:

- Potting media should be loose and open enough to let water and air sink in

- It must not be tight

- Fulfilling the necessary nutrient need

- Material needs to be airy and light for adequate aeration and drainage

- Maintains water in the houseplant so it does not get dry

- Can be customized per plant need

- It doesn't require a lot of labor and is hard to deal with

- Control over pH changing overtime and protecting the houseplant

- Check for the media's CEC to be moderate enough to hold nutrients

It can be a tiring and hectic process to find the correct media which fulfills all requirements. Therefore, we have listed the most used growing media below.

Types of Growth Mediums

Each growth medium has a different type that is suited for a specific kind of plant. In this section, you'll learn about the source, appearance, pros, cons, use, and utilization of different media.

Perlite and Pumice

Perlite and Pumice share similar natures, and you can use them for similar purposes. They are white and incredibly enough to fly away by a little wind stroke. Perlite, aka "volcanic glass," usually constitutes a minor diameter of a few millimeters and is roughly sphere-shaped.

Perlite can float over water and has a porous consistency. It tends to retain a small quantity of water too. On the other hand, Pumice is darker in color and heavier than perlite. You can quickly source them from any gardening shop and retail stores.

Both types are mostly known for gardening. So, there are cheap and easier to find too. Perlite and Pumice share similar natures, and you can use them for similar purposes.

Pros

- Excellent aeration and drainage
- Lightweight and easy to work with

- Encloses moisture

- Affordable

- pH neutral

Cons

- Easily washed away

- Not recommended for plants that require a lot after case (water and nutrients)

1. Vermiculite

A myth among plant parents is that you can use perlite and vermiculite in place of one another. However, we must correct this concept as they both have opposite properties. With its dark orangish-golden color, vermiculite is a tiny particle shaped like a worm.

Vermiculite is an excellent water absorber as compared to perlite. Like the former media, you can obtain it through the heating process. Do you know?

Pros

- Great water retention

- Immune to pests and mold

- Non-toxic and sterile

- Great CEC capacity

- Nearly pH neutral

Cons

- It cannot hold moisture

- Poor aeration

2. Zeolite

Zeolite looks like perlite but is a bit darker in color, such as grey/green. The growing media also have a similar density, but it is relatively expensive and harder to find than other soil types. You may also mistake Zeolite for perlite due to its volcanic region. Still, beware, as their chemical composition is exactly different.

Pros

- Zeolite can absorb water of about 60% of its size

- Optimal nutrient provider

- Avoids over-fertilizing

- Non-toxic carrier

Cons

- High CEC capacity

- You can deactivate it in case of irreversible adsorption

3. Compost

Have you been fooled by compost being soil? Well, you will not be now. Do not be turned off, but it is a well-rotted organic material with a robust earthy odor. Manufacturers mainly extract it from materials likely to be wasted, such as animal waste, fruits, and vegetables.

The decomposition process to finally achieve compost is long. The fun fact is that you can produce this growing media in your residence too. For that, click here.

Pros

- Break down essential nutrients for the plant

- It provides an ideal bacterial environment

- Increased water retention

- Resistant to pests and weeds

Cons

- Small nutrient content (2-4%)

- Less aeration

- Heavy

- Expensive

4. Peat Moss and Coco Coir

You can derive peat as a form of compost by decomposing Sphagnum moss. Online retailers, gardening stores, and supermarkets sell it in large bags.

Peat moss has been controversial for its vital role in nature stability (water retention). Again, it is not a renewable resource, and about 31% of peat is needed to form an excellent growing medium. So, many researchers have been looking for this media substitute.

Hence, manufacturers have successfully come up with an alternative named Coco Coir. The great thing is that they extract this environmentally friendly compost from coconut coir waste. Coco Coir is gaining popularity and is primarily available online.

Pros

- Great for water-loving plants

- Improved water retention

- Holds Nutrients

- Best for houseplants in summer

Cons

- Non-renewable resource

- Expensive

5. Soil Basic: Sand, Silt, and Clay

Have you needed clarification about which types of media are the actual soils? Then, here you go. Sand, Slit, and Clay are the official and natural soils. The composition of all types comprises soil and may be hard to find in retailers and shops. The primary use of soil is in industrial areas.

The medium is small particles. It is beneficial for trapping water and gases for the efficient growth of plants and their roots.

Pros

- Good drainage

- Improved aeration

- Support for the plant

- Nutrients Retention

Cons

- It would help if you replaced it often

- It may vary depending on the area

1. Garden Soil

Garden soil is a unique type of mixture of multiple media. It is a growing medium and can vary according to the soil's location and age. You can find compost, soil, clay, fertilizers, and many other materials; dig any garden to obtain this media type.

Pros

- Free

- Rich in healthy bacteria and organic matter

Cons

- A large number of pests and bacteria

- Not suitable for open areas

- Limited drainage capabilities

- Heavy

2. Wooden Bark

People often use wooden bark in combination with soil at the top. They usually obtain it by cutting the superficial parts of the tree, such as the roots or trunk. It resembles mulch and is sold in pieces (of a few mm in thickness and some cm in size).

You can easily find this media in gardening shops and online retailers. The best part is that they sell it relatively inexpensively in large bags.

Pros

- Trap moisture (especially for summers)

- Keeps the plant cool

- Controls temperature variation

Cons

- It may deplete nitrogen from the houseplant as it decays

- It may attract pests and termites

3. Water

You may be mixed up; what? Is water a growing media? It's unbelievable. If you've been in this hobby for a long time, you know that water alone can grow some plants. People call this wild technique hydroponic, which they can use to grow many fruits and vegetables through water.

Using water as a medium serves excellent benefits, such as saving water, efficient spacing, and fulfilling the essential nutrients. However, if you are new to houseplants, start with the traditional potting method first. It is one cheap and sustainable option for root development for intermediate plant parents.

Pros

- Less use of water

- Yields high-quality product

- Suitable for potting greens and fruits in huge volume

Cons

- It partially depends on electricity

- Expensive to set up

- Waterborne disease

4. Sawdust

Does the growing medium of your plants always become too heavy or light? Then, there is a type of material that can help you adjust your houseplant structure. Sawdust is a refined powder form of wood extracted after cutting and shaping wood.

Experts recommend that most gardeners use Sawdust for planting in open areas. You can easily buy it from any gardening store. They sell it in large bags, kilograms (kgs), and pounds (lbs).

Pros

- Suggested for plants exposed to sunlight

- Good for nitrogen-high fertilizer

- Excellent stabilizer

Cons

- Deprives the houseplants of oxygen and light

- It may deplete nitrogen essential for plants to grow

5. Limestone

Limestone, which looks like white dust, comes from the accumulation of marine life skeletons over decades. The consistency of this medium can vary. Stores often sell it in large bags. It is cheap and can be used to solve many planting problems.

Some houseplants use a soilless medium, which means a lower soil pH. Therefore, gardeners add Limestone to stabilize such mediums as peat moss or compost.

Pros

- Provides a suitable environment for soilless plants

- Affordable

Cons

- Limited durability

- Regular maintenance

Now, you have adapted the best use of all the common types of growing mediums. It is also essential for you to learn about which media is best suited for which houseplant type (which you have seen in Chapter 1).

Checklist of Which Potting Medium is Best Suited to the Houseplants

Categories	Availability	Growing Medium	Reason Why?
• **Flowering Houseplants**	This all-purpose organic mix can be a perfect match for the flowering category	A blend of these growing mediums can help you achieve great results: Perlite, Peat Moss, Compost, and Limestone A good and quality mix may have an addition of bat guano, earthworm castings, sandy loam, granite dust, pH regulators, fish emulsion, crab meal, and shrimp meal	• Retains moisture • Well-drained • Soft • Nutrient-rich
• **Cacti and Succulent**	You can search for "Cacti Soil" over any online store like Amazon or the gardening	A mix of Pine Bark, Compost, Coco Coir, or Potting soil can be an excellent fit for this type	• Provides great drainage • Excellent aeration • Keeps the roots

	shop	of houseplant You can enhance this organic mix with added minerals like Perlite, Chicken Grit, Volcanic Rock, and Fine Gravel. Avoid vermiculite as it stores water	dry
• **Air Plants**	Sand and pebbles are easily available	Sand, tiny pebbles, and any low-nitrogen base can be an excellent mix to support air plants Avoid adding and using soil as a growing medium for the air plants	• Easy to maintain plants • Provides essential nutrients • Appropriate water content
• **Trailing and Climbing Houseplants**	Any well-draining medium can be suitable for this category	A combination of Wood, Wire, Bamboo, and Rattan can assist you to thrive in these houseplants You can also get an additional pack of trellis, round arches, and even spindles. You must have learned that climbing and trailing houseplants are the hanging and container types. So, you make a wire yourself with non-rusting wire or plastic-covered wire	• Plants require water • The mixture drains the water well
• **Indoor Palms**	Indoor plants are container plants	You may try to create a mix of Peat Moss, Leaf	• Loose and porous

	that require this type of mixture	Mold, and Shredded Bark These palm plants can be effectively grown when you get a specific cactus or palm soil mix. Still, the general-purpose soil can work just fine too	• Lowers soil pH • Easy water drainage • Good aeration
• **Narrow-leaf / Broad-leaf Foliage Houseplants**	You can easily get multiple sand mixes from any gardening or retail store	Blend one to two portions of Potting Soil, a part of Coarse Sand, and finally, two portions of damp Peat Moss. You may cut in the pasteurized gardening soil too if available.	• Retain moisture • Supply an appropriate amount of nutrients
• **Ferns**	The mix that is rich in organic matter can be a top match for ferns.	A well-drained mixture of Perlite, Garden Compost, Bark, and Peat Moss Try to get soil that is neutral to alkaline.	• Retains moisture • Light and fluffy mix • Rich in organic matter • Good aeration
• **Bromeliads**	The perfect blend for Bromeliads can be achieved by getting the media through retail stores and mixing all of them well	The mix of medium-grade Perlites, and Sphagnum Peat Moss. Fine Fir Bark can be a great choice for Bromeliads You can also add some other enhancers such as charcoal, orchid mix, and maybe soilless	• Holds moisture • Excellent drainage

		potting mix	

You can go through this checklist when you choose a growing medium next time for a different type of houseplant. Many plant hoarders still need to work on whether they can reuse the potting soil or not.

Compost can help you retain the nutrients and essential bacteria in the soil. The experts advise that you can use the potting soil by mixing it with about 50% of rotted compost. Many millennials have successfully transformed their balconies to Monstera's Instagram aesthetic.

"When all doors were closed over her, she invested in indoor babies and successfully created a 40K+ strong houseplants family on Instagram (@Naomiplanter)."

You can also grow a beautiful green family of houseplants with the proper guidance. There is a story of a mental health counselor in Portland named Naomi Painter. She got inspired by a living stone plant in a florist shop. She has detailed all her struggles with potting mixes and medium with the houseplant pictures.

There has been a misconception that light, water, and a good quality growing medium promise a healthy houseplant. However, the role of temperature and humidity is often neglected and can almost kill your indoor babies.

CHAPTER 4

TEMPERATURE AND HUMIDITY – THE POWER OF FIRE AND WIND

"It was one of those humid days when the atmosphere gets confused. Sitting on the porch, you could feel it: the air wishing it was water."

– Jeffrey Eugenides

J ust like humans can't survive in all abnormal temperature conditions, plants are the same. All indoor plants are primarily native to the environmental conditions in their tropical and sub-tropical regions. Hence, it gets more accessible for the houseplants to grow at room temperature effortlessly.

Still, there can be variations. There can exist many types of houseplants which require different temperature intensities. Houseplants consider a high temperature to be 85-75°F with an improved humidity level. Most foliage and flowering houseplants prefer temperatures ranging from 60-75°F.

Now, there is an exception in the intensity for the daytime and the nighttime. The essential flowering houseplants mostly require 60-75°F in the daylight and 55-60°F in the evening. There are different heat requirements for all houseplants. For instance, the minimum for tender plants is 60°F, 50-55°F for half-hardy ones, and finally, 45°F for hardy plants.

There are many common issues that beginners can face with the optimal temperature for houseplants. You can always use the misting sprays to lower the humidity level for the houseplants. However, too much heat can make the leaves wilt and turn brown. Also, the cold weather can do no good and kill the plant.

Common Issues with Temperatures of the Houseplants

The humidity level is crucial in defining which temperature best suits any houseplant. Here, you can discern which spots to pick and frequently change with the weather through the following guide.

Finding the Right Space for Your Plant

Choosing an excellent place for your houseplants to reside heavily depends on the type of houseplant. If you have a desert-dwelling cactus in your home, you must find a sunny and dry place for your houseplant to grow. Conversely, if your indoor baby is more like a leafy type, you might pick a spot with indirect sunlight and high humidity.

Seasonal Changes

Seasonal changes can always occur, making the need to rotate the places of the plants. The too-hot weather can make the leaves dark and wither with flowers. At the same time, the lower temperature level can make the plants dry and die in the end. You may notice the leaves turning yellow if there is a considerable temperature drop in the night where you live.

Therefore, you must learn to stabilize the temperature with hot and cold drafts for the greenery creatures.

Humidity Levels

You'll find that most houseplants can survive at average indoor humidity levels. However, some tropical houseplants thrive and require a more humid environment. So, you can create the damp condition by grouping the plants, investing in a pebble tray, and getting a humidifier.

Some humidity-loving plants' favorite spots can be the kitchen and bathroom, with a window directly throwing sunlight or a grow light. The plants can also have a hard time surviving in cold conditions. The heating units drop, resulting in less humidity. So, if you find crunchy leaves in this weather, prune them off. Don't worry. You just forced their healthy and new growth.

Using Hot and Cold Drafts

You need to be aware of keeping the humidity optimized in cold weather. Consider placing the houseplants with radiators, heaters, and forced-air vents. Keep the plants in a stable environment.

Do you have a radiator near a window, or the air conditioner is in your window? Then you may hang the plant through a thick rope a few feet above the ground. Some other suggestions are getting an aesthetically pleasing wooden shelf to elevate plants or a radiator cover.

Ideal Indoor Space and Protection from Harsh Sunlight

Houseplants are usually kept indoors and used to less heat and light. Consider placing your plants briefly in direct sun exposure, especially during summer. You should pay closer attention to outdoor weather and let the plants be in direct contact with the sun.

When you leave the plants in direct heat, then there are chances for the growing medium to dry out. It will result in you frequently watering the plants, and the leaves will eventually turn yellow. In this case, you may place the plants away from the window or draw a sheer curtain.

Conversely, when the sun is not that strong in winter, you may keep the plants closer to the window where the sun hits just right. You can make these little adjustments according to your plant type and the weather conditions and change the spots in the rotation.

Tips to Keep the Temperature Neutral for Houseplants

Here are some key things to help you ensure the longevity of indoor plants.

1. You can use the misty sprays to keep the humidity level down and the leaves hydrated.

2. The air temperature should be lower if there is less light in the room (within the permissible range).

3. Ensure the leaves do not touch the window glass, as this may make them burn or cause hypothermia.

4. The plants have similar growing conditions. So, try to keep the temperature, humidity, and light exposure for the plants needed.

There are always many perfect spots for houseplants. You need to make one that suits and fulfills the need of your houseplant best. Plants require care, and you may have little time. Therefore, cold-tolerant plants come in the frame to help you.

Do Cold Tolerant Indoor Plants Exist?

Do you live in challenging chilly conditions? Are you afraid that your houseplants may get dried and die there? You'll be pleased to learn that some tolerant plants can survive your cold-to-death rooms. The best thing is to give significant watering gaps if your room is cooler.

Here is a list of cold, hardy houseplants you can consider while starting your green collection.

ZZ Plant

Zamioculcas Zamiifolia is a resistant and easy-to-maintain type of plant. It is the best choice if you live in a cold climate. Surviving with less sun exposure, light, and dry conditions is challenging enough.

1. Cast Iron Plant

Also known as Aspidistra Elatior, it is another rough and tough plant that can survive below the average ideal conditions for houseplants. Cast Iron plants can survive severe cold conditions above 32°F or 0°C.

2. Geraniums

You can call these Pelargonium too. They are a pleasant type of plant that is capable of bearing cold weather. They only need a few hours of direct contact with sunlight and are ready to grow.

3. Clivia

It is another shade-loving cold hardy houseplant. These houseplants can bear both dry or moist and bright or indirect sunlight. They can grow anywhere but die at temperatures lower than 5°C (40°F).

4. Jade Plant

They work just like Geraniums, and sun exposure for an optimum time is enough for them to thrive. These cold hardy houseplants can stay in severely dry conditions and cool weather without dying or curling up.

5. Maidenhair Ferns

These plants are different as they always require the potting soil to be moist and damp. Hence, you may need to pay attention while watering the plant. Else, it is capable of thriving in lower light conditions too.

6. Sago Palm

Do you know? Sago's palm is, unlike its name, an extremely tough houseplant. Sago can handle a broad range of temperatures, including colder weather conditions. It is also known as Cycas Revoluta and originates from the southern region of Japan.

7. Snake Plant

Have you been in search of an all-rounder and adaptable houseplant? Then, this plant can be your first choice as Snake Plant has of living and growing in all types of weather conditions. The plus point is that even if you're unavailable, this houseplant can take less light, cooler temperatures, and dryer growing medium very well.

8. Dracaena Marginata

These are other cold-tolerant houseplant that can bear the cooler atmosphere up to 10°C (50°F) and more.

9. Philodendrons

They cover a wide variety of lovely foliage houseplants and make excellent houseplants. Philodendrons are famous for thriving in multiple weather conditions indoors. They are highly adaptable to different watering and lightening routines.

They make great air purifiers, and they cannot stay at a temperature below 55°F. It has many other species adding to the collection of cold hardy plants.

Stability and well-balanced care are the only factors that balance the long life of plants. Even though these plants can endure intense weather conditions, keeping the soil wet for a long time can cause the roots to rot. Therefore, it is better to be careful.

It is necessary to do aftercare and keep an eye on the cold hardy plants. It can help you make sure your plant is responding happily to the colder weather or not. When there are cold-tolerating plants, there are some plants that need higher humidity levels too.

Why Does Some Plant Prefer Higher Humidity?

Houseplants primarily originated from the humid forest environment. They grow efficiently and healthily when the air moisture level is high. The ideal humidity level for all houseplants varies as there is 40-60% higher humidity than your home needs for the green babies to grow. Moreover, the houseplant requires a much more humid environment, especially in winter.

Many houseplants like Bamboo, Aloe Vera, Orchid, Monstera, Golden Pothos, English Ivy, and many others are low-maintenance. They promote more growth in humidity as they comprise higher moisture levels. They benefit from the higher heat and moisture via leaf tipping, less transpiration, and reduced mire pests.

The plants that prefer higher humidity are often suitable to keep in kitchens or bathrooms. The foliage plants can absorb the steam as you take a shower daily. If your bathroom has a large window with enough light exposure, this can be ideal for these houseplants.

Although houseplants may prefer certain atmospheric conditions, they can also affect the surrounding temperature.

Plants that Increase or Decrease Humidity in Homes

The overloaded dryness and moisture in the air can lead to many hazardous health problems. Well, different houseplants can do the job both ways for you. Indoor plants can help you retain the humidity in the air and decrease it when needed.

Plants to Increase Humidity

Some houseplants restore humidity, deliver oxygen, and filter the air from harmful chemicals. These houseplants can thwart health concerns such as respiratory issues, wrinkled skin, and even soar throat.

The weather often becomes dry in winter and completely moistureless. On the contrary, air conditioners can dry out the weather when it's hot. It is the case where the houseplants can help you through transpiration. It is a process through which the stomata over the leaves release moisture into the air resulting in increasing humidity.

Here is a relevant list of both types of plants that can help you control humidity in a preferred way.

Areca Palm

- Transpiration rate: 10

- Healthily grown up to 5-6 feet

- Can release 1 quart of water vapors per day

- Removes Toluene, Formaldehyde, and Xylene from the air

Bamboo Palm

- Transpiration rate: 9

- Filter the air through Formaldehyde, and other toxins

- Place Bamboo Palm in a saucer filled with pebbles and water for better results

Ferns

- Transpiration level: 9

- Restore moisture and improve humidity

- Purify air by removing the harmful toxins

Some other houseplants like Peace Lily, Florist's Mum, Lady Palm, Rubber Plant, English Ivy, Parlor Palm, Corn Plant, Dwarf Date Palm, and Golden Pothos can also assist you in keeping the humidity level up.

Plants to Decrease Humidity

There are better conditions than having a high moisture level inside the home. In winter, too much humidity can make the air damp, moist, and clammy. It can cause several respiratory diseases.

Therefore, a strong need arises for a natural solution that can absorb the excess humidity from the environment.

Where the leaves of indoor plants get water content through the air, they can simultaneously harvest much moisture through them too. Here are some efficient houseplants which can work naturally to help you reduce the humidity indoors.

Boston Fern

- Thrives in the more moist climate

- Moisture Absorbent

- Low-maintenance

Palms

- Can grow in humid and tropical areas

- Absorbs moisture from the air

- Filter toxins

- Easy to maintain

Tillandsia

- It needs indirect sunlight to grow

- Lives by absorbing the nutrients and moisture from the surroundings

- It would be best if you watered twice or thrice a week

In addition to these top picks, many other plants like Cactus, Spider Plants, Orchids, Purple Waffle Flower, and Peperomia can work as natural dehumidifiers in your homes without much aftercare.

The Houseplants grow effortlessly at room temperature most of the time. However, some native houseplants require higher humidity. At the same time, there exist plants like cacti and succulents, which bloom in dry environments. All these plants need different levels of moisture to survive and thrive.

Checklist of Relative Humidity Levels of Houseplants

The amount of water in the atmosphere compared to the water vapors in the air measures the relative humidity of the houseplants. Here is a list to help you learn about the humidity levels suitable for common houseplants.

Categories	Humidity Level	Problems	Solutions
Flowering Houseplants	40%-60% of humidity is perfect for flowering houseplants during summer. When the plants reach the flowering stage, the percentage varies from 40%-50%	In winter, the humidity level may drop down.	You can use misting sprays to keep the plants alive
Cacti and Succulent	They are on the drier side and require only 10% of humidity in the home. Therefore, they are considered easy to maintain in winter	Cacti and Succulents can't survive direct sun exposure and heat beyond 35C/95F	It is preferred not to take them out in the strong hot environment
Air Plants	The humidity level of air plant varies from 50%-70%, which is not much more than the average room temperature	They can't survive without water in the supplement	Keep watering the plants regularly
Trailing and Climbing Houseplants	They require a high humidity level to survive such as 60%-80%	Plants need to be moist quite often to grow effectively	Water them every now and then for nice growth
Indoor Palms	Palms prefer the humidity level to be	Sensitive to dry and hot weather	Must be watered in summer and

	around 40%-50%		placed in indirect sunlight for longevity
Narrow-leaf / Broad-leaf Foliage Houseplants	They are humidity-loving plants that grow tremendously with a humidity level of about 60%-80%	They need to be damp but not soggy. So, the watering schedule plays a vital role in their growth	Make sure that there is proper drainage available for these houseplants. An elevated saucer with water and pebbles can slice this problem for you
Ferns	Ferns prefer to be in a less humid environment. Their relative humidity level is 30%-50%	Ferns may turn brown and eventually die down when exposed to direct heat	It is recommended to keep them in a shaded area with filtered sunlight and pot them in a well-draining medium
Bromeliads	Bromeliads prefer 70%-90% humidity to survive well. Nevertheless, they grow just fine at room temperature with a humidity level of 40%-60% indoors	They may require an artificial setting to stay alive with the preferred humidity Direct sunlight can burn the leaves	You may install a humidifier to keep the atmosphere balanced for the houseplants Place them in the shade away from the window

Once you learn their behavior, keeping houseplants becomes relatively easy. All types of houseplants need a customized environment according to their nature. Till now, you have discovered all elements that play a vital role in growing houseplants without making mistakes.

For instance, the standard categories are watering, lighting, potting, and environmental needs. Still, many more issues can endanger your houseplant's natural growth and life. Stay tuned to learn more!

GoodWill

"Where flowers bloom, so does hope."

— Lady Bird Johnson.

A healthy and beautiful home where planters and succulents are thriving, and flowers are blossoming is the desired life of several plant parents. I want to give you the power to convert these dreams into reality. Before doing that, I have a simple question for you.

Would you like to help another millennial trapped in daily struggles to have a plant partner by their side?

If so, you'd be changing the lives of many people you might never know or meet in real life, but they'll always remember you as the helpful 'stranger.'

They are going through problems just like we had a little while ago…Having no idea how to choose houseplants, spending a lot of money but getting no results, and wondering whether they should accept that they have a brown thumb?....... That's when you come into the picture.

The only way for us at Humanity Publications to accomplish our mission of helping plant parents is, first, by reaching them.

Most people are already tired of spending $$$ and getting poor results. They'll likely check the book cover (and its reviews) before buying them directly. If you have found this book worthy so far, would you like to share and leave honest feedback about it?

You can save someone's hard work and hundreds of dollars by typing a review in less than 60 seconds.

Your review will save……

….. A plant parent from losing their plant baby.

……A fellow millennial that wants to nurture life but can't due to a mid-life crisis

…….A person that stays up at night wondering whether his plant will make it to the weekend

To ease their pain….. all you need is to leave an honest review…. by just sparing 60 seconds out of your time.

If you are reading on a kindle or an e-reader, you can scroll to the bottom of the book, then swipe up, and it will automatically prompt a review.

If, for some reason, they have improved in any way - you can go to the book page on amazon. (or wherever you purchased this and leave a review right on the page)

PS - Your honest feedback can save many plants and help plant parents out there

I'm thrilled to invite you to continue reading this "The Houseplant Whisperer." (There are many tactics and methods to uncover)

PPS - Life-saving hack: if you introduce something valuable to someone, they associate that value with you. If you'd like goodwill directly from another plant parent - send this book their way.

Thank you from the bottom of my heart. Now back to our regularly scheduled programming.

—Your biggest fan, Michelle

CHAPTER 5

PEST CONTROL & DISEASES

"Most of the time pests and diseases are just nature's way of telling the farmer he's doing something wrong."

— Michael Pollan

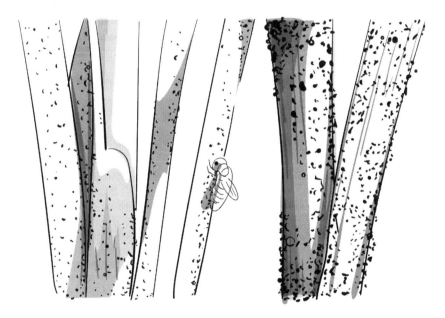

Have you ever noticed that all houseplants have some sort of bugs and crawlies around? Do you think it's because the indoor baby is not correctly cared for? Well, there can be another case. The houseplant growing conditions, such as high humidity and Lack of air, are the ideal climate for the pests.

Even if you religiously follow all rules and regulations, there are chances of your plant attracting pests. You may get upset seeing creepy insects buzzing around your leafy plant. Things can worsen when you realize the pests damage the plant built with love.

Overall, the plants are sturdy enough to tolerate the mild infestation by bugs as they are less harmful. One of the most common insects is the fungus gnat which may not be life-threatening but can be a nuisance. However, their population can grow if you keep looking the other way.

There are a few common indoor pests that you may face while building a green team. The bad news is that this can damage and kill your houseplant eventually. Knowing that you can acquire a few tricks to nip the root cause promoting plant pest growth is excellent.

Most Common Indoor Plant Pests

You must adopt a few techniques, including proper plant care and regular leaf washing, to keep your plant safe. Here is a list of common indoor pests, how they look, and how to eliminate them.

Fungus Gnats

The fungus gnats are tiny gnats that fly around the plants. They mostly look like fruit flies. Hence, it is easier for you to miss them. They mostly prefer damp medium, which is rich in organic matter. Usually, they are harmless, but if they complete a lifecycle around the houseplants, they can cause fungal damage.

The roots can rot when the gnats keep growing in the moist soil. They either eat the fungus or the healthy plant overall. You can eliminate gnats by placing a colorful sticky note/trap anywhere close to the houseplant. It will help you see the population of gnats.

Additionally, you can also use mosquito bits (BTi). Add 4 tbsps of bits in a water gallon and let them soak for an hour. Strain the bits and drench the plant in the water every three days. It will remove the gnats from the roots.

Spider Mites

Spider Mites are very tiny aphid-like-looking insects. You can primarily find them in the undersides of the leaves. They have different types of body colors, i.e., red and yellow. They have eight creepy legs. A magnifying glass could be necessary to see if they exist.

You may not be able to detect spider mites at the beginning of an infestation. Spider mites suck the nutrients and water from the leaves, making them yellow, eventually dying down. So, the tip is to cut and wash the leaves regularly and keep the plant moist. Cut down the infected leaf, wrap it in a bag, and throw it away.

1. Thrips

Thrips are flying pests mostly found in houseplants that are kept indoors after quite an extended outdoor stay. They are hardly noticeable. However, once they start infestation over your plant's leaves, you can see them damaging the upper layer of the leaves.

The pests leave their waste behind, which turns the leaves grey and silverish. So, next time you see discolored leaves, it's probably the thrips harming. You can eliminate them by getting blue sticky traps or minute pirate bugs for chemical-free control.

2. Mealybugs

These pests come from a white cotton cast over the plant roots. They release honeydews which can dangerously attract many insects and pests. They can be disastrous for indoor plants. They are harder to control and get multiplied too.

You may use a bud (Q-tip) and apply a bit of isopropyl alcohol over the bug. Otherwise, you can also use the insects like green lacewings, which can help you eliminate the mealybugs without harm.

3. Whiteflies

These pests are often taken as mealybugs because they have a similar appearance. However, these are flying pests that can take flight. Whiteflies also exude honeydew and tend to be multiplied. They can severely affect the plant by attracting ants and different diseases.

The whitefly-specific pesticides, lacewings, and hard water splashes are enough to keep the whiteflies away occasionally.

4. Scale Insects

Scale insects love indoor plants. They come in various forms, but you may deal with the soft brown scale the most. They mostly look like odd brown growth over the plant's stems. They are very dangerous as they can be multiplied and have spiky mouthpieces.

They can be malicious to your leafy babies. So, before they feed on the houseplant's juices, it's better to take care of them. You can either scrape the scale insects. You can also use insecticidal spray, rubbing alcohol, and regular inspections for better results.

5. Aphids

Aphids are primarily plant-specific. However, the most common type is root aphids. Though tiny insects, their damage can be enormous as they tend to reproduce exceptionally. You can primarily find them in the undersides of the leaves.

You can identify them by the honeydew they secrete, a white waxy substance. They can start from the stems infestation and slowly reach the leaves, making them wither, yellow, or curl. It invites many insects and diseases like mildew.

Make sure that you treat your houseplants correctly. One necessary thing to notice is that you may take aphid infestation as a nutrient deficiency. Always check the soil and the plant stems before adding any more nutrients.

You may use yellow sticky traps or biological insecticides to eliminate aphids. Otherwise, removing the badly infested houseplants is suggested, as the recovery can be impossible.

Now, when you keep houseplants, there are chances that routine care might not be enough to keep the pests away. Hence, besides this timely solution like sticky traps, you need something practical.

Types of Pesticides

Pesticides can be a substance or a mixture that helps repel and prevent pests from infesting your houseplant. They come in three different types, which include synthetic, conventional, and natural pesticides.

Plants' parents often argue that *"they don't want the toxic chemicals to touch their green babies."* Well, this is a sweet myth that "natural pesticides are not harmful to plants." The truth is that both are formulated to kill pests.

A few organic pesticides can be less toxic than commercial ones but not completely harmless. Here is an excellent comparison to help you pick the right option.

Natural Pesticides	Commercial Pesticides
These are repellent that is extracted strictly from natural and organic ingredients.	These pesticides are produced through chemical compositions, which tend to kill pests, fungi, and weeds.
There is absolutely no chance of any chemical alteration, but they are minimally processed.	These substances are formed via the formulation of an active ingredient in the chemical factory.
Effective for pest control	Helps in getting rid of pests easily.
You have to be a bit patient for the organic pesticides to work.	They are chemically engineered and work rapidly in pest killing.
They require reapplications.	They work instantly.
They are expensive as they are derived from natural and organic matter.	They are relatively less costly.
You may need professional to use them	You can see the guide through the pack

correctly.	and handle the pests.
Less odor as they involve organic products.	May release smell as a result of chemical reactions.
Safe with children and animals.	It can be dangerous.
It may only help in pest damage.	They promote growth as well as pest control.
A few organic pesticides include copper sulfate, neem oil, alcohols, hydrogen peroxide, chlorine products, and soaps.	Some popular synthetic pesticides include formulated MetaldehydeDiazinon, Boric Acid, glyphosate, Acephate, Deet, Propoxur, and Dursban.

The key is to choose the pesticides with accurate direction and care. Prevention is always better than cure. Still, if not pests, some environmental conditions can invade your plant's health.

Common Houseplant Disease

You may be wondering whether houseplants actually get sick. Well, the answer is YES. There can be pests infesting the plants, a lack of ventilation, and many conditions like overwatering and underwatering. All these situations can make your plants ill eventually.

Here is a list of the most typical houseplant diseases and the necessary diagnosis and prevention.

Leaf Spot Fungus

This disease can result in your foliage getting oval-shaped browns and black spots outlined with yellow edges. The fungus spots mostly attack the plants like palms, yucca, and orchids. They can make the leaves weak, and cause falls off the plant.

It advised cutting the leaf that shows the fungus prints. You can sweeten the condition by improving the aeration and ventilation of the houseplant. You may try fungicide if the defect pertains.

Gray Mold (Botrytis Cinerea)

It is the easiest to detect and the most common plant disease. They appear as grey patches over the leaves (with furry white holes). The white dots can gradually grow, turn the leaves black, and wither eventually.

You can save your plants from gray mold by not overwatering and keeping the plants at a distance. The damp leaves are in the best condition for these spots to form over the leaves.

Powdery Mildew

If you have African violets, succulents, and begonias as houseplants, then beware. This condition can cause white powdery fungus to cover plant leaves, stems, and flowers. You can keep your plants away from these splashy coatings through adequate aeration and proper watering.

Make sure not to underwater your greenery kids. Cut that leaf instantly at which you notice the powdery mildew. If the problem persists, try fungicide.

Downy Mildew

They can form blotches and mold-like appearances in yellow, brown, green, and purple colors. In the worse case, this disease can also make your leaves pale and wither slowly. Experts recommend removing the infected part of the leaf

Overwatering the leaves can make the plant get downy mildew. You can prevent the situation by not overwatering the houseplant. Other than this, there is no chemical solution for this defect.

1. Rust

Do you have pelargoniums growing inside your house? Then, these rusty nodules give you a headache. These orange patches can appear on the undersides of the leaves. They can make your green-leafed plant turn yellow and eventually die.

This disease is not harmful to houseplants, but prevention is better than cure. You may get rid of any leaf which begins showing rust symptoms. You can avoid this rusty situation by avoiding overfeeding and improving aeration within your plant collection.

2. Sooty Mold

Previously, you learned about aphids, the pests which secrete sugary material. The honeydew released by these mealybugs can halt the beauty of the houseplants. It is another fungal type of disease that can harm your green babies. If left untreated, they can form black and brown patches known as Sooty Mold.

The best suggestion to stay safe is always to check if any pests are infesting the plants. Add a tbsp of detergent in a gallon of water and wash the leaves through it for 15 minutes. You can also give a cleansing wash to the leaves if the situation goes out of hand.

3. Stem & Crown Rot

If you have a history with houseplants, you must have encountered this Stem and Crown Rot. As the name suggests, this disease works by rotting the beautiful stems of the plant around the soil. It does not stop there but moves forward in decaying the whole plant until it reaches the leaves.

You cannot treat this fungal infection. Still, you can avoid the problem by ensuring your soil is well-drained and never soggy. The sad part is that it has been very late when you detect the issue.

4. Root rot

If you notice your leafy baby has stopped responding to watering, Root Rot can be the suspect. Root Rot similarly affects your plant as the former disease. It attacks the roots directly, making them black or brown. You may notice the symptoms in the ending stages.

The potting soil becomes ultimately dark. This type of decay is either your plant being overwatered or underwatered. Hence, you must ensure the potting soil is neither dry nor wet.

We all feel bloated when we eat much, weak when consuming less, and sick when not taken care of properly. Plants are the same. They are also living beings who require a living routine. You must not be afraid, as the plants can be kept and revived with the right action at the right time.

"Ciara faced the resilient mealybugs and did not allow the plant to drop off the twig."

Here is a story of a houseplant savior who never gave up on her green baby. Ciara explains how she had to chop her indoor plant vine by vine with her hands. However, she trusted the process and recovered the more healthy plants within four months. It is an inspiration; you should keep hope. You can always try neem oil and rubbing alcohol mixes for cleaning indoor plants.

Some pests might not be deadly, but they can suck essential growing nutrients out of the leafy babies. Nutrition plays a vital role in the overall appearance and growth of houseplants.

CHAPTER 6

PLANT NUTRITION - GIVE US THIS DAY,

OUR DAILY BREAD

"Plants and flowers taught me how to grow, by growing in secret and in silence."

— **Michael Bassey Johnson.**

Just like humans require calcium, protein, vitamins, oxygen, and nitrogen, all plants need some sort of supplement to develop attractively and lusciously. Nutrients help plants complete their lifecycle efficiently, germinating, growing, fighting diseases, and reproducing.

The question arises plants can survive without plant food or fertilizers. Then, why do we need fertilizer? The answer is that nature alone is not enough to replenish the nutrients in the plant's soil. The fertilizers provide the necessary micronutrients and macronutrients to the houseplants.

The leafy plants absorb microelements such as Nitrogen, Potassium, Phosphorus, magnesium, calcium, and many more from the air and light via fertilizers. Fertilizers make photosynthesis easy for indoor plants.

All the nutrients have distinctive functions for the nourishment of plants. Plants require primary macronutrients in high content, while secondary macronutrients are needed less. 16 elements in total lay out the foundation of the plants. However, the deficiency of any of them can halt plant growth.

Primary Plant Nutrients

Indoor babies need a high concentration of these nutrients for survival. They are responsible for the overall happy growth and appearance of the plants.

Nitrogen (N)

The macronutrient plays a fundamental role in plant development. It is responsible for protein synthesis, energy metabolism, chlorophyll formation, and photosynthesis. Plants take nitrogen in the form of nitrate.

Nitrogen enhances cellular multiplication and beauty of the aerial zone of the plant. The deficiency of nitrogen can result in slow growth and yellow plant leaves.

Phosphorus (P)

Phosphorous is the main character for overall root formation and flowering in houseplants. It makes the plants resistant to environmental changes. It helps shoot growth and promotes energy storage and hassle less photosynthesis process.

Phosphorus plays a crucial role in maintaining the aesthetics of your green babies. Its absence can make the flowering hard and the plant old and die.

Potassium (K)

The macronutrient maintains the overall water supply and reserved substances for the plants. It improves nitrate absorption, stimulates flowering, maximizes photosynthesis capacity, and strengthens the cell tissues. The plants become sturdy enough to tackle all weather.

Potassium works as a balancing agent. Hence, its shortage can result in the wittering of leaves, making the indoor plant an easy target for fungal attacks. Lack of this nutrient may also cause disruptive distribution of nitrogen, magnesium, and calcium.

Secondary Plant Nutrients

Plants need secondary macronutrients in less concentration than N, P, and K. Here is how they play a role in stabilizing the houseplants.

Calcium (Ca)

Calcium binds to the cell walls and ensures effective plant growth and cell development. It helps the plant retain the minerals in the soil. Additionally, seed formation also becomes easy to stabilize the toxic substances in the plants.

Magnesium (Mg)

Magnesium is an indispensable element for the plant. It comprises the core of the chlorophyll element. Therefore, it has a significant role in photosynthesis, storage of sugars, and imparting phosphorus. Magnesium also regulates and activates the enzymes in the plant for better development.

Sulfur (S)

Sulfur is responsible for chlorophyll formation, tissue formation, and distribution of nitrogen. It also intervenes in protein synthesis. Hence, Sulfur also plays a vital role in the overall appearance and beauty of the plant defenses.

All kinds of nutrients fulfill the disparate living needs of the houseplants. Plants require macronutrients in different proportions to promise well-being. There are a few more micronutrients that ensure proper plant growth, strong immunity, and a sustainable lifecycle.

Micronutrients

The plant's healthy growth and practical living require some nutrients in minute content. The following list highlights the necessary nutrients.

Iron (Fe)

Iron contributes to the pigment of your indoor baby. It accelerates photosynthesis and is a factor in many prime enzymes. It is the power unit of the electron in the plant cells. Iron circulates various essential elements through the plant, maintaining its beauty.

Zinc (Zn)

The plant comprises specific enzymes that have multiple functions for development. Zinc is the central component of many enzymes that control indoor plants' metabolic reactions. So, zinc deficiency can halt the plant tissues and result in a shortage of carbohydrates, chlorophyll, and protein.

Manganese (Mn)

The Lack of Manganese is a common issue found in plants. It is an essential micronutrient needed for average plant growth and a stable metabolic rate. You can mainly find it in plants that grow in well-aerated, calcareous, and dry soil. The rich organic matter fertilizer can result in a deficiency of Manganese.

Boron (B)

Boron is another vital micronutrient that forms the tissue and cell walls. Hence, its deficiency can make the plant's roots weak. Therefore, ensure that boron is present in your medium before root intake. There are many more essential nutrients like Chlorine (Cl), Silicon (Si), Molybdenum (Mo), Copper (Cu), Cobalt (Co), and so on, which promote the plant's luscious growth.

Different developments require both macronutrients and micronutrients in various proportions. Choose a medium (fertilizer) according to your plant type and what you expect.

Essential Nutrition Guide for Flowering & Non-flowering Houseplants

Green babies are unlike human babies. They don't whine and cry when hungry, thirsty, or uncomfortable. Plants show signs which may appear too late. Consequently, plant parents can't wait until the plant shows symptoms like wrinkling, getting pale, curling up, rotting, and dying.

Hence, you "require" a fertilizer to can help you schedule your plant over the growing cycle. Therefore, here is how the fertilizer schedule would work for your plans in all seasons.

Scheduling	Spring	Summer	Fall
When to start fertilization?	Recommended to begin 8 weeks before last spring's frost	Summer is the season in which plants actively grow, your growing schedule should get regular here	You may slow down the fertilizer applications in the fall. You can initiate fertilization 8 weeks before the first fall frost is expected

Should you trust the packet guide?	When you start adding fertilizers, it is recommended to use half of the suggested quantity in the first three applications	Refrain from exactly following the pack guide. You can begin by adding ¼ times less fertilizer quantity than suggested	You need to half the fertilizer quantity that you used for the summer fertilization schedule
How to deal with granular fertilizer?	Only add half of the instructions as the indoor baby just begins growing	Their use would likely be less frequent, maybe once a month	Try to add the fertilizer 3-4 times at max with long gaps until the winter arrives
How to add liquid fertilizer?	Only mix the liquid fertilizer to half of the strength as the plants do not require many nutrients when they have just activated	You can apply liquid fertilizers on a bi-weekly or monthly basis. It is preferred to use water-soluble liquid fertilizer for better results	Slow down the schedule by adding fertilizer once a month and in much less content as compared to the summer schedule
Which fertilizer is best?	In spring, you may pick a slow-release and single-application fertilizer (more about this later). Try to choose a fertilizer with high Nitrogen content for foliage plants and Phosphorus rich fertilizer for flowering houseplants	Plants require nutrients for an extended period in summer. Therefore, you must choose a slow-release houseplant. It's one application can last 3-4 months. They break down the nutrients slowly for your houseplants.	As you weaken the fertilizer strength, you save plants from the shock of a seasonal switch. You can continue using the fertilizer that you have been using

There is no fertilization schedule for winter as the plants get deactivated. Further, fertilizing the plants in winter can result in burns. Be careful, as your indoor baby can breathe its last.

Note:

Almost all flowering and non-flowering houseplants need similar fertilizer and nutrient ratios. Ensure the fertilizer has the NPK macronutrients and micronutrients required for any plant type's nourishment and growth.

However, if you deal with flowering categories like African Violets, Gloxinia, or Begonias, try to choose a fertilizer with high Phosphorus ratios like (1-3-1). Moreover, a balanced nutrient supply overall (preferably with a 5-3-3 or 5-5-5 ratio) is necessary. Do you still have questions? Don't worry; here is a bonus point to clear your misconceptions and assumptions.

Tips & Tricks

- Never overfeed your indoor babies with fertilizer. The overuse of nutrient-rich fertilizers can harm the leafy plant. It would be best to build your plant's ability to grow slowly.

- You may start using organic fertilizer as it is the most inexpensive and easy to use.

- The seasonal temperature has less effect on plants as compared to sun exposure.

- If you live in a climate with fewer chances of sun sight, use a fertilizer with half the quantity recommended on the pack (all year long).

- Otherwise, if you are in a summery region, you can keep the summer schedule all year round.

- Choose a fertilizer with Potassium, Phosphorus, and Nitrogen for the best results.

- Only fertilize plants when it is the season.

Fertilizer comes in various forms and types. You can find their specifications in the following.

Types of Fertilizers

There are three prominent fertilizer kinds: liquid, granule, and spikes. All of these types have their pros, cons, and convenience. You can choose whichever suit your plant the best.

Slow Release Granules

Granules provide nutrients for a more extended period. They slowly release the essential elements in the soil for shooting growth. Granules also require fewer reapplications as compared to liquid ones. The only trade-off of using these is your plants don't feed the nutrients instantly.

Here are a few recommended and top-rated granules among plant parents.

- Phosphorus-rich Granules

- Root Zone Granules

- All-purpose Granules

Liquid Fertilizers

Do you need an instantly working fertilizer? Then, liquid fertilizer should be your call. It is water soluble, gets to the roots quickly, and starts working. The only downside is that the liquid fertilizer needs multiple reapplications as it can't feed the houseplants long.

They are available in various forms, such as in a tea bag (brewed), concentrate, and readymade editions. Here are some fantastic suggestions.

- Compost Tea Concentrate

- General Purpose Liquid

- Bouncy Big Plants

Fertilizer Sticks (Spikes)

Are you new to this green realm? Then, give the fertilizer sticks a try. They can make your work easy as you don't need to mix, measure, or mess up any granule and liquid. It would be best if you pushed the spikes in the soil. They work like granules and feed plants slowly but over a long time. Ensure that you don't overuse the fertilizer sticks.

The fertilizer types require different lighting conditions to release nutrients actively. The atmosphere plays a crucial role in improving the absorption of elements. Plants react differently to all seasons. Stay tuned to know more.

CHAPTER 7

LIGHT CONTROL & SEASONAL CHANGES

"All that is gold does not glitter. Not all those who wander are lost: the old that is strong does not wither, deep roots are not reached by the frost."

— J.R.R Tolkien

Light works as the driving force for houseplants. It is the "fuel" needed by plants to grow efficiently. Your indoor babies get food through photosynthesis. They capture light and use it to break down carbon dioxide and water into oxygen. So, light energy is converted into chemical energy, leading to effective plant growth.

Plants need consistent and persistent energy sources, such as light, to bloom. Now, sunlight always fails to fulfill the plant's needs, i.e., after sunset. Your green babies form chlorophylls that are visible to different wavelengths. Therefore, LED (Light emitting diode) comes into the frame.

Houseplants can efficiently utilize disparate wavelengths for multiple purposes. For instance, plants can take wavelengths (430 and 460 nanometers) for vegetative growth when 650 and 700 nanometers of light is enough for flowering.

Before you jump down to get a LED light, it is necessary to learn the lightning propositions. There are specifications about the light requirements given below.

How to Tell if the Lightening is Appropriate for Different Plant Types

Have you ever noticed that all houseplants comprise disparate living requirements? Some indoor greenies are high maintenance and get crimped with a moment of negligence. In contrast, others are not sensitive and need less light and overall care.

Before, you must have seen the houseplants categorized according to the types. Now, we narrow them down to the lighting conditions. This characteristic of inside babies will help you better understand the plant of your dream. There are two things you should consider to discern the light best for your houseplant:

1. Light Intensity

2. Light Amount

Lux (Lumen per square meter) is the unit used to measure *light intensity*. Lumen is the ability of humans to perceive light. Here is a chart showing how you can use a lux meter and discern the intensity.

The plants you keep in your living room get 50 lux, while those in direct sunlight receive 100000 lux. The difference is far more than expected. Here is an easy comparison to show you how much light-intensity houseplants need.

Plants	Intensity
Low Light Plants	Lux 500-2500
Bright Light Plants	Lux 10000-20000
Medium Light Plants	Lux 2500-10000

Very Bright Light Plants	Lux 20000-50000

Plants should take 10+ hours of light for healthy development. They can survive at 10 times lower intensities but won't grow tremendously. All plants have different requirements. Hence, it would be best if you learned about your plant type. You can always get a lux meter to check the lighting spots in your home.

Lightening Conditions for Different Houseplants

If you have ever been a plant parent, you must have seen these tags "place in the partial shade" or "keep in bright light." As a novice, you might not know how much shade is partial and how much direct sun exposure is enough. Every home has different lighting intensities, encouraging plant growth in a particular category. So, choosing plants that fit the sunlight strength and indoor lights' power available in your home is better.

Plants	Optimal Spot	Sunlight Required	Grow Lightening	Tips
Low-light Plants Such as ZZ Plant, Peace Lilly, English Ivy, Chinese Evergreen, Cast Iron Plant, Ponytail Palm, Parlor Palm, Dumb Cane, and Dracaena	Any fairly dark spot can make an optimal place for low-light plants i.e north window, office lighting, sunset on a clear day	Less than 3 hours of sun per day, you can keep them in the same spot far from direct sun exposure	Lower-intensity plants usually do not require such artificial lighting to grow. Still, if you fail to deliver indirect sunlight to the plant. 10 and 15 watts of fluorescent light Is enough for growth Artificial light should ideally be placed 6-12	Low-light plants can survive without direct light exposure as they require time to grow gradually with less water and light intake They can get dry easily but try to avoid overwatering by just feeling the soil

			inches above the plant's growing space	
Medium Light Plants Such as African Violet, Alocasia, Amaryllis, Elephant Ear, Norfolk Island Pine, Asparagus Fern, Rubber Plant, and Fiddleleaf Fig	These plant types also need to be out of direct sunlight. The spots near the west-facing window or east-sided window would be suitable which are in daylight but not direct sunlight You can reduce the direct sunlight effect (approx. 50%) by placing the plant 2-3 feet away from the window	They thrive in 3-6 hours placed in the optimal spot	Medium-light plants require artificial lighting to grow seeds initially. The light power can be 15-20 watts for these plants' effective development	They may not get dry as easily, but it is suggested not to overwater these types
High Light Plants Such as Aloe Barbadensis, Jade Plant, OrchidsTi Plant, Orchid Cactus, Gardenia, Jasmine,	Plants should be placed in bright, lit, and direct sunlight such as in the south-west window (opened) or preferably in a south-facing place	6 hours of direct and bright sunlight is enough for these plant's healthy growth	Bright plants may not need artificial help for seeding but there are a few types such as peppers and tomatoes. They may require some extra indoor light.	Higher-intensity babies usually have a long stay in the warm and right environment. Try to water them more often after

Kalanchoe			Try to take a light with 20+ watts of energy	checking the medium

All houseplants need light to grow, but they prosper at different ranges. In the section above, you can easily discern all plant lighting requirements. All plant parents must know that summer and spring is the prime time for plant growth. The reason is that the plant's growing medium (fertilizer and soil) and water intake absorb nourishment through the light. Here is a detailed scenario of how lighting can change in different situations and how to adjust accordingly.

Adjusting Light Relative to the Changes

The light can change as the day goes by, along with seasonal changes. The plant parents should change the location of the indoor babies as the sun switches direction. It is how you can tell which spot to take when the light travels with time.

Location

The plant's location determines if indoor plants receive ample light. It plays a crucial role in selecting optimal spots for the houseplants with the changing latitudes and building structures, such as the sun rising from the east while resting in the west. East-faced windows direct more sunlight in the morning and west-sided windows in the afternoon.

Things get twisted as in the southern hemisphere, and the southern-facing windows get the least sunlight while the northern-sided windows get the most. The case changes when it comes to the northern hemisphere. Here is a classic direction of windows if you live in the northern hemisphere (such as the UK, US, and Canada).

- **South-Facing Windows**

The south-sided window is heaven for bright light plants. It generally receives direct and intense sunlight in the home. Natural light directly hits it if any building structure, canopy, or trees do not shade the window.

- **West-Facing Windows**

These windows are shady compared to south-sided windows. They receive indirect light in the early morning and early afternoon. At that time, the south-faced windows lead the bright sunlight. Consequently, the sun directly hits the west-side windows in the evening and afternoon.

The intensity of the light is highest at this time. Therefore, beware; it can scorch your indoor babies if not cared for properly.

- **East-Facing Windows**

In the early morning, the east-side windows receive direct sunlight. These windows receive indirect light with lesser intensity. Later, the same window gets shaded light exposure. This site is best for plants that require indirect bright light without burning the plant.

- **North-Facing Windows**

The light hardly glows in the north-side windows. You may notice indirect bright sunlight in the north-facing windows. North-sided windows make the ideal spot for low-light plants like Ferns.

Seasonal Changes

Seasons have an evident effect on the growth of plants. In summer, the sun's rays are intense, and they last for a more extended period. So this makes the perfect condition for the plant's healthy growth. Similarly, the development process halts during winter with less intense sunlight.

Hence, it is necessary to schedule for changing the plant's side. For instance, the daylight brightens highly in the west-facing windows during summer. It might need to change the direction towards the south side for more sunlight in winter.

The plants hardly show any improvement in the north-facing window in winter. While in summer, they can be a good choice for shade-loving plants. It is essential to learn the basic of that how much intensity a plant can bear.

The key is no matter where you live, ensure your plant type gets the required light for survival. Sometimes, you may need something to lower the light intensity in summer.

Making Light Less Intense

Just as choosing the right spot is necessary, making the light less intense for other plant types is also crucial. Here are a few suggestions for creating a place for low-light and medium-light plants.

- **Window Films -** If your plant is sensitive to harsh sunlight, then window films can help you protect your leafy baby. It fights against the UV rays for shade-loving plants.

- **Window Sheers -** These are lightweight curtains blocking the sunlight's intensity through the window.

- **Placement -** This tip is for you if you have low and medium-intensity plants. You can place the plants a few feet far from the window where the room must receive bright sunlight. It will help your babies get indirect sunlight.

This way, you can constantly adjust the place for your plant following the light that hits your home. You must follow your gut and give appropriate lighting care to your leafy babies. Proper lighting can utilize all your efforts. Plant babies may require growth lights to stay alive when they don't have the necessary lighting conditions, like winter, autumn, or a gloomy day.

So, for northern countries' residents and others, it is suggested to use artificial light such as LED, Fluorescent, and Incandescent light. Plants may need 15-18 hours of this light for a healthy life. Here are the signs you might notice when your plant lacks proper care.

Diagnosing Problems in Struggling Plants

Two main reasons your plant can struggle due to light: too much or too little light is needed to grow. You must be extremely careful as the defective lighting symptoms resemble pest infestation and disease. Here is a demonstrative comparison.

Excessive Light

- Leaves will develop brown patches due to scorched heat
- The plant will seem washed out, faded, dull, and pale
- Soil drying out quickly
- It may get hot and wilt eventually
- Feel moisture-less and dried
- Leaves get crunchy and crispy

How to handle it?

If excessive light halts your plant's health, you may remove it from the direct sunlight spot. Place the indoor plant away in the corner of the room or in some window that receives less sunlight.

Less Light

- Plants may look tall and spindly
- Leaves feel leggy as if they have been stretched out
- Poor development and leaf growth
- Little photosynthesis makes the plant dull and dead
- Lower leaves may start getting yellow
- Color might change to dark green, then yellow, and eventually result in death

How to handle it?

If you notice any of these symptoms, do not immediately move your plant in direct sun. They might not be able to tolerate the harsh sun exposure instantly. Instead, you can shift the plant to a brighter spot for a few days tracking the difference.

You can overcome both problems according to the situation and lighting conditions. However, what can you do if proper sunlight can't reach high-intensity plants? Else, the room is brimming with the sun, but your plant is low light? This situation can result in you killing your green baby. Therefore, as discussed before, you must pick an indoor plant per lighting in your home.

Top High Light, Medium Light, and Low Light Plant Picks

If you're confused about choosing the plant that fits available lighting, this section can help you. Here is a list of the best and easy-to-grow houseplants from both categories.

High-Intensity Plants

The plant types demand strong sunlight to complete their natural growth cycle. They usually originate from countries like Australia and South Africa. These regions ensure long sun exposure throughout the day. They require more "food," which means more light.

You can keep high-light plants thriving through appropriate lighting. So, these plants can be a blessing if you reside in a sunny area. Here are a few recommendations.

Aloe Barbadensis (Aloe Vera)

Aloe vera is easier to propagate in houseplants. It requires less water and just bright sun for better propagation. It does not start wrinkling by a moment of negligence. It can lusciously develop even if kept in filtered sunlight. You can report the buds for reproduction.

- Low maintenance

- Requires less water and direct sun (for long periods)

- Sap is beneficial for pain relief (from cuts and burns), and first aid

- Useful for multi-purpose

Jade Plant

Jade Plant is the most loved among the plant parents. They slowly grow and require no special care. A few hours of direct sun exposure is enough for Jade Plant to thrive. They can quickly adapt to different environments, and south-facing windows can be an excellent place.

- Easy to keep throughout the seasonal change

- Tolerate bright, and high-intensity light

- Sturdy stems and fleshy leaves

- No high demands

Thimble Cactus

The cactus type is easy to keep as it needs high-intensity light to survive. It is famous for handling all types of environments well. They do well in high temperatures and live up to down to frost. They are harmless and need a well-drained pot with soil to be happy. They do not mind a little bit of negligence.

- Unique and attractive

- Only require watering when completely dried

- Require well-drained soil and direct bright light

- No need to water in winter

Phalaenopsis (Orchids)

Orchids require high intensity when they start blooming. However, a shady environment is recommended for effective health as they grow. There are specialized planters explicitly designed for this plant type, orchids.

- Popular among beginners

- Requires little water to survive

- Thrives in mild and warm environments

- Great water Purifier

- Good drainage and fresh air flow

Stephanotis (Jasmine)

All plant lovers always love Jasmine as they release a lovely scent. The showy white flowers are the star of the show. They make stunning dark foliage paired with tropical-looking vines. They loathe soggy roots, so avoid that.

- Adds sweet fragrance to the room

- Reacts well to room temperature

- Requires rich and loamy soil

- Incredibly low-maintenance houseplant

Medium Intensity Plants

Many houseplants do not need a bright light or a completely lightless room. There are plenty of medium-intensity plants. These houseplants can survive with a moderate amount of heat and light. These are the best option for plant parents if they don't get a hot summer.

Medium-light plants mostly require indirect light. So, you can place them 4 to 6 feet from sunlight in a room with bright sunshine and no curtains. Here are a few fantastic plant recommendations.

African Violet

African violets make your home a living bouquet as they flower beautifully. Although, they are a bit fussy and only require moderate light to live. They can scorch in high intensity and get leggy with too less light. In case you have medium light to offer, chef's kiss!

- Colorful blooms

- low maintenance

- Requires less watering

Alocasia

Alocasia is a beautiful broad-leafed baby known as an elephant ear plant. Plant parents especially adore their stunning foliage. Indoor plants prefer an indoor environment with efficient indirect light and humidity. They like living in the pots and require watering sessions every week.

- 100+ varieties available

- The soil must be moist

- Can be toxic for kids and pets

Bamboo Palm

Are you fond of tall and thriving houseplants? Then, the bamboo palm must get on your list. The cherry on top is that they can grow in multiple lighting and environments. The only drawback is that Bamboo Palms require frequent watering.

- Can grow up to 20+ feet tall

- Low-maintenance

- Pinnately divided leaves with fresh yellow blooms

Monstera

The Hall of Fame houseplant comprises huge split leaves. It is species of evergreen tropical shrubs and vines. They are slow in growth, but the after-results are worth it. Netizens also call it the "Swiss Cheese Plant" as it has natural holes, making them a must-get.

- Great home purifier

- Prefer lightly moist soil

- Thrive in east-facing windows

Begonia

Begonia is the favorite from the list because of its pink bloom. Their natural habitats are humid subtropical and tropical areas. The plus point of these houseplants is that they have many species which can survive and thrive in disparate climates.

- Grown for foliage and flowers

- 2000+ different plant types

- Require medium light and well-drained soil

Low Light Plants

Have you got no sunny sills? Don't worry; low-light plants can make a spot in your home. They can live in any shady place with indirect light. You don't need to worry about west or east-facing windows for low-light plants.

Low-intensity plants prefer the tropical forest environment with lower light and shady areas. These plants can be an optimum option if you don't want to invest in supplementary growth lights. Here are a few low-light plants suggestions for you.

ZZ Plant

It is a low-maintenance plant that is cold-tolerant and requires less light. It requires a warmer environment for luscious growth. Still, it can survive low light intensity and sprout slowly. It seems sturdy and comprises upright thrust branches. Additionally, the glossy foliage and fleshy roots add to the beauty.

- Grow without natural sunlight, i.e., windowless offices
- Shiny, wide, and oval-shaped leaves
- Tolerates drought well
- The plant may be toxic for kids

Peace Lily

Peace Lilies are the best houseplants as their growth continues throughout the year. They require little to no attention. They constitute large dark green leaves with graceful white flowers. Water intake is a must for lilies as their foliage may wilt.

- Low maintenance
- Requires less water for survival
- Can thrive in low light
- Keep children away from these plants

English Ivy

English Ivy is also an easy-to-keep indoor baby. It requires indirect sunlight. Hanging baskets make an optimal home for these plants. Their hanging branches give a trailing effect to your balconies. You need to spray them with water now and then for refreshment.

- Can live in indirect light

- Spreads as a ground cover outdoors

- Aesthetic decor

- Requires humidity and a cool room at night

Chinese Evergreen

Chinese Evergreen give a beautiful effect to the corners as they have smaller branches but oval and glossy green leaves. They are excellent low-intensity plants as their foliage can burn in high heat. They require indirect light for best-blooming results but also do fine in low-light areas.

- Low-maintenance

- Partial shade to full shade

- Dark green to silver foliage

- Keep pets away from them

Cast Iron

Cast Iron Plant is well-reputed for being indestructible. They can survive without proper lighting and regular water intake. The north-facing window is the favorite place for Cast Irons. They comprise handsome and arched-shaped deep green leaves. They require you to water them once the soil gets dry.

- Survive in little light

- Partial shade to full shade

- Lush-leaved with slow growth

- Adds elegance to the home

The plant usually thrives in a warm climate. However, the situation changes during winter. The chilly season brings a lot of environmental changes, such as lighting, temperature, and humidity. So, your babies need your special care in these cold times.

Care Routine for Plants in the "Quiet Season"

Houseplants stop growing in the winter. The quiet season asks for a few minimal changes in the overall nourishing schedule of the plants. Here is a complete instructive guide to help you step by step.

1. Less light means less water

It is essential to remember that the more sunlight a plant gets, the thirstier it will be. So, it's better to cut on water intake for houseplants in winter. The plants that usually require to be watered every week in summer may need to take water every two weeks in winter.

Another essential suggestion would be to check the potting medium before adding water to the plant. Let it sit and wait a few more days if it feels moist. Only water the plant when it feels dry. You can get a moisture meter if you wish not to make your finger dirty.

2. Focus on the sunlight pattern

The sun rises later and sets earlier in the winter. Indoor babies get no time to take plenty of sunlight. Therefore, you should take your plants out and closer to the window. Additionally, it would be best if you also changed the direction of the pot each week so that the plant can grow from all sides. Don't worry about the plant's propagation; bountiful houseplant options adapt to all seasons.

3. Leaves may "witter"

When winter arrives, the houseplants regulate themselves according to the lower temperature. Hence, this light and environmental drop make them shed some leaves, which is perfectly alright.

4. Don't fright your leafy littles

The room temperature is ideal for your plant's healthy growth. The extreme cold or hot temperature you replicate via hot air vents, radiators, and conditioners can stress them. Hence, avoid using hot and cold drafts. The sudden temperature rise or drop can take your indoor baby's life.

5. Stop fertilization

As you must have learned in the previous chapter, fertilization does not occur in winter. So, even if you add fertilizers, it can only damage the plants.

6. Beware of pests

Winter is the favorite season for sap-sucking pests and spider mites. So, inspecting the undersides of the leaves and stems each time you water the plant is highly advised. Taking the pest out of your hands is suggested if you notice any infestation. Else, you can wipe them off with an alcohol-soaked cotton pad. Other than this, neem oil and insecticidal soaps are also great options.

7. Try raising the humidity level

The air gets dry in winter resulting in 10-20% humidity. Houseplants from tropical climates may need about 40-50% humidity for adequate growth. In this case, you can increase the moisture by clustering the plants. Also, you can use a tray filled with water and pebbles beneath the plants. But, ensure that the pot is above water level to avoid root rot.

There's a myth that misting the plants increase the humidity level. You better not believe it. The final recommendation would be investing in a humidifier.

8. Clean the leaves

It is a crucial tip to kip your plant clean and neat. You can use a microfiber dusting glove or a damp cloth for wiping the foliage. Keep the dust and grime away from the green baby. You may also give a quick rinsing bath to leaves if you got no time.

9. Say "no" to repotting

Resist getting cabin fever about repotting the plant during winter. Spring and summer are ideal for repotting plants as they show maximum growth.

Taking care of your plant's diet must be your priority. Houseplants are living beings. They require changing skin and body care routines in different seasons, just like you do. Following all the precautions, you can successfully establish a healthy houseplant. You can recreate and even propagate it to share with friends.

CHAPTER 8

HOUSEPLANT PROPAGATION

"A man doesn't plant a tree for himself. He plants it for posterity."

— Alexander Smith

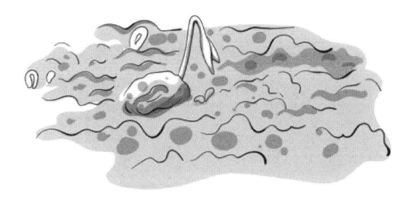

H ealthy houseplants can give "birth" to new plant babies. Yes, you read it right. The plants can propagate. It is widespread for houseplants to be asexual, meaning that the plants comprise the reproductive cells in their stems, leaves, or roots. Hence, nurturing any part of your houseplant can reproduce dozen of new babies.

Propagation is an adventurous and forward approach to the green world. It does require patience and effort, but the results are tremendous. Many houseplant parents encourage the reproduction of plants due to all valid reasons.

The idea is both eco-friendly and cost-effective. You can extend your green collection without going bankrupt. You can seal a deal with green-thumbed besties if you want different plants in your group. Also, it will feel like a thrift offer, and you can give away the houseplants to family and friends.

Here are some fantastic cutting techniques to kickstart your propagation journey. You can ask the plant parent mates to swap the propagated babies. It can help you have a diverse collection to showcase. Additionally, once the houseplants have matured, they may look overgrown and big. So, it's better to cut there some parts and plant a new life.

Types of Houseplant Propagation

Many techniques help you bring a new plant to this world. The most common strategy is "cutting." It requires you to be skilled enough to trim different plants of the plant for nurturing.

Cutting Methods

This method requires a lot of attention and careful use of the equipment. You need to follow specific rules for cutting different parts.

Stem Cuttings

Stems comprise most of the plant's structure as they grow from it. Trimming the stems while the plant is still growing but not yet flowering is advisable. It's suggested to propagate during spring and summer to achieve the best results. Here's a guide on how to cut the stems.

- Take a very sharp knife or blade

- Place it just below the node (leaf joint)

- Cut about 3in-5 in a while, removing the lower leaves (let the leaves at the top be)

- Dip the lower inch of the stem in rooting hormone

- Fill a pot with cutting soil and make a wide hole through a pencil and place a few inches of trimmed stem in it

Leaf Cutting

You can try leaf cutting if your plant has no main stem. There are three ways you can cut the leave for the propagation of a baby plant.

- Cut the whole leaf

- Take a part of it

- The leaf with an inch of its shoot (most commonly used)

All these processes work the same, but different plants propagate accordingly. For instance, the cacti and succulents prefer to be reproduced via leaf only. At the same time, African violets and rubber plants require a leaf with the shoot. Finally, snake plants need only a trimmed leaf.

Root Cutting

The cutting technique requires you to trim a decent amount of root. Then, you can cut it into 2-4 inches sections. It is crucial to place the root (with its end closest to the plant's crown) just below the surface (while repotting). Planting up to 5 root parts can increase the chances of propagation success.

It will enhance the new shoot growth. Cutting the root in the winter when the Parent and Baby Plants are ready for healthy development is advised.

Cane Cutting

There are two ways to use a cane for reproduction. Many plants, like dumb cane and dragon plants, propagate via cane cutting. In this process, you need to cut a stem with buds. Trim the whole stem into 3-inch pieces. The roots will grow below that cane while the shoot will sprout from above.

- Place the stem pieces horizontally halfway into the soil

- Insert the cane in the soil vertically

There are ample options to help you propagate other than these cutting techniques. Here is a list of those approaches.

Air Layering

Air Layering is an interesting process of making baby plants through the stems (still attached to the plants). You need to follow a particular stem-cutting style. The roots of the new plant will propagate over the parent plant.

Many large stemmed plants, such as Rubber and Swiss Cheese Plants, may propagate through Air Layering (more about it in upcoming sections). After that, you can replant them. It can result in a huge baby plant.

Division

Division is a specialized approach involving the separation of a portion from the parent plant. Careful repotting of the section leads to successful propagation. Houseplants such as Ferns, Spider plants, and African violets provide good options for experimenting with this procedure.

Plantlets and Offsets

Few plants produce plantlets on their small stems, known as Stolons. The plantlets are baby plants. You can plant the plantlets. Taking these plantlets out and potting them in moist soil can reproduce plant babies. Many plants, like spiders and mothers of thousands, release plantlets in the plant body. It makes propagation easy.

Many houseplants have offsets produced at the side of the main stem. They are also called pups and are only removed from the parent plant after they have matured. The pups can be repotted in the similarly for further propagation.

Sowing Seeds

Sowing seeds is also a propagation method. It requires particular environmental conditions for successful results. The process needs you to:

- Place seeds with space between over the soil (in the pot with plastic covering)

- Water the pot or tray thoroughly

- Add compost layer over the large seeds

It would be best to have the seeds covered until they show a sign of life (after a week). You may keep plants at 60 – 75°F with little light contact. After the germination stages, you can take the green babies out in indirect sunlight.

Professionals and gardening nurseries prefer the seeding method for propagation. They usually have devices and tools for creating a favorable environment for germination. Beginners can have a hard time seeding the baby plant.

10 Easy Steps to Home/Indoor Propagation

It is an extended version of Air Layering propagation. It requires more steps than cutting techniques but promises steady results. Suppose you want to propagate a thriving and luscious houseplant. Follow the tips given below:

1. Gather rooting hormones, black plastic, tape or twist ties, and Sphagnum Moss.

2. Select a healthy stem from the plant.

3. Remove the bark strip from its surrounding.

4. Make two girdling cuts over the stem, maintaining an inch of space.

5. Ensure the incision is deep enough to remove the bark's upper layer.

6. Peel the stem scraping off the green phloem and the cambium layer of the leaf. Remove woody material from the bark.

7. Take rooting hormone and coat the exposed area.

8. Pick Sphagnum Moss and wrap it around the coated space.

9. Apply the rooting hormone over the moss again with a bit of pressure. Press the substances into the naked bark.

10. Finally, secure the area with plastic to hold the moss in one place. Conceal the area with twist ties or Tape to sustain moisture.

Roots usually take a few weeks or more to propagate. Once the root mass has developed enough, sever the branch from the layering site (about 1 inch deep). Replant the roots for successful propagation. Choose a pot with good aeration to discourage root rot. After that, you can follow the same schedule for plant care as you did for the parent plant.

Now that you have been introduced to critical growth control factors, it's time to consider your first Plant Companion.

CHAPTER 9

UNDERSTANDING WHICH PLANT IS RIGHT FOR YOU

"In some Native languages, the term for plants translates to those who take care of us."

— Robin Wall Kimmerer

Getting yourself a plant baby is a fun yet budget-friendly hobby. There is a wide array of available houseplants. They come with numerous benefits that promise your overall well-being elevating your mood. However, a single mistake can convince you to be a brown thumb: a lack of research.

With one wrong move, you can end up getting a plant that is not suitable for your lifestyle. For instance, the climate or surroundings might not work for your plant's growth. As a result, your houseplant breathes its last.

Thus, even if you're considering the cheapest succulent in the aisle, conducting a little research is recommended. This little background digging can help your plant baby enjoy a good life under needed care.

Hence, you must pick a houseplant with the conditions you can provide. Finding the right plant for you as a beginner may be tricky. In that case, below are some essential steps that you need to consider:

Care and Maintenance

Different plant types need varying care and commitment to thrive. Reading all the living requirements of the plant that makes a place in your heart is suggested. It is also crucial to keep in mind that houseplants are living beings. You have to take time out for these green mates

Ensure that the plant you have chosen is healthy and growing. Some signs of a fresh plant are well-anchored stems, well-formed leaves or buds, and normal-sized growth. Avoid planters having mushy stems, soggy soil, or limply leaves. Only puck a plant from a trustworthy and licensed vendor.

An important factor that many beginners forget is choosing a healthy potting soil mix. Getting the wrong combination can rot the roots of the plant. (You can check Chapter 3 for a more in-depth explanation)

As a beginner, you should prefer plants that can be grown easily. Some good examples are Aloe, Snake Plants, Bromeliads, and Chinese Money Plants, which require a minimal care routine. Before you jump into getting any of these, go ahead and explore the critical aspects of plant survival.

Light

Plants live longer lives with efficient light. They need it to grow, survive, and thrive. Therefore, ensure that you choose the right plant for your available light, even though a plant might be able to grow in low-light conditions. It may need more light for flowering and dense foliage.

The most common mistake you should avoid is choosing a plant that isn't suitable for the room in light. Thus, start by determining your space's hours and quality of light. You can also consider artificial lights to boost your plants' light needs.

Here is a list of light conditions that provide the optimum indoor growing environment.

Low-light Plants

Many describe Low light as "bright enough to read the newspaper." The majority of the low-light plants tend to grow foliage instead of flowers. This plant will suit a reasonably dark corner or a north window. In their natural habitat, they act as "understory plants."

It indicates that they are growing underneath the branches of larger plants. Some good examples of low-light plants include Parlor Palm (Chamaedorea), Chinese Evergreen (Aglaonema), Pothos (Epipremnum), and English ivy (Hedera helix).

Medium-light Plants

These plants are fond of well-lit spaces such as east and west-facing windows. Yet, they are not a fan of direct sunlight. You can also keep these plants where fluorescent lights are present, such as in your office building, parking garage, hotels, or nearby grocery store.

Some recommended medium-light indoor houseplants include Cast Iron Plants (Aspidistra), Ponytail Palms (Beaucarnea Recurvata), and Parlor Palms (Chamaedorea).

High-light Plants

This plant type thrives in direct light, and keeping it in a brightly lit location is recommended. The window facing south or southwest is the best spot for these plants. The planters belonging to this category mostly grow flowers.

Some common high-light plants include hibiscus, Cacti and succulents, and Citrus such as calamondin orange, kumquat, and Meyer lemon.

Besides, it would help if you considered a few factors while assessing the light.

Light Evaluation

Sometimes, you choose a perfect plant kept in optimum light conditions. Even after that, it still dies. If you need help, here are some things you must notice.

Light Quality

Light quality defines as the color or wavelength of light. The light spectrum comprises yellow, green, blue, red, orange, indigo, and violet light. Our sunlight provides light of all these colors.

The light part plants use to grow is known as Photosynthetically Active Radiation. It is primarily composed of red along with blue light. With the advancement of technology, grow lamps have become more common. These lights only omit light from the red and blue wavelengths of the light spectrum.

Ensure you figure out the kind of light emitted by a grow light before buying it. These lights are usually labeled red, blue, white, or balanced light.

- Looking for a quick way to grow green leaves and start seeding? Blue light and mixed light bulbs can be great options for non-flowering plants.

- Mixed-light bulbs or red light are suggested to accelerate bud formation in flowering plants and keep them shorter.

- Balanced, white, or mixed light bulbs would suit your plant in any growth stage.

Light Duration

The photoperiod is the number of hours your plant needs light within the 24-hour time frame. According to the photoperiod, plants divide into three categories based on their flowering response: long days, short days, or neutral days.

Long-day plants - Thrive when daylight hours exceed night-time hours, such as Gloxinia, Tuberous Begonias, and African Violets.

Short-day plants - Poinsettia, Chrysanthemum, Thanksgiving, and Christmas Cacti require shorter days for flowering.

Neutral Day Plants - They don't care about day length differences as they are insensitive to them. Some common examples include Crossandra, Flowering Maple (Abutilon), and Gerbera Daisies.

Lastly, set a timer if you're using an artificial light where natural light is unavailable. Doing so will ensure that plants receive the optimum light hours.

Flowering Houseplants	14 to 16 hours per day
Hydroponic Lettuce and Herbs	12 to 14 hours per day
Seedlings	16 to 18 hours per day
Foliage Houseplants	12 to 14 hours per day

Space

Sometimes your complete focus is on the maintenance of the plant. Ensure a sufficient distance between the light source and the plant is present. You might ignore the safe space between the light source and your plant baby.

For example, bulbs produce much heat, like high-pressure sodium and incandescent. Additionally, with fluorescent and led lights, you must maintain a healthy distance, which ensures a healthy plant baby. Here is a small chart to help you with it.

Flowering Houseplants	6-12 inches
Hydroponic Lettuce and Herbs	6-12 inches
Seedlings	4-6 inches (keep moving your light during the growth time)
Foliage Houseplants	12-24 inches

Positioning

Don't just randomly place your plant baby anywhere without giving it a thought. The only reason is that fitting perfectly with a specific place's house decor is not enough.

It would be best to ask questions before deciding on your indoor houseplant's position. For instance, "Which room gets the most sunlight in my house?", "What is the direction of the window in that room?", "how far is it from my heaters (drafts)?", "What is the temperature of my place roughly on average?"

Another thing you should consider is the height of the plant. Whether it will fit into that given space? Or it would help if you trailed down. Additionally, consider its weight as well. It should be light enough to lift from the shelf each week. Lastly, make sure that your plant pet is easily accessible to you.

How is the View?

Once you have figured out the first two factors, it's time to consider the aesthetics. Indoor plants are renowned for beautifying the space where you place them. They can easily change the vibe of your place per your taste. The great thing is that they come in all shapes and various sizes. So you can effortlessly adjust them almost anywhere.

However, choosing the wrong size for an incorrect place will defeat the whole purpose. For instance, you have placed large majesty palms in a studio apartment. It will make the room look cluttered and disorganized. Instead, an air plant or baby toes plant would be better relative to the position. Some more recommended plants for small spaces include Peperomia, Oxalis Triangularis, Succulents, Polka Dot Plant, Snake Plant, and Peace Lily.

You can also opt for succulents and planters hanging from a shelf. Some friendly options are Pothos, Philodendron, String of Pearls, Spider Plant, and Monstera Adansonii.

Alternatively, go with a single statement piece in your room's corner. Another great tip would be to place the plants away from the center and around the perimeter. It will make the room space appear larger.

On the other hand, some good options for large spaces include Palms, Calathea, Rubber Tree, Fiddle Leaf Fig, Monstera, Birds of Paradise, and Dracaena.

Start slowly, and you'll eventually find the right style for your place.

Temperature and Humidity

Imagine yourself as an indoor houseplant. You grew up in a greenhouse filled with humidity. Suddenly, you shift to a new house where the air conditioner blowing cold air is sucking all the moisture. On the contrary, winter heaters make the air toasty and dry.

This change in temperature and humidity will impact the growth of plants. Too many low levels can turn the leaf's tips brown and edges yellow, while the flowers might die quickly.

Similarly, higher temperature and humidity levels would cause grey mold to appear on leaves, stems, and flowers. Thus, the indoor planters and succulents end up getting rotted. The great news is that most indoor houseplants can tolerate these fluctuations.

Generally, the foliage plants thrive between 70° and 80°F at day time and from 60° to 68°F at night time. At the same time, most flowering plants prefer the same range during the day but grow the best at night around temperatures of 55° to 60°F.

A good rule you can follow is to keep the temperature around 10 to 15°F at night time. Setting a temperature lower than the daytime will intensify flower color and accelerate physiological recovery from lack of moisture. Along with that, it will assist in prolonging your plant's life.

Flowering plants are the most sensitive to heat. Protect them from abrupt temperature changes caused by registers and drafts. Therefore, don't place your indoor plants near air conditioning sources or heat.

Talking about humidity, most indoor plants lack sufficient levels, especially in winter. All planters and succulents except cacti massively benefit from raised humidity levels. However, misting plants to increase humidity is questionable. If you want to do so, using tepid water is suggested.

If you're wondering when to mist plants, do so in the early morning. It will allow leaves to get dry before evening time. However, avoid misting plants with fuzzy leaves, such as African violets.

Alternatively, take a tray and place the pots over it. Fill the tray with water and pebbles. It will raise the humidity levels in the area around the plant. Placing a couple of plants in the room will automatically increase humidity levels. Besides that, you can also use an automatic humidifier for extra moisture for plants and your family.

Now you know all basics that can help you make a sound choice. Besides these factors, select a plant that fits your aesthetics. For that, here is a pictorial representation of the main houseplant types. It will make the selection process even easier for you.

Pictorial Representation of Main Houseplant Types

1. Flowering Houseplants

It is one of the most popular categories of houseplants. Many plant parents enjoy having them because of their blooming flowers and attractive colors.

- **African Violet (Saintpaulia)**

These plants are fond of indirect sunlight and usually come in white, purple, and red.

- **Begonias**

Begonias tend almost constantly to bloom in favorable conditions. They require medium to high light for growing and come in various colors.

- **Chenille Plant (Acalypha Hispida)**

This plant from the pineapple family has quite a quirky appearance. They are known as show-stoppers due to their showy flowers and colorful basal rosettes. You can get them in orange, red, pink, and yellow.

- **Christmas Cactus (Schlumbergera x Buckleyi)**

Set yourself for a holiday feeling the whole year through Christmas cactus. These plants can thrive even after complete neglect. You can get them in the colors pink and red.

- **Clivia or Kaffir Lily (Clivia Miniata)**

This plant baby enjoys sitting in a shady spot with no direct sun exposure. It usually comes in shades of orange and yellow.

- **Kalanchoe (Kalanchoe Blossfeldiana)**

You can get as many houseplants as you want. They thrive in bright indirect sun and come in various colors, such as pink, yellow, red, and white. Yet, only a few would look as mesmerizing as a blooming Kalanchoe.

- **Peace Lily (Spathiphyllum Floribundum)**

This attractive houseplant has dark green luscious leaves and white bracts enclosing beautifully into tiny flower clusters. You can get these flowering plants in the colors white or yellow.

- **Pelargoniums**

This houseplant can be a great option if you're not all about flowers. The majority of people enjoy them due to their scented leaves and foliage.

- **Madagascar jasmine(Stephanotis Floribunda)**

This beautiful climbing vine species can grow indoors as well as outdoors. They will beautify your space with shiny-oval-shaped leaves and scented blooms.

- **False shamrock (Oxalis Triangularis Subsp. Papilionaceae)**

Add an oomph factor to your living room with this plant having deep maroon leaves. Their flowers are usually five-petalled of pale pink or white color.

- **Hoyas**

Hoyas will be a great option if you're looking for trailing vines. They have waxy, thick leaves with star-shaped fragrant flowers. They come in red and light-pink flowers. The unique texture of this plant makes it stand out.

- **Streptocarpus**

These plants make a great decor piece with primrose-like flowers and fresh green leaves. They come in various hues like blue, white, purple, pink, and red. They are also bicolored on occasion.

2. Cacti and Succulents

Are you looking for a budget-friendly option that is budget friendly as well? If so, cacti and succulents are great options. They are fascinating and collected by several plant parents.

- **Kalanchoe Daigremontiana - Mexican Hat Plant**

The Mexican Hat Plant has grey-green leaves with brown spotting. The triangular lance-shaped leaves give a unique touch to this houseplant. At the same time, its tubular greyish-pink flowers are cherry on top.

- **Aloe Vera - Barbados Aloe**

Aloe Vera, also known as Barbados Aloe, has dull green leaves with spiny margins and forms narrow yellow rosettes. In addition to that, its tubular greenish-yellow flowers (around 3cm in length) are a treat to the eyes.

- **Lithops Karasmontana - Karas Mountains Living Stone**

Lithops are a great option if you're into tiny cute succulents that don't take up much of your space. These clump-forming succulents are around 4cm in height. In autumn, it blooms white flowers spread across 3 to 4cm.

- **Mammillaria Bombycine - Silken Pincushion Cactus**

Do you want a cactus plant but with a twist? If so, this plant would be the right fit for you. This houseplant from the cactus family comes with dense white hairs and cylindrical stems. In addition, they have white radial tubercles with long central spines. The deep rose-pink flowers make this plant extremely appealing to the eye.

- ### Ferocactus Glaucescens - Glaucous Barrel Cactus

It is another excellent option from the Cacti Plant family. It is cylindrical with grey-green stems (60cm in height). The spines are typically yellow-colored and may sometimes cluster together. At the same time, its flowers are also yellow and funnel-shaped.

- ### Aeonium Arboreum Atropurpureum - Dark Purple Houseleek Tree

This evergreen houseplant will make your space look beautiful throughout the year. In the late spring, it blooms conical panicles of small yellow flowers. The deep-red purple leaves will add a striking color to your home decor.

- ### Dancing Bones Cactus (Hatiora Salicornioides)

This small scrubbing plant has a slender shape with segmented stems. In the springtime, it produces bottle-shaped stem items and yellow-orange blooms. It is also known as bottle cactus, drunkard's dream, and spice cactus.

- ### Dragon Fruit Plant (Selenicereus Monacanthus)

If your home gets direct sunlight for about 6-8 hours, the dragon fruit houseplant can be the next favorite plant baby. The greenery mate bears tropical fruit and has become immensely popular recently. Several people enjoy them for their taste and unique color. Other names for them are strawberry pear, pitaya, and pitahaya. Their exotic look and tempting flavor make this plant a fantastic choice. The most common variety has black seeds and white pulp. However, you might come with black seeds and red pulp. The two main types come with green scales and bright red skin.

- ### Joseph's Coat (Opuntia Monacantha)

This prickly pear cactus has an interesting combination of creamy white and green variegation. Sometimes, it displays a flush of pink color. What distinguishes these plants are their offshoots. If given enough room, these offshoots are stacked up and look appealing to the eye.

- ### Panda Plant – Kalanchoe Tomentosa

Panda Plant is a velvety green succulent with having greenish color with brown spots on leaf tips. It is an excellent option for beginners as it is low maintenance and care, making it a perfect indoor choice.

3. Air Plants Tillandsia Spp.

Air plants are here to give you a fuzzy feel with their texture and grey-green appearance. They typically possess thick leaves covered with scales. They have cute little flowers which grow roughly 2 inches in size. As they can anchor on places other than soil, you can adjust them on various surfaces.

4. Trailing and Climbing Houseplants

Are you looking for a houseplant that can decorate your windows and fence? If so, trailing and climbing houseplants can be a great option. You can hang them in different places with the help of hooks and curtain rods.

- **Golden Pothos, Epipremnum Aureum**

Golden Pothos, a money plant, is an evergreen plant with thick waxy heart-shaped leaves. The name "money plant" is a common name given to several plant species, including Epipremnum Aureum (Golden Pothos), in some regions, particularly Asia. Some believe these plants can bring the owner good luck, prosperity, and financial success. The yellow splashes on these leaves make this plant unique and eye-catching. As a houseplant, it is most famous as a hanging plant.

- ## Heart-Leaf Philodendron, Philodendron Scandens

Just like Golden Pothos, Philodendrons are great climbers. They overgrow and require little to no care to thrive. These houseplants usually have green foliage, while sometimes they have purplish, green, or coppery color. By looking closely, you'll see visible veins of white or red color running in a parallel direction. The size and shape of the plant will vary depending on its maturity and species.

- ## Orchid Cactus

This unusual cactus plant has fat and long leaves which fold and twist as they grow. Its trailing quality makes it a perfect choice for tall planters and hanging baskets. If you plan to get one, use the foliage texture by setting it in a sleek, smooth ceramic container.

- ## Satin Pothos, Scindapsus Pictus 'Exotica'

As the name explains, exotica has a lush tropical look. The variegated cordate leaves have silver markings appearing like splashes of paint. They also have large heart-shaped leaves that catch your eyes in the right light.

- ## Red Herringbone Plant Maranta Leuconeura Var. Erythroneura

This indoor houseplant is popular because of its attractive patterned foliage. The ovate-shaped leaves of this indoor houseplant resemble praying hands. The underside of these leaves is purple-green to gay-green. The news leaves appear to be rolled tubes. However, pale central variegation, prominent red fishbone-patterned veins, and pale underside are the superior characteristics of this plant.

- **Staghorn Fern, Platycerium Bifurcatum**

This plant type is widely cultivated as an ornamental plant as it is super easy to grow. Staghorn fern looks like elk antlers or deer, which explains its unusual name. Even if they grow slowly, they grow into a large statement piece. They have two specific leaf types - green fronds that extend from the base and flat, small leaves covering the root ball structure.

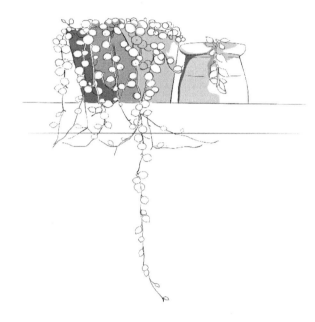

- **String of Beads (Senecio Rowleyanus)**

This unusual plant is known for its nearly spherical leaves. This plant grows from weak roots that can produce around three feet long trailing stems. It usually grows between rocks and under bushes for protection against direct sunlight. The leaves have a pea-like shape with a diameter of 1/4 inch. This round shape allows lesser water evaporation and minimizes the area exposed to the dry desert air.

- **Burro's Tail Sedum Morganianum**

Covered with overlapping green leaves, this bountiful trailing plant adds to its charm. It is usually silvery lime-green, which might give a yellow tint in the bright sun. Burro's tail usually grows in hanging baskets or is seen cascading out of pots.

- **String of Hearts or Rosary Vine Ceropegia Woodli**

Love will be in the air with this mesmerizing semi-succulent vine! Ceropegia Woodii Ssp. Woodii has a delightful green lace pattern growing in opposite pairs along a trailing vine and heart-shaped leaves. The pinkish-purple undersides of stems and leaves add a romantic touch to this plant. Even though this plant is genuinely not succulent, it can store water in its stems.

5. Indoor Palms

Are you looking for a houseplant that instills a feeling of peace and relaxation in your place? If so, indoor palms would be a great option. Under the right conditions, they can thrive with minimal effort. Indoor palms come in a wide variety.

• Parlor Palm (Chamaedorea Elegans)

Bring texture, color, and vibrance to any dull room with parlor palm. This plant comprises a single-trunk palm, arching green pinnate leaves, and narrow leaflets. This plant can produce clusters of yellow flowers if given enough light in spring. Indoors, this plant can grow up to 4 feet but reach 8 feet in ideal conditions. They are immensely suitable options as kitchen top counters and nightstands plants.

• Areca Palm (Dypsis Lutescens)

Topped with arching feather-shaped fronds, this plant has smooth silver-green trunks. The long petioles have seven to eight yellow-green leaves curved upwards into a butterfly look. Usually, it grows in clusters, forming clumps of many stems.

• Pygmy Date Palm (Phoenix r\Roebelenii)

Being part of the Arecaceae family, this planter is a true palm. It is 2 to 4 feet long and comprises bright cherry green fronds. These plants grow straight vertically, while some curve sidewards.

• Chinese Fan Palm (Livistona Chinensis)

This evergreen palm has a beautiful cascading appearance. It is a medium-sized planter having a slender trunk and emerald-green, coarse-textured palm leaves that can grow 3 to 6ft across. The thin log lobes of the leaves dop gracefully, giving a fountain-like look.

- **Ponytail Palm (Beaucarnea Recurvata)**

This houseplant gives a distinctive look through a swollen thick brown stem where it stores water. It has dark green leaves that are long, curly, and narrow, mimicking a plume of water in a fountain.

- **Majestic Palm (Ravenea Rivularis)**

Symmetrical leaves, a slightly swollen base, and an untidy crown characterize Majestic Palms (Ravenea Rivularis). It's beautiful fronds make it a first-choice interior houseplant. Among gardening enthusiasts and plant parents, this is a popular choice. The reason is the tropical island vibes radiated by them.

- **Sago Palm (Cycas Revoluta)**

This beautiful indoor house plant comes with some mischievous twists. First, even if it goes by the name "Sago Palm," this planter is a cycad. Secondly, it has gained popularity as an indoor houseplant, but in reality, it is an outdoor plant. Thirdly, it is known as a new and fancy plant. However, people have been growing it in their houses for millions of years. The only drawback is that this plant has a slow growth speed compared to similar options.

- **Kentia Palm (Howea Forsteriana)**

Welcome Kentia Palm into your house for a calm and relaxed atmosphere. This plant tolerates conditions in which other houseplants might die down. This trouble-free plant can tolerate neglect and is adaptable to various temperatures. This plant can add an exotic element to your place with its tropical, lush, and leafy foliage. It has erect, arching, feather-like fronds, green leaves, and oval fruits. This plant might grow slowly but can eventually reach 40 feet in height.

- **Yucca Palm (Yucca Elephantipes)**

Yucca is a houseplant native to the Southwest United States and Mexico. It is also present in the West Indies and the Eastern United States. Characterized by live green leaves, it can describe as a small tree or shrub. On its lower portion, you might see its dead brown leaves. It is known as a woody plant similar to lilies.

- **Cascade Palm (Chamaedorea Cataractarum)**

This adorable compact plant has a cascading form and green foliage. It is an ideal plant for indoor and other shady areas. This plant will survive the best in fertile soil away from the sun. The cascade plant cannot tolerate direct sunlight and prefers natural or filtered light.

6. Narrow-Leaf / Broad-Leaf Holiage Houseplants

A popular choice among plant parents is the foliage plant. The reason is that they are low maintenance and can withstand most environmental changes. Additionally, they come in a large variety and are easily accessible.

Here are some fantastic types of narrow-leaf/broad-leaf foliage houseplants listed below

- **Epipremnum Aureum - Marble Queen Pothos**

Marble Queen Pothos is a striking plant that is an immensely variegated cultivator of the classic Pothos plant. It appears to have bright, creamy white variegation with colorful green leaves. Some plants are entirely white, while others contain larger green patches. This plant has gained popularity due to its trait of handling some neglect and a variety of conditions. It will be a great option if you're looking for a hanging plant.

- ### Epipremnum - Global Green Pothos

The Global Green Pothos is rare and originates from the South Pacific Island. It has a glossy interior mixed with lime and emerald green patterns. The surface is covered with light green, while the edges are dark green. They have an intricate texture giving a vibrant appearance to the plant. In recent years, it has shown tremendous growth in appeal as a decorative indoor hanging plant and corner specimen.

- ### Alocasia Baginda - Silver Dragon

As the name Silver Dragon indicates, this plant has silver markings all over it that resembles the dragon's scales. By keeping this plant under dappled light conditions, this pattern extends to the leaves. Besides that, the venations also develop a deep green color. The shape of leaves resembles most of the aroid species. However, some of them take note of the pointy edge of the leaves. Botanically, these spade-like leaves are called peltate.

- ### Epipremnum Aureum Neon; Neon Pothos

This houseplant is a super vibrant type of Golden pathos. Neon Pathos has no variegation with bright yellow chartreuse leaves. It will look great as a hanging plant. If you're looking for an option with air purifying quality, this plant would be a great match.

- ### Sansevieria Cylindrica Twisted, African Spear

This houseplant is a succulent that can grow up to 2 meters tall. It has a slender shape with striped leaves, just like a snake. The leaves of the African spear are of grey-green color with horizontal variable stripes of cylindrical shape. These leaves emerge into a rosette that can grow up to 1" inch in width and 6" in length. It grows well in low light and is low maintenance in nature.

- ## Philodendron Brandtianum, Silver Leaf Phily

This climbing tropical vine is known for its attractive leaves. As the name indicates, this houseplant has leaves splashed with a silvery tint. They are small in size and can easily fit into your studio apartment to add a touch of silver and green.

- ## Sansevieria Superba - Snake Plant

Popular indoor plants like the Snake Plant can survive sunlight of nearly any intensity. It has a slightly thick foliage of silver and green color with golden edges. This plant can grow up to 6 to 10" in length. It exhibits sword-like, exceptional long green leaf blades that have decorative markings. They come in various colors: yellow, silver, green, and white. It is a long-time favorite of several home designers as it instantly jazzes up your space.

- ## Dypsis Lutescens - Areca Palm

Areca palm has a smooth stem that extends up to 7.5 centimeters in diameter. It is greyish-green with distinct leaf scars and a yellowish crown shaft. Its foliage forms a graceful spiral arrangement. As a rough estimate, this plant has around 40 to 50 pairs of narrowly lanceolate leaflets.

- ## Alocasia Baginda - Dragon Scale

Are you curious why this plant is named dragon scale? It receives this name because its leaves resemble dragon scales. The leaves have a hard texture and a purple-red venation at the underside. This plant is easy to grow indoors with a reasonable amount of humidity. In the winter, it shreds some leaves for a certain period. During that time, keep the watering intensity to a moderate level to prevent root rotting from excessive moisture.

- ## Cast Iron Plant - Aspidistra Elatior

Aspidistra Elatior features shiny, dark, corn-like leaves. On average, these leaves can grow up to 24 inches. It usually produces purple-brown flowers close to the plant base. The glossy, lanceolate, arching dark green leaves (4" wide and 24" long) can grow directly from rootstock on long stems.

- ## Dumb Cane - Amoena

This tropical perennial plant is native to the Caribbean and South America. It has large leaves that emerge from large, green stems. These large leaves have yellow and stunning cream markings similar to leopard spots. They are available in numerous sizes and styles. Under favorable conditions, it can produce green flowers that resemble peace lilies. However, this rarely happens when you're growing them indoors.

- **Lucky Bamboo - Dracaena Braunii**

This indoor houseplant has naked branches in tufts of thin, long leaves. The leaves have widely distributed strappy leaves along with upright stems. With time, this plant will develop into a plant stalk. In case you have cut the stem, it will not be able to grow longer. You can train the stems of this plant into a variety of shapes. The lucky bamboo is usually green, but the plant is not doing well if any part seems yellow.

- **Madagascar Dragon Tree - Dracaena Marginata**

Dracaena Marginata, the dragon tree, is an eye-captivating plant with red-edge sword-like leaves. This spiky plant can be a great option in your houseplant collection. It is drought-tolerant, low-maintenance, and nearly impossible to destroy.

- **Swiss Cheese Plant - Monstera Deliciosa**

Monstera Deliciosa is a well-known plant with glossy, large-sized, dark green leaves with holes and deep splits. It has a dense, busy shape when young but wants to vine out when it grows. With regular pruning, you can keep the houseplant bushy. Besides that, you can also make it climb a vertical support for a tropical or bold look.

- **Braided Money Tree - Pachira Aquatica**

The money tree planter is the optimum choice for giving your house an exotic look. It comes with bright green palm-looking leaves and a braided stem. In the wilderness, this plant can grow up to 18 m (59.1 ft) in height. It features smooth bark, shiny green palmate leaves, and lanceolate leaflets. This plant's root system is slightly thickened and serves as a reservoir.

- **Zebra Plant - Calathea Zebrina**

Calathea Zebrina has sure decorative leaves with fresh green zebra-like stripes giving a luxurious look to the dark green background. The underside of these leaves has a purplish-red color. This stunning Calathea will have a high decorative and bold element to your place.

7. Ferns

Ferns come in a wide variety. The ones that cannot high temperatures are usually grown indoors as houseplants. Usually, these plants can withstand temperatures lower than 10°C (50°F). They are most suitable for closed rooms, such as bathrooms with high humidity levels or those out of direct sunlight.

- **Nephrolepis Exaltata Bostoniensis - Boston Fern**

Sword fern or Boston fern, Nephrolepis Exaltata, is a native of Mexico, Central America, Florida, the West Indies, Africa, and Polynesia. This evergreen Fern can grow 3′ wide as well as tall. However, it can grow as much as 7′ tall in the wild. Usually, the Boston fern has sword-shaped fronds that are shallow-toothed to the entire pinnae. Initially, the fronds grow upright and gradually arch down as they age. As an indoor fern, it is best for hanging baskets or pedestals. The location should be near kitchens or bathrooms where the air is moister.

- ## Asparagus Setaceus - Lace Fern

This elegant Fern comes with long wiry stems and frond-like sprays scrambled outwards in a horizontal direction. Initially, it is pretty bushy, but as it grows, this plant develops into feathery, bright green fronds. In late summer, lace ferns produce small green-white flowers that sometimes develop into blueberries.

- ## Asplenium Osaka - Japanese Bird's Nest Fern

Asplenium Antiquum Osaka is a widely cultivated compact Japanese Bird's Nest Fern variety. It produces an upright rosette of long luscious green leaves with a wavy, ruffled edge, exhibiting a highly decorative appearance.

- ## Humata Tyermanii - White Rabbit's Foot Fern

Superb plants but with a twist! This indoor houseplant has deep green delicate fronds, featuring a bronze flush when it starts life. This Fern comprises furry silvery rhizomes which grow outside the pot and spreads over the side, giving this plant other common names: Silver Hare's Foot, Bears Paw Fern, and White Rabbit's Tooth. The Fern would look amazing as a hanging houseplant.

8. Bromeliads

A bromeliad can be your house baby if you're looking for an unusual plant. This exclusive family of flowering plants is native to America, while some types exist in the American subtropics. They have striking, almost unbelievably beautiful-looking leaves and astounding flowers. They come in a wide color variety that will easily merge into the aesthetics of your place. This houseplant will fit into nearly any position of your house.

All of these plants are beautiful in their own way. However, keeping their needs and requirements is necessary before choosing one. Below is a chart through which you can easily go for an indoor houseplant that checks all your boxes.

Maintenance Chart for Main Indoor Houseplants

Categories	Maintenance Level	Growth Requirements
• **Flowering Houseplants**	Low-maintenance (Thrives with minimal care)	• Regular misting so the moisture is maintained • 40%-60% of humidity during summer (40%-50% at the flowering stage) • 12 to 16 hours of light per day

		• Grows at 70-80° F during the day time and 65-70° F at night time
• **Cacti and Succulent**	Low-maintenance	• Water only once per month, retain water during the flowering season • 10% of humidity indoors would be enough • 4-6 hours of daily indirect sunlight • Thrives in temperature ranged from 40-80°F
• **Air Plants**	Medium-maintenance	• Mist water only two or three times a week • Humidity level varies from 50%-70% • Bright, indirect sunlight or under fluorescent home/office lighting for a few hours • Grows the best in temperature ranging from 10°C and 32°C (50°F-90°F).
• **Trailing and Climbing Houseplants**	Low-maintenance	• Water weekly, make sure the soil is dry to touch before watering • High humidity level 60%-80% • The light needs vary. On average, they thrive in low to medium light. While others like Philodendrons, need direct sunlight for a few hours to

		grow • Require 65-75°F during the day, and are about 10 degrees cooler at night.
• **Indoor Palms**	Low-maintenance	• Water every day in its first week, every other day in the next week, and 2-3 times per week once settled. Ensure 1 to 2 inches of soil is completely dry before watering. • 40%-50% humidity level • Prefers bright, indirect light near a west or south-facing window • 70 and 80 °F during the day and 60 °F at night
• **Narrow-Leaf / Broad-Leaf Foliage Houseplants**	Medium-maintenance	• Water regularly (roughly after every 5-10 days) • For these humidity-loving plants, 60%-80% of moisture level in air recommended • Needs around 14-16 hours of light per day and 8 hours of total darkness a day. • Generally, 60-80 degrees F (15 - 27°C)
• **Ferns**	Low-maintenance	• Water twice a week. Don't let the soil get soggy. • 30%-50% humidity is required for optimum growth.

		• Fond of indirect light otherwise could turn crispy, burnt, and dry • Thrives in an average temperature range of 55–75 degrees.
• **Bromeliads**	Low-maintenance	• Lightly spray water roughly every two weeks. • High level (70%-90%) of humidity makes these plants thrive. • Prefers indirect bright light indoors as well as outdoors • Optimal temperature range between 50-65°F in daytime and 70-90°F at night time.

Plants are just like babies. The only thing is that they can't cry or throw tantrums when they're going through a rough patch. As a parent, you are responsible for caring for their needs and hoping this guideline will help you keep them happy and healthy for longer.

CONCLUSION

"Let's root for each other and watch each other grow"

—Unknown Author

You would like to have some plantlings in your home for various reasons. They can range from practical needs to subjective reasons. One of the most common objective factors is visual attraction. Surrounding yourself with greenery every single day will promote psychological fitness and well-being.

The air we breathe is full of toxins and pollutants. Getting exposed to these toxins can impact your immune system. The great news is houseplants can absorb all these impurities and save you from these harmful problems. Besides that, they can also improve your health and the environment.

Plants not only stabilize your physical health, but they also affect your mental health. They promote confidence and relax your mood. These plant babies can also combat environmental changes that won't work in your favor, such as humidity control and relief from seasonal allergies.

Apart from enhancing the aesthetics of a corner and creating a cleaner environment in your home, you can also use these plants for culinary purposes. You can grow healthy organic foods like cilantro, basil, carrots, peppers, and onions.

The modern, fast-paced world has left no time to sit back and relax. You might also always be in a rush to get things done. This hassle can lead to stress and FOMO (fear of missing out). Thankfully, indoor houseplants can also reduce tension levels caused by this uncertain life. Moreover, having plants can also relieve your anxiety.

Aside from these practical benefits, you can keep plants due to numerous personal preferences. For instance, you want to decorate your house but are on a budget. In that case, indoor houseplants can be your best friend. There are plenty of cheap, easy-to-care options available in the market. Simply adding a striking piece to your living space will do. That will instantly uplift the outlook of your room.

Often you feel hostile, depressed, and lose hope because of daily life struggles. Adding houseplants to your life will act as a breeze of fresh air. It will help you eliminate the negative aura and instill peace. Moreover, you can also set up some succulents and planters to restore peace and harmony in your space.

You can place small planters near your bed or around you for a calm and peaceful sleep. In no time, you'll feel a difference in your life. The reason behind this is the innate tendency of humans to connect with other living beings.

Starting a family and having children can be problematic in the current economic situation. Even having a pet can be challenging if you work long hours. In that scenario, having plant babies can fulfill your need to nurture someone with love and little maintenance. Taking care of them also allows you to introduce yourself to the beautiful green realm.

There are around 435,000 plant species all around the world. By working with essential plants, you'll be able to get insights into complicated and advanced plants. You might even be able to use this passion to get a professional job in the relevant domain.

However, this is only possible when you firmly grasp the basics. This book is a complete guide that covers all the essentials required to grow plants as a beginner. It includes choosing your first houseplant, their needs (watering, growing medium, temperature, humidity, light), and protection against harmful diseases till their propagation.

The ultimate goal of this book is to build your connection strong with the natural order while making Earth more sustainable. Once you develop a green thumb, this hobby can be a life-changing experience.

"One year ago, my life hit rock bottom. My jewelry business failed, and I was on the verge of bankruptcy. I was hallucinating and couldn't stop crying! Then I started growing plants again."

Monty Don has been working in the fashion industry for eight years. He was immensely successful and had a luxurious life and a stunning wife. Everything seemed to be great. In reality, Monty was getting unwell, becoming short-tempered, and his mental health was hanging by a string. Soon, he was unable to focus and gradually lost everything.

That's when he thought of doing gardening again. He started to look up for some advice and found this book. After going through this book, this is what he said to us:

> **Monty Don, Male, 34 years old (Ottawa, Canada):**
>
> *I started growing plants with my father when I was eight years old. With time, I got so busy with my practical life that I couldn't keep up with this hobby. After excessive stress and anxiety, I thought of giving this book a go and thankfully I did. This book motivated me to start over and today I'm in a much better place mentally. Thank you so much!*

Hoping this book will help you change your life, just like Monty. Don't be shy to share a review!

FINAL THOUGHTS

"The seed that fell on good soil represents those who truly hear and understand God's word and produce a harvest of thirty, sixty, or even a hundred times as much as had been planted!"

—Matthew 13:23 (NLT)

A s someone who loves books, you know the power they hold. They can change lives, spark joy, and provide hope. If you've found this read a book that will be helpful and inspiring; consider leaving a review to help others searching for something similar.

Imagine how many people you could impact by sharing your thoughts and opinions. Perhaps there's someone out there who is struggling with the same issues we once had just a short time ago.

They're looking for guidance and advice but must figure out where to turn.

Your review could be the light they need to find their way. It could help them make an informed decision about which book to choose and guide them towards finding the perfect plant for themselves, naturing their plants to thrive for a lifetime.

Think about the last time you read a book that touched your heart. How did it make you feel? Did it give you hope for the future? If so, why not pay it forward and share that hope with others?

As a self-published author with a limited marketing budget, reviews on this platform are essential to my survival. If "The Houseplant Whisperer" is a book that you believe could benefit others, take a moment to leave an honest review. Leaving a review takes a few minutes of your time, but the impact it could have is immeasurable. Your words could be the spark of hope someone needs.

You can do so by scanning the QR code below. I love hearing from my readers and I personally read every single review.

Blessings to you. Happy Planting!

Michelle Rosa

ACKNOWLEDGMENTS

Thank you to the wonderfully creative book cover designer who realized my idea and perfectly encapsulated the tone of this book. Your creativity and attention to detail have resulted in a cover that beautifully represents the contents. I appreciate your effort and commitment to this project. *Designed by Wonderburg Creations, Digital assets by Freepik.*

I also extend my gratitude to the gifted illustrator who worked so hard to make the book's pages come to life with their magnificent illustrations. Your illustrations perfectly complement the text, making this book more visually appealing. Thank you for your beautiful contributions and for sharing your talents with us, *Fatima Tuzzohra.*

To both of you, thank you for making this book an actual work of art. Your contributions have been invaluable, and I could not have done it without you.

Blessings,

Michelle

REFERENCES

1. "The Greatest Gift of the Garden Is the Restoration of the Five Senses." ~Hanna Rion at Wellness Words of Wisdom. blogs.smith.edu/blog/wordsofwisdom/2012/03/22/the-greatest-gift-of-the-garden-is-the-restoration-of-the-five-senses-hanna-rion/. Accessed 3 Mar. 2023.

2. Cubista, Joshua. "The Practice of Biophilia." Biophilia Foundation, 20 Feb. 2018, www.biophiliafoundation.org/practice-biophilia/.

3. claire. "The Plant-Crazy Generation: Why Millennials Are Leading the Houseplant Trend." Houseplant Resource Center, 27 Jan. 2020, houseplantresourcecenter.com/2020/01/the-plant-crazy-generation-why-millennials-are-leading-the-houseplant-trend/.

4. Stanborough, Rebecca. "7 Science-Backed Benefits of Indoor Plants." Healthline, 18 Sept. 2020, www.healthline.com/health/healthy-home-guide/benefits-of-indoor-plants#7-benefits.

5. "What Houseplants Can Do for Your Mental Health during Lockdown." Verywell Mind, www.verywellmind.com/mental-health-benefits-of-houseplants-5097479.

6. Dzhambov, Angel M., et al. "Does Greenery Experienced Indoors and Outdoors Provide an Escape and Support Mental Health during the COVID-19 Quarantine?" Environmental Research, vol. 196, Nov. 2020, p. 110420, https://doi.org/10.1016/j.envres.2020.110420.

7. "What Houseplants Can Do for Your Mental Health during Lockdown." Verywell Mind, www.verywellmind.com/mental-health-benefits-of-houseplants-5097479.

8. "Quarantine (Google) Trends: 10 Crazy Houseplant Stats." Terrarium Tribe, 27 Apr. 2020, terrariumtribe.com/houseplant-statistics/.

9. "12 Strange, but Also Beautiful, Houseplants You Never Knew Existed." Country Living, 16 Feb. 2017, www.countryliving.com/gardening/g4106/weird-indoor-plants/. Accessed 3 Mar. 2023.

10. "E. O. Wilson Quotes." BrainyQuote, www.brainyquote.com/quotes/e_o_wilson_133730. Accessed 3 Mar. 2023.

11. Davies, Taylor. "Why More Millennials Are Buying into "Plant Parenthood."" NBC News, NBC News, 19 Nov. 2018, www.nbcnews.com/better/health/why-more-millennials-are-buying-plant-parenthood-ncna935836.

12. "10 Good Reasons to Surround Yourself with Houseplants!" Perfect Plants, perfectplants.co.uk/blog/10-good-reasons-to-surround-yourself-with-houseplants. Accessed 3 Mar. 2023.

13. Gaumond, Andrew. "18 Proven Benefits of Plants (Leading Research Studies)." Petal Republic, 8 Nov. 2021, www.petalrepublic.com/benefits-of-plants/. Accessed 3 Mar. 2023.

14. Keith, Jessie. "The Benefits of Having Plants at Home | Plants.com." The Greenhouse Blog by Plants.com, 29 Dec. 2020, www.plants.com/greenhouse/plant-care/benefits-of-having-plants-at-home/. Accessed 3 Mar. 2023.

15. "8 Flowering Houseplants That Provide Color without Much Fuss." The Spruce, www.thespruce.com/the-best-flowering-houseplants-1402664.

16. "Seven of the Best Flowering House Plants to Grow." BBC Gardeners World Magazine, www.gardenersworld.com/how-to/grow-plants/best-flowering-house-plants-to-grow/. Accessed 3 Mar. 2023.

17. "Cacti & Succulent Houseplants / RHS Gardening." Www.rhs.org.uk, www.rhs.org.uk/plants/types/cacti-succulents/houseplants. Accessed 3 Mar. 2023.

18. M, Jon. "Cactus House Plants (10 Cacti You Can Keep Indoors)." GreenUpSide, greenupside.com/cactus-house-plants-10-cacti-you-can-keep-indoors/. Accessed 3 Mar. 2023.

19. "Air Plants (Tillandsia) Guide | Our House Plants." Www.ourhouseplants.com, www.ourhouseplants.com/plants/air-plants. Accessed 3 Mar. 2023.

20. "25 Great Air Plants to Grow Indoors." The Spruce, www.thespruce.com/best-air-plant-varieties-4158871. Accessed 3 Mar. 2023.

21. "Trailing & Hanging Plants." Houseplant.co.uk, www.houseplant.co.uk/collections/trailing-hanging-plants. Accessed 3 Mar. 2023.

22. "15 of the Best Trailing House Plants." BBC Gardeners' World Magazine, www.gardenersworld.com/how-to/grow-plants/15-of-the-best-trailing-house-plants/.

23. Moulton, Madison. "10 Best Indoor Palm Trees to Grow at Home." Petal Republic, 8 Mar. 2022, www.petalrepublic.com/indoor-palm-trees/. Accessed 3 Mar. 2023.

24. "Palms: Indoors / RHS Gardening." Www.rhs.org.uk, www.rhs.org.uk/plants/types/trees/indoor-palms. Accessed 3 Mar. 2023.

25. "37 Small Indoor Plants to Bring Beauty into Your Home." Smart Garden Guide, 2 July 2019, smartgardenguide.com/small-indoor-plants/.

26. Lloyster, Mary. "Selection of Foliage House Plants." House Plants Guide and Tips, 11 Jan. 2023, www.houseplantsexpert.com/foliage-house-plants.html. Accessed 3 Mar. 2023.

27. Hortology. "Ferns." Hortology, hortology.co.uk/collections/ferns. Accessed 3 Mar. 2023.

28. "How to Grow Ferns." BBC Gardeners' World Magazine, www.gardenersworld.com/how-to/grow-plants/how-to-grow-ferns/.

29. "Growing a Bromeliad and How to Care for a Bromeliad Plant." Gardening Know How, www.gardeningknowhow.com/houseplants/bromeliad/growing-bromeliad-plants.htm.

30. "Grow Bromeliads as House Plants / RHS Gardening." Www.rhs.org.uk, www.rhs.org.uk/plants/articles/wisley/brilliant-bromeliads. Accessed 3 Mar. 2023.

31. "Choosing House Plants - How to Choose." Www.houseplantsexpert.com, www.houseplantsexpert.com/choosing-house-plants.html.

32. "Houseplants: Choosing the Best / RHS Gardening." Www.rhs.org.uk, www.rhs.org.uk/plants/types/houseplants/choosing-the-best. Accessed 3 Mar. 2023.

33. "Getting to the Root of the Millennial Plant Obsession." Cosmopolitan, 7 Sept. 2017, www.cosmopolitan.com/lifestyle/a10337665/millennial-plant-lifestyle-trend-instagram-houseplants-gardening/. Accessed 3 Mar. 2023.

34. "Mitch Hedberg Quotes." BrainyQuote, www.brainyquote.com/quotes/mitch_hedberg_297485. Accessed 3 Mar. 2023.

35. "Keeping Houseplants Happy: Our Guide to Watering Your Houseplants." Burgon and Ball, www.burgonandball.com/blogs/journal/guide-to-watering-houseplants. Accessed 3 Mar. 2023.

36. "The Essential Guide to Watering Your Houseplants | WallyGro." WallyGrow, wallygrow.com/blogs/feature/essential-watering-guide. Accessed 3 Mar. 2023.

37. Over or under Watering? The Ultimate Guide to Watering Your Houseplants | Spalding Bulb. spaldingbulb.co.uk/ultimate-watering-guide/. Accessed 3 Mar. 2023.

38. "A Guide to Watering Indoor Plants." The Stem, thestem.co.uk/plant-academy/plant-parent-courses/indoor-plants/a-guide-to-watering-indoor-plants. Accessed 3 Mar. 2023.

39. "10 Golden Rules for Watering." Gardena, www.gardena.com/uk/garden-life/garden-magazine/10-golden-rules-for-watering/. Accessed 3 Mar. 2023.

40. "Soil Quotes (120 Quotes)." Www.goodreads.com, www.goodreads.com/quotes/tag/soil. Accessed 3 Mar. 2023.

41. "Houseplant Growing Mediums and Potting Soil | Our House Plants." Www.ourhouseplants.com, www.ourhouseplants.com/guides/house-plant-potting-soils. Accessed 3 Mar. 2023.

42. "Growing Medium for Plants: The Ultimate Guide." Humboldts Secret Supplies, humboldtssecretsupplies.com/blogs/articles/growing-medium-for-plants-the-ultimate-guide. Accessed 3 Mar. 2023.

43. What Is a Growing Medium? Materials with Photos and Infographic – Your Indoor Herbs and Garden. 21 Feb. 2020, www.yourindoorherbs.com/what-is-a-growing-medium-materials-photos/.

44. Parmar, Bimal. "Choosing a Growing Medium." VegWall Gardening, 5 Mar. 2021, www.vegwallgarden.com/post/choosing-a-growing-medium. Accessed 3 Mar. 2023.

45. "Selecting Grow Medium for Your Plants." Steve & Leif, 25 Oct. 2019, stevenleif.com/blog/selecting-grow-medium-for-your-plants/. Accessed 3 Mar. 2023.

46. "HuffPost Is Now a Part of Verizon Media." Consent.yahoo.com, www.huffingtonpost.co.uk/entry/millennials-obsessed-houseplants-instagram_l_5d7a976de4b01c1970c433b9.

47. "Jeffrey Eugenides Quote." A-Z Quotes, www.azquotes.com/quote/387819?ref=humidity. Accessed 3 Mar. 2023.

48. "House and Indoor Plants Temperature Guide." Www.houseplantsexpert.com, www.houseplantsexpert.com/indoor-plants-temperature-guide.html.

49. What Is Best Temperature for Indoor Plants? Houseplants Pro. 14 Mar. 2021, houseplantspro.com/best-temperature-for-indoor-plants/. Accessed 3 Mar. 2023.

50. "Cold Tolerant Houseplants – Winter Houseplants for Cold Rooms." Gardening Know How, www.gardeningknowhow.com/houseplants/hpgen/cold-tolerant-indoor-plants.htm. Accessed 3 Mar. 2023.

51. "Here's How to Grow Beautiful, Tropical Philodendron Indoors." The Spruce, www.thespruce.com/grow-philodendron-houseplants-1902768.

52. Zimmer, Fred. "Which Indoor Plants like Humidity?" Indoor Plants for Beginners, 6 Sept. 2020, www.indoorplantsforbeginners.com/indoor-plants-that-like-humidity/. Accessed 3 Mar. 2023.

53. "Humidity and Indoor Plants Guide." Www.ourhouseplants.com, www.ourhouseplants.com/guides/humidity.

54. "Indoor & House Plants Humidty Guide." Www.houseplantsexpert.com, www.houseplantsexpert.com/house-plants-humidity-guide.html.

55. Gardening, Indoor. "12 Best Houseplants for High Humidity." Indoor Gardening, 1 Nov. 2021, indoorgardening.com/best-houseplants-for-high-humidity/. Accessed 3 Mar. 2023.

56. Santos-Longhurst, Adrienne. "12 Houseplants to Refresh Dry Indoor Air." Healthline, Healthline Media, 29 May 2020, www.healthline.com/health/humidifying-plants.

57. admin. "20 Proven Houseplants That Increase Indoor Humidity!" Balcony Garden Web, 17 Aug. 2020, balconygardenweb.com/houseplants-that-increase-humidity-indoors/. Accessed 3 Mar. 2023.

58. Staff, Author Homestratosphere's Editorial, and Writers. 8 Houseplants That Help Lower Indoor Humidity (Natural Dehumidifier). 27 Apr. 2018, www.homestratosphere.com/plants-lower-humidity/. Accessed 3 Mar. 2023.

59. "TOP 25 PESTS QUOTES (of 69)." A-Z Quotes, www.azquotes.com/quotes/topics/pests.html. Accessed 3 Mar. 2023.

60. Williams, Diane. "7 Common Indoor Plant Pests (& How to Kill Them) -." The Contented Plant, 31 Dec. 2021, thecontentedplant.com/7-common-indoor-plant-pests-and-treatments/. Accessed 3 Mar. 2023.

61. 10 Indoor Plant Pests You Can Easily Identify and Eliminate. 12 Apr. 2021, morningchores.com/indoor-plant-pests/. Accessed 3 Mar. 2023.

62. Mommers, Hannie. 8 Natural Pesticides for Plants That Are Useful in Our Garden. 16 July 2021, ourgreenhealth.com/natural-pesticides-for-plants/.

63. Zimmerman, Jesse. "21 Pros and Cons of Natural Pesticides vs. Synthetic Pesticides." Pest Control FAQ, Pest Control FAQ, 21 Feb. 2019, pestcontrolfaq.com/natural-pesticides-vs-synthetic-pesticides/.

64. "Natural Pesticides: Using Organic vs. Synthetic Pest Control." Modern Pest, 18 July 2017, www.modernpest.com/blog/what-are-natural-pesticides/.

65. "Pest and Disease Problems of Indoor Plants." Penn State Extension, extension.psu.edu/pest-and-disease-problems-of-indoor-plants.

66. "A List of Houseplant Diseases & Viruses." Ukhouseplants, www.ukhouseplants.com/helpful-tips/identifying-common-houseplant-pests-diseases.

67. "9 Common Plant Diseases: Identification and Treatment | Blossom." Blossomplant.com, blossomplant.com/blog/plant-diseases/common-indoor-plant-diseases. Accessed 3 Mar. 2023.

68. "5 Real Plant Pest Infestation Stories You Can Learn From." The Spruce, www.thespruce.com/nightmare-stories-of-plant-pest-infestations-5116922. Accessed 3 Mar. 2023.

69. Mattner, Christine. "Indoor Plant Diseases: Discover the 10 Most Common." Indoor Plant Center, 13 Mar. 2021, indoorplantcenter.com/indoor-plant-diseases/. Accessed 3 Mar. 2023.

70. "A Quote from Song of a Nature Lover." Www.goodreads.com, www.goodreads.com/quotes/10683065-plants-and-flowers-taught-me-how-to-grow-by-growing. Accessed 3 Mar. 2023.

71. "Basic Nutrients for Healthy Indoor Plants." Dummies, www.dummies.com/article/home-auto-hobbies/garden-green-living/gardening/containers/basic-nutrients-for-healthy-indoor-plants-180945/. Accessed 3 Mar. 2023.

72. "Plant Nutrition - Macronutrients & Micronutrients - an Overview." Seacliff Organics, seaclifforganics.nz/blogs/news/plant-nutrition-macronutrients-micronutrients-an-overview. Accessed 3 Mar. 2023.

73. Dubaniewicz, Kasha. "Common Nutrient Deficiencies in Plants - and How to Fix Them." Blog.bluelab.com, 19 Feb. 2021, blog.bluelab.com/common-nutrient-deficiencies-in-plants.

74. Qiuyun, Jiang. "Identifying Nutrient Deficiency in Plants." Identifying Nutrient Deficiency in Plants, Oct. 2020, www.nparks.gov.sg/nparksbuzz/oct-issue-2020/gardening/identifying-nutrient-deficiency-in-plants.

75. Andrychowicz, Amy. "How to Fertilize Houseplants: The Ultimate Guide." Get Busy Gardening, 19 Dec. 2019, getbusygardening.com/fertilizing-houseplants/. Accessed 3 Mar. 2023.

76. "J. R. R. Tolkien – All That Is Gold Does Not Glitter." Genius, genius.com/J-r-r-tolkien-all-that-is-gold-does-not-glitter-annotated. Accessed 3 Mar. 2023.

77. Leone, Jay. "LED Lights for Plant Growth." Sciencing, 2010, sciencing.com/led-lights-plant-growth-5958172.html.

78. Robinson, Paul. How Much Light Do My Indoor Plants Need? - PlantMaid. www.plantmaid.com/how-much-light-do-my-indoor-plants-need/.

79. "Light Levels for Plants Explained - Best 101 Guide Ever | Plantophiles." Plantophiles.com, 2020, plantophiles.com/houseplant-tips/light-levels-for-plants/.

80. "Understanding Light Requirements for Indoor Plants - Smart Garden Guide." Smartgardenguide.com, smartgardenguide.com/light-requirements-for-indoor-plants. Accessed 3 Mar. 2023.

81. 10 of the Best Houseplants for Low Light Conditions | Simply Indoor Gardens. 9 Mar. 2021, simplyindoorgardens.co.uk/houseplants/10-houseplants-for-low-light-conditions/. Accessed 3 Mar. 2023.

82. Nast, Condé. "31 Best Low-Light Indoor Plants and How to Care for Them." Architectural Digest, 15 May 2020, www.architecturaldigest.com/gallery/best-low-light-indoor-plants. Accessed 3 Mar. 2023.

83. Daniel, Author. 10 Best High Light Houseplants. 22 Jan. 2021, plantophiles.com/plant-care/high-light-houseplants/. Accessed 3 Mar. 2023.

84. "High Light Houseplants." Sunnyside Nursery, www.sunnysidenursery.net/high-light-houseplants. Accessed 3 Mar. 2023.

85. "Learn How to Care for Houseplants in the Winter." The Spruce, www.thespruce.com/tips-on-caring-for-houseplants-in-the-winter-1403001.

86. Beginners, Plant care for. "How to Care for Houseplants in the Winter." Plant Care for Beginners, plantcareforbeginners.com/articles/how-to-care-for-houseplants-in-the-winter. Accessed 3 Mar. 2023.

87. "9 Must-Know Tips for Keeping Your Houseplants Happy in Winter." Better Homes & Gardens, www.bhg.com/gardening/houseplants/care/winter-houseplants-care-tips/.

88. "Winter Houseplant Care: How to Look after Your Houseplants This Season." The English Garden, 6 Nov. 2020, www.theenglishgarden.co.uk/expert-advice/gardeners-tips/winter-houseplant-care/. Accessed 3 Mar. 2023.

89. "Alexander Smith Quotes." BrainyQuote, www.brainyquote.com/quotes/alexander_smith_383683. Accessed 3 Mar. 2023.

90. Frigeri, Peter. "The Beginner's Guide to Propagating Plants." Gaia Flowers, Plants & Gifts, 27 Apr. 2021, www.gaiaflowers.com/blog-flower-shop/flower-shop/plants/houseplant-propagation-the-beginners-guide-to-propagating-plants/. Accessed 3 Mar. 2023.

91. "Propagating House Plants - Methods and Instructions." Www.houseplantsexpert.com, www.houseplantsexpert.com/propagating-house-plants.html.

92. "Houseplant Propagation Guide – Learn How to Propagate Your Favorite Houseplants." Gardening Know How, www.gardeningknowhow.com/featuring/houseplant-propagation-guide-learn-how-to-propagate-your-favorite-houseplants. Accessed 3 Mar. 2023.

93. "How to Propagate Your Houseplants | Kew." Www.kew.org, www.kew.org/read-and-watch/propagate-houseplants.

94. "How to Propagate Houseplants: Complete Guide with Pictures - Smart Garden Guide." Smartgardenguide.com, smartgardenguide.com/how-to-propagate-houseplants/. Accessed 3 Mar. 2023.

95. "Plants Quotes (267 Quotes)." Www.goodreads.com, www.goodreads.com/quotes/tag/plants.

96. "How Do You Know Which Plant to Choose? - Thejunglecollective." The Jungle Collective, www.thejunglecollective.com.au/how-do-you-know-which-plant-to-choose/. Accessed 3 Mar. 2023.

97. "Seven of the Best Flowering House Plants to Grow." BBC Gardeners World Magazine, www.gardenersworld.com/how-to/grow-plants/best-flowering-house-plants-to-grow/.

98. "Cacti & Succulent Houseplants / RHS Gardening." Www.rhs.org.uk, www.rhs.org.uk/plants/types/cacti-succulents/houseplants.

99. M, Jon. "Cactus House Plants (10 Cacti You Can Keep Indoors)." GreenUpSide, greenupside.com/cactus-house-plants-10-cacti-you-can-keep-indoors/.

100. WoS. "Cacti and Succulents as Houseplants." World of Succulents, 19 July 2015, worldofsucculents.com/cacti-and-succulents-as-houseplants/. Accessed 3 Mar. 2023.

101. BH&G Garden Editors. "Grow Air Plants like a Pro—Here's How." Better Homes & Gardens, Better Homes & Gardens, 26 Feb. 2016, www.bhg.com/gardening/houseplants/care/grow-air-plants/.

102. "Tender Ferns - Houseplants / RHS Gardening." Www.rhs.org.uk, www.rhs.org.uk/plants/types/ferns/tender-ferns-houseplants. Accessed 3 Mar. 2023.

103. Quotations, SearchQuotes com. "My Green Thumb Came Only as a Result of the Mistakes I Made While Learning to See Things from the Pl Quotes, Quotations & Sayings 2023." Search Quotes, www.searchquotes.com/search/My_Green_Thumb_Came_Only_As_A_Result_Of_The_Mistakes_I_Made_While_Learning_To_See_Things_From_The_Pl/. Accessed 3 Mar. 2023.

104. Borges, Anna. "19 Heartwarming Stories That Will Make You Want to Start a Garden." BuzzFeed, www.buzzfeed.com/annaborges/reasons-to-garden.

Printed in Great Britain
by Amazon

39392516R00092